TRANSLATION

The various dimensions of translation studies, too often studied independently, are here brought into conversation: Translation practice, including the various crafts employed by its practitioners; the specialized contexts in which translation occurs or against which translation can be considered; and the ethico-political consequences of translations or the manner of their making. Including exciting new work from leading translation theorists, practicing literary translators, and prominent thinkers from adjoining disciplines such as psychoanalysis and neuroscience, the essays gathered here demonstrate many rich areas of overlap, with translation pedagogy, the fundamental nature of translation, the translator's creativity, retranslation, canon formation, and the geopolitical stakes of literary translation among them.

JAN STEYN is a scholar and literary translator working from Afrikaans, Dutch, English, and French. He is a lecturer in the Literary Translation Master of Fine Arts and the Department of French and Italian at the University of Iowa.

TRANSLATION

Crafts, Contexts, Consequences

EDITED BY

JAN STEYN

University of Iowa

Shaftesbury Road, Cambridge CB2 8EA, United Kingdom

One Liberty Plaza, 20th Floor, New York, NY 10006, USA

477 Williamstown Road, Port Melbourne, VIC 3207, Australia

314–321, 3rd Floor, Plot 3, Splendor Forum, Jasola District Centre, New Delhi – 110025, India

103 Penang Road, #05–06/07, Visioncrest Commercial, Singapore 238467

Cambridge University Press is part of Cambridge University Press & Assessment, a department of the University of Cambridge.

We share the University's mission to contribute to society through the pursuit of education, learning and research at the highest international levels of excellence.

www.cambridge.org
Information on this title: www.cambridge.org/9781108706933

DOI: 10.1017/9781108756846

© Cambridge University Press & Assessment 2022

This publication is in copyright. Subject to statutory exception and to the provisions of relevant collective licensing agreements, no reproduction of any part may take place without the written permission of Cambridge University Press & Assessment.

First published 2022
First paperback edition 2025

A catalogue record for this publication is available from the British Library

Library of Congress Cataloging-in-Publication data
NAMES: Steyn, Jan, editor.
TITLE: Translation : crafts, contexts, consequences / edited by Jan Steyn.
DESCRIPTION: Cambridge, United Kingdom ; New York, NY : Cambridge University Press, 2022. | Includes bibliographical references and index.
IDENTIFIERS: LCCN 2022016871 | ISBN 9781108485395 (hardback) | ISBN 9781108756846 (ebook)
SUBJECTS: LCSH: Translating and interpreting. | BISAC: LITERARY CRITICISM / European / English, Irish, Scottish, Welsh | LCGFT: Essays.
CLASSIFICATION: LCC P306 .T733 2022 | DDC 418/.02–dc23/eng/20220609
LC record available at https://lccn.loc.gov/2022016871

ISBN 978-1-108-48539-5 Hardback
ISBN 978-1-108-70693-3 Paperback

Cambridge University Press & Assessment has no responsibility for the persistence or accuracy of URLs for external or third-party internet websites referred to in this publication and does not guarantee that any content on such websites is, or will remain, accurate or appropriate.

For George Craig (1939–2019)

Contents

List of Figures		*page* ix
Notes on Contributors		x
Acknowledgements		xv

	Introduction Jan Steyn	1
1	Solitude of the Translator George Craig	7
2	Translation, Creativity, Awareness Franco Nasi	15
3	Anatomy of a Day in the Life of a Translator Bernard Turle, Translated by Michael Overstreet	32
4	Sturm, Drang and Slang: Writing Translations of Teenage Fiction Clémentine Beauvais	47
5	On X: Embodied Retranslation and Defacement in Brandon Brown's Catullus 85 Adrienne K. H. Rose	64
6	Translating the Greeks Katerina Stergiopoulou	82
7	Beyond Faithfulness: Retranslating Classic Texts Susan Bassnett	112
8	Translation in and of Psychoanalysis: *Kulturarbeit* as Transliteration Jean-Michel Rabaté	126

9	Translation across Brains and across Time *Christopher Honey and Janice Chen*	140
10	Covalent Effect: Literary Translation Practice and the Pedagogy of the Multilingual Workshop *Aron Aji*	162
11	Notes on the Translator's Space/The Editor's Place *Dan Gunn*	179
12	The State of Things *Chad Post*	194
13	Translating into a Minor Language *Rumena Bužarovska*	209
14	An Other Language: Translation and Internationality *Naoki Sakai*	227
15	Five Entries on Translation and Loss *Michael Cronin*	251
16	'A Kind of Radical Positivity': Reflections on the Craft, Contexts, and Consequences of Writing Translations *Kate Briggs, Jen Calleja, Sophie Collins, Katrina Dodson, and Natasha Soobramanien*	266

Bibliography   284
Index   297

Figures

9.1 Maps of brain regions that respond in a similar manner across different listeners, some listeners hearing the same auditory narrative, and others hearing a translation of the narrative. *page* 142

9.2 (a) Illustration of the network structure of the human cerebral cortex. (b) Illustration of the primary gradient across the human cerebral cortex, spanning from more sensory regions to more abstracted regions of the cerebral cortex. 148

14.1 Illustrations of dialectal features. 234

Contributors

ARON AJI is Director of the Master of Fine Arts (MFA) in Literary Translation programme at the University of Iowa, where he teaches workshops and theory courses. A native of Turkey, he has translated works by Bilge Karasu, Murathan Mungan, Elif Shafak, Ferit Edgü, and others. Aji has written a companion essay on his translation of Karasu's *A Long Day's Evening*, for *This is Classic!*, a forthcoming volume of critical essays edited by Regina Galasso.

SUSAN BASSNETT is Professor of Comparative Literature at the University of Glasgow. Her books include *Translation Studies* (4th ed., Routledge, 2013), *Comparative Literature* (Blackwell, 1993), and, most recently, *Translation and World Literature* (Routledge, 2018). Bassnett is also a well-known journalist, poet, and translator. She has served as a judge of many international literary prizes, including the Independent Foreign Fiction Prize, the Spender Poetry in Translation Prize, the IMPAC Dublin Prize, and the Women Writers in Translation Prize. She is an elected Fellow of the Academia Europaea, the Institute of Linguists, and the Royal Society of Literature. Since 2016 she has been President of the British Comparative Literature Association.

CLÉMENTINE BEAUVAIS is a senior lecturer in English in Education at the University of York (UK), as well as an author and translator (English to French). Her research revolves around the theory and practice of translation with children and young people. She also works on children's literature and is an associate editor for *Children's Literature in Education*.

KATE BRIGGS is the translator of two volumes of lecture and seminar notes by Roland Barthes and co-translator (with Roberto Nigro) of an early work by Michel Foucault. She is the author of *This Little Art* (Fitzcarraldo Editions, 2017), a finalist for a Believer Book Award and a book of the year in the *Times Literary Supplement*, *The White Review*, and *The Paris Review*. She holds a DPhil in French Studies from the University of Sussex and is a core tutor on the MFA at the Piet Zwart Institute, Rotterdam. Her next book, *The Long Form*, will be published by Fitzcarraldo Editions.

RUMENA BUŽAROVSKA is a fiction writer and literary translator from Skopje, North Macedonia. An author of four volumes of short stories translated into several languages, her collection *My Husband* was published by Dalkey Archive Press in 2020. She teaches American literature at the State University in Skopje.

JEN CALLEJA has translated full-length works by German-language authors including Marion Poschmann, Kerstin Hensel, Michelle Steinbeck, Gregor Hens, and Wim Wenders, among others. She was shortlisted for the Man Booker International Prize 2019 and the Schlegel Tieck Prize 2018 for her translations. Her translations have appeared in *The New Yorker*, *The White Review*, and *The Literary Hub*, and she writes a column on literary translation for the *Brixton Review of Books*. She is the author of *Serious Justice* (Test Centre, 2016) and *I'm Afraid That's All We've Got Time For* (Prototype, 2020), and she is currently working on her first novel.

JANICE CHEN is an assistant professor of Psychological and Brain Sciences at Johns Hopkins University. She studied Brain and Cognitive Sciences at the Massachusetts Institute of Technology, received her PhD in psychology from Stanford University, and completed her postdoctoral research at the Princeton Neuroscience Institute. Dr Chen was a 2018 Sloan Research Fellow and a 2020 Kavli Fellow.

SOPHIE COLLINS is the editor of *Currently & Emotion* (Test Centre, 2016), an anthology of contemporary poetry translations, and author of *small white monkeys* (Book Works, 2017) and *Who Is Mary Sue?* (Faber, 2018). *The Following Scan Will Last Five Minutes*, her translation, from the Dutch, of Lieke Marsman's *De volgende scan duurt vijf minuten*, is published by Pavilion Poetry and was named the Poetry Book Society's Summer Translation Choice 2019. She is a lecturer at the University of Glasgow and a fellow of the Royal Society of Literature.

GEORGE CRAIG was born in Belfast in 1931 and studied at Trinity College Dublin and the École Normale Supérieure in Paris. After working as a journalist, translating Russian broadcasts for Agence France-Presse in

Paris, he joined the University of Sussex, where he taught French for thirty years. He translated and co-edited the four volumes of Beckett's letters published by Cambridge University Press.

MICHAEL CRONIN is 1776 Professor of French and Director of the Centre for Literary and Cultural Translation in Trinity College Dublin. Among his published titles are *Translating Ireland: Translation, Languages and Identity* (Cork University Press, 1996), *Across the Lines: Travel, Language, Translation* (Cork University Press, 2000), *Translation and Globalization* (Routledge, 2003), *Translation and Identity* (Routledge, 2006), *Translation Goes to the Movies* (Routledge, 2009), *Translation in the Digital Age* (Routledge, 2013), *Eco-Translation: Translation and Ecology in the Age of the Anthropocene* (Routledge, 2017), and *Irish and Ecology: An Ghaeilge agus an Éiceolaíocht* (Foilseacháin Ábhair Spioradálta, 2019). He is a member of the Royal Irish Academy and a fellow of Trinity College Dublin.

KATRINA DODSON is the translator of *The Complete Stories* (2015), by Clarice Lispector, winner of the 2016 PEN Translation Prize and other awards. She is currently adapting her Lispector translation journal into a book and translating the 1928 Brazilian modernist classic *Macunaíma, the Hero With No Character*, by Mário de Andrade (New Directions). Her writing has appeared in *The Believer, McSweeney's, Guernica*, and elsewhere. Dodson holds a PhD in Comparative Literature from the University of California, Berkeley, and has been a fellow of the Fulbright Program, National Endowment for the Arts, MacDowell Colony, and Banff Centre. She teaches translation at Columbia University.

DAN GUNN is a novelist, critic, and translator, as well as being one of the editors of the four-volume *Letters of Samuel Beckett* and editor of the Cahiers Series. He is Distinguished Professor of Comparative Literature and English at the American University of Paris where he directs the Center for Writers and Translators. He was designated in 2017 as editor of Muriel Spark's letters.

CHRISTOPHER HONEY is an assistant professor of Psychological and Brain Sciences at Johns Hopkins University. After studying mathematics and literature at the University of Cape Town, he obtained his PhD in psychology and cognitive science at Indiana University before undergoing postdoctoral training at Princeton University. Dr Honey received the James McKeen Cattell Award in 2010 and was a 2016 Sloan Research Fellow.

FRANCO NASI is the author of numerous books on translation, several anthologies of poetry in translation, and is himself the translator into Italian of, among others, the Liverpool poet Roger McGough.

CHAD POST is the publisher of Open Letter Books at the University of Rochester, where he oversees the Three Percent website, the Translation Database, and the Best Translated Book Awards. In addition to many articles and reviews, he is the author of *The Three Percent Problem* (Open Letter, 2011).

JEAN-MICHEL RABATÉ is one of the world's foremost literary theorists. He is Professor of English and Comparative Literature at the University of Pennsylvania. Rabaté has authored or edited more than thirty books on modernism, psychoanalysis, contemporary art, philosophy, and writers such as Beckett, Pound, and Joyce. His recent books include *Crimes of the Future* (Bloomsbury, 2014), *The Cambridge Introduction to Psychoanalysis and Literature* (Cambridge University Press, 2014), *The Pathos of Distance* (Bloomsbury, 2016), and *Rust* (Bloomsbury, 2018). He is one of the founders and curators of Slought Foundation in Philadelphia and the managing editor of the *Journal of Modern Literature*. Since 2008, he has been a fellow of the American Academy of Arts and Sciences.

ADRIENNE K. H. ROSE teaches in the Classics department and the MFA in Literary Translation at the University of Iowa. She is the editor of *Ancient Exchanges*.

NAOKI SAKAI is Goldwin Smith Professor of Asian Studies at Cornell University, where he teaches comparative literature, Asian studies, and history. He has published in the fields of comparative literature, intellectual history, translation studies, the studies of racism and nationalism, and the histories of textuality. His book-length publications include *Translation and Subjectivity* (University of Minnesota Press, 1997), *Voices of the Past* (Cornell University Press, 1991), and *The Stillbirth of the Japanese as a Language and as an Ethos* (Shinyô-sha, 1995). He serves on the editorial boards of numerous publications in the United States and abroad, and he is the founding editor of the project TRACES, a multilingual series in five languages: Korean, Chinese, English, Spanish, and Japanese.

NATASHA SOOBRAMANIEN is a British-Mauritian writer living in Brussels. She holds a PhD in creative writing from the University of

East Anglia. Her first novel, *Genie and Paul* (Myriad Editions, 2012) is a reworking (or 'cannibalistic translation') of the eighteenth-century French novel by Bernardin de Saint-Pierre, *Paul et Virginie*. This was translated into French by the Mauritian novelist Nathacha Appanah and published by Gallimard in 2018. Her collaborative novel with Luke Williams, *Diego Garcia*, was published by Random House in 2022.

KATERINA STERGIOPOULOU is Assistant Professor of Classics at Princeton University. Much of her work focusses on questions of translation, and especially on the many afterlives of Greek antiquity in twentieth-century literature and thought.

JAN STEYN is a scholar and literary translator working from Afrikaans, Dutch, English, and French. He is a lecturer in the Literary Translation MFA and the Department of French and Italian at the University of Iowa.

BERNARD TURLE translates from English into French. His close to 200 translations include works of art history (by Harold Acton, Bernard Berenson, Rudolf Wittkower), British essays, biographies, novels (by Lytton Strachey, Cyril Connolly, Anthony Burgess, Barbara Pym, Peter Ackroyd, Martin Amis, Alan Hollinghurst), and works from around the globe, particularly, in recent years, from India and Pakistan (V. S. Naipaul, Sudhir Kakar, Siddharth D. Shanghvi, Mohammed Hanif). From among American authors, he has translated W. M. Spackman, John Edgar Wideman, and T. C. Boyle; from South Africa he has translated Andre Brink, from Australia Helen Garner, and from New Zealand Christine Leunens. He has won the Prix Coindreau and the Prix Baudelaire for translation.

Acknowledgements

Thanks to Dan Gunn for initiating this project. To Yoko Nakamura for copyediting and intellectual support. To Bethany Thomas at Cambridge University Press for her patience and guidance. And to the countless, often unnamed, translators and translation scholars whose contributions to the ongoing conversation about our strange field, in writing and in person, are reflected here without credit.

Introduction

Jan Steyn

Translation is an engine of contemporaneity. A translator makes 'present' texts from an original language, culture, and time to a receiving context, though in transmuted form. This is particularly obvious in the case of retranslations, which are 'updated' to reflect and intervene in a new receiving situation, with a new constellation of dominant, residual, or emergent norms. But it is also true of first translations, even when they are of very recent works, since those too posit their translated authors as our contemporaries, and their translated texts as of contemporary relevance. *Translation: Crafts, Contexts, Consequences*, consisting not of translations but of writings about translation, shares in this contemporizing work, each chapter implicitly making an argument for relevance – that *this* perspective on translation is urgent and necessary *now*.

Of course, the *now* of an edited volume is stretchable. No intervention into any area of study can hope to remain relevant forever; yet one may hope that scholars and practitioners will find interest in the essays gathered here long after recent fads, scandals, and controversies have been forgotten. This book begins with a backward-looking piece by our late colleague George Craig written in 2019 at the end of a long and illustrious career, and it ends with a forward-looking piece by five early-to-mid-career women in translation, coordinated and edited by Kate Briggs in 2018. Most of the fourteen pieces in between were written between then and early 2021; all were produced specifically for this volume; all, in some way, address the present situation. For example, Clémentine Beauvais writes of the challenges of translating rapidly dating slang for a contemporary teenage readership; Christopher Honey and Janice Chen attempt to forge entirely novel links between translation and neuroscience; Jean-Michel Rabaté discusses the new version of the Standard Edition of Freud's works; and Chad Post entitles his survey of the current publishing market for literary translation simply 'The State of Things'. While the reader will find a variety of approaches to translation here – from the scholarly to the professional, the theoretical to the testimonial, the celebratory to the resistant – they all speak to present realities and future paths for the discipline.

No book of sixteen essays dealing with translation today could aspire to 'full coverage'. This is a sign of the triumph of translation studies, which has spread beyond its initial literary focus to cover several subfields, upon most of which the present volume will barely touch. What this book aims to do instead is to put a limited number of interesting and interested perspectives into dialogue. Consider the question of vocation and permission – who is called and who is allowed to translate a text – much on the minds of the translation community of late, judging from social media exchanges, blogs, online articles, and statements via mass email.[1] We see the issue arise in different guises in this volume. Natasha Soobramanien, a British novelist with Mauritian roots, reflects on what she describes as the 'intimacy' of having her novel *Genie and Paul* (itself modelled on, versioned after, but let's not say 'translated' from, Jacques-Henri Bernardin de Saint-Pierre's *Paul et Virginie*), translated by the Mauritian novelist Nathacha Appanah. This closeness between writer and translator, Natasha and Nathacha, is something that she finds absent in the case of Jeffrey Zuckerman (a talented white, male, American translator) bringing another Mauritian, Ananda Devi, into English, and Soobramanien asks us to consider the implications of 'who gets to translate what'. Elsewhere in this volume, George Craig attests to another intimacy, one that allows him to translate Samuel Beckett's letters. This goes beyond the fact that they had the same educational and geographical path (from Trinity College in Dublin to the Ecole Normale Supérieure in Paris), or spoke many of the same languages, to a fundamental question of a translator being able to hear and render a writer's voice. The reader can find and imagine a multitude of dialogues between the chapters gathered here, touching on translation pedagogy, translatorly invention, canon formation, variations and idea(l)s of invariance, to name a few topics, each salient in our current debates, and each regularly recurrent in translation discourse over a much longer period.

The diversity of perspectives gathered in this volume ranges across generations, with eminent scholars and translators appearing alongside urgent new voices; across languages, with different parts of the world and different directionalities among languages represented; across the theory/praxis divide, with translators, scholars of translation, and scholars in other fields with an interest in translation brought together; across periods, with ancient works and older translations discussed alongside contemporary ones; and across disciplines, with literary translation at the fulcrum, but including insights from fields such as neuroscience, psychoanalysis, linguistics, and geopolitics. What's excluded from the wide range represented here are those discourses that use translation merely as a metaphor to discuss other matters. It is true that translation (etymologically linked to metaphor) makes for a great metaphor to explain other things and endlessly gathers metaphors to explain itself (translation as performance, conducting, acting, exchange, mimicry, ventriloquism, skinwalking, revivification, channelling ghosts, copying, transformation, cloning, grafting, map-making, a game of chess, a game of go, a game of charades, adoption, adaptation, reflection, reading …). Rather than reduce translation to a metaphor for something else, each of the essays gathered here discusses the material practice of linguistic translation; even when they question the individuation and countability of languages between which we translate (Sakai), or when they give a speculative account of what happens in the brain while we translate (Honey and Chen), the chapters of this volume ultimately pertain to linguistic translation as practised by humans.

The book's subtitle is intended as shorthand for some of the variety of viewpoints represented here. *Crafts* signals our interest in translation practice, or rather the set of practices that leads to the production of literary translations. Literary translators are the only translators represented here – regrettably there are no interpreters, medical or legal translators, or experts on machine translation in this volume. Kate Briggs and George Craig are translators from French; Bernard Turle and Clémentine Beauvais from English (into French); Franco Nasi from English (into Italian); Dan Gunn from both French and Italian; Rumena Bužarovska from English (into Macedonian); Aron Aji from Turkish; Katrina Dodson from (especially Brazilian) Portuguese; Sophie Collins from Dutch; Jen Calleja from German; and Adrienne Rose from Latin, Greek, and Classical Chinese. Each of these translators gives some insight into literary translation practice, but it is clear from this volume that this practice is not one, that it cannot be reduced to the singular. Sophie Collins writes here that the term 'craft' tends 'to be deployed as a euphemism for a set of so-called universal aesthetic standards'; Jen Calleja, in the same piece, sharpens the critique, pointing out that a 'craft' standard can be exclusionary – 'patriarchal, sexist, classist'. The pluralization of the term in our title is meant to counter that possibility of exclusivity: our interest is in the multiple crafts of practising translators today, not in setting, or promoting, one particular craft as the norm. The pluralisation is also meant to capture the fact that we are interested in multiple literary genres in translation (see, for instance, Clémentine Beauvais on translating children's and teenage fiction) and in the other craft-like practices that go into producing literary translation, notably editing (discussed by Dan Gunn) and publishing (discussed by Chad Post).

These practices all take place in historical, linguistic, cultural, national, disciplinary, and publishing *Contexts*. Three of our chapters – those by Susan Bassnett, Katerina Stergiopoulou, and Adrienne K. H. Rose – deal with the particular context of retranslation: translations of classical texts in conversation with the other translations of those texts that have come before (or that will follow). Retranslation in particular shines a light on the transmission/transmutation poles of translation and, collectively, this cluster of essays probes the fundamental nature of translation, of heritage, and of the contemporaneity of translations. Jean-Michel Rabaté's chapter on translation and psychoanalysis and the chapter by Christopher Honey and Janice Chen on translation and neuroscience consider translation from the perspective of an outside discipline, tracing overlaps and mutual impacts, showing how translation and the discourse about translation function within different contexts, and asking us to consider the lessons to be derived from these contexts for our own.

Finally, we hope to indicate the importance of the impacts, or *Consequences*, of translations themselves, of the manners in which they are made, and of the ways in which we talk about them. Naoki Sakai, in an at once highly personal and highly theoretical essay, traces and reformulates what he has hoped to achieve with his translation theory over the past three decades. He once more makes a plea for revising our understanding of the distinctions we make between 'our' language and 'an other' language. This is important not only because we risk being historically blinded (by the specific 'regime of translation' that we live in) or logically at fault (taking the divisions between languages and dialects to be in some way formally, rather than socially, motivated), but also because of the geopolitical consequences following on from how we formulate translation and the 'difference' it is meant to overcome (yet might in fact reinforce). Michael Cronin does fruitful work in seemingly fallow ground, taking what is perhaps translation's most overused metaphor – translation as 'loss' and, relatedly, 'mourning' – but linking it to deep, theoretical translation questions (the question of a translation's 'life' and its relation to a translation's 'completeness', for instance) as well as to concrete translation practices and their ethical and political impacts on issues such as migration, class, wealth inequality, and the construction of a culture. Rumena Bužarovska writes about the tangible effects of translations into Macedonian: economic, social, academic, canon-building, and nation-building. Her thorough, detailed, and positioned investigation into the outsized effects of literary translations – many of which she herself has produced – into one 'small' language after the dissolution of the former Yugoslavia is eye-opening and an important corrective to any sense we might derive of the stakes of translation had we only considered traffic among the world's major vehicular languages.

The rubrics of 'crafts', 'contexts', and 'consequences' are not meant to imply that there is no overlap between the essays gathered here. Aron Aji, for instance, writes about his own practice as a literary translator and, notably, as a teacher of translation (on which topic the reader can, and should, look also at Franco Nasi's splendidly playful contribution on playful translation and his practice of assigning 'extreme texts' to his translation workshop in Modena, or Clémentine Beauvais's discussion of teaching translation workshops to teenagers). Aji would be an obvious contributor to the 'crafts' discussion. But in discussing his literary translation and teaching situation, he also gives an image of, and argues for a sensitivity to, particular 'contexts' (Turkish literature in American English, and the institutional context of the 'translation workshop' at the site of its founding, in Iowa City, Iowa). And we could just as legitimately see Aji's contribution as falling under the aegis of 'consequences' since his notion of the 'covalent effect' has both aesthetic and ethical horizons. The book ends with an exciting piece by five young but established women translators – Kate Briggs, Jen Calleja, Sophie Collins, Katrina Dodson, and Natasha Soobramanien – that explicitly touches on all three rubrics.[2] This final chapter advances the debate about literary translation today, addressing several 'hot button' issues in a manner that is relational and conversational, grounded in experiences and perspectives of the contributors, and at the same time considered and written for the important slow-form, long-form, think-together object that, whether in the hands or on the screen, is a book.

Notes

1 See, for example, the debate over the (young, nonbinary, white) Dutch author Marieke Lucas Rijneveld opting not to translate the (young, black, female) American poet Amanda Gorman following a public outcry (in the Dutch media and on social media) after they received the contract to do so from a Dutch publisher. The debate began with a newspaper opinion piece by Janice Deul in *De Volkskrant*, which can be found in Haidee Kotze's translation as 'A White Translator for the Poetry of Amanda Gorman: Incomprehensible', 18 March 2021, accessed 29 October 2021, www.monabaker.org/2021/03/18/

english-translation-janice-deuls-opinion-piece-about-gorman-rijneveld/. It was soon avidly discussed by translators and translation scholars on social media, resulting in a debate so bitter that, for example, the administrator of the 'Literary Translation' Facebook page, which has more than 4,000 members, had to sift through over 1,000 comments posted on the matter in the space of a week, remove fifteen of them for policy violation, and make changes to the community guidelines. Several fast think pieces emerged in both blogs and newspapers: many reactionary, some misinformed, several deliberately distorting, few of them measured. (A recommended piece written in the midst of this would be a piece on *Medium* by Haidee Kotze, 'Translation Is the Canary in the Coalmine', 15 March 2021, accessed 29 October 2021, https://haidee-kotze.medium.com/translation-is-the-canary-in-the-coalmine-c11c75a97660. The American Literary Translators Association sent out a statement by email to all of its members, clarifying its position and supporting the inclusion of more translators of colour in their community. It should be noted that some more traditional academic writing also benefited from the debate, with many sharing and reading, for example, Şebnem Susam-Saraeva, 'Representing Experiential Knowledge: Who May Translate Whom?', *Translation Studies* 14, no. 1 (2021), 84–95.

2 Natasha Soobramanien is not strictly speaking a literary translator, but she is an author who has worked with translators and whose work is closely engaged with translation.

CHAPTER I

Solitude of the Translator

George Craig

Solitude of the translator? Well, *of course*, I hear you say: what else? (Image of a single figure – St Jerome, or Scott Moncrieff, as it might be, poised in thought over a piece of papyrus or paper covered in alien letters.) I have in mind something less predictable. 'The translator' is a functionary, like a printer, or a publisher, and may or may not be an interesting person; but by the act of *translating* he or she intervenes directly in *our* life. His/her affective processes *matter*, since we come up against, find ourselves living with, some of their consequences.

One more preliminary. It will normally be the case that the translator has taken on the translating out of admiration, perhaps even love, for the original text, but we have to allow for the possibility that it has been undertaken out of disapproval or even hatred. Our ideologically divided world makes that quite possible. Imagine yourself translating the memoirs of a Goebbels, or a Mengele....

I should, as they say, 'declare an interest': one way or another, I have been actively (and happily) concerned with language and languages, spoken and written, for most of my eighty-plus years, first as learner, then as teacher, always as enthusiast. Central to this fascination is a curious sensory imbalance: by far the most important (and effective) of my senses is *hearing*. I note, ruefully, that while many people of my age need and rely on hearing aids, I have to keep earplugs with me all the time, and find the world a very noisy place. But this imbalance has its advantages, allowing me above all to register and be interested in even small variations of tone and accent, in speech and in music.

I first found myself involved in translation when, as a schoolboy, I went youth-hostelling in France with a friend. Suddenly, simple survival depended on finding the right words: an exciting but scary prospect. A year later I went with my father to the Olympic Games in London, 1948. I was mad keen on sport, but was also fascinated by the announcements of events, names of competitors, and results: first in English, *then in French* (ah, those were the – diplomatic – days). As it happened, a man sitting behind me had noticed that I was particularly attentive to these announcements – not least, on my side, because of the way in which the French announcer pronounced the names of non-French athletes. The man tapped me on the shoulder and asked me, very politely, why I was so interested; I explained that I was learning French, but to my amazement he said: 'Well, I advise you not to imitate him when you speak: he has a very vulgar Paris accent.' I had no idea at the time that there *were* such things as local or group accents in French, but his comment stayed with me. I had myself been mocked when I was very young for having a provincial (West of Ireland) accent, and I can remember promising myself that one day I would speak a language so well that nobody would know where I came from. On such tiny details the orientation of a whole life can depend.

And so, by easy steps, to translating; first as the solving of practical difficulties that had arisen in my work as a teacher of French over my thirty years in the University of Sussex; then when I undertook to translate for publication. Two ventures warrant attention here: the translation of a work by Christiane Olivier, *Les Enfants de Jocaste* (published as *Jocasta's Children*, 1989); and that of the French-language letters of Samuel Beckett (published 2009–2016). And with these two ventures we come a little closer to the title of this piece.

First, the Olivier. It had been passed to me by my psychotherapist wife who wanted to know whether it could be of interest to non-specialist readers. So far, so neutral-sensible. I set to to read, and within a few pages, I was hooked. The voice that I heard was so unlike anything I might have expected, so unaggressive (and of how many therapist arguers can *that* be said?), that I wanted at once to translate it and get it out for an English readership. Anyone who has had experience of French intellectual argument will know that it is sustained by what seems total confidence: 'Here is how it is; there are other arguments, but they don't matter.'

In Christiane Olivier I found something entirely different: she was clearly (if diffidently) aware that there were competing theoretical approaches in anything to do with therapy, but she saw herself as focussing entirely on her dealings with the client. It felt like a humble, enquiring approach rather than a demonstration of professional confidence. What were at issue were the patient's needs. Familiar with the muscular certainties of the theorists, I felt obliged to push them out of the way – and, of course, face down a not-easily-convinced publisher. That struggle itself took a couple of years. (I was later to see a review which, among other things, asked 'Why was this not published sooner?')

But from my point of view, what mattered was the fact that Christiane Olivier's writing had spoken to me in a way that went beyond approval or interest. I had been *singled out* by her writing and *had* to respond. I was on my own. I wanted, I needed to represent her, even though I was an outsider, a non-therapist. What might have been a simple professional involvement, a job, had become a strong personal responsibility, a one-man crusade – my first experience of solitude in translation.

And so to a very different work: one that was to take twenty years. Different in virtually every respect, not least the contrast in fame: a Christiane Olivier whom virtually nobody knew, and a Samuel Beckett whom everybody knew. But there were more important differences, particularly the fact that Beckett could and did write not only in English but in French: the French-speaking world knows *En attendant Godot*, the English-speaking world knows *Waiting for Godot*; and that's just the beginning. So what need for a translator? The answer is simple enough: Beckett's letters to his French friends and acquaintances, and to other European correspondents, are in French, and those to his Anglophone friends and relations (Irish, English, American) are, of course, in English.

I was delighted to be asked to join the editorial team. I knew Beckett's work well, and there were other links: not least the shared Irishness (both of us born, brought up, and educated in Ireland). But this is not flag-flying: what matters is that Irish English is not identical with English English; not just the sounds but the *rhythms* of Irish speech are different. A simple example will show something of what I mean: the standard English sentence 'I haven't seen him for a long time' becomes in Irish speech 'I haven't seen him this long time', where the word 'long' has to be spoken a tone higher than the two words on either side. But, just as it's essential to be aware of this difference, I repeat my point about flag-flying: nothing could be further from Beckett's mind and feelings than a glorying in things Irish: the 'Gaelic revival' meant less than nothing to him. And he is very much aware of the danger of overindulging in Irishries: in a letter to Barbara Bray he mentions a translation he himself has done (of a play by his friend Robert Pinget), and says of his own contribution: 'a bit too free and Irish'.[1] Only once have I come across the kind of Irishism that jumps out almost aggressively. It occurs in a letter to an ex-student of his, and refers to exchanges they'd had in those far-off days: 'when you went and wrote the wild poem'.[2] It is the 'went and wrote' that catches the eye, more than the 'wild poem'.

Anyone setting out to translate Beckett must negotiate all such differences. Something of that 'negotiation' is what I want to show here.

I should make clear that Beckett and I never met. Three times we arranged to meet: the first time, it didn't happen because he was ill; the second, same story but my turn to be ill; the final time, he was hauled away at short notice to deal with a crisis in a German production of one of the plays. There had been an earlier failure, on my side. As I was leaving Trinity College Dublin for Paris in 1953, one of my tutors (Owen Sheehy Skeffington, an old friend of Beckett's) had handed me a letter of introduction to Beckett. Sadly (dismally) I was too shy to take it up; and, by the time I'd got my nerve back, he was so famous that access was virtually impossible. The publisher Jérôme Lindon, whose taking up of three of Beckett's unpublished novels had virtually launched him, saw to that.

Now to the work. Perhaps the most remarkable fact about the letters is their sheer *number* (they are to be counted in thousands): if you wrote to him, he answered. Even when the incoming letter amounted to little more than 'Dear Mr Beckett, I think you're wonderful', it would get at least its 'Thank you so much.' So deeply ingrained was the habit that the writing day took a recognisable form: letters in the morning, his own work in the afternoon. And, of course, the incoming letters covered a colossal range; one has only to think of (in English) his thirty-year correspondence with Alan Schneider, who directed his plays in America, or (in French) his exchanges with the art-historian and critic Georges Duthuit, the publisher Jérôme Lindon, or the painter Avigdor Arikha. My task was to translate some at least of these letters into English.

But what English? These are not any old letters, and not simply a set of polite replies to earlier messages; they are the letters of a great writer to his friends and colleagues. This is a classic translator's challenge. What do I do?

I start from an extraordinary fact: Beckett could be said to show, and live with, a barely believable combination of propensities usually seen as irreconcilable – those of the introvert and those of the extrovert. Beckett the drinking companion (back at dawn from a drinking session with, say, Harold Pinter); Beckett the delighter in the otherness of other people, the man who knew every decent restaurant in Paris, and where one might find Tullamore Dew; and Beckett the man who needed to sit in silence, waiting for the promptings that could only come in that silence, and which would issue in that body of writing which was *not* the letters, all the long way to *Worstward Ho*. As an incorrigible introvert, I had to mind my step.

But there was one possibility of common ground. It was speech. Everything about the words, as they hit me, told me that, before they had been written, they had been *spoken*. One way of suggesting how much that mattered is to remind readers how Beckett could not rest until he had found performers who could speak his words as he had heard them in his head – and how he loved those performers for their ability to do so: Jack MacGowran, Pat Magee, Billie Whitelaw (just read the letters in which he speaks of the many performers who could *not* get it right, whether famous like Joan Plowright, or up-and-coming like Albert Finney or Brenda Bruce). Or look at the photograph of Beckett coaching an attentive Billie Whitelaw.[3]

But the importance of speech runs far beyond actors and public performance. When I read Beckett, I am instinctively listening out for what I can only call the *voice of the text*. This it is that drives the words, but also prompts *me*: promoting this, playing down that, boldly advancing, hastily retreating, asserting, qualifying, *suggesting*. And how am I to represent these -ings?

This is where we come back to Irishness: not, I hasten to say, as some simple this-rather-than-that. For the Irish, there is always a tension between local and official, and between standard English and usages familiar since childhood. The questions for me will be: 'How will Beckett have *said* these words *at that moment*? With what stress? What volume or insistence?' Only when I feel I am sure of that can I move to the next stage: how to *represent* what I have heard; how to find an English that can somehow convey these emphases, these allusions, these reachings, these reminders, these compromises. But what is essential is my hearing the voice of the text, with its particular characteristics *that day*, its emphases, its *tone*. Then and then only can I reach for some sort of equivalent, drawing on the resources of both standard and Irish English. And, as I hope that makes clear, there can be no other voice present: I am alone with Beckett. It is in the solitude that that brings that I find what allows me, indeed impels me, to put out these and not other words.

What complicates matters is that Beckett is at ease in more than one foreign language – French of course, but also Italian and German. (Anne Atik, the wife of the painter Avigdor Arikha, tells of how Beckett and Avigdor would talk to each other in any of several languages, but usually finished up in German.) There is no 'rule' other than his own sense of the *appropriate*, always at work, something that shows in how he handles the addressee (as friend, as collaborator, as authority, as victim of circumstance). In short, he doesn't need a translator to help him out. It is always his voice that I need to hear: to reach a sense of how he would have said this or that *in English* to that person on that day. He enters the world of the Arikhas, or Jacoba van Velde, or Roger Blin, or Ludovic Janvier and engages with each in an eager sharing. The relative closeness of the relationship varies, of course, from one case to another, but Beckett's side is abundantly clear, and it is for that that I listen: to have the sense that that day, to that person, he would have spoken like *this*, because this is how his written words work: their meaning and their tone. Here are two small examples of how it works. In a letter to the Arikhas he writes, of holiday arrangements, 'Avons fini par bien nous loger'; and my translation is 'Eventually found somewhere nice to stay.'[4] And to Josette Hayden he writes 'Je partirai après-demain passer 48 heures avec les cousines'; and my translation is 'I'll be going away the day after tomorrow to spend a couple of days with the cousins.'[5] Beckett, then, knows perfectly well what he wants to say, and how he wants to say it; my task is just to try to catch that.

But there is one major exception: a set of letters in which Beckett does *not* know what he wants to say, or whether he is able to say it. These are the letters to Georges Duthuit.[6] In these long, impulsive, almost desperate venturings, Beckett is facing down his unrecognised demons, searching for new ways of saying/writing; wondering whether *this* is possible, *that* desirable or necessary. He trusts Duthuit, so holds nothing back: doubts, hopes, fears, memories fill page after page, in sentences that go on and on, tumbling over each other. As readers we know only the urgency they had for Beckett: they are about whether he can and how he might or should write. Amazingly, Duthuit can take all this. But one would almost want to say that we as readers can take it only because we *know* that Beckett overcame the demons, and went on to produce new work: new novels, new plays. We are being given a glimpse into the crucible where the words are formed and aligned, and of his casting about in that crucible. As translator, I could only listen and try to follow him.

These letters to Duthuit I have called a 'major exception' to the general run. There is also a minor exception: the small number of letters in which Beckett acts as critic or adviser. We all know, from *Godot*, what to think of 'crrritics'. At the same time, Beckett himself never loses his sense of the appropriate, the acceptable, and has no hesitation in amending or correcting the words of friends or protégé(e)s who have sent him texts of theirs to read – even if he has to say, with almost comical discomfort: 'No, no: don't thank me.'

Whichever way we turn, I come back to *voice* as the single most important of the elements that make up the oeuvre. I realise that, in using a phrase like 'the voice of the text', I am begging several questions: implying that there *is* a 'voice of the text', claiming that I hear it and respond to it in and by my translation, and that that translation – by an English speaker – of the words of another English speaker, Samuel Beckett, can stand in for his words. That is a very large claim, or set of claims. I can only assert that I am, successively, hearing and transcribing what I *hear*, and that what I hear *is* the voice of the text.

But how can this be? Virtually all literature reaches us as letters printed on a page, and that reality never goes away: the next time we open the book, those letters are still there. Surely *this* is the central reality? I grew up at a time when the primacy of the eye was unquestioned. English teachers dealt with obtrusively non-visual collocations like the Tennysonian 'and the long glories of the winter moon' by invoking category words such as 'assonance' or 'onomatopoeia'. (I concluded at the time that, in thinking such words deadening and unhelpful, I had simply got it all wrong.) Well, we may have moved on since then, but something remains of the tendency: after all, the printed page *invites* the eye. I can only go back to those English teachers of long ago and play a similar game, encouraging people to think of these printed characters also as a *score*: an instruction to let the symbols be *heard*, as musical notes played on an instrument are heard.

But what, it would be reasonable to ask, does all this come to as *experience*? What is it like to listen for and to the voice of the text across a thousand samples covering more than thirty years of Beckett's life? Who is the Beckett with whom I have been closeted for nearly as long? This solitude, this private, one-way relationship has its own reality. I already had the highest admiration for his *work*, but this was different: this was Beckett off duty, so to speak.

The issue of voice doesn't arise, for the most part, with what one might call the 'business' letters – to publishers, publicists, 'officials' of various kinds; but even within these there is a small but interesting subgroup: the letters which show him dealing with the problems of professional acquaintances, for example the admirably argued letter he writes to the court in Franco's Spain in support of Fernando Arrabal, on trial for blasphemy and every kind of turpitude. Or again the letter he writes to one Connie Ricono in support of an Italian actress who had been refused (for contract reasons) permission to perform *Giorni felici* (the Italian translation of *Happy Days*). He is careful to say that he doesn't know the actress (Clara Colosimo), but that 'it is impossible for me not to be touched by her attachment to my plays and poems',[7] and he asks that permission be, exceptionally, granted. What is apparent, in these and other similar cases, is, quite simply, his generosity of spirit. It is enough for him to hear of someone's distress for him to offer help or sympathy or both. Fame (and, of course, there was to be no shortage of that) made no difference. It is enough for him to hear that, for example, Djuna Barnes (of *Nightwood* fame) has run into financial difficulty: at once he jumps in to help. To use an almost forgotten expression, he had no 'side'. The clearest illustration, of course, is his response to the award of the Nobel: it is 'a disaster', and all ceremony must be avoided. What is needed is anonymity and distance, so he and Suzanne hide in Tunisia (although even there newshounds are in pursuit).

Small wonder, then, that the correspondence in general maintains and deepens his commitment to family and friends, in France, or England, or Ireland, or America. Then again, one of his most endearing traits is his readiness to encourage younger artists: one thinks of the warmth of his support for Harold Pinter, whose *The Caretaker* had been coolly, even dismissively, received in Paris – Beckett ashamed of, and apologising for the ineptitude of French reviewers. And the young French writers who benefited from his support or advice were beyond counting.

It is impossible to read these letters without being moved by this readiness to reach out to others, his lack of vanity, and, before, during, and after all this, his pursuit of the word through a lifetime. Even in the late letters, body now failing, mind clouded, memory fading, and without hope of a future, we still hear the voice; not just in the regrets and the mocking of the irreversible feebleness, but in the simple human warmth that never leaves him. 'I hope words have now failed me', he writes in 1989. They have not.

And, finally, I go back to saying that listening in silence for the sound of a voice, and the words that that voice carries (from familiar to desperate), is an utterly – and matchless – solitary experience. That solitude has been, for me, a gift beyond price.

Notes

1 Letter of 13 November 1959 to Barbara Bray, in Samuel Beckett, *The Letters of Samuel Becket* (henceforth *LSB*) *III: 1957–1966*, ed. George Craig, Martha Fehsenfeld, Dan Gunn, and Lois More Overbeck (Cambridge: Cambridge University Press, 2014), 254.
2 Letter 28 August 1981 to Elizabeth Stockton, *LSB IV: 1967–1989*, ed. George Craig, Martha Fehsenfeld, Dan Gunn, and Lois More Overbeck (Cambridge: Cambridge University Press, 2016), 556.
3 *LSB IV*, 317.
4 Letter of 15 October 1966 to Avigdor Arikha and Anne Atik, *LSB IV*, 50.
5 Letter of 28 December 1972 to Josette Hayden, *LSB IV*, 316.
6 *LSB II: 1941–1956*, ed. George Craig, Martha Fehsenfeld, Dan Gunn, and Lois More Overbeck (Cambridge: Cambridge University Press, 2011).
7 Letter of 3 July 1967 to Connie Ricono, *LSB IV*, 75.

CHAPTER 2

Translation, Creativity, Awareness

Franco Nasi

> For, you see, so many out-of-the-way things had happened lately that Alice had begun to think that very few things indeed were really impossible.
> – Lewis Carroll, *Alice's Adventures in Wonderland*

'Wordfish' is the title of a short poem for children written by Roger McGough:

> Wordfish
> are swordfish
> in a state of undress
>
> Criss-crossing
> the ocean
> in search of an S.[1]

McGough's ditty is a witty and moving story of worried wordfish in search of their lost identity. If, instead of an S, our wandering fish happened to run into an L, they could suddenly assume the new, unexpected identity of worldfish. Words can indeed open doors to surprising worlds, as we are frequently taught by children, poets, and whoever has the ingenuity to look at languages in an oblique or divergent way.

Leaving the wordfish to their search, we might wonder whether in another language – Italian for instance – words (*parole*) can generate worlds (*mondi*). They do not have many letters in common; nonetheless, *parole* can easily generate a *prole* (children, progeny). With the loss of a single letter, they can create offspring, a commitment for the future, hopefully new and better words. It is just a coincidence, but it could come in handy to a future translator who might stumble in the translation of the paronomasia word-world. Obviously, this is not the only solution nor a 'perfect' one: the translator could adopt different strategies, opting for a synonym for world and trying out a new play on words – such as *terra* (earth) and *erra* (third person of the polysemic verb *errare*, meaning both to wander

15

and to make a mistake, an error); or *mondo* (world) and *modo* (mode or way) – or just leave *parole* and *mondo* and be satisfied with them ... This is the beauty and ugliness of translation, its *splendour* and *misery*, as José Ortega y Gasset entitled an enlightened and always enlightening essay on translation, published in 1937.[2]

Each translation carries with itself the awareness of its own limits. Even if people still insist on using meaningless adjectives such as faithful or unfaithful as a critical paradigm to evaluate translations, a faithful, perfect translation does not exist, simply because it would be a paradox, a contradiction in terms. It could be no more than a mere copy, provided it is elaborated in the same language, in the same place, and at the same time as the original, and therefore an original itself or a non-translation ('Pierre Menard, Author of the Quixote' by Jorge Luis Borges, on the one hand, and digital texts, on the other). However defective and tentative translations might be, they are nonetheless vital and necessary, because they are movements not only from one culture to another, from one language to another, or from one language to its variations in time and register (such as intralingual translations of Shakespeare's plays into contemporary English), but also from a thought to a word, or from a text to an idea. Translation preserves by creating and creates by preserving.

We all live immersed in a perennial translational movement, from a past that becomes present and future, remembrance and projection into the not-yet, as Enrico Terrinoni, the Italian translator with Fabio Pedone of the last three books of *Finnegans Wake*, argues in his pyrotechnic and hypnotizing recent book *Oltre abita il silenzio*: 'We must begin to think that we are all *translating beings*, and that our life is actually an infinite and inexorable translation.'[3] With regard to the alleged limit of any translation, Terrinoni adds, 'Translating is not a perfect equation, because the idea of change does not provide for this possibility. As we are never the same in two different places-moments in space-time, in the same way two distant points of sound-sense will never, ever coincide. And this is why in translation, rendering sometimes involves surrendering.'[4]

Translating the Impassible

From a linguistic point of view, today, probably more than ever before, we are 'translating beings'. We are exposed to foreign languages every day, and new technologies are working hard to help us to survive in our multilingual world. It is not uncommon to read ads for a little device the size of a mobile phone that claims to be able to translate any oral text into a variety of languages in real time. Not many decades ago, an instant automatic translator was a figment of the imagination, maybe that of a skilful science-fiction writer. Certainly, it was not something purchasable online. David Bellos titles his successful 2011 book on translation *Is That a Fish in Your Ear*, after a somewhat similar translating tool imagined by Douglas Adams in his *The Hitchhiker's Guide to the Galaxy*, a series first broadcast on BBC Radio 4 in 1978. The magic object was a curious earplug, a Babel fish – a wordfish, if you wish – that, once stuffed in one's ear, was able to translate from and into many languages. What was a dreamed tool half a century ago is now a real device.

Even without using handheld linguistic interpreters, our daily interaction with the computer allows each of us to handle translating situations with languages we barely know. Accustomed to heavy, old paper dictionaries, but having experienced such wonderful technological progress and having seen 'so many out-of-the-way things', we are likely to think, with Alice, that very few things are impossible in the realm of translation.[5]

In Lewis Carroll's book, Alice thinks about the 'impossible' at the beginning of her journey underground, when she realizes that the door to which she has the key is too little for her to pass through. She needs to become smaller to succeed, and so she does become smaller. In Walt Disney's adaptation, or intersemiotic translation, of the book, there is a curious new piece of dialogue between the girl and the door. Alice asks why she cannot pass through, and the door answers:

DOOR: Why it's simply impassible!
ALICE: Why, don't you mean impossible?
DOOR: No, I do mean impassible. *(chuckles)* Nothing's impossible!

It is an easy pun and probably can be translated with no trouble in many neo-Latin languages. But a closer consideration of the word might render the translation more complicated. The *Merriam-Webster Dictionary* has the following definition for *impassible*: '1. a: incapable of suffering or of experiencing pain; b: inaccessible to injury; 2. incapable of feeling: impassive', and with the less common spelling *impassable*: 'incapable of being passed, traveled, crossed, or surmounted'. When we hear the conversation in the Disney film, we probably choose the second meaning (i.e. that Alice simply cannot pass through). Nonetheless, the door is also heartless and impassible to Alice's request. The passage of the pun from English to another language is definitely more complicated if we try to maintain in a single word both the different nuances of *impassible*. In Italian, for instance, we have *impassibile* and *impassabile*. In this case, the act of translation, of transposition, or, as we say in most neo-Latin languages, after Leonardo Bruni, the act of *traductio*, of leading through, and therefore of passing through, is almost impossible.

In a way, what I just wrote about the homonymy in English of the term *impassible*, and the apparent impossibility of carrying it over into Italian, is in itself a way to inform the reader about a specific feature of the source text and its problematic rendition in another language, and therefore a highly 'expanded' and 'clarified' translation, to adopt a couple of Berman's deforming tendencies.[6] The sword/word/worldfish and the impassible door are just two examples of a self-evident commonplace: no present-day Babel fish is able to find an efficient, economic, and aesthetically convincing translation of McGough's poem or of Alice's pun on the impassable door. The poem 'A Valentine' by Edgar Allan Poe can be used as a third example. The composition, with rhymes and metric cadence, states clearly that it is a riddle, that the solution is the name of the lady to whom the valentine is dedicated, and that her name can be found hidden in the poem. Here is the beginning of the twenty-line poem:

> For her this rhyme is penned, whose luminous eyes,
> Brightly expressive as the twins of Leda,
> Shall find her own sweet name, that nestling lies
> Upon the page, enwrapped from every reader.[7]

After a careful perusal of the text, and maybe with the essential help of an editor's footnote, a reader might see that the name is hidden in a very original, diagonal acrostic: first letter first verse, second letter second verse, third letter third verse, and on, for twenty lines to form Frances Sargent Osgood. Most people, like the automatic translation tool, might be able to grasp the meaning of the horizontal sentences, but they are unlikely to identify the diagonally written solution. Before we try to solve the problem of the translation, we need to *set the problem* properly: we need to have a clear idea of the bidirectional complexity of the text, its metrical form, its rhythm, and the aim or *skopos* of our translating act.[8]

Translating the 'Remainders'

No doubt the world continues to exist without these bizarre compositions and their tentative translations, but it would be very different if writers and translators were forced or decided not to use our languages in divergent and oblique ways; if they ignored the 'remainders', the 'dark side' of language;⁹ if they went on strike, ceasing to force the language, and lived within the reassuring barbed-wire borders of standard, communicative, unambiguous language, with our Babel fish finally able to solve every translation problem.

This might have been what Orwell's Big Brother had in mind when he reformed the language and introduced Newspeak in the superstate of Oceania. With *Ingsoc*, the name of the new language, no divergent thought could be uttered, and perhaps not even thought. This is what we read in the appendix of *1984*:

> The purpose of Newspeak was not only to provide a medium of expression for the world-view and mental habits proper to the devotees of Ingsoc, but to make all other modes of thought impossible. It was intended that when Newspeak had been adopted once and for all and Oldspeak forgotten, a heretical thought – that is, a thought diverging from the principles of Ingsoc – should be literally unthinkable, at least so far as thought is dependent on words.¹⁰

The goal is clearly stated: 'Newspeak was designed not to extend but to diminish the range of thought' and could be reached by 'cutting the choice of words down to a minimum'. In addition to the programmatic statements, the *1984* appendix gives instructions on how this new denotative, economic, and pragmatic language could be forged. The new language (which would become the only language by 2050) is based on Oldspeak but transforms it radically, through a sort of intralinguistic translation. It reduces (and eventually eliminates) all its ambiguities and interpretative possibilities. In Newspeak, for example, the word 'free' can be used only in the sense of 'devoid of', as in the phrase 'a field free from weeds', but not in the sense of 'free man', since in the state of Oceania this concept (or state of being) no longer exists. Useless words have therefore to be eliminated, starting with synonyms and opposites, thus favouring an enormous contraction of the dictionary. An example that clarifies how the grammarians of the Newspeak intend to proceed is offered by the word 'good'. It is not necessary to have a contrary word with a different sound and etymology, such as 'bad'. It would suffice to put the prefix 'un': so we would have the much more economical pair of opposites, 'good' and 'ungood'. Beyond Orwell's examples, we could take another similar pair such as 'right' and 'left' and translate them into Newspeak 'right' and 'unright'. If we exit the semantic field 'left-right' and look laterally, we might see 'right' as opposite to 'wrong'. Since we do not want to have any ambiguities in our language, we could apply to the new pair of opposites the same rule suggested by Oceania Newspeak, this time using the second term as dominant:

'wrong' as opposite of 'unwrong' (for right/correct). If we look carefully, we realize that a root is left over from the two oppositions: obviously, the word 'left' that we can now use in its meaning of the past participle of the verb *to leave*, as opposed to exhausted, consumed completely, now 'unleft'. This way of proceeding, disambiguating, and economizing would be an automatic machine translation delight. The following table, to which I have added the Italian translation, might help make the new lexicon even clearer.

Right	Right	Destra
Left	Unright	Sinistra
Right	Unwrong	Giusto
Wrong	Wrong	Sbagliato
Left	Left	Rimasto
Exhausted	Unleft	Consumato

All this just to introduce another poem for children by McGough:

> The dentist drilled my teeth
> Left right left right
> But he didn't do it right
> Left right left right
> So I've only got one left
> Right left right left[11]

As in jokes, no explanation is needed. But what would a Newspeak translation be like?

> The dentist drilled my teeth
> unright right unright right
> But he didn't do it unwrong
> unright right unright right
> So I've only got one left
> unright right unright right

Perplexity is the reaction one might have when faced with a 'composition' of this kind. What is it? An avant-garde poem? A nonsense verse for children? Or just an intralingual translation that, as Henri Meschonnic would have said, instead of ferrying a living text safely from one bank of the river to another, is delivering a dead body? To add another piece to the puzzle, when I read McGough's poem for the first time, I thought the right and left refrain was the obsessive back-and-forth of the drill on the teeth of the patient, which could have been a plausible interpretation. But to a native English speaker, or at least in McGough's mind, the left/

right is the cadence of a military march. All those different interpretations (more or less legitimate or immediate) are possible simply because the language of the original poem has not been reduced to a 1984 Newspeak, flat, unanimated, monochromatic, grey, unambiguous message. Human languages, as long as they stay human, live with their ambiguities, playfulness, overlappings, allusions. In specific communicative situations, as in poetry, language urges word somersaults, and in so doing, stimulates thinking, wakes it from the slumber of linguistic clichés and standardized habits, solicits interpretative wit and imagination. Newspeak, on the contrary, far from wanting to stimulate anybody, aims to transform language into something standard and automatic, 'as much as possible independent from self-awareness'.[12] The new language would also make every diachronic intralingual translation impossible, in particular of literary texts. The passage devoted to this topic in the novel is indeed frightening:

> When Oldspeak had been once and for all superseded, the last link with the past would have been severed. History had already been rewritten, but fragments of the literature of the past survived here and there, imperfectly censored, and so long as one retained one's knowledge of Oldspeak it was possible to read them. In the future such fragments, even if they chanced to survive, would be unintelligible and untranslatable. It was impossible to translate any passage of Oldspeak into Newspeak unless it either referred to some technical process or some very simple everyday action, or was already orthodox (GOODTHINKFUL would be the Newspeak expression) in tendency. In practice this meant that no book written before approximately 1960 could be translated as a whole. Pre-revolutionary literature could only be subjected to ideological translation – that is, alteration in sense as well as language.[13]

Newspeak does not allow any ideological opposition to the dominant power and at the same time annihilates the historical memory and heritage of a civilization. 'A little more than kin, and less than kind.'[14] Like Claudius in *Hamlet*, Newspeak committed a murder. To sum up – parodying a contemporary flag-waving chauvinist slogan – 'Meaning First!' Aesthetic forms and allusions, ambiguities and remainders are to be left out, as hopeless migrants.

Translating Extreme Texts

My point is that the analysis and translation of what I have called extreme texts,[15] or highly constrained texts, such as acronyms, anagrams, lipograms, pangrams, plays on words, and puns, but also poems, lyrics, and even novels, are not just useful teaching practices that can allow students to improve their linguistic competence, both in their native and foreign languages. I believe that these activities have a fundamental pedagogical and political value. Today, perhaps more than ever, it is necessary to activate learning experiences that can stimulate the acquisition of a habit of autonomous thinking, a critical thinking that is able to grasp the complexity of a problem, or of a text, through a rigorous and yet open-minded perusal and scrutiny and at the same time render/translate the complexity in a different, original form. The translation of extreme texts requires both an active approach or insight, and complex analytical work; it forces us to understand the divergent and non-standard ways in which foreign language is used and the mechanisms that allow linguistic and cultural systems to be elusive and surprising, and, at the same time, it urges an original, creative rewriting of the text and a thorough scrutiny of the endless possibilities of the target language. In a classroom setting, it can also be a highly motivating and pleasant activity, and a perfect way to train the mind, to improve our human ability to comprehend the complexity of a problem, define it, and be aware of our responsibility as active mediators as we look for an original and creative translation. Furthermore, the translation of extreme texts questions and challenges the power of the instructor – the teacher will assign a translation without having the answer from the teacher's edition, simply because there is no single right solution, and there is no unique strategy to be followed. The teacher becomes a maestro collaboratively working with his pupils in a Renaissance artist's workshop rather than a chalk-and-talk authority dispensing truth and definite solutions.

In his still valuable 1963 essay, 'Da tradução como criação e como crítica', Haroldo de Campos highlights the pedagogical relevance of the act of translating. Translation is not a mere reformulation in a different language of a text, but an active educational process of critical thinking and creativity, and a critical act directly performed.[16]

Even apparently unambiguous expressions can hide unexpected potential meanings. I have come across the title of Nathaniel Hawthorne's masterpiece *The Scarlet Letter* many times over the years, and the image has always been that of a red *A* sewn on Hester Prynne's dress. But one day, while talking about the A-shaped 'mark' or 'stigma', to use Hawthorne's words, on Dimmesdale's chest, I noticed that the mark was his Scar, his Scar-let letter. I have not been able to find any passage in Hawthorne's writings or in critical literature on his work that says anything about that 'coincidence', but after that lateral reading or insight into the title, the scar is now always right there, on the front page of the book. And if I were to translate even only the title of the novel, I'd be facing a very complex problem, as I did when I was asked to translate the 'Dentist Poem' by McGough. Needless to say, the English homonyms (right/left) do not work in Italian, as shown in the table. With this kind of translation, we are often on the verge of throwing in the towel. The more you think about it, the more the translation seems impossible. Then a plausible solution might come unexpectedly, maybe while walking, riding a bicycle, or drinking a cup of tea. Then out of the blue came the Italian 'a destra e a manca', an idiomatic expression meaning the same as 'destra e sinistra', but 'manca' means both 'left' and 'missing', so, since the drill left no teeth in the mouth, all the teeth were missing. Once the first lateral solution is perceived, then it is only a matter of experience and craft to find a *maldestro* (clumsy, maladroit) for 'not right', and to give a metrical cadence to the text with an alternation of hendecasyllabic and enneasyllabic lines.

> Il dentista mi ha trapanato i denti
> A destra e a manca a destra e a manca
> Ma la sua azione è stata assai maldestra
> A manca e a destra a manca e a destra
> Ora dalla bocca ogni dente manca
> A destra e a manca a destra e a manca[17]

Somebody might say that this is not a faithful translation of McGough's poetry, because 'clumsy' is not in the source text, 'a destra e a manca' is formal and a bit obsolete, whereas 'left right' has a martial ring to it. They are probably right, even if it is difficult to define the boundary between a translation, a paraphrase, an adaptation, a rewrite, and a transcreation. Perhaps, as Gideon Toury said, it is a matter of 'Norms',[18] which, like almost everything, change over time and space. And this, after all, is not negative: movement has something to do with life and our nature and allows us to laugh every now and then, which does not seem to happen in the superstate of Oceania.

To establish connections between the secondary, potential, and hidden meanings of several signs requires a critical, non-mechanical ability and, above all, an open mind accustomed to perceiving words as something other than clichés. Children are masters of re-elaboration and enjoy assembling and disassembling words. John Pollack wrote a very pleasant informative book on word games, with a title that in itself is a nice play on words and at the same time a puzzle for those who would try to translate it: *The Pun Also Rises*. The challenge is even more difficult if, as in Italy, Ernest Hemingway's parodied book *The Sun Also Rises* is known by its British title

Fiesta. Pollock writes about the importance of looking at language in a divergent way in order to improve one's own critical thinking:

> As children gleefully learn to spot and evaluate secondary meanings in common words and phrases, they're really learning how to think critically. To get the joke, they have to overlook the obvious to explore other possible interpretations of what they have just heard, and fast.[19]

Teaching Extreme Translation

A pedagogy of translation aimed not only at the acquisition of a technical skill but also at the improvement of wider and deeper critical thinking about the translating act is the subject of many recent international studies and experiments. This is witnessed also by the interest aroused by Lawrence Venuti's project to publish a collective volume that gathers together significant experiences of translation teaching. Venuti's call for papers, which required 'descriptions of courses and pedagogies for teaching the translation into English of humanistic, pragmatic, and technical texts', received a hundred and sixty-four proposals from twenty-four countries. A selection of twenty-six articles was published in the very useful volume *Teaching Translation: Programs, Courses, Pedagogies*. In a substantial introductory essay ('Translation, Interpretation, and the Humanities'), Venuti identifies three contradictions, or 'institutional antinomies', in the university system. The first is that many translation courses are taught by teachers who neither translate nor conduct research on translation. The second is that 'to dedicate one's research and scholarship to translation in any form continues to be tantamount to jeopardizing one's academic career'.[20] These two antinomies emphasize the 'prevalent notion' that translation is 'a one-to-one correspondence with the source text' and is therefore reduced to 'a process of mechanical substitution',[21] and is not regarded 'as scholarship or as art, as a kind of writing that should be valued for its learning or its creativity, or that might be learned and creative at the same time'.[22] This leads to a third pivotal contradiction: notwithstanding the fact that the hermeneutic approach to translation as an interpretative act, following, among others, George Steiner's *After Babel*, has been assumed as a diffused and shared model in literary and cultural studies, the prevailing paradigm as far as translation is concerned is an 'instrumental model, in which translation is seen as a reproduction or transfer of an invariant that is contained in or caused by the source text, whether its form, its meaning, or its effect'.[23] This is proved by the fact that the authors of many academic studies quote and comment on texts in translation without even recognizing that they are working on translated texts and therefore on texts that are the result of an interpretative act, almost always omitting the translator's name.

The volume's theoretical approach is more clearly stated by Venuti in his previous *Translation Changes Everything*, a title that sounds like a catch-phrase for a new manifesto. Without denying the political importance of his 'foreignizing' approach to translation – extensively explained in his *The Translator's Invisibility* of 1995, which owed much to the hermeneutical line of thinking of Friedrich Schleiermacher and Antoine Berman – in *Translation Changes Everything*, Venuti asserts that the Schleiermacher–Berman line, 'although apparently hermeneutical in its approach, although apparently treating translations as an interpretation, rests uneasily on an instrumental model of translation'.[24]

Venuti's hermeneutic model, which we could define as radical, looks at Jacques Derrida's notion of inscription and Charles Peirce's interpretant in his unlimited semiosis and can be applied to every literary genre and all types of text: humanities, pragmatic, or technical. 'The inscription and the interpretant' become 'the key factors in a hermeneutic model that eschews the German tradition of hermeneutics – notably the work of Martin Heidegger and Hans-Georg Gadamer – where the aim is to disclose an essential meaning in the source text'.[25] To be respectful of the source text does not consist in a rigid foreignizing translation but in establishing 'the ground of an ethics of innovation in the translating culture'.[26]

'A Survey of Translation Pedagogies' by Sonia Colina and Venuti is the closing essay of *Teaching Translation*. The excursus identifies two main pedagogical approaches to translation. In the first, based on a positivist epistemology, the teacher's knowledge is to be transmitted to the learner in a more or less automatic way, with a 'chalk-and-talk' teaching strategy – in other words: 'look at what I write on the board, take notes and do as I did'. Opposite to this approach, recent translation studies, more receptive to a socio-constructivist epistemology, has pushed for a radical shift from a positivist to a constructivist epistemology in the teaching of translation: 'the translator and the translation process' and not the 'veneration of the source and target texts' is now the focus of pedagogical activity.[27]

The objective of translation courses is no longer to show a correct and definitive translation of a text and to induce students to reproduce that unique and standardized *problem-solving* procedure. Its main objective is to develop translating awareness and skill. If translation is a 'decision-making process', and if its choices are to be made in a conscious and situated way (i.e. in a particular context, in which the linguistic aspects must be considered together with the cultural, economic, social aspects, etc.), teachers in the classroom will have to abdicate the title of supreme legislators or judges, to assume the more modest and fruitful function of facilitators or guides.[28]

The need for an opening to a didactic method based on a socio-constructivist approach in the field of translator training had already been stated by Donald Kiraly in his convincing and scientifically solid *A Social Constructivist Approach to Translator Education*. In the book, cognitivist pedagogy seems to intertwine with the assumptions of American hermeneutics, and its notion of interpretative community, and the active role of the reader in creating the meaning of a text:

> Translators today cannot afford to be linguistic hermits, sitting alone behind a typewriter and surrounded only by dusty tomes. Translators are embedded in a complex network of social and professional activity ... Translators are professional text interpreters and communicators. They do not transfer meaning; they *make* meaning as they work.[29]

Kiraly insists on the difference between translation competence and translator's competence. To have translation competence means being able to produce an acceptable text in a target language based on a text written in another language. To acquire translator's competence means to be able to interact in different communicative situations, with different speakers and different communication systems. Translators should therefore be aware of the responsibility they have in the communication process, since their role is not only to transfer a meaning from one language to another but to create it.

Consequently, in training translators, 'chalk-and-talk lectures should be replaced by collaborative workshops, attended not only by teachers and students but also by experts and actors in the editorial productive chain (professional translators, editors, publishers, or clients). The 'guide' should be careful to situate the translation act in a real context, making explicit to students the purpose of translation (why it is done, for whom), coherent with the principles of *Skopostheorie* and other functionalist approaches to translation. Moreover, ethical considerations implicit in every translation act should not be neglected. And finally, it would be necessary for pragmatic translation choices always to be followed by a theoretical reflection, in order to strengthen the awareness of the translators.

It is not uncommon to hear, from colleagues who are experts in specialized translations and corpora, criticism about the uselessness of theoretical reflection on translation. An excess of theory, especially if not directly connected to the experience of translating, can indeed be tautological, self-referential, and ultimately useless. But if by theory we mean a rational and self-aware reflection on our own action, in an attempt to comprehend its complexity and social/ethical relevance, then theory is an essential moment in the development of a translator's competence.

When I read about this apparently recent turn from a positivist to a socio-constructivist epistemology, some pages by one of the greatest positivist thinkers of the nineteenth century, John Stuart Mill, come to mind. The essay 'On Genius' appeared in the *Monthly Repository* in 1832 and deals with the problem of the acquisition of knowledge. Mill's position is very clear: what is learned passively is not true knowledge. It is necessary that each person 'discovers' the 'truth' directly, by direct experience. We can learn to repeat 'like a parrot' knowledge that someone else has communicated to us with words, but if we really want to know something, we must 'discover' that something in an autonomous way, we must be sure that the thought is our thought: 'I must verify the fact by my own observation, or by interrogating my own consciousness.'[30] The purpose of education is not to fill the minds of the pupils with information: 'Never trouble yourself about giving knowledge – train the mind – keep it supplied with materials, and knowledge will come of itself. ... Let the feelings of society cease to stigmatize independent thinking.'[31] That was written almost 200 years ago, by a positivist philosopher, yet it has the urgency of a recommendation that fits well with our contemporaneity, which, as we know, is marked by endless movements and changes that require flexibility and competence rather than knowledge.

Yet you can go even further back in time and find other similar pages. Plutarch, for example, in *The Art of Listening* asserts that the learning process is not reducible to stacking knowledge: 'The mind does not need to be filled like a vase, but rather, like wood, needs a spark that ignites it, giving you the impulse to search and an ardent love for the truth.' It often happens, continues Plutarch, that one goes to the neighbours to ask for fire, but then, finding their large and luminous flame, one remains there to warm up, without lighting one's own torch, without taking possession of the fire, without being autonomous. It is necessary 'to practice a personal research, to acquire a mental habit not of sophists or pure scholars, but deeply rooted and philosophical'.[32]

It is reassuring to note that supposedly new acquisitions in the most recent pedagogy have always been at the centre of the reflection of enlightened minds, like those of Mill or Plutarch, and not just another recent pedagogical *turn*.

Conclusion: Defining the Game

A brief description of a teaching experience that took place during a workshop on translation for advanced students in an undergraduate programme in Modern Foreign Languages at the University of Modena and Reggio Emilia. The first part of the workshop was led by Laura Gavioli and dealt with translating using corpus aids. Topics varied from current news to tourism to public service leaflets. I was in charge of the second part of the workshop that dealt with the translation from English into Italian of 'extreme texts', mostly children's books to be translated into Italian. We began with texts like the Swordfish/wordfish or 'The Dentist' poem by McGough, trying to identify what we can call the intratextual constraints (puns, metric, rhythm, rhymes, etc.) of the source text and comparing the numerous solutions of the students. The same was done with picture books, where the paratextual constraints, such as images or the performability of the text, are essential parts of the book to be translated. At the end, we worked on texts with allusions and parodies (intertextual constraints) such as Alice's poem 'How Doth the Little Crocodile'. The most rewarding experience, however, was the collaborative translation of a popular picture book recently published in England and not yet translated into Italian. *Oi Frog!*, written by Kes Gray and illustrated by Jim Field, is the first of a series of four very witty 'dialogues' between animals. The first one is between a frog and a cat and is described on the cover of this colourful book as 'a hilarious rhyming tale about a frog who discovers that all animals have their special places to sit!'

What happens is quite simple: the cat tells the frog to sit on the log. The frog doesn't like the idea and asks to sit on the mat. Of course, cats sit on mats, says the cat. The frog tries something else: 'what about a chair?' And the cat answers back that hares sit on chairs. And from then on, there is a lively and surprising list of places where the different animals must sit, simply because their names and the names of the object are phonetically connected by rhymes. Thus, Mules sit on Stools, Parrots on Carrots, Foxes on Boxes, Gorillas on Pillars, Rats on Hats ... The frog at the end of the book seems to be convinced that there must be a rule but has a last question for the cat: 'What do dogs sit on?' 'I was hoping you weren't going to ask that', is the cat's answer. And the last image closes the circle with the dog sitting on the frog that was supposed to sit on the log. The second book of the series, *Oi Dog!*, is the revenge of the poor frog. It begins by changing the rules – it is not frogs but rather dogs that must sit on logs, and this is only the start of a number of surprising new combinations of places and animals. This is a brief description of the written text, which could be easily translated without the 'impassible' constraint of Field's beautiful illustrations.

A few months before the beginning of my workshop, an Italian publisher specializing in children's books, Carlo Gallucci, asked me first whether these books were translatable and, second, if I was willing to do it. Since I tend to think that theoretically everything is translatable, I was tempted to accept the job. But the more I thought about it, the more hopeless I felt. I simply could not find the right key to unlock the text, all my solitary walks, cups of tea, and bicycle rides waiting for some lateral insight to happen notwithstanding. So I said to the publisher that I was going to give it to my class as a collaborative assignment and see if something would come out of it. The text was given to the students at the end of our semester workshop, after they already had the opportunity to face many other challenging translations. They were informed and aware that the assignment was a real project, with a real publisher interested in the translation and a teacher who was unable to do it. The class was quite large (about seventy students). They worked in class for two hours in small groups of three, exchanging first impressions and 'setting the problem' together. Then they finished their translation individually at home. When I began to read their solutions, I was astonished by their creativity under these constraints. Using the images, and well aware of the logic and stylistic structure of the composition, they were able to solve all the different challenging rhymes and images in a smooth, highly readable, and funny translation. We discussed the different solutions in class, decided which were the most convincing, and tried to polish the text by working on the number of syllables, the alliterations, and other details. An example: in Italian, parrots is *pappagalli* and carrots is *carote*. No way two *pappagalli* can sit on *carote* and rhyme. The illustration of the picture book has two parrots, one big and the other small, sitting on a heap of carrots. The solution: 'Il pappagallo e suo nipote siedono sulle carote', 'A parrot and his nephew sit on carrots'. Icing on the cake: The publisher and the English writer accepted the translation, which will be published and signed as a collaborative translation.

I may not have been the goal-scoring star of the match, but at the end I felt like a satisfied and proud coach, not able to run as fast as his players or to kick the ball hard enough, but perhaps useful in setting up the game, in defining the problem, giving the players the opportunity to display their talent and ingenuity in solving it.

Notes

1. Roger McGough, *An Imaginary Menagerie* (London: Frances Lincoln, 2011), 88.
2. José Ortega y Gasset, 'The Misery and the Splendor of Translation', trans. Elizabeth Gamble Miller, in *Theories of Translation: An Anthology of Essays from Dryden to Derrida*, ed. Rainer Schulte and John Biguenet (Chicago: University of Chicago Press, 1992), 93–112.
3. Enrico Terrinoni, *Oltre abita il silenzio* (Milan: Il Saggiatore, 2019), 62.
4. Terrinoni, *Oltre abita il silenzio*, 179.
5. Lewis Carroll, *The Annotated Alice*, ed. Martin Gardner (Harmondsworth: Penguin, 1970), 30.
6. Antoine Berman, *La Traduction et la lettre ou l'auberge du lointain* (Paris: Seuil, 1999).
7. Edgar Allan Poe, *The Works of the Late Edgar Allan Poe*, vol. 2, *Poems and Miscellanies*, ed. N. P. Willis, J. R. Lowell, and R. W. Griswold (New York: Redfield, 1850), 14.
8. Franco Nasi, '"Per lei, il cui nome è scritto qui sotto": sulla traduzione di un acrostico obliquo di Edgar Allan Poe', *Griseldaonline* 17 (2018), accessed 29 October 2021, https://griseldaonline.unibo.it/article/view/8980.
9. Jean-Jacques Lecercle, *The Violence of Language* (London: Routledge, 1990).
10. Erich Fromm, 'Afterword', in George Orwell, *1984* (Harmondsworth: Penguin, 1981), 246.
11. Roger McGough, *Bad Bad Cats* (London: Puffin, 1997), 35.
12. Fromm, 'Afterword', 253.
13. Ibid., 255–6.
14. William Shakespeare, *Hamlet*, ed. David Bevington (New York: Bantam Books, 1988), 1.2.65.
15. Franco Nasi, *Traduzioni estreme* (Macerata: Quodlibet, 2015).
16. Haroldo de Campos, *Traduzione, transcreazione. Saggi*, Italian trans. A. Lombardi and G. D'Itria (Salerno: Oèdipus, 2016), 46.
17. Roger McGough, *Gattacci*, Italian trans. Franco Nasi (San Dorligo: Einaudi Ragazzi, 2001), 53.
18. Gideon Toury, *Descriptive Translation Studies – and Beyond* (Amsterdam: John Benjamins, 1995).
19. John Pollack, *The Pun Also Rises: How the Humble Pun Revolutionized Language, Changed History, and Made Wordplay More Than Some Antics* (New York: Gotham Books, 2012), xxiii.
20. Lawrence Venuti, 'Translation, Interpretation, and the Humanities', introduction to *Teaching Translation: Programs, Courses, Pedagogies*, ed. Lawrence Venuti (London: Routledge, 2017), 4.
21. Venuti, 'Translation, Interpretation, and the Humanities', 5.
22. Venuti, 'Translation, Interpretation, and the Humanities', 6.
23. Venuti, 'Translation, Interpretation, and the Humanities', 6.
24. Lawrence Venuti, *Translation Changes Everything: Theory and Practice* (London: Routledge, 2013), 3.

25 Venuti, *Translation Changes Everything*, 4.
26 Venuti, *Translation Changes Everything*, 8.
27 Sonia Colina and Lawrence Venuti, 'A Survey of Translation Pedagogies', in *Teaching Translation: Programs, Courses, Pedagogies*, 203.
28 Rosemary Arrojo, 'Deconstruction and the Teaching of Translation', *Translation and Interpreting Studies* 7, no 1 (2012): 96–110.
29 Don Kiraly, *A Social Constructivist Approach to Translator Education: Empowerment from Theory to Practice* (New York: Routledge, 2014), 12; italics in the original.
30 John Stuart Mill, *Literary Essays*, ed. E. Alexander (Indianapolis, IN: Bobbs-Merrill, 1967), 34.
31 Mill, *Literary Essays*, 45.
32 Plutarch, *L'arte di ascoltare, Tutti i moralia*, ed. E. Lelli and G. Pisani (Milan, Italy: Bompiani, 2019), 86–7.

CHAPTER 3

Anatomy of a Day in the Life of a Translator
Bernard Turle
Translated by Michael Overstreet

> To Christiane Besse, pygmalioness in thanks for the plushness of the wing under which she took me and others
>
> *'We never live our own lives; we always live those of others.'*
> Antoine de Saint-Exupéry, *Southern Mail*

Another translatorly night of sleep. Which is to say another night haunted by Frenglish morsels, those I'd failed to purge out onto the computer screen the night before: the reason why, between one and two thirty in the morning, and then again before daybreak, at four, my brain, already weakened by an extensive bout of insomnia riddled with everyday aches and pains, became plagued with dreams of yapping, delicate monsters.

It is in Frenglish that my delirious hallucinations assault me, and it is in Frenglish that you should read these lines, ' – hypocrite lectrice, – ma semblable, – ma soeur!', for, given the Globish of the modern world, the pidgin I use while thinking is the dialect that best reveals my state of mind. However, a translator is meant to have neither a state of mind nor a condition of the soul. Due to the vagaries of the world of publishing, to which critics all too often forget professional translators are indentured, I wrote these lines in French and my French was translated into English.

The catalogue of the Bibliothèque Nationale in Paris states that, to date, I, who by birthright (if the political history of my native Provence had gone differently and had not been so bridled by Parisian centralisation) ought to be a speaker of Occitan, have translated 180 works from English into French. However, this is only the second time that the inverse has occurred: that I have been translated. You will not be surprised, then, that as a taciturn Mediterranean, I am taking full advantage of the opportunity to set my translator a task I hope will be as arduous for him as these sleepless nights have been for me. Dear *lectrice* (finally, in my unusual role as author writing for a specific occasion, I take licence to address you directly or, rather, *quasi* directly, as if it were my voice that were reaching you and not that of my translator), I implore you to practise, on behalf of my young colleague Michael Overstreet, a goodwill that critics have not always shown towards me – hence my recurring nightmarish visions.

1:30 a.m. I am awoken by a scream that I let out in the middle of the night after a disturbing dream wherein an ectoplasmic blogger brandishing a weapon in each hand told me he had finally discovered a return to form for T. C. Boyle in *The Harder They Come* (2015), Boyle back at his best, writing as he did 'in his greatest novels, those from his early years (1981–2000)'; in a sequel to my disturbed dream, a second waking nightmare, I qualify: 'his greatest novels, *those that I have not translated*'. Indeed, I have only been translating Boyle since *Drop City* (2003). This is what I call my Amis–Boyle–Brink Syndrome: publishers entrusting authors to me only after their reputation has been established, and whose later works are reviewed with eager displays of a painful nostalgia for the novels that secured their fame in the first place (i.e. those I did not translate). To be sure, these are prestigious authors, but I had shown up after the *fête*. Furthermore, I feel a certain guilt: what if I was responsible for the disaffection of the francophone blogger towards his favourite American author? Just as I might be guilty of the fact that Peter Ackroyd, a bestseller in English (and whose fifteen titles I have translated), only ever appealed to the critics in the French-speaking world. Will my biography rattle off a litany of failures one after the other? And if so, would it be considered the story of a paranoiac?

2:30 a.m. I drift back to sleep and begin to wander. I owe my most harrowing nocturnal screams to my Leghorn Syndrome. 'Leghorn' was one of my most persistent recurring night terrors, persistent, that is, until it was replaced by another, similar but worse, nightmare – aka 'du François' (more about which soon, dear *lectrice*). An eternity ago, before the computerised twenty-first century, an attentive reader had contacted me by post, care of the publisher – a common practice at the time. He had enjoyed my translation of an art book on Tuscan villas, by Harold Acton, but what a pity, he exclaimed in his letter, that I had left Leghorn in English, when it should have been written in French: *Livourne*!

4:00 a.m. 'And what to say concerning the toponym "Le François" (a municipality of Martinique), the prefix "Le" systematically used there like it is in English, as if one said in French, apropos the port of Le Havre, "à Le Havre" and "de Le Havre" (instead of the grammatically correct contractions "au Havre", "du Havre")?' And thus I am awoken once again, this time a little before dawn, by my own scream echoing the motto of the chivalric Order of the Garter: 'Au François qui mal y pense!' In my translation of *Fanon* (2008), by John Edgar Wideman, *Le Projet Fanon* (2013), I had committed this gaffe which was fiercely highlighted on the blog of an economist and exponent of the French language (a rebuke that continues to admonish me to this very day, since the internet possesses not only the gift of imbecility but also that of indelibility). The economist and specialist-of-works-written-by-French-speaking-authors-who-live-in-regions-that-may-or-may-not-politically-qualify-as-French-but-are-usually-almost-always-outside-of-hexagonal-France, or *francophoniste*, working out of Melanesia, when reading my African American author in the French I rendered, disliked 'the verbal deluge and the tangential observations of this novelistic text'. When critics are disappointed by a work in translation, they have a tendency to direct their hostility toward the translator, predictably claiming that 'the translation is not always up to the standard of the original'.

O expected and urticant verdict.

Do I practise this trade so that I may be infantilised in this way? To have my wrist slapped because of one supposedly inaccurate word, lost amongst the 125,000 others? I am dying to retract my wrists and regain control of my life.

Is it not the common belief that a translation can *never* be up to the standard of the original, that it can only ever be a third-rate remake, a contestant doomed to the B-league? One could, incidentally, ask how high this standard could possibly be, given the low opinion the *francophoniste* economist had of the non-novel. 'The word "*blancheuse*" is used several times. Is this a pseudo-creolism in the American text?' Here, too, a mundane 'gotcha' remark. Whenever we translators risk using deviant vocabulary (in this case an insular variation of '*blanchisseuse*') or whenever we seem to neologise or take any sort of linguistic initiative, someone always finds a good reason to strike it out. This happens to authors too. When the British press reproached Martin Amis for having, in *Lionel Asbo: State of England* (2012), invented a slang word that did not exist in contemporary reality, he replied quite fittingly, something along the lines of: 'Why use a word that would only be valid for a few months? My book would be démodé before it even came out.' The French press laughed (I was relieved) reading my adaptation of the false slang of Amis I reinvented in French by listening to the kids who always take the same Provence–Alps–French Riviera Regional Express Train (TER) as I do, kids whose ideology and idiolect reminded me of those of the protagonist. If it is possible that the (necessarily) external bodies the translator injects into the original text contaminate it, it is nevertheless these bodies that, throughout its 400, 500, or 600 pages, breathe new existence into the work. Critics rarely draw attention to this virtue of respiratory aid brought to a book via its translation. They no doubt take it for granted.

A translator is supposed to possess an encyclopaedic knowledge, but we have our limits. We are humans, not machines, the tendency of millennials in newly assumed positions of power to view us as mere gadgets, subordinate tools to be kept away from any serious editorial process, notwithstanding. (Is this the first step toward our replacement by automated translation and the final step of the erasure of our biographies?) We occasionally have someone on hand who knows the answer, but not always. As a last resort, for better or for worse, we frantically coast along the far reaches of the Web – O great and fallible navigation. (Before, we spent lifetimes at the library, a practice no longer feasible.) Some sites write 'au François'; others, such as the official website of the city, 'à Le François'. Am I right in remembering that I had once found the phrase 'I arrived à Le François' in one of the works of Frantz Fanon that I had read to try to shed some light on the antinovel of Wideman and to instil my translation with a bit of his Negritude? Why had I preferred 'à Le François' to 'au François'? Had I thought that it would make for a better 'pseudo-creole'? I go to the train station *des* Arcs(-en-Provence) and refer to it as such, but I then hear the train conductor articulate through the loudspeaker, 'destination *de Les* Arcs'. I was thus, at the time of the translation of *Projet Fanon*, perfectly aware of the contention. Was I like the fearful pupil that systematically chooses the wrong answer, or was I like a hapless victim of Dracula, subconsciously drawn to the wrong, dead-end street? Perhaps, in the case of 'à Le/au François', my brain had asked itself whether administrative jargon was in the process of evolving (or anglicising – americanising – exactly what the *francophoniste* economist was accusing me of). In these neoliberal times, the names of municipalities are more like labels or logos, and if they are composites, they seem to want to appear in their entirety under any circumstance. Where I am going with this is to say that my blunder did not bear witness to my having committed a sin of anglicisation, nor did it testify to a moment of disgraceful laziness or inattention but rather to the shifts in language that I spend all day – no doubt inappropriately and excessively – investigating and questioning, even at this very moment as my groggy mind meanders, perhaps affected by ergot of rye.

5:00 a.m. The problem with critics is that they, looking through their opera glasses from their high loge, cry out 'To arms!', but only once the battle has already been decided. Their work would be more helpful if they could somehow intervene beforehand, while editors are still fastidiously laying siege day after day. Whatever the case may be, it is I, the translator, and not the critic, who woke up screaming a few minutes ago. It is I who have, concerning these lines, already used the last of my ammunition and am already at half the number of pages that are allotted to me in this group publication, while not fulfilling the promise of my title (my own personal *Projet Fanon*), seeing that I have not even begun to recount my day in the life of a translator – only my night. Anxious awakening at 4:00 in the morning. Thus, I, like a hard-working and erring (but also impassioned, attentive, and monastic – and perhaps occasionally combatant) scribe, am ready for my morning rituals.

5:07 a.m. At least, to soften the blow of my awakening, I can reminisce on how a collection editor purchased the rights of a novel and gave it specifically to me to translate. After reading my translation, he exclaimed: 'Ah, I finally know what he means!' 'It is not easy', writes Vladimir Jankélévitch, 'to perceive the infinitely doubtful glimmer, nor to understand its meaning. This glimmer is the flickering lustre of insight by which the unknown is suddenly discerned'.[1] (No doubt that the translation apps that enable you to 'speak forty-three different languages' will soon advertise having such 'insight'.) During a radio exchange on France Culture, Antoine Perraud, a distinguished journalist (as well as anglicist and musicologist), congratulated me for having been able to recognise and then follow the jazzy rhythm of Wideman throughout *Projet Fanon*. Self-gratifying reverie.

6:00 a.m. As it happens, after such a night and rude awakening, I find myself needing to reconnect as quickly as possible with the music of the book that I am translating these days, the latest Boyle, *Outside Looking In* (2019), about the inventor of LSD. By 'music' I mean something like its breath and rhythm: the bass notes in the original that sustain me during my months of work and that it's my duty to diligently breathe back into the translation. I am now awake, and so must I start chipping away at my translatorly day.

6:21 a.m. Before leaving for his shift at the hospital, my husband takes my blood pressure, and it is not first-rate. Is the 'À le François/Au François' nightmare to blame? Not entirely. Sitting all day long. A life spent translating paper tigers, not living my tiger life, not singing my own song. When will I live my own life to feed my own biography? 'I would very much like to see Syracuse / so as to remember it in Paris.'[2]

6:37 a.m. Turning on my computer with the rising sun, I open straight away my folder *Translations* and click on the description *Outside Looking In*. (Not an easy title to translate. Will it be necessary to follow the example of the Germans? Boyle is the one who suggested to me the alternative title for the novel, *The Light*, saying: 'The Germans called it "Das

Licht". Perhaps "*La Lumiere*"?', without the accent – there is often an error, included in the original printed book, when my authors risk writing French words.) Before translating a single line, I prepare myself to return to the thread of his story, the thread of a life that it not mine. The rhythm of my breathing is not my own; I breathe adulterated, artificial air. I latch on to my computer as if my nightmares and nightly repose (or absence thereof) were of no consequence, as if only the words of the author were important; I do not solve my own faults, only those belonging to others.

6:45 a.m. In order to relieve my shoulders of the weight of the night, it is best that I do not immediately start translating. I tackle my correspondence, which means checking my mailbox, answering the emails that call for an answer, and avoiding, on the periphery of the screen, the clickbait inviting me to translate some or other statement using some or other translation app. My life at that moment is comprised entirely of the emails that I received while having my nightmares and that seem twice as virtual.

7:15 a.m. Hence the desire to stuff myself with an excessively greasy, sugary, and indulgent breakfast in order to physically confront the weight of the text, a quick snack that calms me momentarily but worsens my hypertension. I feel as if I am looking to fill the tank, to become a tank, an engine. Rest assured, dear *lectrice*, I will not expand upon the composition of my communal morning *agape*. I will not give in to the culinary lyricism of Boyle, or André Brink, or of one of my Indian authors, in whose writing the description of dishes triggers an orgy of aromas – descriptions comprised of either French gastronomical terms, which, far too quotidian to impress the francophone reader, are unable in French to evoke the exoticism they take on for an American or a South African audience (they would be received in France as merely irritating, something that would drip off the tongues of some nouveau riche discovering good taste for the first time), or of Hindi, Gujarati, or Bengali terms that have not yet entered into the vocabularies of francophone bon vivants. Instead of salivating, I spit. Because how can taste be conveyed through writing, particularly in the language that gave us *La Physiologie du goût* (*The Physiology of Taste*) and Camembert, particularly when it concerns the preference of taste buds that are the polar opposites, the very antipodes, of those of Brillat-Savarin? Even if I, personally, have such antipodally inclined taste buds upon my tongue, how can my French words possibly articulate the delicate, savourous palate of baingan bharta, rogan josh, and gulab jamun?

7:56 a.m. After stuffing myself, and after, maybe, a quick jaunt in the garden (which I will have to resign myself to enjoying only via the occasional observation from my office window throughout the day), instead of watering the aubergines that will supply my husband with the makings for a potential baingan bharta tomorrow, I get to translating. That is to say that I remove myself from my physical environment. I eject myself from my life in order to dedicate myself entirely to the book and life of another.

But why not to my own book, to my own life? To my own biography: *Scenes from Provincial Life*? I am reminded of Sophie Mayoux, one of the French translators of J. M. Coetzee, enthusiast of his 'autrebiography': oscillating between biography (not lying) and fiction (lying). Translation: a double lie. Yes, to write my biography, to at last no longer be someone else, to no longer lie.

Translation, a double lie: is it a sensible and honest way of being in the world? Yes, if I have an Indian conception of translation (India: republic of multilingualism, land of translation) – namely, where translation is a pragmatic need that is as self-evident as it is nonchalant, a daily tool that permits me to understand others and them to understand me in a multilingual context. Here, in the heart of my Provençal, Maylesque community, which is subscribing more and more to a sort of interlanguage, people do not understand my work; they cannot even *conceive* of what it is. Why would someone need to translate? This does not prevent Neo-Provençals from translating ceaselessly as well as unconsciously, akin to, à la Molière, M. Jourdain speaking in prose, burying their ancestral tongue (whatever it was) under their blissful assimilation to a new language that is now slowly heading toward universalism (i.e. Globish): 'J'ai *checké* ton *combo* sur le *web*. *Fun*! Génial pour *binger* toutes les *séries* que tu veux. Tu vas *customiser* tes meubles? Et en plus, t'as un *parking* pour ton *SUV*, c'est *top*!' In case of emergency (if they go abroad), Neo-Provençals think translation apps are *top*. They could not care less that 75 per cent of the 'target language' output is gobbledygook. In India, at my friends' apartment in Maharashtra or at the Andhra Pradesh orphanage where I sometimes stay, when I am translating directly under the air vent, cloistered up in my room, I feel as though it is I who am an untouchable or disabled child and, on top of it all, a crook. All the people around me, even the most illiterate minds, seem to speak multiple languages as a matter of course. It is social context that imposes these mental gymnastics.

8:15 a.m. In short, to come back to the here and now, I must get to work on my translation. *Outside Looking In* is the tenth Boyle that I have translated; it first appeared in German, in Germany, where he has an enormous fan club – certain commentators go so far as to say that Boyle is an American *and* German author. My face goes pale once more; another failure to add to my unwritten biography? Boyle has a large following in France, but not to the point of holding his 'première' in Paris in *my* translation.

8:32 a.m. I come across the phrase 'the doctor applied his stethoscope'.

8:34 a.m. I send a text to my husband, who, on his break (at 9:30), reports that in French medical parlance one would say, 'the doctor listened to the heart of his patient' or 'the doctor listened to the lungs of his patient'. English opts for the visual, the gestural ('applied'), the object ('stethoscope'). All morning long, examples come up one after another, gestures comprised of two actions condensed into a single term: 'The book she had slipped from the shelf ... shrugging off her coat ... pushed herself up from the chair ... she swung a leg over the crossbar of her bike'. French opts for intent ('listened'), which will thus be reflected in the translation, letting gestural precision fall by the wayside. It is important to remark that English (the author), too, sometimes leaves out what French makes clear: the stethoscope can be used to listen to the heart *or* the lungs. Must the translator choose between the heart or lungs, which the author was able to elide? Must I ask myself a question that the author did not even think about and also proceed to answer it? On to the next problem.

9:51 a.m. To get back to my grub, what I *would* prefer is an Icelandic or Scottish breakfast. *Hafragrautur*/porridge, herring, black pudding, fried tomatoes, eggs, bacon, beans, toast, honey ... It would seem that this is not too terrible a choice for a person suffering from hypertension. Perhaps it is even recommended, especially for those translators who subscribe to the Translators Studio method, the one that tries to get you into peak physical condition like Robert De Niro in *Raging Bull*, who knows? In any case, it is probably better than trying LSD to better immerse myself in the ambiance of *Outside Looking In*. And my morning ablutions? Maybe I will skip them today. I know, an aberration and a sin for most believers, American and americanised, but not for this Mediterranean translator – I, who prefer to preserve the bite marks of my sleepless night and remain trapped in the envelope of the words of yesterday, the words of the book that has become my very life. I will wash when I have truly penetrated the pulsation of *Outside Looking In* and have allowed myself to take a step back and distance myself, physically, from the text. Then maybe will I discover errors of viewpoint. Only then will I be able to remove what has remained too visceral and idiosyncratic from the translation – that which has remained too Provençal *cabrier*, which is to say, that which is myself; only then will I be able to remove myself from the story even more. Which is, at the moment, a pleasure and a relief, because to work in the morning is the happiness of recovering an illusory world, a world à la Jacques Demy, cut off from my physical reality: a quasi-magical universe, regardless of the content of the book. It is the happiness of not existing, the excitement of returning to a story and style that I steep in for several months, with a new perspective each morning brought on by the contradictory desire to appropriate them because, each day, I insensitively metamorphose them, unweaving and reweaving them so that the original text resembles me more and more – without my trickery being noticed, naturally. A bit like how, as children, upon discovering a new word, we would enter a brand-new world that we were free to inhabit as we pleased. Eventually though, we would believe that we ourselves created what we discovered. Then an all-powerful feeling would come when credulous, admiring adults began to believe in this world themselves. It is the same thing here, now: in what has become my language, I say what the author said in his, which is *almost* the equivalent of having thought it first. I consume authors and their source language; their blood becomes my blood. Translators have a trace of vampire in them. Translations of novels are accompanied by dark, incomprehensible forms and forces, just as much as those of poetry.

It is often said that poetry is more difficult to translate than novels. However, the latter is an epic that is just as elusive, just as rhythmic or unbalanced; it has rhymes without end and ends without rhyme, or reason, a structure similar to the 'line of beauty' mentioned by Ackroyd in *English Music* (1992),[3] undulations, in the ocean of words, from the dolphin on which the translator must sit astride for several months. (Did Norman Douglas mention in *Siren Land* [1911] the legend of a boy who, mounting a dolphin in the bay of Naples, ended up wounding himself on the pointed fin of the porpoise and dying? I translated it so long ago – so many sentences, pages, books ago – that I no longer know.) And what does my splashing around with dolphins, in Kailua-Kona, Hawaiʻi, or Coral Bay, Western Australia, have to do with my 'real' life (the one my biography that will never be written will be based on) as an adventuring anglicist curious of every last anglophone land? Or even better: a dolphin of the Ganges glimpsed in the brown waters under the Howrah Bridge? The entire anglophone world, with its plethora of accents, mixes in my kaleidoscopic brain and moves in lexemes. Accompanied by the dolphin memory, I advance, as if pushed by the sacred Fire, into the vapours of *Outside Looking In*.

11:00 a.m. Break time. An apple from the Durance river valley, a piece of cheese from Salers. An ergot of rye (lol).

11:18 a.m. Pre-lunch break. The more effectively and expeditiously I type, the faster I will get the first step over with, and the more time I will have to take care of the translation problems that are not necessarily where I think they are (the Le François-esque difficulties are the trees that conceal the forest), and the longer I will be able to extend my lunch break. The more effectively and expeditiously I type, the more I resemble the hordes of stenographers that we humans of the cross-contaminating information age have become. So yes, it is now (11:27) possible to answer the questions: 'What do you think of translation software? Do you believe that it will supplant you one day?'

Oh, it will not supplant me personally; I will supplant myself all by myself: I am on the last stretch, in both my private and translation lives. My successors however ... I have seen typographers, assistants, proofreaders, copy-editors, so many secretaries sacrificed on the altar of changing times, an entire personnel that was still integral to the publishing world of the 1980s. Today, in the twenty-first century, everyone can make a book without the help of others because of the good graces of the internet. The Association of Literary Translators of France campaigns to have the status of author attributed to its members, no doubt believing that this is the way to save them from the purge, which, at the same time, turns a blind eye to the fact that even authors are no longer safe from being devoured. Translation software threatens translators; there is no denying it. We can jeer at the absurdity of the idea, but the technology is evolving and will swallow us all; the internet is engulfing the human in every domain. The internet promulgates internet culture. Literary culture will be lost in, and by, the masses; what other future can we expect at the heart of mass-market thought?

12:00 p.m. I persevere; my translating continues.

1:00 p.m. Let us redress the most pressing matters. Lunch time.

1:12 p.m. Digestion. Occasionally, the TV/nap break turns out to be fruitful. This somnolence is not necessarily wasted time, but rather a time of maturation, research, and sometimes unexpected revelation. I disengage and stay alert. Even while dozing, I do not withdraw from my translation, for translation *is* my life. Every now and again, half-listening, I chance upon a fruit ripe for the picking. I lift myself up from my chaise longue and rush to the pencil permanently stationed in front of the television set so as to enable my jotting down words or expressions before they vanish into oblivion as abruptly as they had appeared.

1:57 p.m. Rough awakening after another recurring nightmare. It was about 'brands' (probably due to the deluge of TV ads for 'seniors' at this time of day); brands, one of the heartbreakers when I am awake and when I am translating. Amis invents pseudo brand names. Boyle, he uses real names, which never fails to abrade my secular, republican disposition. In short, I dream that I am both deaf and mute, getting thrashed by baton blows and taser. This scene alludes to my translation of the 2007 Boyle, *Talk Talk*, and, more precisely, to the reproaches that a professor at Lille University addressed to me (in a review) because, among other things, I had translated the word 'Mace' as 'baton' (*matraque*). He sought, as he explained it, to

> illustrate how the task of the translator, in [his] conception, has a 'visual purpose'. One must find a balance that could also be said to be a focus, in the cinematographic or photographic meaning of the word, ranging from blurry to clear – which in no way means that the translator must render clear that which is blurry, of course, the translator makes visible to the reader what the original makes visible, no more, no less, and most importantly, 'no less'!

The incriminating passage in question is the following: 'She watched the cop – the patrol man – in her side mirror as he sliced open the door, hitched up his belt (they all did that, as if the belt with its Mace and handcuffs and hard black-handled revolver were all the badge they needed) and walked stiffly to her car.' One thing the professor from Lille University reproached me for was using the French word for 'truncheon', which he took as me not having *seen* the capitalisation of 'Mace'. It is clear that I had asked Boyle about this *while translating* the book, long before the nasty remark was made by the professor in his review, and that Boyle gave me a description of the object, but it is certainly possible that I indeed did not see or, rather, did not *want to see* the capitalisation, since I associate the integration of brand names into a text as product placement and am loath to provide publicity without recompense. The professor reproached me for having read 'mace' with a lower case as a blunt weapon (the item that the 'mace bearer' of Westminster wears – this here is a troubling fact, because I personally knew the 'mace bearer' of the time … *Had my private life meddled in my work? Gnawing desire for an autobiography?*). Furthermore, among other sins, for 'black-handled revolver', I had used 'black-handled Colt' (*colt à poignée noire*), which seems, in Lille, to be a product name and an aberration, because 'Colt' would send the reader to the Wild West. Had I been blinded by a hopeless, Gallic anti-American liberalism during the seventies? Not to the point where I would have been unconscious of what I was doing. I had chosen 'black-handled Colt' intentionally; in no way did it just come to me out of the blue. As for the cinematographic visualisation exercises forwarded by the professor from Lille University, which seem to me to be a statement of the obvious (how can there be a description without having the setting, place, etc. reveal itself in the process?), I am sure that most translators constantly practise it – except that everyone sees in their own way, no? If I misled the reader, which remains to be proven, did I see, in the scene where a police officer wrongfully arrests a woman, an act of timeless violence? Is timeless American violence always a repeat, in my eyes, of Wild West culture? Hence, perhaps, this shift to 'Colt'?

2:08 17" p.m. I am a hair's breadth away from throwing in the towel, from letting university professors and *francophoniste* bloggers make do with translation apps. And, moreover, I am, in this text, currently surpassing my quota of authorised pages.

2:08 23" p.m. Fortunately (for me), the Lille University professor continued describing (himself): 'The translator, attentive and discreet, explicit here, implicit there, a focusing he hopes is perfect, in perfect balance'. He then gives his version of the passage in question. Because it is useless to reproduce it here for an anglophone audience, I will instead content myself with a simple quantitative comparison. The original passage contains fifty-two words, mine fifty-six, that of the professor seventy-two.

2:11 p.m. My publisher would be delighted (particularly from a financial point of view) if I gave him a text fattened up to that extent (even if, in French, it is estimated that a translation from English will witness a 15 per cent increase in length, something that I find to be debatable and, frankly, undesirable). As for the francophone reader, who, in the translation of the professor from Lille University, is certainly on the right path thanks to his indispensable 'paralysing gas spray' (*bombe de gaz paralysant*) for 'Mace', does she/he not run the risk of being bored to tears, if not by my 'baton', then by slowing the rhythm of the language to a crawl? The professor and I manifestly do not share the same *cinécriture*, to borrow a term from Agnès Varda.

I confess, I detest firearms (I cannot even stand the term 'target language', so you can imagine …). In *Talk Talk*, I was again no doubt the fearful pupil or victim of Dracula that makes a mistake because he *wants* to. Mea culpa. My mistranslation was the acting out of a pacifist. It oozed the nausea I experience whenever I hear the Second Amendment; it came about, I know, I confess, from my opposition to the interference of firearms in life and in writing. I am a Gandhian translator who, from time to time, has the duty of translating the lexical field in which firearms reside and who, every now and again, merits a gun barrel held to the temple by a Lille University professor.

2:16 p.m. How many francophone readers have, to date, suffered from my mistranslation? How many francophone readers would have suffered through a *Talk Talk* that was more than a third longer?

2:17 p.m. I drive this digression and the NRA from my mind and get back to translating. I pass quickly from *Talk Talk* to *Outside Looking In*, from guns to LSD. I visualise things cinematographically. My paranoid ramblings risk being a pernicious influence on my postprandial productivity. I must reinvigorate myself. It is that time of day when hyper- and hypotensives enter into the most tenacious battle. Do not squander energy with regrets and remorse but channel it into words, damned words, splendid words, breadwinners, comforts, palliatives, jubilations, all at once and entirely. An unremitting game of balance ('perfect focusing, perfect [cinematographic] balance'? No, I am leaning towards velocipedic). Conserving the rhythm of the translation while conserving that of my own life and vice versa. Pondering, translating all the while, the possible traversals/transferrals of one by/into the other.

3:13 p.m. I am in front of my screen but I am also on a plane, boat, train, bus. People are often surprised to hear that I can work on public transport. They think that the noises of the world are a handicap. Far from it. Is vagrancy not the m.o. of the translator? I, a true jacklondonian, must tap my science from the wide-open world.

4:00 p.m. Break time. The 'after-school snack', or the 'four o'clock snack', as we used to say as kids. I take advantage of the respite to go down to the patio and give myself over to my favourite pastime, mosaics. At first, I started mosaics or, more precisely, 'picassiettes', as an antidote to translating, to de-stress. The 'pique assiette' picks at the plates (*assiette*) of other people. Using mortar, the picassiette cements, upon surfaces of his or her choosing, fragments, bits of broken 'assiettes', shattered remnants of porcelain, pieces of figurines, shards of glass, and buttons. It is a raw art, based on the imagination of the fingers and is subject to guided improvisation. I quickly noticed that, in my picassiette performance, all I was doing was transposing the mechanism of translation; I pick at the plate of the author. With the help of old pieces, fragments, and Brexitian morphemes, I create a new francophone 'work'. Like a patchworker, I pick through garbage, glean what there is to grab. I work only with what is secondhand, broken, dusty. I write only in quotes; everything has been said, everything has been written, everything already exists; all I do is bend down and pick it up, reorder it, and revamp it. Translation and picassiette are the achievements in my office and on my patio, respectively. The culmination of my gleaner wanderings on this planet.

4:36 p.m. I cease my picassietterly translation of the world.

4:39 p.m. And take back up my scriberly translation. My end-of-afternoon work is benefiting from my sojourn in the garden as well as from the act of cementing together coloured pieces of a bygone universe, fragments on which I bestow a second life. A sort of serene peace settles within me.

As if lulled by a tropical breeze, I abandon the pages I translated prior that are at the moment still immediately followed by the terra incognita of the original text, in order to go back and even further polish a preceding, already worked passage, a task that takes less energy than artistry, and that corresponds more to the waning hours of the day. I have my translatorly actions of the morning and my translatorly actions of the evening, just as there are morning ragas and evening ragas.

5:51 p.m. As the sun begins to set, I am assailed by melancholy. I take a count of my progress for the day: a day of translating = one leg of an arduous hike. By dint of the tapping of my phalanges on the square buttons of my keyboard, by way of incessant erasing and replacing, I have gallicised a new parcel of terra incognita from the source language. I have inched even closer to the end of the book. To the end of human translation.

5:57 p.m. I rethink a thought that I thought this morning: even authors are no longer safe from being devoured. I will forever be grateful that my life has been measured in the works of prestigious authors, but I regret having 'lost' Rupert Thomson. He was one of my favourite authors. Tortured, certainly, but, perhaps because we are the same age, he bonded to my contemporaneity – or rather I bonded to his. Perhaps I should have translated only those who were my exact contemporaries to the very year. From 1996 to 2007, I translated his *The Insult* (1996), *The Book of Revelation* (2000), and *Death of a Murderer* (2007). Several of his books have not been translated into French; he had a dry spell between 2007 and 2013. In 2005, my publisher asked for my opinion of his novel *Divided Kingdom* (2005). I had written an enthusiastic review, but the publishing house took it no more seriously than a dissenting opinion penned by the minority. And yet I had found it to be visionary (on the Brexitian explosion). *Secrecy* (2013), to my knowledge, had not been translated, but my publisher had me once again translate *Death of a Murderer* and then abandoned Thomson entirely, whose *Katherine Carlyle* (2015) was then translated with Denoël, but not by me. I do not know what happened with *Never Anyone But You* (2018), which I would have dearly liked to translate.

6:03 p.m. I continue translating Boyle with no regrets while forgetting everything that I have been unable to translate during my career. I will keep going till nightfall and then some.

6:59 p.m. Didier is home and is preparing dinner.

7:30 p.m. We eat while watching a Marseillais sitcom. We digest while watching an episode of *The Good Fight* (of *The* – du? – *Good Fight*). I remark in passing the audio description, displayed God knows why on-screen tonight (perhaps an ironic wink to *Talk Talk*, its deaf and mute protagonist and its apparently equally deaf mute translator). *Door hisses open.*

8:50 p.m. Following the dinner/TV break, reinvigorated by the energy of the characters from *The* (or *du?*) *Good Fight*, I translate again for a little less than an hour.

9:47 p.m. I return to my dawn activity, to my correspondence, as if to close the parentheses of the day, during which I did not live my own life but rather that of another.

10:13 p.m. Before going to bed, I read a page or two. A biography. I have just learned that Leon de Kock is publishing a biography of André Brink, who died four years ago during the return flight from Brussels to Cape Town after receiving an umpteenth prize. Which brings to an end, mere collateral damage, our collaboration of fourteen years and eight books. I feel as though 'de Kock is daring to publish' would be a more apt phrasing, for it would be difficult to surpass *A Fork in the Road* (2009), Brink's autobiography. And yet I am nevertheless looking forward to reading it because I will be reading a portion of my own life. Will this finally be the right moment to open the bottle that Brink gifted me the last time we saw each other? A Solms Astor wine, the viticolore domaine – ha! *viticolore*! the veritable domain of the translator is indeed the Freudian slip – of *Philida* (2012), the final opus written by Brink. So our crus will be able to mix – his Western Cape and my familial Côtes de Provence.

I translate; therefore, I am a viticulturist.

Perhaps, one day, I will sit down to write my autobiography, the day when I am no longer a translator. Either because translation apps will have won the day earlier than expected or because I will have finally become translator of the text of my own life. My life. My autobiography. Only then will I be Dracula and not one of his victims, thinking beyond the two languages wherein I have shackled myself; only then will I be able to twist my linguistic tethers in every which way, worrying only about what I would like to express.

Only then will I be freed from saying that which I do not want to say.

Notes

1 Vladimir Jankélévitch, *La Méconnaissance, le malentendu*, vol. 2 of *Le Je-ne-sais-quoi et le presque-rien* (Paris: Seuil, 1980), 179.
2 Bernard Dimey, 'Syracuse', music composed by Henri Salvador, 1963.
3 Peter Ackroyd, *English Music* (London: Penguin, 1992), 308.

CHAPTER 4

Sturm, Drang and Slang
Writing Translations of Teenage Fiction

Clémentine Beauvais

Nobody in the world understands me! whines the Stereotypical Teenager (when not asleep, drunk or masturbating). Whether or not that cliché is correct, teenage literature does often take as a major narrative drive the idea that adolescence is characterised by a fundamental breakdown in communication. Where meaning used to circulate, it no longer does: the teenager's slang, picked up among peers and sharpened on the street, is impenetrable to parents; adult speech, filtered by teenage ears, suddenly sounds full of authoritarian demands; as voices change – boys' darkening, girls' speeding up – so does body language as limbs grow, chests swell and faces turn unreadable. The teenage character of adolescent literature, emerging from the blissful trust of childhood, becomes a master of suspicion, Foucault-shrewd in seeing through institutional lingo:

> They have come up with a
> Civil way for saying we are slow,
> But it all means the same thing:
> I get extra time because
> I have *special needs*.[1]

Meanwhile, best-friends-forever are no longer forever, or only intermittently forever. New friendships are born – though the signs, again, are difficult to interpret:

> 'Hi, Cassie!' she says,
> Blinking.
> That's all.
> And I wonder if
> This means
> We're friends.[2]

When did the world become so desperately undecipherable? asks the teenager of adolescent literature. Still, friends are not as complicated as potential romantic partners; there is no glossary for love, the most crucial signals of which slip into silences, sighs, the interstices of casual conversations – or, as in Elizabeth Acevedo's *The Poet X* (2018), notes in a biology lab book:

A: You ever messed with anyone in school?
X: Nah, never really be into anyone.
A: We not cute enough for you?
X: Nope. Ya ain't.
A: Damn. Shit on my whole life!
X: You just want me to say you cute.
A: Do you think I am?
X: I'm still deciding:)[3]

In short, adolescence – or so teenage literature tells us – is about being perpetually lost in translation. Or, more optimistically, perhaps it's about becoming an obsessive translator of everyday life. Everyone and everything is suddenly a potential object of interpretation. Each adult utterance is subjected to ruthless deconstruction. Friends' words are decrypted, reused, misused, defined and redefined; with them, language begins to be perceived as context-dependent (the trope of a teenager going to a new school gives ample opportunity for linguistic exploration) and linked to socio-economic class. Fragments of a lover's discourse are zealously dissected, and the lovesick teenager struggles to package into words all their feelings. Here they bump against the outer frontiers of language.

No wonder Xiomara, Acevedo's rebellious protagonist, philosophically concludes:

> The world is almost peaceful
> when you stop trying
> to understand it.[4]

How can a literary translator of teenage literature – examples above are taken from books I have myself translated into French – render a type of text so focused on the (mis)understandings, (mis)translation, (mis)interpretation of others' discourses and the early formulation of one's own?[5] In this chapter, I talk about the translation of contemporary teenage literature through its focus on language as a *problem*. Literature's polyphonic, often multimodal characteristics are in permanent tension with the fact that it is also highly commercial, with the kinds of editorial demands that inhabit children's literature more generally.[6] Translating teenage literature implies navigating spaces between languages as a place of both acculturation and experimentation.

In the first part, I look at elements within teenage fiction that invite the translator to treat language as resistant, alien, difficult. I next show that those literary nudges are counterbalanced by editorial drives towards naturalness and domestication. This leads to the necessity for the translator to commit not just politically, but also *didactically*, to the text. In the last part, I look at what creative translation workshops with teenagers themselves might bring the translator in this endeavour, offering a meeting point for aesthetic and didactic considerations in the translation of adolescent fiction.

An Aesthetics of Linguistic Resistance...

Most teenage fiction is fundamentally about finding a place in the world; it stages young characters negotiating their roles in the social and political spheres and getting to grips with the riddles of interpersonal relationships and institutions.[7] Many of those problems are discursively inscribed, dependent as they are on the world's many tongues (in the figurative sense of *tongue*, though the teenagers of adolescent literature are quite curious about the literal too). The teenage character writes, speaks, stays silent in many ways and across a wide range of platforms, registers and voices. Teenage literature today joyfully jumps from messaging to secret diary, letter to internal monologue, lyrical poetry to cartoons, lists to maps. Generic hybridity is common, with novels in verse, novels in comics and other hybrids gaining commercial traction, while authors experiment with language in sometimes postmodern ways.[8] This polyphony (after Bakhtin), arguably, both shapes and responds to real reading experiences of multi-literate contemporary teenagers, who are quite receptive to rapid switches of register, perspective or mode (e.g. through images, maps, layout etc.). Thus, the (interlinguistic) translation of adolescent fiction today is bound up with questions of intralinguistic and, often, intersemiotic translation too (to take Jakobson's terms).

An example is Acevedo's National Book Award winner, *The Poet X*. The novel, composed of chapters in verse from a first-person perspective, also contains 'schoolwork' in prose, such as text messages, notes passed in class, prayers, lists; poems, including an entire poem in Spanish and its English translation; visual poetry; haikus; a 'song'. Much of the novel, across those different types of writing, is in American English with occurrences of Dominican Spanish, sometimes explained, sometimes translated, sometimes neither, mirroring the translinguistic fluency of bilinguals. In the story, Xiomara Batista, a Harlem teen of Dominican heritage, develops a passion for slam poetry and begins to write and speak her own texts. Because her mother does not speak English, Xiomara's life also involves simultaneous translation, transmitting – or refusing to transmit – or only partially transmitting – important messages:

> 'No es nada. It's nothing.
> It was just a misunderstanding.'[9]

Xiomara also engages in translating her own feelings – love for the handsome Aman, frustration towards her mother, fear for her brother, tenderness towards her friend Caridad – into poetry. And that poetry does not remain on paper; she 'translates' it back into her body by performing it. Academically, too, Xiomara learns to switch registers; the novel provides readers with two versions of schoolwork: the 'draft' – highly poetic, idiosyncratic and intense – and the school-polished version, in prose, the character's fiery temperament gleaming under a slightly stolid patina. Xiomara thus constantly goes from body to words and back, from family to social life, from school language to private language and across various types of text.

This boundary-bending approach to language is quite typical of contemporary adolescent literature.[10] Adolescent fiction is intensely concerned with learning about boundaries, and how to bend or break them. As Lydia Kokkola analyses, adolescence symbolises a kind of 'buffer zone' between childhood and adulthood.[11] During that time, the body opens up – for carnal reasons, among others – and closes down; frontiers between the self and the world become more sharply defined and problematized. So, too, on a linguistic level. Many adolescent novels play with frontiers between registers, languages and voices; controlling those frontiers – choosing when and how to release words – often means exerting power.[12] The teenage novel is thus not just often polyphonic but also presents characters at an age where the polyphonic aspects of existence emerge as an ardent problem.

For the translator, this emphasis on the gradual acquisition and mastery of multiple voices encourages an approach that stresses the tension between self and words – the reluctance of language to signify straightforwardly. If the teenage character is, metaphorically speaking, experiencing the resistance of language, then the work of the translator can, indeed should, render that sense. In terms more familiar to translation theory, we could talk here of a nudge, present in that category of text within its characterisation, structures, narration, style, genres etc., towards an 'ethics of difference', a foreignisation.[13] Here the *foreign* is both inter- and intra-linguistic; *foreign* of another country, but also the foreign within the self, the person inside who struggles to speak.

In the following extract from Sarah Crossan's *The Weight of Water* (2012), Kasienka, a Polish teenager living in Coventry, overhears two Polish classmates:

> They laugh, loudly, because the teacher
> Is right there listening,
> Not understanding,
> Thinking they are being
> Good
> When really they are being
> Horrible,
> When really they are talking about
> Her chest.[14]

This passage piles up unwieldy gerunds and repetitive adverbs; Kasienka's efforts to find the right words for the boys' attitude – landing on simple, strong adjectives – reveal not just that her English is imperfect but that she is struggling to find the right words for the situation. Her plain, but powerful, choppy English is difficult to render in French, a language that requires more grammatical machinery.

Elle les écoute	*She listens to them*
Sans les comprendre;	*Without understanding;*
Elle croit qu'ils sont	*She thinks they're being / they are*
Sages,	*Nice (/well-behaved)*
Alors qu'ils sont	*Whereas they're being*
Sales,	*Dirty,*
Alors qu'ils parlent	*Whereas they're talking / they talk*
De sa poitrine.[15]	*About her chest.*
	('Literal' back-translation)

My translation choice was to preserve the straightforwardness, roughness and slight clunkiness through the clumsily vague present construction 'ils sont/sages/ils sont/sales', and to weave alliterations of harsh [k] and soft [s] sounds, expressing the coexistence, in Kasienka's speech, of resistance and fluency. I opted to render the awkward internal gerundive rhyme through a system of quasi rhymes (sages / sales / parlent), which does not provide perfectly satisfying closure, and where the poetic stumbles, frustratingly.

Even as the syntax is simple and the vocabulary basic, the text – as in many instances of adolescent literature – calls for an aesthetics of resistance, an experience of the teenager's frustration that language does not quite exactly cover reality.

... but a Didactics of Domestication

Yet, of course, while there are *literary* reasons to consider teenage fiction a good candidate for an aesthetics of linguistic resistance, there are also pressing *editorial and didactic* reasons to privilege naturalness and domestication. Teenage fiction is a closely controlled, reviewed, surveyed strand of publishing. At least on the Anglophone market, a domesticating tendency dominates,[16] due in part to the highly commercial nature of teenage literature and to the fact that translated works in Anglophone countries are an exception; numbers of translated texts are still very low, and publishers aim at an aesthetic of naturalness and transparency.

Alongside those commercial aspects, the domesticating tendencies are also a question of ideological (and, as I argue, didactic) stakes. Teenage literature is read by many adults, but it is put under much stronger ideological scrutiny than adult fiction. In recent years, notably under the impulse of movements seeking to widen representation and diversity within children's and adolescent fiction, an influential para-academic discourse on teenage literature has emerged, through blogs, social media etc.[17] Correspondingly, politically committed academic work on the matter has noticeably increased, including scholarly analysis of controversies,[18] or interventions with a view to changing the current publishing status quo or pedagogical practices around the mediation of such texts.[19] This discourse on teenage literature has enabled an emerging strand of teenage fiction representing the previously ignored experiences of characters from minority ethnic or cultural backgrounds, people of colour, women, LGBTQ+ people and people with disabilities. This cultural diversification of teenage literature has led to discursive diversification, with political as well as literary ramifications – *The Poet X*, for instance, is, arguably, ideologically and aesthetically inscribed within this movement.

In this context, the translator cannot just engage with the 'usual' challenges of translating speech (challenges well described by van Coillie). They must also be receptive to the quickly evolving, culturally variable discourses of youth culture, youth activism and identity politics, which are constantly developing their own vocabulary, narratives, characters (both real and fictional) and multimodal forms of communication. Much contemporary teenage literature follows closely the development of discourses emerging online and in activist circles, and novels are a strong channel by which those politics become normalised, aestheticised and integrated within dominant youth culture. A worldwide bestselling teenage book such as Angie Thomas's *The Hate U Give* (2017), for instance, cannot be read – or translated – without close familiarity with the development, discourses and stakes of the #BlackLivesMatter movement as well as fluency with a longer history of African American writing.[20] The kind of discursive agility required of translators – reaching into the far past and the immediate present, into youth and internet cultures – makes teenage literature probably one of the most demanding kinds of literary translation today from the point of view of intralinguistic and metalinguistic skill.

But there exist significant discrepancies in the degree of penetration of such discourses in different cultures, leading to tensions, in translatorial decisions, between aesthetic and political choices. For instance, Tillie Walden, the author of comics for young people, in her recent graphic novel *On a Sunbeam* (2018), has a nonbinary character, Elliot, who goes by the pronoun 'they'. In the French version, issued by the prestigious publisher Gallimard and translated by Alice Marchand, Elliot is referred to, throughout, as 'iel', which is one of the French equivalent pronouns of the singular 'they'. Yet the French translation introduces, and maintains throughout the book, inverted commas around 'iel'. This decision has the effect of making the pronoun conspicuous, giving, within the speech bubbles, an impression of air quotes.

This editorial–translatorial decision says a lot about the difficulty, for the textual aspects of teenage literature that are closely linked to emerging political discourses, of translating happily to other cultural contexts where they are barely known. Evidently, in 2018, the use of the term 'iel' was far less familiar to a French audience than the singular 'they' for an Anglo-American one, and the scare quotes arguably highlight it as an abnormal pronoun. Where including a gender-neutral character was a passively political act in the American version (one tending towards normalisation), it becomes, in the French version, depending on one's interpretation, either militantly political or permanently othering. Reactions from bloggers to this one aspect of the text have been mixed, with the book being praised for its representation of queer identities, but the scare quotes attracting some negative comments.[21] The translator of teenage literature today must show not just familiarity but also critical engagement with the many discourses involved; this requires adopting at all points an ethical/political position.

Because that political commitment is directed towards a young audience, it belongs to a wider sphere of discourse infused with age-related power imbalances. As childhood scholar D. T. Cook argues,

> Tensions of voice, of persona, and of the locus of decision-making are present in every personal interaction with a child, in every depiction of a child, in every iteration of childhood, and in every gesture made by, toward, and about children. Each word to a child ... each decision made on its behalf ... favors some aspects of the world over others; every lifestyle choice is potentially didactic.[22]

Any translatorial decision in children's and teenage fiction is of necessity didactic – a term that should not be taken, however, in its pejorative sense. Scholars of children's and teenage literature have long discussed what is known as the literary/didactic split in texts for the young,[23] namely, the fact that this kind of literature is characterised by a double drive towards pleasuring and teaching. In the driving seat is the adult, a composite entity that has been defined as 'hidden.'[24] This entity is also sometimes perceived as perverse and domineering (since Rose in 1984), or more neutrally as a normative authority.[25] Discussions of tensions between adult authority and child potential have constituted the core of children's literature theory since its inception. The didacticism of literature for the young is less a fault to be bemoaned, however, than an aspect of that literature's aesthetics – and can, in fact, be celebrated. Literature targeted at young people, namely, at people (in theory) equipped with a longer future than the creators of that literature, cannot sever itself from its engagement with futurity, as I discuss elsewhere.[26] It is didactic insofar as its utterances attempt to reach out, through the younger readership, into a future inaccessible to the older authorship. Thus the term 'didactic', in the theoretical framework of youth literature, emerges not as a defect but rather as a characteristic of children's fiction, which signals it as a category of text engaged in the cultivation of its primary readership's future actions.

From this theoretical perspective, the translator of adolescent fiction, like the writer of such fiction, is thus not just politically but *didactically* committed by the text they are translating: they may opt to endorse or eschew that commitment, but in either case, they will have made a choice of a didactic nature. And those choices are, of course, strongly connected to editorial and other material configurations. In the current international market of children's publishing, the United States, it is fair to say, controls the ideological and, therefore, didactic agenda of teenage fiction, including its translated imports into English. I will take here the example of a didactic translatorial choice with one of my own teenage novels in verse, *Songe à la douceur* (2017), whose translation into English (as *In Paris with You* [2018]) I followed closely: Sam Taylor, the translator, and I corresponded much about it while it was being edited, simultaneously, by a UK editor and a US editor. The translation required some rewriting, especially of moments considered ideologically problematic in the Anglophone world.

One clear example was a passage where young Tatiana, aged fourteen, among other night-time reveries, imagines herself as the victim of attempted rape, from which a fantasy husband-to-be saves her heroically. The passage is told by the (female) narrator:

> Tatiana est une jeune fille très à l'ancienne.
> Je l'imagine s'imaginant un homme peu amène,
> > voire sombre et même cruel au début,
> > le genre d'homme qui a vécu
> > des choses qu'on ne sait pas,
> mais cet homme-là, rencontrant Tatiana,
> > sous l'effet de sa beauté et de sa vertu
> > se verrait infusé d'un perplexe et vibrant amour,
> > auquel feraient obstacle bien des aventures
> et des péripéties,
> > y compris la plupart du temps une sorte de tentative de viol par
> > un autre homme qu'au départ elle aurait trouvé assez charmant ;
> > tentative de laquelle elle serait sauvée, in extremis, hymen toujours
> > en condition optimale, vêtements un peu déchirés mais cachant
> > adroitement ses tétons,
> > > par l'homme qui l'aime,
> et ils partiraient main dans la main pour être mariés ...²⁷

Taylor's first translation was as follows:

> Tatiana is a very old-fashioned young girl.
> I imagine her imagining a rather surly heartthrob,
> dark-eyed, rough, even cruel to start with;
> the kind of man who's been through things
> that no young girl can even imagine,
> Encountering Tatiana, however,
> > this noble savage,
> > transfixed by her beauty and her virtue,
> > falls prey to a pulsating, life-changing love
> > which will of course be thwarted by various incidents
> and events,
>
> generally including a sort of attempted rape by another man whom she
> did at first find rather charming; an attack from which she will be saved at
> the last second, her hymen still in top condition, her clothes a little torn
> but draped in such a way as to hide her nipples,
> > by the man who loves her
> and they will walk off hand in hand into the sunset to be wed ...²⁸

From editorial feedback, it was clear that the attempted rape (and, arguably, the very word 'rape') was impossible to keep in the English version. The passage, it was assumed, might be (mis)interpreted as advocating rape; the very acknowledgement that teenage girls might have rape-attempt fantasies was problematic. The mention of the word 'rape' was also considered unnecessarily triggering. I rewrote the passage in French, and Taylor provided another translation, to make it clear that Tatiana was in fact having *torture*-attempt fantasies, which are quite acceptable:

> For example:
> One time, she might be kidnapped by the mafia (or some sort of hoodlums
>   anyway)
> – in the shape of three very bad (but not bad-looking) men,
> who want to dig up dirt
> on her mystery man,
> because he's working as a spy for their enemy
> (or something);
> so they threaten to hurt
>   Tatiana,
>   to torture her, even,
>   unless
>   she confesses
>   everything she knows about him!
> (Though in fact it's not the kind of torture
> that would actually hurt her:
> electrical wires that aren't plugged in;
> ropes not tied so tightly that they burn her skin;
> her torturer too susceptible to her beauty
> to really do his duty.)
> And suddenly one of the gangsters will stop
> and stare
> and shout in a panicked voice:
>   *Who's there?*
>   And she will be saved in the nick of time
>   by the man who loves her,
> and they will walk off hand in hand into the sunset
> to be wed (etc.).[29]

The rewriting is not, in literary terms, inferior to the first version (in fact, it is arguably funnier). The modification here has not literary, but didactic, implications. By replacing a fourteen-year-old character's cartoonish rape fantasy by a cartoonish torture fantasy, the English version is making a different didactic utterance – speaking into existence a quite different world of adolescent reverie. To stress the point, I do *not* consider this rewriting an artistic concession: it is a decision driven by a specific didactic commitment to an audience who indeed would not have received the 'original' version as the French audience did. That fantasy would have stood out, unsettled, caught the attention of the young Anglophone readership in a way that it did not for a French one. Such translatorial decisions, of course, also commit not just the translator and editor but also the author. Reactions of shock or outrage from young readers in the United States would reflect badly on the original author; thus the translator cannot eschew thinking about such didactic choices in translating a text with no adjustment. There is no default solution that would be ideologically – and thus didactically – neutral.

However, this translatorial decision is by nature didactic (and not 'just' political or ideological) because it most certainly would *not* have been made had the book been intended for adults. As such, it is a didactic utterance: it states, 'I do not want *young people* to be reading about a fourteen-year-old's rape fantasies'. It implies, too, that the book's readers will be literarily immature – incapable, here, of operations of reading such as sensitivity to unreliable narration and to humour. Those decisions, by reflecting back on the work, and forward onto the audience, make statements about teenage literature and its readers, which may be to a degree performative. We can bemoan this fact, but we can also rejoice in the fact that it makes ethical demands on the translators, encouraging self-reflectiveness and a dynamism in their practice. Still, it is extremely difficult, always, as a translator of teenage fiction, to draw the line between didactic domestication for the purpose of ideological conservatism and for aesthetic–didactic purposes – here, preservation of effect linked to consideration of audience.

Translating Teenage Novels with Teenagers

Between the aesthetic and the didactic, there is, in the reflective work of a translator in teenage fiction, an empirical possibility of working out some of those questions. In this last part, I turn to the translator's contact with their target audience. That contact is very much a privilege of children's and adolescent literature. Adult readers live their lives scattered around the world, and only a self-selecting group come to literary events; teenagers, however, are conveniently locked up and packed into schools every day. This allows authors and, sometimes, translators direct access to roomfuls of their (in-theory) target audience, captive, to test things on them and work with them – namely, to do writing workshops. Since the 2000s, the practice of literary translation workshops has risen in Anglophone countries and is budding in others, with translators visiting schools and book fairs and getting children and teenagers (either monolingual or bilingual) to translate literary texts. I will talk here not about the potential benefits of that practice for young people but about what it might bring the translator, and translation, of adolescent fiction.

Let me describe briefly the kind of translation workshop I do with teenagers. I first talk to the teenagers about translation before showing them a video of Acevedo doing a slam poetry performance. I then give out a poem by her, from *The Poet X*, and read it out loud. This is the stanza we translate:

> It happens when I'm at bodegas.
> It happens when I'm at school.
> It happens when I'm on the train.
> It happens when I'm standing on the platform.
> It happens when I'm sitting on the stoop.
> It happens when I'm turning the corner.
> It happens when I forget to be on guard.
> It happens all the time.[30]

The 'it' that happens is explained later: various instances of sexual harassment or catcalling. We talk about what they hear and, perhaps, already begin to understand in the poem: sounds, beat, rhythm. We then seek to intuit some of the meaning. After this semantic stage, teenagers work in groups to propose literary translations (into French) of the poem, which they then perform and discuss in class.

Just because teenagers are translating does not mean, obviously, that their words are more valid than the adult translator's. Teenagers often say 'we would/wouldn't say that', but they are of course talking from within their own contexts, and they are not representative of their whole age group. Writing teenage literature, even highly realistic teenage literature, is a literary move, not a journalistic one: a literary dialogue is not a transcript of a 'real' dialogue, and the teenage character is not a direct reflection of a 'real' teenager. Yet much of teenage literature does seek to achieve a 'pseudo-orality', a literary rendering of oral language with a concern for real-life plausibility.[31] Teenage literature, with ancestors such as J. D. Salinger's *The Catcher in the Rye* (1951) or S. E. Hinton's *The Outsiders* (1967), sought from its early years to blur the boundaries between ethnographic and sociological observation of teenagers and their literary rendering. Thus, it is evidently enriching for the translator to come into contact with contemporary teenage speech.[32] Furthermore, the co-constructed nature of the exercise – they have to work together and negotiate a solution – means that it invites them to the kind of polyphonic thinking, and dialogic work, that adolescent fiction itself is so concerned about. Writing the translation is a way of, so to speak, activating and adopting the polyphonic potential of the source text.

As such, the teenage translator is mirroring what the teenage narrator is doing: finding the best words in the best order for the cacophony of feelings, meanings and gestures in their heads. Some words are clear, some less so; some feelings are straightforward, others do not appear to exist in 'our' native language – do they even exist in *any* language? Rendering all this in a literary way recapitulates the protagonist's experiences. Working this out with actual teenagers helps the translator gauge how stretchable the target audience's tolerance of linguistic estrangement can be, when subjected to the pull of literary artifice, and what kinds of didactic utterances emerge in that encounter. The answer is, often, very stretchable and also, paradoxically, quite didactic indeed. The target audience, in short, is often quite satisfied with high linguistic experimentation *and* explicitly didactic content.

In the case of the Acevedo poem, French teenagers routinely propose translations for 'It happens' ranging from the immediate 'Ça arrive' and 'Ça se passe' to much freer and/or more politically loaded interpretations – interpretations, that is, that put a more didactic stamp on the text. Those who treat sexual harassment with the kind of matter-of-fact resignation one would have about the weather might suggest 'C'est là' (it is there); those who want to lay the emphasis on the victim will reach for 'Ça m'arrive' (it happens to me); those who focus on the perpetrators offer 'Ils le font' (they do it). Teenagers not only come up with such suggestions but also explain their choices well and are fully aware of the political connotations. Simply, they often do not seem to feel that the spelt-out, actively political commitment restricts their freedom of thought. Translatorial choices emerge that are both aesthetically complex *and* didactically explicit.

Teenagers of all backgrounds generally intuit very well the central questions of translation theory from the practice of translation. They launch into discussions about, for instance, the transformation of 'bodega' into 'café', 'bar' etc., the mysterious 'sitting on the stoop' (a practice unknown, and architecturally impossible, in France) and so on. I have observed that teenage translators often proceed from domestication to foreignisation in their strategies. They might first, for instance, translate 'train' as 'RER', not just a very French but a very Parisian denomination for suburban trains; they then modify their approach, opining that we cannot Parisianise this very New York story. They move from a literal translation of each verse to a more poetic one by stretching the field of lexical possibilities, deciding that rhyme and rhythm may trump semantics. I would argue, though more extensive research is currently being done, that teenagers put in a situation of literary translation will often move outwards, so to speak, from an aesthetics of naturalness to an aesthetics of linguistic resistance and experimentation, with a stronger and stronger focus on the literary. But, importantly, they do *not* shirk away from political, and therefore didactic, decisions. In the process, they can come up with texts arguably more actively committed than the source text.

For the translator of adolescent fiction, these encounters are precious not only because they provide very many fresh pairs of eyes on a text but because they are a window onto the linguistic, metalinguistic and literary ability, as well as the political sagacity, of that target audience. They show that teenagers are not just passive consumers of text but fluent users of language, and social and political thinkers. Often, such workshops reflect, in short, exactly what teenage fiction is about: that linguistic resistance, wordplay and awareness of the political nature of language are facts of everyday life for teenagers, and ones they are quite equipped to deal with.

Conclusion: Beyond the Aesthetic and the Didactic

Christiane Nord's insistence on 'loyalty', as opposed to fidelity, in the task of the translator is applicable, too, to teenage literature today, which seeks to be *loyal* to the teenage experience, though not claiming to be a faithful reflection of it.[33] Like translation, it is less a question of direct equivalence than of alternating strategies; sometimes contemporary teenage jargon will be used to activate identification (what Rudine Sims Bishop might term the 'mirroring' mission of youth literature[34]), and sometimes the characters will speak in ways that are primarily aspirational or foreign (the 'window' mission, in Bishop's view[35]).

Similarly, the translator of teenage fiction must determine, often on a case-by-case basis, whether the 'pseudo-orality' of the text, or its occasionally meteoric switches to another register or the use of textspeak etc., should be made natural – to spur on the plot – or left discursively disturbing, slowing down the pace of reading. Teenage literature remains, arguably, a primarily target-oriented market, a didactically committed and a didactically committing kind of literature, and so, therefore, does its translation. Its postmodern polyphony, a joy and a challenge to tackle as a translator, is counterbalanced by tight control – authorial, editorial and translatorial – over its ideological agenda.

But even in that control we can find creative pleasure and an opportunity for inventiveness, as working with teenagers themselves reveals. A precious practice for translators (as well as for teenagers), it reconnects one to a live (and lively) target audience. With them, we witness directly the linguistic and literary agility of that audience, their readerly maturity, their literary sense and their expertise in register- and code-switching. While questions of an aesthetic and didactic order precede and supersede those encounters, they find in them a place to meet, less conflictually than constructively. Because that audience, in fact, is not against being taught while it is being entertained – and not against committing to a vision of the world and to the words that express it.

Notes

1 Sarah Crossan, *The Weight of Water* (London: Bloomsbury, 2015), 57.
2 Crossan, *Weight of Water*, 89.
3 Elizabeth Acevedo, *The Poet X* (New York: HarperCollins, 2018), 106.
4 Acevedo, *Poet X*, 223.
5 Throughout this article I refer to teenage or adolescent fiction to mean works whose target audience is roughly in the thirteen-to-eighteen age bracket. This literature is also known as 'young adult' and 'new adult' in its higher age ranges. Distinctions between the three labels are of little relevance to this article (for a discussion, see Amy Pattee, 'Between Youth and Adulthood: Young Adult and New Adult Literature', *Children's Literature Association Quarterly* 42, no. 2 [Summer 2017]).
6 See Riitta Oittinen, *Translating for Children* (New York: Routledge, 2002); Gillian Lathey, *Translating Children's Literature* (London: Routledge, 2016).
7 Roberta Seelinger Trites, *Disturbing the Universe: Power and Repression in Adolescent Literature* (Iowa City: University of Iowa Press, 2000).
8 Eve Tandoi, 'Hybrid Novels for Children and Young Adults', in *The Edinburgh Companion to Children's Literature*, ed. Clémentine Beauvais and Maria Nikolajeva (Edinburgh: Edinburgh University Press, 2017); Mike Cadden, 'The Verse Novel and the Question of Genre', *ALAN Review* 39, no. 1 (Fall 2011); Ebony Daley-Carey, 'Testing the Limits: Postmodern Adolescent Identities in Contemporary Coming-of-Age Stories', *Children's Literature in Education* 49 (2018).
9 Acevedo, *Poet X*, 158.
10 For the verse novel in particular, see Mike Cadden, 'Rhetorical Technique in the Young Adult Verse Novel', *Lion and the Unicorn* 42, no. 2 (2018), and Richard Flynn, 'Why Genre Matters: A Case for the Importance of Aesthetics in the Verse Memoirs of Marilyn Nelson and Jacqueline Woodson', *Lion and the Unicorn* 42, no. 2 (2018); see also Sara K. Day, 'Power and Polyphony in Young Adult Literature: Rob Thomas's *Slave Day*', *Studies in the Novel* 42, nos. 1/2 (Spring and Summer 2010).

11 Lydia Kokkola, *Fictions of Adolescent Carnality: Sexy Sinners and Delinquent Deviants* (Amsterdam: John Benjamins, 2013).
12 See Robyn McCallum, *Ideologies of Identity in Adolescent Fiction: The Dialogic Construction of Subjectivity* (New York: Garland, 1999).
13 Lawrence Venuti, *The Scandals of Translation: Towards an Ethics of Difference* (London: Routledge, 2002).
14 Crossan, *Weight of Water*, 15.
15 Sarah Crossan, *Swimming Pool*, trans. Clémentine Beauvais (Paris: Rageot, 2018), 23.
16 See Lathey, *Translating Children's Literature*.
17 See Karen Coats, 'Teaching the Conflicts: Diverse Responses to Diverse Children's Books', in *The Edinburgh Companion to Children's Literature*, ed. Clémentine Beauvais and Maria Nikolajeva (Edinburgh: Edinburgh University Press, 2017).
18 See, for example, Ebony Elizabeth Thomas, Debbie Reese and Kathleen T. Horning, 'Much Ado about *A Fine Dessert*: The Cultural Politics of Representing Slavery in Children's Literature', *Journal of Children's Literature* 42, no. 2 (2016).
19 For the publishing status quo, see, for example, Philip Nel, *Was the Cat in the Hat Black? The Hidden Racism of Children's Literature, and the Need for Diverse Books* (Oxford: Oxford University Press, 2017). For the pedagogical practices around the mediation of such texts, see, for example, Sean P. Connors and Ryan M. Rish, 'Troubling Ideologies: Creating Opportunities for Students to Interrogate Cultural Models in YA Literature', *ALAN Review* 42, no. 3 (Summer 2015).
20 See Vincent Haddad, 'Nobody's Protest Novel: Novelistic Strategies of the Black Lives Matter Movement', *Comparatist* 42 (2018).
21 See, for example, 'Dans un rayon de soleil, de Tillie Walden', *biblioqueer*, 5 May 2019, accessed 31 May 2019, https://biblioqueerblog.wordpress.com/tag/gallimard-bd/.
22 Daniel Thomas Cook, 'Interrogating Symbolic Childhood', introduction to his *Symbolic Childhood* (New York: Peter Lang, 2002), 7.
23 Maria Nikolajeva, *Power, Voice and Subjectivity in Literature for Young Readers* (London: Routledge, 2010).
24 Perry Nodelman, *The Hidden Adult: Defining Children's Literature* (Baltimore, MD: Johns Hopkins University Press, 2008).
25 Nikolajeva, *Power, Voice and Subjectivity*.
26 Clémentine Beauvais, *The Mighty Child: Time and Power in Children's Literature* (Amsterdam: John Benjamins, 2015); Clémentine Beauvais, 'Didacticism', in *Keywords for Children's Literature 2.0*, ed. Nina Christensen, Lissa Paul and Philip Nel (New York: New York University Press, forthcoming 2021).
27 Beauvais, *Mighty Child*, 32.
28 Clémentine Beauvais, *In Paris with You: A Novel*, trans. Sam Taylor (London: Faber, 2018), unpublished version.

29 Beauvais, *In Paris with You*, trans. Taylor, 36.
30 Acevedo, *Poet X*, 52.
31 See Monika Fludernik, 'Conversational Narration – Oral Narration', in *Handbook of Narratology*, ed. Peter Hühn, Jan Christoph Meister, John Pier and Wolf Schmid, 2nd ed. (Gottingen, Germany: De Gruyter, 2014).
32 Lathey, *Translating Children's Literature*, 70.
33 Christiane Nord, 'Scopos, Loyalty, and Translational Conventions', *Target: International Journal of Translation Studies* 3, no. 1 (1991).
34 Rudine Sims Bishop, 'Mirrors, Windows, and Sliding Glass Doors', *Perspectives* 6, no. 3 (1990).
35 Bishop, 'Mirrors, Windows, and Sliding Glass Doors'.

CHAPTER 5

On X
Embodied Retranslation and Defacement in Brandon Brown's Catullus 85

Adrienne K. H. Rose

Retranslations of Catullus 85 (*odi et amo*) abound, in part due to the poem's brevity (2 lines), subject matter (human condition), and epigrammatic tone (interpreted variously as laconic to angsty). Even those writing with Dryden's presumption that translations should bear specific, local distinctions such that Vergil adopt the sounds and sensibilities of an English gentleman,[1] yield versions in English that, if done literally, with lexical fidelity front of mind, resemble one another to a fault.[2] In his book *The Poems of Gaius Valerius Catullus*, American poet Brandon Brown writes, 'The inane repetition of alienated labor is the opposite of what this translation is hoping to accomplish'.[3] This boldly self-aware twentieth-/twenty-first-century literary translation Republican Roman poet Catullus's *carmina* (poems) enlists contemporary Anglo-American vernacular while embedding a reception history of Catullus's *libellus* (little book/booklet) into the translation itself. Reading Dryden today, we might ask: how close does Brandon Brown come to Dryden's position in making Catullus speak as if the Roman poet were living in Oakland, California, in the twenty-first century? In his formal interventions, what is gained by augmenting the original's elegiac couplet by exponential proportions? How is repetition in *this sense* different from the kind of repetition in Classical retranslations that quote old versions verbatim? Brown's meta-translation, bolstered by his embodied translation practices, corroborates a rupture in both the received norms of translating ancient poetry and the practices of reading such translations. Poem 85, in particular, in Brown's translation ingeniously pays tribute to Catullus's famous *odi et amo* ('I hate and I love') epigram by enlisting repetition and amplification. In addition to creating a sophisticated and stylized soundscape comprised of the translated words of the original poem, Brown amplifies the formal and rhetorical features of poem 85, while schooling the reader in *odi et amo*'s reception history. Finally, Brown modulates the topic of Catullus's poem from 'Lesbia' (Catullus's beloved) to 'translation' in a self-referential gesture. Brown's remarkable innovations are significant because they use repetition and amplification to offer the reader new, perhaps shocking ways of experiencing Catullus's poems, ways that venture beyond the translation of their words and sense, yet remain very closely attuned to the formal, rhetorical, and topical features of the originals.

To appreciate the full extent of Brown's accomplishments, it is helpful to bear in mind the numerous retranslations of Catullus that earlier poets and translators have produced. In the *Oxford Book of Classical Verse in Translation*,[4] which includes translations of Classical poetry ranging from Homer (*c*. eighth century BCE) to Boethius (480–524 CE), there are eighteen *carmina* excerpted from Catullus's *libellus*. However, the total number of included translations of Catullus's *carmina* tally up at thirty-one, since nine of the eighteen poems are represented with multiple versions by different translators. This is rather abundant for a poet whose entire extant opus consists of only 116 poems. A quarter of these are short two- and four-line epigrams, a form that Martial, a later Latin epigrammatist, regards as the lowest in the hierarchy of the literary genres: 'What could be humbler/smaller? I start to make epigrams' (*Quid minus esse potest? Epigrammata fingere coepi* XII.94.9). In contemporary creative writing lingo, Catullus produced a mere 'slim volume'. Yet, those poems have been powerful in generating a multitude of retranslations in English by later literati. His famous poem 5 (*Vivamus mea Lesbia* ...) accounts for five different renditions in the *Oxford Book*, interestingly all from the seventeenth to eighteenth centuries:

Thomas Campion (1601):

> My sweetest Lesbia, let us live and love,
> And, though the sager sort our deeds reprove,
> Let us not weigh them ...

William Corkine (1612):

> My deerest Mistrisse, let us live and love,
> And care not what old doting fooles reprove.
> Let us not feare their censures, nor esteeme
> What they of us and of our loves shall deeme.

In Rainer Schulte's anthology devoted to multiple English-language retranslations,[5] Catullus 5 receives its own section comprised of twenty-three different versions. There is surprisingly little overlap between the two anthologies, since Schulte's selections are focused on retranslations by poets from the twentieth century. The one exception is Thomas Campion's Catullus 5, which appears in both collections.

Beyond these anthologized versions, Leonard Smithers's 1894 retranslation of lines 1–2 of *carmen* 5 reads: 'Let us live, my Lesbia, and let us love, and count all the rumors of stern old men at a penny's fee.' About one hundred years later, Guy Lee's 1990 translation of the same lines reads:

> We should live, my Lesbia, and love
> And value all the talk of stricter
> Old men at a single penny.[6]

Ryan Gallagher's retranslation, simply titled '5' (2008):

> We must live now my Lesbia and love.
> We'll appraise all rumors at once
> of the serious and senile.[7]

David Mulroy's lines:

> Let us live and love, my Lesbia. Here's
> a copper coin for the criticism
> of elderly men with exalted morals.[8]

Restricting each translated line to roughly ten syllables, Mulroy attempts to approximate the hendecasyllabic (eleven-syllable) metre of the Latin poem. The alliteration above (let, live, love, Lesbia; copper, coin, criticism; elderly, exalted; men, morals) mimics the consonant and assonant soundplay with the letters 'a', 'm', 'u', 'r', 's', and 'i' in the original's opening lines. And Mulroy nearly pulls it off, save for the awkwardly phrased 'elderly men with exalted morals'.

The examples from Schulte's collection and the individual selections above corroborate the landscape represented in the *Oxford Book* of ancient Classical poets whose poems most frequently continue to invite retranslation in later literary eras. Among the ancient poets included in the *Oxford Book*, Catullus is surpassed in the number of original poems represented by multiple retranslations only by Homer (who is represented by ten) and Horace (twelve). Beyond the covers of the *Oxford Book*, one need not look very far to discover dozens more, truly several dozen more, Homeric, Horatian, and Catullan retranslations. And many more which have continued to be published after 1995, when the Oxford anthology went to print.

Homer's iconic status as a literary and cultural obelisk for Renaissance and Victorian elites explains the long tradition of English-language retranslations of the *Iliad* and *Odyssey*. Horace's vast corpus – his Epicureanism, satirical 'blame poetry', air of moral uprightness, and technical elegance

– might account for some retranslation appeal at later historical times of social and political turmoil. From Horace's *Odes* III.2.13 comes Wilfred Owen's poem 'Dulce et decorum est', condemning World War I and the 'desperate glory' sought by its young casualties. The same line protesting the same war appears in line 70 of Ezra Pound's 'Hugh Selwyn Mauberley': 'Died some, pro patria,/ non "dulce" non "et decor".'[9] Horace imported into Latin poetry the difficult Greek lyric metres used by Sappho, Alcaeus, and Pindar, and it seems reasonable to expect that some English Horatian versions are also driven by the same sort of philhellenism so ardently embraced by Lord Byron.

As for Catullus, he lived to see the politically contentious 50s BCE in Rome, when rival dynasts Caesar and Pompey competed for political supremacy in campaigns characterized by violence and social unrest. Unlike Martial (38/41–103 CE), whose status under Domitian as 'an impoverished citizen from Bilbilis in Spain' limited the object of his vitriol to lay folk, Catullus's wealthy aristocratic familial status meant his contemporaries were 'the great and powerful',[10] and in his poems he attacks real people holding actual positions in political office. His poems respond to current events, and those people who appear in his poems include Cicero, Memmnius, governor of Bithynia, and of course the singularly notorious Clodia Metelli (a.k.a. Lesbia), sister of the infamous aristocrat P. Clodius Pulcher. Catullus poem 29 engages explicitly with contemporary events, satirizing the political marriage of Caesar's daughter Julia to Pompey. Poem 49 'gives thanks' to Cicero for some favour unknown to us.

Many of his poems are flippant, rude, abusive, and decidedly unprofound. The opening poem of his *libellus* labels his poems *nugas* (1.4) – literally 'nuggets,' trifles, stuff – quick verses jotted down on a napkin en route to a dinner party.[11] Catullus's love poems declare his infatuation with and subsequent contempt for Lesbia and later Juventius, and strike twenty-first-century undergraduate readers as 'emo' – excessively brooding and self-involved – even for a generation of readers reared on the 'selfie'. His poems express 'an emotional immediacy and urgency that claim the reader's sympathy'.[12] For example, when he finds occasion to address a backstabbing friend in *carmen* 77, Catullus writes:

> *Rufe mihi frustra ac nequiquam credite amice*
> *(frustra? immo magno cum pretio atque malo),*
> *sicine subrepsti mi atque intestina perurens*
> *hei misero eripuisti omnia nostra bona?*
> *eripuisti, eheu nostrae crudele venenum*
> *vitae, eheu nostrae pestis amicitiae*

> Rufus, my so-called friend for nothing, my 'friend' and all for what –
> For nothing? No, just a sickening price.
> Is this how you've snuck up on me, burning my guts,
> stealing my one last good thing?
> You cheated me of that nasty infection, for fuck's sake,
> that horrible ulcer of our friendship.[13]

This kind of visceral expression is in part responsible for Catullus as a literary mainstay over time. His poems feel consistently modern, not two millennia old. They 'have an air of freshness and novelty'.[14] For example, Catullus's forthright pronouncement in *carmen* 43 of how, compared to Lesbia, all other women fall short:

> *Salve, nec minimo puella naso*
> *nec bello pede nec nigris ocellis*
> *nec longis digitis nec ore sicco*
> *nec sane nimis elegante lingua,*
> *decoctoris amica Formiani.*
> *ten provincia narrat esse bellam?*
> *tecum Lesbia nostra comparatur?*
> *o saeclum insapiens et infacetum!*

> Hey, girl. Your nose is huge,
> your camel toe, your eyes – the unsultriest.
> Ham-fisted, drooling, troll.
> I've heard you're all that in the commuter towns.
> How do you stand next to Lesbia? Asking for a friend.

The saturation of existing English-language retranslations of Catullus's poems challenges the contemporary poet/translator to enlist enterprising strategies to render new Catullan versions for twenty-first-century readers that bear some unique, post-modern features and sensibilities.[15] For example, the simple matter of doing away with predictable end-rhymes and regular metrics, along with the likes of *thee*s and *thou*s employed by elitist Victorians intent on preserving Classics and venerating antiquity on pedestals, yields a free verse more palatable to current readers. Translators in favour of fragmentation, expository techniques, such as documenting the process of translation in/as the translation itself, stream of consciousness, and experiments which enlist technology, are commonly writers themselves who are interested in stepping into the creative psyche of the ancient poet while seeking to gain access to some innovative expression by working within the constraints of another writer's voice, subject matter, and historicity.

Faced with this challenge, Brandon Brown's *The Poems of Gaius Valerius Catullus* (2011) proceeds fully aware of its place at the end of this long and exhausted tradition. Rejecting prior retranslations of Classical texts, Brown writes that 'The inane repetition of alienated labor is the opposite of what this translation is hoping to accomplish'.[16] Like Catullus, Brown's learned, purposefully venomous, hyperactive, colloquial poetic voices bombard the reader with a barrage of emotions. In contrast to my own fairly literal retranslation of *carmen* 77 above, Brown's version of the diatribe against backstabbing Rufus, excerpted here, erupts with a more vitriolic urgency:

> Goddamn it Rufus. Fucking Rufus. Rufus! So Rufus and I, we were friends ... Rufus. Pffft. He ripped me off, became my blood brother and then disowned me and all my blood, borrowed my copy of *Arcades Project* and bailed, etc. Ouch! Ouch![17]

Brown's retranslation of Catullus 43, which touts the features of the inelegant, unbeautiful woman, reads:

> Love can't save necks, minimize the girth of a nose or bellow pedicure. It can't make a black eye fade after a good ass kick. Love can't make digits long for ore, or keep insane sickos from turning your tongue into an elegant *pâté en croûte*. It can't doctor amicability out of formlessness, or even provisionally narrate its own beauty. Love is comparative, monstrous. How stupid. How on the face of it.[18]

Like Catullus, Brown takes aim at political and popular culture figures. For example, 'My apartment's name is Trump, my broker's name is Princess. You can call my apartment Prick Palace' and 'Watching the inauguration of Barack Obama, for example, I thought a lot about ancient Rome, which is where Catullus lived'.[19] With reference to popular celebrities, Brown writes, 'And I care about one want more than gold: that Lindsay / Lohan moves in with me and spackles my want. / Move in with Catullus who wants but never hopes' and 'Robert Pattinson is pretty, whatever. Lindsay tweets / *Robert Pattinson is hotter than Catullus and his whole family*'.[20] The anachronistic features may be unsettling, but they make Catullus a more accessible, curious figure for a new generation of readers who aren't able to read the original Latin. Reciprocally, Brown makes Lindsay Lohan more accessible to a generation of Catullus scholars who might not be able to read the original pop culture.

Brown gives acknowledgement to fellow translators of Catullus, such as Peter Whigham, Bernadette Mayer, Ryan Gallagher, and Louis Zukofsky, while distinguishing himself from these other translators by using exegetical, commentarial, situational strategies and his own embodied experience to transform selected Catullan poems into a conglomerate of its reception history firmly situated in the present moment. He also uses raw language, which goes beyond the register of previous translators. To give the reader a sense of one of the ways Brown's *Catullus* differs from those mentioned above, an excerpt of Brown's *carmen* 5 reads:

> Revive, my lovebird. I've got an aim to muss. Sure, the rumors will sound severe, but right now sock it to me with your *duende*. We'll fiercely cum a million times. Then we'll ... Catullus asserts that he and the lovebird will kiss many thousands of times and then he shall *conturbabimus* them. *Conturbabimus* literally means something like 'to throw into a mob.'[21]

Often his retranslations describe the thought processes leading up to and during the acts of retranslation, or consist of commentarial notes reminiscent of Mayer's renditions of Catullus in *Eruditio ex Memoria* (1977):

> "Vivamus mea Lesbia ...!" Sound: look for elisions, running feet, connotative words (conturbabimus, dormienda) predominance of a's, m's. "Vivamus mea Lesbia atque amemus..." balanced ideas in a balanced construction, placing of words first for emphasis (Omnes, Soles Nobis, Nox), structural shifts in tone., Imagery: "Lesbia" – "senum"; brevis lux et perpetua nox mille ... centum, tantum. The mysteriousness of others, "rumores ... invicere," "senum severiorum," "nequis malus," the evil-eyed world, the cruel and severe old world, Catullus and Lesbia, "my beautiful love," "gratum est" and "tua opera" (by your doing).[22]

Brown's retranslation of Catullus's famous poem 51 (*Ille mi par esse deo videtur...*), which Catullus translated from the Greek of Sappho 31, consists of 'a list of possible ways to translate' in place of rendering the actual lines of Catullus 51:

> 1. Given that Catullus was clearly attracted to the work of Sappho (viz. its privileged status in *Sparrow* as the only complete translation), translate some other work of a poet to whom I am similarly attracted.
> 2. Translate the Sappho poem from the Greek and, like Catullus, add an extra stanza about my laziness.
> ...
> 12. Substitute discursive short list of possibilities as the translation, and include the four extra Catullan lines as a sort of consolation prize for the reader.
> Otium molests Catullus. Otium he exulted in and what does he get? Otium beats up his Prius in the suburbs.[23]

Brown's is by no means the first Catullan experiment in translation, but his is the most recent and perhaps the most outrageous. Louis and Celia

Zukofsky's 1964 homophonic translation matches Catullus's Latin words with similar-sounding English syllables. Bernadette Mayer's *The Formal Field of Kissing* (1990) includes translations of a selection of Catullus's poems, as well as several poems titled 'Epigram' written in the punchy, wry, invective style of Catullus's short verses. Anne Carson's 'Catullus: Carmina' in *Men in the Off Hours* (2000) presents the *nugae* in the laconic, casual tone characteristic of Carson's other writing. Her 'Odi et amo' whittles away all the words except 'hate', 'love', 'why', and 'I', which she arranges into a visually arresting, emotionally compelling concrete poem. Carson's *Nox* (2010) uses Catullus 101 (*Multas per gentes et multa per aequora vectus* ...) to structure a meditative, mourning, accordion-format book-length collage on her brother's death by glossing the poem word by word, and by using the full dictionary entry for each Latin word as a guide for the work's direction and movement. These examples illustrate the many different approaches writers use in rendering Catullus's work, as well as the range of writers Catullus's poems can attract.

Brown's books include *Top 40* (2014), *Flowering Mall* (2012), and *The Persians by Aeschylus* (2011), and all engage in some way with translation. *The Persians by Aeschylus* is a 'literal' translation produced from Brown's belief that 'the text which proceeded from my body should report on my total experience of reading *The Persians* by Aeschylus, not simply report on the "meanings" of the "words" of that work'.[24] Accordingly, he revises the conventional meaning of 'literal' in translation to reach beyond 'meanings' and 'words' to include a 'total experience of reading'.[25] This 'total experience' is truly a full body experience, as Brown incorporates his physical sensations, appetites, and struggles into his retranslation. *Flowering Mall* is a selection of 'elongated' versions of Baudelaire's *Fleurs du mal*. Brown refers to them as 'conceptual translations'.[26] A recent review of *Top 40* describes it as 'a biography of an American moment'.[27] Brown is quoted in this review as saying, 'The structure of the *Top 40* is not seismically safe, it cannot survive / unagitated longer than one week',[28] and yet the review seems to suggest that 'the poems survive, even as they shift. The book is meant to become dated, but also to live on', and Brown envisions his own poetry as material for future translation.

Repetition can lead to experiments, creativity, and renewed originality. Catullus 85 expresses the paradoxical feelings of love and hate with a remarkably economic use of language: a total of fourteen words, eight of which are verbs, and not a single noun or adjective to behold.

> Odi et amo. Quare id faciam, fortasse requiris?
> Nescio, sed fieri sentio et excrucior.

The words in the poem form a chiastic structure that reflects the paradoxical sensations the poem's persona presents. The only second-person verb in the poem, *requiris* ('you ask'), at the end of line 1 is answered at the beginning of line 2 by the first-person verb *nescio* ('I don't know'). The first-person verbs *odi* and *amo* ('I hate' and 'I love') in line 1 are reinforced in line 2 by *excrucior* ('I am tormented'). Because there are so few words to work with, most of the retranslations appear in a limited number of oddly similar ways. Retranslations of the *odi et amo* epigram are so numerous and the possibilities for innovations so exhausted by now that new retranslations appear nearly identical to old ones, and merely repeat the words and phrasing of previous versions.

Havelock (1929):

> I loathe her, and I love her. 'Can I show
> How both should be?'
> I loathe and love, and nothing else I know
> But agony.[29]

Gregory (1956):

> I hate and love.
> And if you ask me why,
> I have no answer, but I discern,
> can feel, my senses rooted in eternal torture.[30]

Goold (1962):

> I hate and love. Why I do so, perhaps you ask. I know not,
> but I feel it, and I am in torment.

Martin (1979):

> I hate & love. And if you should ask how I can do both,
> I couldn't say; but I feel it, and it shivers me.[31]

Green (2005):

> I hate and love. You wonder, perhaps, why I'd do that?
> I have no idea. I just feel it. I am crucified.[32]

Through internal repetition, Brown's version of Catullus 85 extends this two-line epigram by building on the original's single couplet. Mimicking the hexameter of the epigram's first line, Brown keeps a 15-syllable line throughout, as he augments and inflates his retranslation to eighty-five couplets, a total of 168 lines, including one photographic version, which I will discuss at the end of this chapter.

Brown's version of *carmen* 85 can be divided into roughly three sections. The first is a fugue-like contrapuntal meditation on the individual words of the Latin poem – he echoes the phonemes of the Latin words to generate a kind of sonic feedback loop ('Perhaps you'll ask. / Perhaps you'll ask, purring hapfully. Perhaps I'll hop …'). Brown's version begins to play with iterations of these core components: 'I hate. I hate and. I hate "and." I hate love. I hate questions.' He continues: 'I hate forts. I "hate" forts. I hate fortitude. I hate perhaps', multiplying the total number of words in the poem while repeating the same core words. 'Forts' echoes the Latin's *fortasse*, which Brown morphs into 'fortitude', before landing on its literal translation, 'perhaps'. The effect is a shifting pattern of utterances that builds and moves sonically like the transposed subject or theme in a fugal composition. At times Brown tickles the reader by modulating a little wildly:

> Your hate is a fort, but I require loving it. Requisite
> you-love mocks my energy for producing commodities.
>
> I love producing commodities. I love 'and.' I love hating and I love hats. I love mock hats, and mock smirks. I love smocks.
>
> I love *socks*…[33]

The element of sonic play and improvisational riffing is indebted in part to Zukofsky's homophonic versions of Catullus. While Zukofky's phonetic equivalence yields more sombre poems, Brown's sonic progression, although not an exact analogue to the Latin text, moves in increments and playful modulations a reader can mostly follow. Brown's delightful sonic play on the Latin words brings him to 'O, diet you mock', 'I mock morass', 'why are you doing it? For / more ass? To mock death, perhaps, I say. I wear a fat smock.'[34]

Once Brown establishes the timbre of his version and moves through various permutations of 'hate', 'love', 'knowing', and 'perhaps', he introduces a didactic commentary mode, whereby he pauses the wordplay to address the reader. The second section of Brown's poem is in part comprised of instructions on how to read, including commentary on the literary, linguistic, theoretical, rhetorical, metrical features of this Latin poem. One learns, from his version, the pertinent tools for poetic interpretation and appreciation of *carmen* 85 as they would be given in a classroom lesson.

> I know what you're thinking: where are all the *adjectives*? Well, I hope you won't think my project abject when I inform you that
>
> this translation of the 85th poem in the corpus
> of Catullus is adjectiveless. Bold I know, but that be-
>
> fits the boldness of the text, the most famous of the forty-eight epigrams, often simply called the *odi et amo*.[35]

Brown quotes the original poem in Latin in his retranslation before embarking on a lesson in Catullus's economic poetic language and the couplet's chiastic structure. He refers to Catullus as a translator, doing 'two things at once. Although not at the same time. The translator is torn apart, but later.' He teaches and explains the elegiac couplet as 'a poetic form that's al- / ways torn apart, Six feet surging in the first and five is how / it quiets down. In between is blank space, which is how grapho- / lects express the idea of silence.'[36] A lengthy interpretation of the individual lines follows, with excursions into mild translation theory: 'When / the translator reads the text and asks "What are you?" there is not / going to be an answer. There are going to be many / answers, but none are going to be found in the text' and 'The translator reads and writes, deciphers and names, but there's more. / Absorbing the preceding writing and housing it as de- / lay alters the structure of the translator's body, perhaps'.[37] Like the characters in Anne Carson's *Antigonick*, who speak as fictional figures aware of their own reception history, Brown's 85 makes reference to moments in the interpretive and translation history of *odi et amo*.

Finally, Brown shifts and transforms the amatory context of Catullus's poem. Readers familiar with Catullus understand that Clodia/Lesbia is the direct object of those verbs 'I hate and I love'. However, in Brown's version, the conflicted expressions of love/hate pertain instead to the process of retranslation. Brown takes the reader on a 'detour' from the Latin poem with an extended stay in a suspended, liminal translational space: the 'dangling space between ... reading the preceding / writing and writing the marks, "I hate", "I hate and", and so on'. This space, where neither original nor retranslation occurs, is inhabited entirely by a process that resembles 'a stray and like totally rabid dog, perhaps. Doing laps.' Doing precisely eighty-five laps. Brown's mention of writing that 'goes awry' 'in a scene of detours ... called translation' proposes a fascinating commentary on the status of Classical texts and the current climate in which their retranslations circulate. This contextual shift in Brown's version of *carmen* 85 from 'love' to 'translation' is important and significant because it highlights the possibilities for retranslations to contribute to and expand the original poem's range of references.

Included in the contextual shift are the whimsical, seemingly nonsensical, modern American cultural references Brown introduces into his version – such as the inclusion of fad diets, a 'cuddly pooch', video games, and getting 'crunk' – that certainly don't appear in the original text, and may strike even a progressive reader as absurd. Referring to Catullus's *cognomen* (last name), which means 'puppy/young dog', Brown comes up with 'Cute dog that hugs' and later 'Cuddly pooch'.[38] He pushes this further: 'I feel bearded. / I feel groomed. I feel like a cuddly dog accidentally / foaming at the jowls, ripping the skin off your calves like a chick- / en wing.' The final couplets of Brown's 85 are excerpted below:

> I call
> you on your landline, I call you like I'm Catullus, confused,
>
> ambivalent, uninterested in your fucking questions.
> Like I'm nailed to the X. I dunno ... *I feel like I'm on X.*[39]

Building up to this, he uses modern interjections, like 'Cedar Sigo', the name of Brown's real-life poet friend, 'e-mail', a 'landline', 'NES' (Nintendo Entertainment System) video games, and the concept of getting 'crunk'. These moments when Brown makes himself most 'visible' as a twenty-first-century reader and translator of Catullus reveal the 'total experience' of translation as em*bodied*. Brown's version of Catullus 85 ends with a culmination of his own confusion and frustration, an *excrucior* (torment) from Brown's personal context of *odi et amo*. Like Catullus's poem, Brown introduces the impersonal 'you'. Brown's 'you' is 'dangling there' like the pentameter line of an elegiac couplet, like the defunct landline telephone. Like Catullus, Brown expresses confusion and ambivalence. However, Brown's context for 'I hate and I love' is not inspired by the tribulations of romance, as it is for Catullus, but by the exhausting process of retranslating Catullus. His expression of feeling 'confused, ambivalent, uninterested' is compounded with the lines 'I don't know why I do anything. Why I ... write elegiac couplets or translate Catullus.' This is followed by the comment 'Two texts to mean the same thing, but the second time with feeling'. There is a number of ways to interpret this particular expression, which suggests to me a view of the relationship between original text and translated text ('two texts to mean the same thing'). This imbues the translation ('the second time') with more emotion, feeling that is amplified by repetition. It also suggests a view of how the many retranslations of *carmen* 85 in English repeat the text of a previous retranslation almost verbatim, as I illustrated earlier in this chapter.[40]

At this particular cultural and literary moment when there exist so many retranslations of Catullus 85, 'Why bother?' Brown seems to gesticulate. 'I dunno.' His solution appears to be distraction and self-obliteration by way of getting 'crunk'. His expression of creative and existential despair arrives at the conclusion of Brown's completed retranslation of *carmen* 85 – 'I'm doing it. I hate doing it', 'I don't know why ... But I did it. I do it. I hated it / and loved it', where 'it' refers to the retranslation itself.

Brown's outrageous, provocative approach is effective in expressing the core emotions (hate, love, uncertainty) and their conflicting natures in such a way that exceeds the weary and worn-out conventional approaches to translating Catullus's poem. Brown's poem concludes with a crescendo of conflicting feelings (*excrucior*) expressed by two contrasting uses of 'X'. Brown enlists the letter 'X' as a visual symbol of the cross used in the act of *excrucior*, as well as for the figure of chiasmus, named after the Greek letter chi χ. The image of a long, slow, painful crucifixion as a method of execution, 'Like I'm nailed to the X', (sacrificed for his art) is followed by a dramatic pendulum swing to the other end of the spectrum of emotions with an ecstatic effect: 'I feel like I'm on X.' Brown's letter 'X' represents Catullus's paradoxical *odi et amo* in one instance in the final line of the poem, while his use of 'X' in twenty-first-century parlance lends new extremes with which to interpret *carmen* 85. That said, this particular augmentative, repetitive, fugue-like approach would not be sustainable very far beyond a singular virtuosic display such as Brown's 85. The economy of words in Catullus 85 and the Latin poem's status as the most translated of Catullus's epigrams provide a literary and translation context hospitable to precisely the sort of experiment Brown offers. It wouldn't work with another poem. In her 2010 article on Brown's *Sparrow* (the section of Brown's book devoted to retranslations of Catullus's polymetric poems 1–60), Judith Goldman recalls Yves Bonnefoy's statement that translation is a matter of declaration: 'You can translate by simply declaring one poem a translation of another.'[41] That said, she goes on to concede that 'to call "Revive my lovebird" a translation is clearly a provocation'.[42] Goldman writes that while the term 'adaptation' is easier, 'Brown's text emerges as a translation *par excellence*' since Brown's translations of Catullus powerfully throw down a response to the challenge posed by Charles Bernstein '[to take] translation as its own medium'. Bernstein asks, 'what is the translation doing that can't be done in any other medium?'[43]

In this sense, Brown's retranslations make sense only in the medium of translation. Without the interface of retranslation, Brown's 85 would be devoid of context and their provocative *flâneur* utterly deflated. While useful in general, these subordinate distinctions, such as 'adaptation', 'transcreation', 'imitation'; 'pseudotranslation', pander to the conventional, traditional categories of what is acceptable as translation. While sub-categories can be useful, continuing to invent creative terminologies for innovative kinds of translation confirms the inflexibility of certain readerly biases.

I have deferred until now any discussion about the photograph included among Brown's retranslations of Catullus 85. The photograph depicts a white outdoor wall made of concrete or stucco that features subtle, regular geometric patterns moulded into its surface. The wall displays various markings applied by hand using spray paint or paint markers. Atop the swift, interlocking strokes that are characteristic of a street painter's tag, Catullus's Latin epigram is inscribed in full in black ink. All caps. The photograph is black and white, and the wall conjures graffiti in the typographic style of its letterforms and in the accompanying inscribed marks, such as the sweeping, exaggerated features of individual letters of the alphabet. The other visible orthographic features include the letters 'M' and 'A', followed by what looks like a capital Greek gamma 'Γ' and a lowercase gamma 'γ'. While the wall seems to offer a suggestion of the year and perhaps month when some of the markings were made – the numbers '-01-09' are visible at the top left of the wall – the photo appears in Brown's book undocumented. No date, location, or provenance. It appears quite simply on its own page as part of the retranslation, as one of the eighty-five couplets Brown offers as part of his augmented version of Catullus 85.

Graffiti is a form of street art that at the very basic level consists of inscribing a 'tag' that depicts an individual's moniker in a stylized typographical manner. Ancient graffiti from Pompeii and Herculaneum feature spontaneous, hand-written compositions by the everyday man on the street, such as 'Marcus for consul' or 'Calvus smells'. Since the 1990s the realm of graffiti has expanded to include street artists, such as the United Kingdom's Banksy or Greece's Sonke, who paint expansive murals on the walls of public edifices. Other artists use stencils, which allow for more intricate details while economizing on the time required to spray an image. Both Banksy and Sonke create elaborate murals on public edifices. Banksy's overtly political, satirical, and subversive pieces are a form of social commentary. By contrast, Sonke's beautiful, wistful women depicted in effusive swirls reminiscent of Van Gogh's starry nights are appreciated for their aesthetic appeal. Before uncommissioned street art became gentrified via its entry into the curated, white-walled gallery establishments it sought to disenfranchise, graffiti was considered by some to be vandalism. 'Unauthorized' graffiti is still considered illegal, an eyesore and a nuisance. Wielding a marker or penknife against a bathroom stall, or on a larger scale throwing up a tag on a city building, train car, bridge, or other prominent public property is an act of defacement that is criminally punishable for trespassing and vandalism. The activity of tagging is performed illicitly, often hastily under the cover of night. Graffiti artists use tags in order to maintain personal anonymity while registering recognition and 'street cred' by marking territory, kind of like a signature that declares 'X was here'. Rival artists will paint over another artist's tag, obscuring it with their own signature.

Graffiti is a clandestine and subversive form of public protest. People write hate-graffiti on bathroom stalls and in more prominent public places, just as they are inclined to declare love. On the train line that runs from Paisley to Glasgow is painted:

>   MY DARLING FLOPS
>   I LOVE YOU[44]

In *Men in the Off Hours* (2000), Anne Carson introduces her retranslations of Catullus with a graffiti excerpt originally inscribed on a bridge:

>   I LOVE YOU JOHNNY AND I DIDN'T DO ANYTHING[45]

Graffiti and Brown's retranslations have in common that they are publicly inscribed announcements of private feeling, defacements in protest of establishment, and an over-writing of existing text. Brown's works aim to retranslate the Latin poems of Catullus, yet at the same time the retranslations include Brown's individual modern views and experiences in addition to those conveyed in Catullus's poems. Brown shifts the subject matter and context of the original poems from 'love and hate' to 'translation' in poem 85 in order to convey his personalized reading and interpretive experiences of these Catullan poems. These public, published retranslations of Catullus express Brown's mixed feelings and experiences of love and hate about the process of retranslation. They also comment on how traditional retranslation practices have become perverse in that new retranslations repeatedly resemble previous retranslations of the same original text, resulting in tedium and lack of innovation. By repetitively playing with the individual words of poem 85 thereby expanding and inflating the text, Brown raises a protest/rupture against the traditional, conventional, established practices of retranslating canonical Classical poems I mentioned earlier in this chapter. He also increases the possibilities of the text, previously stifled by the inflexible notions that an acceptable translation should consist of one-to-one correspondences. Brown's self-expression and defacement/shifting of the original texts' subject matter and context re-inscribes poems 85 with new interpretations that self-reflexively highlight the translator's individuality and the need for creativity and experimentation in the retranslation of Classical texts.

Notes

1. 'I may presume to say … I have endeavoured to make Virgil speak such English as he would himself have spoken, if he had been born in England, and in this present age'. Virgil, *Aeneid*, trans. John Dryden (New York: P. F. Collier and Son, 1909).
2. See Adrienne Rose, 'Odi et Amo: A Brief History in Translation', www.academia.edu/35988545/ODI_ET_AMO_A_BRIEF_HISTORY_IN_TRANSLATION, accessed 29 October 2021.
3. Brandon Brown, *The Poems of Gaius Valerius Catullus* (San Francisco: Krupskaya Press, 2011), 54.
4. Adrian Poole and Jeremy Maule, eds., *Oxford Book of Classical Verse in Translation* (Oxford: Oxford University Press, 1995).
5. Rainer Schulte, *Comparative Perspectives: An Anthology of Multiple Translations* (Rockville, MD: American Heritage Publishing Group, 1994).
6. Guy Lee, *Catullus: The Complete Poems* (Oxford: Oxford University Press, 1990), 7.
7. Ryan Gallagher, *The Complete Poems of Gaius Valerius Catullus* (Lowell, MA: Bootstrap Press, 2008), 19.
8. David Mulroy, *The Complete Poetry of Catullus* (Milwaukee: University of Madison Press, 2002), 6.
9. Ezra Pound, *New Selected Poems and Translations* (New York: New Directions, 2010), 113.
10. Guy Lee, *Catullus: The Complete Poems* (Oxford: Oxford University Press, 1990), xvii.
11. Petty napkin-theft is the topic of *carmen* 12. BYOD (Bring Your Own Dinner) is the topic of *carmen* 13, in which Catullus emphasizes that Fabullus will dine well (*Cenabis bene, mi Fabulle, apud me*), provided he brings along with him his own food, wine, and attractive, witty dinner guests.
12. Julia Gaisser, *Catullus* (Oxford: Wiley-Blackwell, 2009), I.
13. This and the following three translations are by Adrienne Rose. My retranslations convey the tone of the Latin poems I perceive by selecting English words and phrases that may produce comparable emotional and rhetorical effects while remaining well within semantic range of the original words.
14. Gaisser, *Catullus*, 14.
15. Catullus is 'the most accessible of the ancient poets', and the most translated Latin poet, with new editions of translations being published nearly every few years. The American Philological Association's bibliographical guide to *Greek and Latin Lyric Poetry in Translation* (1972) lists nine new published retranslations between 1956 and 1969. More recent years have seen David Mulroy's *The Complete Poetry of Catullus* (2002), Josephine Balmer's *Catullus: Poems of Love and Hate* (2004), Daniel Garrison's *The Student's Catullus*

(2004), Danièle Robert's *Le Livre de Catulle de Vérone* (2004), Olivier Sers's *Le Roman de Catulle* (2004), Peter Green's *The Poems of Catullus* (2005), Ryan Gallagher's *The Complete Poems of Gaius Valerius Catullus* (2008), Len Krisak's *Gaius Valerius Catullus: Carmina* (2014), and Jeanine Diddle Uzzi and Jeffrey Thomson's *The Poems of Catullus* (2015). As the titles of these books suggest, each edition offers slight variations on the heavily trodden Catullan lines already bearing the translation boot marks of successive previous generations.

16 Brown, *The Poems of Gaius Valerius Catullus*, 54.
17 Brown, *The Poems of Gaius Valerius Catullus*, 164.
18 Brown, *The Poems of Gaius Valerius Catullus*, 18.
19 Brown, *The Poems of Gaius Valerius Catullus*, 132, 133.
20 Brown, *The Poems of Gaius Valerius Catullus*, 138, 134.
21 Brown, *The Poems of Gaius Valerius Catullus*, 12.
22 Bernadette Mayer, *Eruditio ex Memoria* (New York: Angel Hair Books, 1977), 28–9.
23 Brown, *The Poems of Gaius Valerius Catullus*, 59–60.
24 John Bloomberg-Rissman, 'Two Publications by Brandon Brown', review of *908–1078* and *The Persians by Aeschylus* by Brandon Brown, *Galatea Resurrects #17 (a poetry engagement)*, 19 December 2011, http://galatearesurrection17.blogspot.com/2011/12/two-publications-by-brandon brown.html.
25 Bloomberg-Rissman, 'Two Publications'.
26 'Brandon Brown with Andy Fitch', interview by Andy Fitch, *The Conversant*. n.d., http://theconversant.org/?p=2809
27 Davy Knittle, 'Pretty Information', review of *Top 40* by Brandon Brown, *Jacket2*, 22 June 2015, http://jacket2.org/reviews/pretty-information
28 Brandon Brown, *Top 40* (New York: Roof Books, 2014), 57.
29 E. A. Havelock, *The Lyric Genius of Catullus* (Oxford, 1939) 59.
30 Horace Gregory, *The Poems of Catullus* (New York: Grove Press, 1956), 151.
31 Charles Martin, *The Poems of Catullus* (Baltimore: Johns Hopkins University Press, 1979), 122.
32 Peter Green, *The Poems of Catullus* (Berkeley: University of California Press, 2005), 191.
33 Brown, *The Poems of Gaius Valerius Catullus*, 155–63.
34 Brown, *The Poems of Gaius Valerius Catullus*, 156.
35 Brown, *The Poems of Gaius Valerius Catullus*, 157.
36 Brown, *The Poems of Gaius Valerius Catullus*, 157–8.
37 Brown, *The Poems of Gaius Valerius Catullus*, 160.
38 Brown, *The Poems of Gaius Valerius Catullus*, 160, 161.
39 Brown, *The Poems of Gaius Valerius Catullus*, 163.
40 Echoed in Brown's phrase 'the second time with feeling', any Broadway enthusiast or *Buffy the Vampire* fan will recognize the familiar exhortation that one play again 'once more, with feeling!'
41 Yves Bonnefoy, 'Translating Poetry', in *Theories of Translation: An Anthology of Essays from Dryden to Derrida*, ed. Reiner Schulte and John Biguenet (Chicago: University of Chicago Press, 1992), 186–92.

42 Judith Goldman, 'On Brandon Brown, "Sparrow," from *The Poems of Gaius Valerius Catullus*', *Postmodern Culture* 20, no. 2 (January 2010), 6.
43 Charles Bernstein, *Attack of the Difficult Poems: Essays and Inventions* (Chicago: University of Chicago Press, 2011), 65.
44 Alison Young, *Street Art, Public City: Law, Crime and the Urban Imagination* (New York: Routledge, 2013), 1.
45 Anne Carson, *Men in the Off Hours* (New York: Knopf, 2000), 38.

CHAPTER 6

Translating the Greeks

Katerina Stergiopoulou

'May I / Also survive its meanings, and my own': so ends James Merrill's 'After Greece', a 1962 poem deftly interweaving Merrill's own time in Greece and his particular interest in otherworldly spirits with the classical tradition.[1] Merrill begins with a Greece that signifies transformation ('Light into the olive entered / And was oil') – translation too perhaps – before launching into a series of more familiar images: 'pale stones / Shine from within', 'old ideas / Found lying open to the elements', 'Of the gods' houses only / A minor premise here and there', while 'The rest / Lay spilled, their fluted drums half sunk in cyclamen'.[2] Though the tone here is more playful, we are not far from the Byronic Childe Harold's exclamations on both Greece's absence ('Fair Greece! sad relic of departed worth! / Immortal, though no more; though fallen, great!') and its surprisingly continuing beauty: 'And yet how lovely in thine age of woe, / Land of lost gods and godlike men, art thou!'[3] Merrill's poem's speaker then contrasts both his fantasy of ancient Greece after his return ('I some days flee in dream / Back to the exposed porch of the maidens') and his own 'country's warm, lit halls' to his desire for 'Essentials: salt, wine, olive, the light, the scream' – for the metamorphic, bare Greece on which the poem had opened.[4] But the poem has one more move left, for the identification of Greece with nature or with 'primitive' forces is no less a trope than the romantic one:

> No! I have scarcely named you,
> And look, in a flash you stand full-grown before me,
> Row upon row, Essentials,
> Dressed like your sister caryatids[5]

A silence marked by ellipses soon threatens the poetic voice as it trails off: is there, then, no 'after Greece', no possibility of relating to or approaching Greece authentically, or individually, not even as a real physical place to which one has been, without the obfuscation of centuries of such attempted approaches? Baudelaire might have ended here, on Merrill's 'faultless eyes gone blank beneath the immense / Zinc and gunmetal northern sky'.[6] The American poet instead makes his peace with his condition without idealizing its bleakness. 'Stay then. Perhaps the system / Calls for spirits', he tells these now reified, indeed personified and capitalized 'Essentials', and we realize that, by dint of the typographical conventions Merrill follows, they were never non-reified; already in its first appearance quoted above the word 'Essentials' was capitalized because placed at the beginning of a line. There is no escape, the poem knows, if not yet the poet, from the systems already in place and constantly newly put in place, recapitalized by us as we live in them, but there may yet be room for a paradoxical survival within: 'May I / Also survive its meanings, and my own.'[7]

In 'The Task of the Translator', his famous preface to his translation of Baudelaire, Walter Benjamin speaks of translation in terms of survival. The translation, he argues, arises not from the life of original, but from its over-life, its 'Überleben'.[8] Benjamin is not here making the somewhat straightforward claim that the original text gets an over-life, survives beyond its original context of production, through a translation of the kind he envisions; rather, the original already possesses this 'over-life' and that is what gives rise to the translation.[9] The original's *über* of life, of textual life, enables the *über* of translation, its literally interpreted over-setting (*über*setzen, 'translate') or carry-over (*über*tragen, 'translate');[10] thus the translation designates ('bezeichnet') or proves the original's living on ('Fortleben'). What Benjamin adds to the Merrillian idea of survival is certainty as to the translation's contribution. The original and translation are mutually indebted to each other, but the translation, he claims, realizes for the first time and solely 'in embryonic form' that excessive element that could only have been latent in the original: what Benjamin calls 'pure language' (*reine Sprache*) and equates to 'the innermost relationship of languages to one another'.[11]

The American modernist poet H.D. (Hilda Doolittle), an avid reader and translator of ancient Greek texts (mostly lyric and drama), suggested that the relationship of her works – many adaptations or partial versions and not what we might call straightforward complete translations – to their originals was palimpsestic.[12] She defined a palimpsest as 'a parchment from which one writing has been erased to make room for another'.[13] The striking difference between the *Oxford English Dictionary*'s definitions and H.D.'s is the idea of 'making room';[14] rather than presenting the palimpsest as the product of forceful erasure, of 'conquest' or destruction, she proposes a gentler, more symbiotic relationship between the two writings.

While seeing the erasure of the old as the condition of possibility of the new, she nonetheless doesn't state that the newer writing will be done, or emphasize the mixed product that will be the result of this process. She insists only on the gesture of making room without guarantee of the completion or success of future writing. Through the image of the palimpsest H.D. grounds materially (and historically) Merrill's and Benjamin's survivals. A translation would be the result of a double process of preservation and erasure: it would retain – and work within – an older structure (which has both survived and faded) under a newer one, and thus both arise from and exceed the bounds of its original, showing something about it (its relation to time par excellence, but also to linguistic change) for the first time.

After first tracing, necessarily in brief, some key moments and motifs in the history of the translation of Greek texts primarily into English, it is some cases of such making room – of translations from Greek surviving both their originals' meanings, and potentially their own – that this essay will focus on. Specifically, I will argue that modernist writers make use of such an understanding of translation in order to evade or even subvert 'systems' or stereotypes both of 'Greece' and of translation, and thus change the landscape, allowing for the plethora of approaches and experiments characterizing Greek translation today. I will highlight how Greek translation becomes paradigmatic for translation *tout court*, informing both translation rhetoric and practice, and then tackle the particular and model cases of Homer and Sappho, the former diachronically, the latter synchronically through several case studies from the first half of the twentieth century. The chapter concludes with a cautionary note as I examine the programmatic resistance to Greek translation displayed by Virginia Woolf and Greek modernist poet Yorgos Seferis. Both writers illuminate some of the dangers of thinking that the classical past is available for our appropriation and draw to our attention the ever-present issues of privilege, access, and exclusion. Surviving thus more clearly becomes a matter of inscribing futurity into both one's own translation and, through and despite the particular translation, into the original.[15]

History/Rhetoric

The history of Western translation begins with two moments involving Greek as target and source language: the translation of the Hebrew Scriptures into Greek in the version known as the Septuagint (third century BCE to first century CE), and the translation of Greek texts into Latin, starting with Livius Andronicus's versions of Homer and Greek drama in the third century BCE. The first, though momentous in its own right, also eventually facilitated the spread of Christianity in the West, guiding, moreover, the composition of the New Testament in Greek; the second gave rise to Latin literature.[16] One might then easily jump to the claim that the Greek language is the lightning rod for the evolution of Western culture (as defined by religion and literature). I am not going to make such a loaded claim here, choosing to focus instead on the vagaries of translation and its practice, both historically and rhetorically. For the Septuagint and Roman translation culture bequeathed us not only texts, but also theories and ways of approach to both the act of translation itself and the conception of language(s) as such. The Septuagint produced the famous legends of miraculous, divinely inspired and sanctioned translation – implicitly encoding translation as a dangerous and essentially impossible pursuit – while Cicero's first-century BCE comments on processes of translation that were then taken up and elaborated by other Latin rhetoricians were the first attempt to articulate a methodology of translation and a sense of its cultural – and in some ways proto-national – value.

These two translational moments were crucial in shaping still commonly prevalent – if not in the now burgeoning field of translation studies – modes of thinking about translation both practically and metaphorically. In the initial account of the 'letter of Aristeas' (c. 130 BCE), the Septuagint translation is presented in more worldly terms, as jointly authorized by Ptolemy, the pagan Greek king of Alexandria, and the Jewish high priest Eleazar. This complementarity is emphasized in the way the translation unfolds: the seventy-two translators 'proceeded to carry out [the business of translation], making all details harmonize by mutual comparison'.[17] Still, the sacrality of the original transfers onto the Greek translated text itself: 'Inasmuch as the translation has been well and piously made and is in every respect accurate, it is right that it should remain in its present form and that no revision of any sort take place.'[18] About one hundred years later, both the original impulse and the process of the Septuagint translation have become divinely sanctioned: the high priest, writes Philo Judaeus, detects 'God's guiding care' in Ptolemy's proposal of translation, and the now seventy translators

> became as it were possessed, and, under inspiration, wrote, not each several scribe something different, but the same word for word, as though dictated to each by an invisible prompter ... the Greek words used corresponded literally with the Chaldean, exactly suited to the things they indicated.[19]

Even more miraculously, the original has remained the same though translated: people who speak both languages view original and translation as 'one and the same, both in matter and words'.[20] From here it is a straight line to the controversies caused by each major translation of the Scriptures into a vulgar tongue, beginning with Saint Jerome's fourth-century Vulgate and culminating in the Reformation. Translation is too risky a task to undertake without proper authorization (and such defensive self-authorizing characterizes almost every translator's account of their work) – leading to a successive and slow transfer of sacrality from original to a translation which is canonized as the original's double (so Jerome should not dare contradict the Septuagint, so Luther is lambasted for altering Jerome's interpretation, and so Buber and Rosenzweig go to great lengths in the early twentieth century to justify a new German translation) – and the only successful translation is one which changes nothing. These strictures are transferred to secular translation as well, as a simple glance at the *OED* makes clear. Examples of historical usage under the verb *translate* (I.1a) progressively limit the act's possibilities, at least where poetry is concerned. Dryden in 1693 claimed that "Tis only for a Poet to Translate a Poet', while a century later, Dr Johnson and Boswell agree that 'Poetry ... cannot be translated; and, therefore, it is the poets that preserve languages' by honing them into untranslatability. By the early twentieth century, the Johnsonian maxim has crystallized into even more negative form: per the much-(mis)quoted Robert Frost, 'poetry ... is that which is lost out of both prose and verse in translation.'[21] And it is Greek poetry that becomes an emblem of the untranslatable par excellence.

The Roman orators left an equally familiar yet more practical legacy. For them, there seem to be two primary modes of undertaking translation. As Cicero writes,

> I did not translate them [Greek orations] as an interpreter but as an orator keeping the same ideas and the forms ... but in language which conforms to our usage ... I did not hold it necessary to render *word for word* [verbum pro verbo], but I preserved the general style and force of the language.[22]

Jerome, writing of his own translation of the Bible into Latin several centuries later, supplies the other now familiar term that was implied but absent in Cicero (to whom he refers): 'sense for sense' ('sensum ... de sensu').[23] Undercutting the seemingly more passive Biblical model, the Romans also bring an explicitly agonistic sense into their translations, best encapsulated by Nietzsche: 'translation was a form of conquest ... [one] struck out the name of the poet and replaced it with one's own – not with any sense of theft but with the very best conscience of the *imperium Romanum*.'[24] The tendency towards artful paraphrase – which, per Quintilian, would 'vie with and rival our original in the expression of the same thoughts'[25] – or imitation would later reach more fertile ground in France than in the Germanic/ Anglo-Saxon literary traditions. Still, many of the metaphors used to express it inevitably find their way in the writings of classically educated translators: so, for example, Dryden and Goethe speak of translation in Cicero's economic terms, while Pope borrows Horace's fire analogies, and Dryden relies on the plant/grafting similes of Pliny.[26]

I linger on these early examples, Biblical and Roman, not only because they form the basis for how we still talk about translation,[27] but because they are uniquely operative in discussions of *Greek* translation. George Chapman in the early seventeenth century both tries to passionately defend the scholarly authority of his translation of Homer's *Iliad*, and claims, with false modesty perhaps, to be unworthy of the task.[28] A hundred years later, Alexander Pope berates Chapman for his freedoms ('loose and rambling', 'paraphrase'), but nonetheless uses the same rhetoric ('I must confess myself utterly incapable of doing justice to Homer').[29] Despite, moreover, his proclamation to 'follow modestly in [Homer's] footsteps' and choose an in-between way between a literal translation and a paraphrase, Pope's *Iliad* is best remembered through Richard Bentley's contemporaneous quip: 'it is a pretty poem, Mr. Pope, [but] you must not call it Homer.'[30] Contrarians, like Abraham Cowley in the late seventeenth century and Robert Browning in the late nineteenth, disdain the middle way that most translators into English at least profess, yet still rely on the tropes highlighted above. Cowley unapologetically defends his 'imitation' of Pindar – 'I have ... taken, left out, and added what I please' – for 'if a man should undertake to translate Pindar word for word, it would be thought that one madman had translated another', while Browning becomes that madman in his translation of Aeschylus's *Agamemnon*, aiming 'to be literal at every cost save that of absolute violence to our language' and attempting to translate 'the very turn of each phrase in as Greek a fashion as English will bear'.[31] Despite the difference in method, though, both translators venerate the obscurity and almost divine authority of their original: Cowley speaks of Pindar's odes as 'the noblest and highest kind of writing in verse', while Browning boasts of Salmasius's characterization of the *Agamemnon* as more obscure than any passage in 'the sacred books'.[32]

History/Practice: The Case of Homer

The comparison between pagan Greek writing and the Bible was already present at the beginning of the relatively brief history of translation from Greek into English – and it is for Homer that both sacrality and its usual corollary of untranslatability are most frequently reserved, with the paradoxical result that the Homeric epics are also the most translated ancient Greek texts. Chapman attempts to justify the very project of translating Homer by claiming for the epic bard a 'sacred' authority.[33] This trend continues especially in Homeric translation until it reaches its apex in the late nineteenth century, in a translation very different in spirit from many that had preceded it: Butcher and Lang, after surveying in the preface to their influential 1879 translation of the *Odyssey* the trends in Homeric translation of the past 350 years, claim to aim instead for the 'historical truth' – an approach that would allow 'the story', as well as the 'manners and institutions' of Homeric Greece to shine through 'without modern ornament'.[34] Formally, however, they do away with verse and choose instead the 'the English of our [= King James] Bible' as the appropriate equivalent to Homeric Greek.[35]

Even though explicit references to Homer's divinity have abated since the dawn of the twentieth century, the treatment of his poems suggests otherwise. For, despite the relative stability of the Homeric text and the canonicity of its purported creator, what Homer says and sounds like – and thus, by extension, who Homer is envisioned to be – varied greatly in the first three centuries of Homeric translation. Every translator highlighted the faults of his predecessors and the almost complete faultlessness of Homer, but then went on his own daring – we might say Roman – way.[36] As George Steiner has noted, translations of Homer into English provide an index of linguistic and poetic fashions across time – fashions and oddities.[37] That is, the rhetoric of fidelity and sacrality, even of untranslatability, in effect sanctioned renderings that now strike us as 'pictures drawn from a lost point of view'.[38] Chapman inaugurates this tradition by translating his *Iliads* (1612) and his *Odysseys* (1614–15) in different metres. When John Ogilby (1665) and Thomas Hobbes (1673) both choose rhymed iambic pentameter for their versions, it may appear that 'Homeric' form has been settled, but only until Pope's neat heroic couplets come along. In the nineteenth century, alongside the rise of textual scholarship, we nonetheless have Homer in ballad stanzas (William Maginn, 1850), Spenserian stanzas (P. S. Worsley, 1861–62), Anglo-Saxon-inspired verse (Francis Newman, 1861), and archaic, Norse-saga-flavoured stanzaic verse (William Morris, 1887). Even Butcher-Lang's prose version (1879) doesn't quite put a stop to the experimentation, and by professional scholars no less, with J. W. Mackail's quatrain and Francis Cotterill's dactylic hexameter versions appearing in 1903–10 and 1911 respectively. But starting in the 1930s, Homer increasingly settles into prose or into what Christopher Logue has called 'blank-verse prose',[39] the reverential treatment moving from rhetoric to experimentation-averse practice and to the almost mechanical settling for earlier solutions.[40]

The celebrated Homeric translators of the second half of the twentieth century each approach the task differently of course, but all nonetheless recall the rhetorical motifs and modes of thinking about translation outlined above. Richmond Lattimore aims for the Homeric qualities identified by Matthew Arnold a century earlier, with a special emphasis on 'nobility', while also noting the limiting absence of an English 'poetic dialect'; Robert Fitzgerald insists, like Francis Newman, that Homer is 'to be appreciated only in Greek'; Robert Fagles also returns to Arnold and refers knowingly to the 'risky business' of outlining one's translation principles (he too, like Pope, aims for a 'middle ground').[41] It's not until Emily Wilson that we get a frank admission that 'all modern translations [of ancient texts] are equally modern'; she not only resists the tradition of 'bewail[ing] one's own inadequacy when trying to be faithful to the original' but also acknowledges frankly what Philo and many translators following in his conceptual footsteps could not admit: that to translate necessarily implies change.[42] As translations of Homer continue to appear apace – I counted seventeen *Odysseys* since 2000 on the shelf at my university library in the fall of 2019 – it seems that a satisfactory Homer has not yet been found.

Paradoxically, though, the stagnation in what has come to be designated translation proper – a task relegated increasingly to professional scholars – has been accompanied by an expansion in more creative engagements that are often, in their ways, no less scholarly; 'it is an over-simplification to see scholarly and poetic aims as *necessarily* opposed', warns Lorna Hardwick, and indeed the history of Homeric translation backs her up.[43] Chapman advertises his academic credentials, perhaps protesting too much as to his knowledge of Greek, and at the same time attacks 'pedants'; Pope, whose translation drowns in footnotes and who berates Chapman for his freedom, nonetheless also singles out pedants for particular scorn; even our stereotypical pedant Matthew Arnold has snide remarks for others of his kind.[44] Though many writers in the last hundred years have used Greek mythical images or phrases or motifs freely, without reworking specific texts, a particular subset actually engage in what might be called scholarly work. Ezra Pound's first canto, a version of *Odyssey* 11, is an attempt to 'at least … translat[e] Homer into *something*', as Pound had said of Pope,[45] continuing in some ways Francis Newman's effort to present a foreignized, Anglo-Saxon Homer but with an added emphasis on the 'original' Homer as a product of scholarly mediation.[46] James Joyce's *Ulysses*, an experiment on a different scale that is not beholden to a single prototype, was nonetheless heavily influenced by, for instance, Jacques Bérard's provocative tomes on Homeric geography and on the indebtedness of the *Odyssey* itself as a narrative to Phoenician journeys that, Bérard argued, are linguistically encoded within it.[47] Such modernist examples – which I will analyse further below – pave the way for writers like Christopher Logue and Alice Oswald, whose respective versions of the *Iliad* in *War Music* (1959–2005) and *Memorial* (2011) both seek to capture Homeric orality, though the Homeric voice each primarily hears is a very different one indeed. Logue is more interested in the often fast-paced action narration and in the artificial texture of the epic dialect,[48] while Oswald sees the poem as an 'oral cemetery'; staying within a single register, intent on transmitting both vivid Homeric detail and the somewhat distant narrative tone, she seems to suggest that each voicing of the same words is both a commemoration of an older one and a new one altogether.[49] Neither is wrong: both Oswald and Logue make space within Homer's text as received, and survive – by overwriting and writing over – Homeric conventions that other translators list as problems impossible to overcome. Homeric repetitions and similes, epithets and patronyms, the hard-to-convey mixed dialect, the unrealistic or unseemly divine interference are all embraced and forcefully and creatively conveyed in translation rather than lamented as vestiges of a different age and culture that will only cause the modern reader to stumble. Such writers enact Homer's renewability in a way that more traditional modern translations often do not.[50]

Sappho's Survivals

The productive alignment between poet and scholar – the way in which poetry can both highlight and put in particular perspective the frames and systems through which an ancient text is known, interpreted, and transmitted – is seen most readily through the figure of Sappho, the Greek poet who in the twentieth century (and into the twenty-first), after the discoveries of a vast trove of fragments of her work at Oxyrhynchus, has required the most rigorous textual methods to be read at all. Like Homer, she has had a very active life in English;[51] unlike with Homer, translations of her work have flourished especially in the last century. In a literal way, Sappho is still new; we are still, in this twenty-first century, being reached by new poems attributed to her, so much so that the poet-translator-classicist Josephine Balmer recently reissued her earlier volume of translations to include these new findings.⁵² As Yopie Prins and others have shown, Sappho is first a figure fascinating as a biographical person and as a name, her life indistinguishable from her poetry. The materiality of her work, however, comes to the fore in the late nineteenth and early twentieth centuries, and Sappho becomes ever more 'a space for filling in the gaps, joining up the dots, making something out of nothing'.⁵³ Surviving for most of history through selective quotations in other authors (who may have quoted incorrectly, or cherry-picked, and who often provide frustratingly little context for even the most provocative utterances), or now through barely legible papyrus scraps painstakingly reconstructed and debated by textual scholars, with the shadow of forgery or inauthenticity ever lurking in the background,⁵⁴ and perhaps primarily through voicings and appropriations by artists and ordinary people who are drawn to elements of her putative life or to 'sapphism' but who may know or care little about Sappho's meagre body of work in a difficult Greek dialect or about its historical context of production and transmission – surviving in these ways, Sappho 'may once have performed, but, ever since, others have performed her'.⁵⁵

In the preface to her Sappho translation Josephine Balmer makes a strong case for taking into account contemporary scholarship even as she elsewhere calls for 'transgressive translation'.⁵⁶ For Balmer, as for Hardwick, the two need not be opposed. Practising translation 'not as a branch of philology but as a means of looking at a text anew', she aims to produce a version of a classical text (say, *Iliad* 22) which 'could not exist without a translator's close knowledge and understanding of the original text, not only of its language, but also of its historical and social conventions' and relies too on the model of the palimpsest; her work, she writes, would 'offe[r] a reading as well as a writing'.⁵⁷ Sappho isn't, or isn't only, divinely unapproachable, untranslatable, but a function or a role other poets can play, a space they can inhabit, a question they can all answer 'correctly', as Pound writes in Canto 13 translating Confucius, 'That is to say, each in his nature'.⁵⁸ I want to examine here a few such cases that offer an implicit or explicit example to Balmer (as well as to other contemporary translators from Greek, including Anne Carson) but that have mostly not been recognized as performing this kind of palimpsestic work, pulled usually towards the pole of 'free' translation or adaptation instead.

For a group of American writers, all friends in their youth, the same Greek poet can mean and appear in different ways in translation, even as they all still exemplify the same palimpsestic mode of engagement. While Pound, fascinated by recent papyrological discoveries, produces a translation of Sappho with no apparent original, his erstwhile fiancée and fellow imagist H.D. turns to Sappho a few years later with an apparently opposite agenda, while his lifelong friend and antagonist William Carlos Williams, resistant to the lure of Greek throughout his career, tackles Sappho in the last book of his epic *Paterson* (1958) and is, surprisingly, the only one of the three to fully and recognizably translate a poem: Fr. 31, Sappho's best-known, most translated work, adapted already in antiquity. Mary Barnard, a younger American poet and correspondent of both Pound and Williams, produces her own translation of Sappho (1958), much celebrated thereafter, incorporating elements from her predecessors' practices yet crafting a Sappho that appears both less and more scholarly: small, concise, but complete poems (no brackets or ellipses here), coherently organized, dot her white pages, but an extensive afterword documents their tumultuous and tenuous textual existence in a way that is unusual for a non-academic volume. Each poet-translator, however, differently reflects the community of scholars, artists, and anonymous others that shaped what Sappho is, but also the simultaneously deliberate and accidental nature of such shaping.

When faced with Pound's 1916 poem 'Papyrus' or Barnard's 'It was you, Atthis, who said', we might indeed think of them as creative versions, or even as transgressions. Pound's title thematizes the fragmentation displayed in the poem, suggesting that he is imitating this new 'genre'.

> Spring ...
> Too long ...
> Gongula ...[59]

Gongula, the well-known name of Sappho's companion, as well as the title pointing us to the Oxyrhynchus finds, evokes the image of 'the muse in tatters':[60] inspiring but at a distance, never to be grasped. Sappho's erotic longing is perfectly mapped onto modernity's longing for her, and it is up to the reader to decide whether this represents genuine nostalgia on the part of Pound or a well-executed parody of such feelings. Similarly, Barnard's twenty-three-line 'It was you, Atthis, who said' (poem 43 in the numeration of her edition) – a version of Sappho Fr. 92, which consists only of seven legible words in Greek (and a few more illegible ones), each the opening of a different line – may be attributed to her poetic imagination, and to her desire to give Sappho a (twentieth-century) voice. That Barnard's poem itself is about the imagined return of Sappho from exile back to Mytilene – a fact we discover only at the end, after Sappho has been sensually described by one of her companions, presumably the Atthis of Barnard's title – makes it the perfect response to Pound's poem: Sappho, named twice in Barnard, 'will walk / among us like a mother with / all her daughters around her'.⁶¹ Though Barnard's translations are generally hardly wordy, her tendency is to complete the fragments (often with good evidence) into whole poems rather than fill them with ellipses; she is telling Pound, her erstwhile mentor in this long-gestating Sappho translation project,⁶² that Sappho doesn't have to be coded as absent, and, perhaps more provocatively, that he, a man, could not properly hear her voice or would not let her speak.

Once we dig a little deeper into the texts that Pound and Barnard were looking at when producing their poems, however, we realize that, though the interpretations I have offered above hold, they need to be qualified. For behind both of these versions lies a scholar's own creative act: J. M. Edmonds's daring reconstructions, now rejected by more cautious philologists. Pound's poem isn't 'inspired' by Sappho but in fact translating the opening of Sappho Fr. 95,⁶³ as published by Edmonds:

....
του[.......
ἦρ'ἀ[.......
δῆρατο[.......
Γογγύλατ[.......⁶⁴

Edmonds doesn't translate these lines when he first publishes the fragment in 1909, though in a separate publication in 1916, which postdates the composition of Pound's 'Papyrus', he gives this rendering: '"[It cannot be] long now" [said I]. "Surely," said Gongula.' Without Edmonds's guide, Pounds consults the dictionary: he reads ἦρ' (legitimately) as a contraction for ἔαρ 'spring' and δῆρα as δηρός 'long, too long'. But Pound is also attentive to other features of the extant text (though surprisingly not its material, which is parchment rather than papyrus). In the fragment, as in Pound's poem, the lines get slightly longer; r's give way to l's; the whole Greek words in the first two translated lines rhyme, echoed in Pound's *ng*; the articles beginning with τ are also symmetrically placed at the cut-off ends of the last two lines. Pound's 'too' sonically replicates the fragment's first word (genitive article του), which otherwise has to be left out because it is meaningless on its own. So, a poem ostensibly about absence becomes a poem about what remains: these letters, not nothing. For Pound, then, Sappho is, yes, an emblem of loss, but also of material contingency,⁶⁵ and thus a potential emblem of success. Pound may somewhat facetiously claim in 'How to Read' (1929) that you only need to know a few hundred words in a given language to read a good poem written in it,⁶⁶ yet Sappho is proof not only that he was right to insist on concise and precise writing ('use absolutely no word that does not contribute to the presentation'[67]) when he launched the Imagist movement in late 1912, but also that a good poem can make it through even with only a quarter of its words semi-intact. One word alone could be enough – so βροδοδάκτυλος, 'rosy-fingered' in Sappho's Aeolic dialect, evocatively recalled late in Pound's *Cantos*.[68] Though it comes from a poem (Fr. 96) that is lengthy by Sappho standards, Pound suggests that that added initial β which distinguishes Sappho's word from Homer's stock epithet for the dawn is already enough of a poetic intervention. It implies already the extent of Sappho's revision and, in some ways translation, of his epic voice into her own,[69] telling us that, far from treating epic language as canonical and not daring to change it, she does not hesitate to adapt it to a pattern of speech belonging to her own time and place. The modernist poet, translating her words, only follows in her footsteps.

The case of Barnard's poem is more curious still. Rather than backtrack from his initial speculations in 1909 as he eventually did with the opening of Fr. 95, Edmonds actually publishes his reconstruction of Fr. 92 (82 in his numeration) into a full twenty-line poem in his revised 1928 Sappho edition for the Loeb Classical Library, the current edition in Barnard's time. While in 1909 he hoped to have 'guarded effectively against seeing what is not there', by 1928 he can only say that the poem is 'very tentatively restored' and that 'many words *even outside the brackets* are very doubtfully legible'.[70] It is, obviously, this poem – a Sapphic imitation by a scholar of Greek – that Barnard then translates, even choosing to judiciously cut a very doubtful line. This is not to say that Pound and Barnard are following Edmonds blindly, not realizing his own agency in the production of these poems (which he makes clear, especially in the case of Fr. 92). But what they are doing with Sappho is different from what may initially appear to be the case: they cling more closely to that ill-defined boundary between translation and adaptation and put into question the very status of an 'original' text. If we stop reading them as 'translations with no originals',[71] as only Pound's 'Papyrus' and Barnard's 'It was you, Atthis, who said', we can begin to see how they survive both the 'system's' meanings – whether the system is philological scholarship, the cult of Sappho, or imagism – and their authors' own, pointing us instead to that transitional space where meaning is constantly created and undone. This is how Sappho comes to us: painstakingly, letter by letter, with sound or metre often as a deciding aid in reconstruction (Pound), and by first being imagined, literally called into being, through a space that is created for her not just in scholarship but fundamentally, as the ancient *testimonia* or vase depictions of her betray, in lore, through word of mouth (Barnard). She comes because we need her and she needs us; as Barnard's Atthis puts it, 'Sappho, if you will not get / up and let us look at you / I shall never love you again!'

H.D.'s Sappho-based poems, each titled 'Fragment xx' and bearing a translated Sapphic fragment as an epigraph,[72] foreground the tension between the lack implied by the title and the fulsomeness of the poems themselves.[73] They represent on the one hand a version of Edmonds's tendency to prolix supplementation, while on the other they enact the gesture of contextualization that has contributed to the lines' survival; as H.D. wrote in her unpublished essay 'The Wise Sappho', 'each fragment [bears] witness to the love of some scholar or hectic antiquary among the funeral glories of the sand-strewn Pharaohs.'[74] That is, just as Hephaestion quotes Sappho on love being 'bitter-sweet' (Fr. 130, H.D.'s 'Fragment Forty') because he is interested in the lines' metre, Tryphon transmits 'neither honey nor bee for me' (Fr. 146, H.D.'s 'Fragment 113') because it is an example of a proverb, and Athenaeus in *Scholars at Dinner* informs us that Sappho wrote about chick-peas (Fr. 143), so H.D. implies that 'my mind is divided' (Fr. 51, H.D.'s 'Fragment Thirty-Six') speaks to her because it expresses the split between the personas of lover and poet.[75] H.D.'s version of the split, moreover, is not unfamiliar to Sappho herself, or at least to her subsequent history. Her reputation by the tenth century had become so divided that the Suda, a Byzantine encyclopaedia, records entries for two Sapphos: one the famous poet, the other a heterosexual love-struck woman.[76]

H.D.'s ostensibly new poems, however, remain Sapphic in their syntactic or structural core. So, 'Fragment Thirty-Six' ('I know not what to do: my mind is divided') embodies division, as the speaker's thoughts go back and forth, while the speaker of 'Fragment Forty-One' (= Fr. 131, 'Atthis, the thought of me has grown hateful to you, and you fly off to Andromeda') similarly wavers between two figures, the presence of the latter only revealed at the very end, just as in Sappho's much shorter fragment.[77] But this is most obvious in the very first Sappho poem H.D. published, 'Fragment 113', 'neither honey nor bee for me' [μήτε μοι μέλι μήτε μέλισσα]. As Wharton's translation quoted by H.D. in the epigraph suggests, Sappho's phrase is verbless – not a particularly noteworthy feature in Greek, especially in such a short phrase. Astonishingly, though, so is 'Fragment 113': this page-long poem is composed of a single sentence, in which there is never a main verb. The first twenty-six lines contain a sole verb in line 14 in a subordinate clause ('*though* rapture *blind* my eyes'),[78] while the remaining seventeen have seven verbs, again all in subordinate clauses that depend on the poem's repeated 'not ... not/nor' skeleton (e.g. 'not iris ... /... / not this, nor any flower, / but *if* you *turn* again'). Like Sappho's fragment, H.D.'s poem is propelled forward only by the 'not-not' syntactic frame – clearly an intentional variation on the more customary 'neither ... nor' to echo the repeated Greek conjunction μήτε μήτε – and by recursive sonic effects that reflect the heavy alliteration in Sappho's phrase. When the poem concludes by praising the lyre 'frame' and its 'heat, more passionate / of bone and the white shell' rather than 'the lyre-note' or the 'trembling of the string', we realize that the frame must be Sappho's alliterating and assonant verblessness: that concrete structure, rather than an absent, always imagined trembling lyric voice, is what produces the fire of this poem first and foremost – what H.D. traces over in her palimpsestic rewriting.[79]

Williams introduces *Paterson* with a note, grasping towards a definition of his epic poem; among the terms offered is '*a reply to Greek and Latin with the bare hands*'.[80] Consistently throughout the poem Greek is offered up as a temptation to avoid because it takes one out the sense of '*a local pride*' that Williams wants to delineate and celebrate.[81] Yet the second part of *Paterson*'s fifth and last book opens with a translation of Sappho Fr. 31, and closes with a quoted interview with Williams himself on the nature of poetry, in which he insists that 'anything is good material for poetry'.[82] If *Paterson*'s intention is 'To make a start, / out of particulars / and make them general', to quote the poem's first three lines, what kind of particular is Sappho and how does she allow the poet to build up to this general statement?[83]

The six-page section alternates between lyric poems and a variety of contemporary records (three letters and the interview). The first letter from 'A.P.' introduces the Sappho translation with a gesture of self-denial that echoes, and yet in its complete abnegation points up the false modesty of, the standard translation preface: 'I am no authority on Sappho and do not read her poetry particularly well.'[84] Indeed, A.P.'s misunderstanding becomes very clear through the poem that follows; for where A.P. finds Sappho's voice 'clear gentle tinkling', avoiding 'all roughness' and akin to 'the silence that is in the starry sky', Fr. 31 is violent, jagged, and visceral, its speaker insistent on voicing her own experience. Despite its potentially gentle, idyllic opening ('Peer of the gods is that man, who / face to face, sits listening / to your sweet speech and lovely / laughter'), the poem's next three stanzas are devoted to the effects of 'limb-loosening' eros.[85] They describe the speaker's emotional and bodily turmoil when *she*, and not 'that man', sees the poem's addressee: 'my voice falters, my tongue / is broken', 'my eyes / are blinded and my ears / thunder', 'a trembling hunts me down', 'I ... lack little / of dying'.[86] Williams's taut version of the poem (seventy-seven words to Sappho's seventy-nine[87]) is especially attentive to spatial arrangement: both to the Sapphic stanza, which he replicates, and to the crucial placement of the poem's protagonists, with the speaker off to the side.[88] Like Sappho herself, Williams depicts the temporal unfolding of the speaker's symptoms of disintegration through rhythmic shifts. While the first stanza, which focuses on 'that man', follows a rising rhythm, consisting like his Greek original of dactyls, spondees, and trochees, the second switches gears entirely: dactyls become anapaests, trochees iambs. The remaining two mix rising and falling tempos (with each of the last stanza's lines falling into a different foot pattern) and scramble the until-then consistent stress apportionment in each line.[89] Though Sappho the speaker seems dead to herself at the end of her poem and though she has already proclaimed that her tongue is broken, clearly it is not, for this song is being sung: by her, and by Williams, whose own tongue falters in sympathy two thousand years later. As Sappho the poet exceeds herself in Fr. 31, so in Williams the received, stable image of Sappho (insofar as it might be contained in her most typical metre, which he imitates in the first stanza, and in A.P.'s letter) is overcome.

The rest of this section of *Paterson* reflects, I wager (though I don't have space to show it here), the broader modes of Sappho's survival: through the Baudelairean glimpse of a female passer-by in an urban space, 'dressed in male attire, / as much as to say to hell // with you', and through the celebration of African-American blues singer Bessie Smith by the jazz musician Mezz Mezzrow ('Every note that woman wailed vibrated on the tight strings of my nervous system; every word she sang answered a question I was asking. You couldn't drag me away from the victrola, even to eat').[90] As a counterpart to the male gaze that objectifies the unattainable androgynous woman in the city, imagining 'a / thousand questions' – all relevant for Sappho herself on both the metapoetic and the factual levels: 'What are you doing on the // streets of Paterson?', 'Are you married? Have you any // children?'[91] – the musician Mezzrow completes the transformation implied by Williams the translator. He *becomes* Sappho the poetic persona of Fr. 31 in being paralysed by Smith's songs, while Smith is praised for the controlled modulation of intense passion in her singing, thus turning into Sappho the poet/performer of Fr. 31: 'I was put in a trance by Bessie's mournful stories and the patterns of true harmony.'[92] Each of Sappho's two personas evident in Fr. 31 leads to a different set of afterlives: on the one hand, Sappho the woman memorializing herself and remembered by others as hopelessly in love and, because of her homosexuality (sometimes dwelled on, sometimes suppressed) the object of male fascination, both erotically desired and condemned,[93] and, on the other, Sappho the celebrated lyric poet supremely in control of her poetic voice. This double Sappho then perfectly exemplifies Williams's definition of poetry, offered in the first response of his quoted interview: "A poem is a complete little universe ... Any poem that has worth expresses the whole life of the poet. It gives a view of what the poet is."[94] The poetry and the life, the poet and his or her community, the lyric and the documentary, inside and outside (however each is construed), but also the moment and history, the utterance and its transmission, the poem and its translation, the life and the afterlife, are inextricably intertwined – this is what Sappho teaches.

On Not Translating Greek

The 'untranslatability' of Greek is proverbial, as seen earlier with Homer: Wilhelm von Humboldt even writes in the introduction to his own translation of the *Agamemnon* that 'a poem of this inimitable nature is ... untranslatable.'[95] Friedrich Hölderlin's translations of Sophocles were famously said to have plunged him into the abyss of madness – too extreme in their attempt to forge a link between Greek and German for even Walter Benjamin – while Ezra Pound felt compelled to translate Sophocles's *Elektra* by leaving half of it in transliterated Greek.[96] But what I want to close with here are two notable cases of intentional non-translation. Unlike the authors above, and the many other translators who proclaim their originals untranslatable even though they have themselves translated them, Virginia Woolf and Greek modernist poet Yorgos Seferis both refuse to translate; their decision presents us with an alternative mode of survival when faced with the ever-present pernicious nationalist, military, and/or patriarchal 'systems' that Greece can come to signify.[97] Translation, it turns out, might not only be too difficult but too easy, the Greeks too conveniently appropriated by those who claim privileged access to them.

In her 1925 essay 'On Not Knowing Greek' Woolf deploys some of the clichés about Greek that are always swirling around translators' prefaces: the untranslatability of Greek, its absolute distance from us, and its extreme musicality that approximates birdsong. Woolf, however, extends the claim implicit in her title from a feminist one – women, even of Woolf's class, were not given the same opportunities to study Greek as their brothers – to a more radical undermining of the whole enterprise of 'knowing Greek'. No one, regardless of schooling, knows it well enough. The hints of false modesty in prefaces actually reveal a deeper truth: 'We can never hope to get the whole fling of a sentence in Greek as we do in English. We cannot hear it.'[98] Woolf's novel *Jacob's Room* (1922) dramatizes this tension: her protagonist, Cambridge-educated Jacob, brags that he and his friend 'are the only people in the world who know what the Greeks meant' while the narrator tells us, 'Jacob knew no more Greek than served him to stumble through a play' and knew no ancient history.[99] Nonetheless, Jacob very easily takes possession of Greek space when he visits the Acropolis. A 'drum of marble', he notes, is 'conveniently placed' for him to sit on and write down his musings, only to then be disturbed and irrationally angered by Woolf's favourite constituency, two middle-aged women also taking in the site: '"Damn these women – damn these women" he thought ... "How they spoil things."'[100] Jacob literally stands himself in the stead of the ruined temple: 'There they are', he exclaims upon first seeing the Parthenon columns, but shortly thereafter he concludes that 'Greece was over; the Parthenon in ruins; yet there *he* was.'[101] Jacob *is* Greece indeed, insofar as he exerts a gravitational pull on every character including the narrator for no particular reason – other than perhaps that a young man of his kind has always done so – and thus prevents other kinds of stories from being pursued.[102] After his (non-narrated) death in the First World War, which directly follows his Greek trip,[103] all Jacob leaves behind is a pair of shoes, the tragedy of the moment modulated by the possibility of someone else finally filling them. The parsing of Greek and the privilege and illusions it confers must be painfully let go of together with Jacob, Woolf seems to suggest, in favour of a different kind of novelistic and cultural future.

At the same time, though, Jacob is not entirely unredeemable, and perhaps neither is Greek.[104] One of the final insights from his Athens trip echoes that of 'On Not Knowing Greek': 'As for reaching the Acropolis who shall say that we ever do it, or that when Jacob woke next morning he found anything hard and durable to keep for ever?'[105] By keeping her own intense engagement with Greek mostly private – emerging in the confines of her private notebooks or in the oblique structural presence of Greek tragedies in her major novels[106] – Woolf intentionally keeps Greek at a distance and thus in a space of malleability. Latent in Jacob's 'yet there he was' is his sense that he himself constructs the space he alternately admires and sees ruined. As Woolf asks in 'On Not Knowing

Greek', are we not 'reading into Greek poetry not what they have but what we lack'?[107] That 'the Greeks remain in a fastness of their own' is not only a cause for despair because one is faced with a difficult Aeschylian line, but also the marking of the contingency and tenuousness of all knowledge and all meaning: 'There is an ambiguity which is the mark of highest poetry; we cannot know exactly what it means,' Woolf writes.[108] In her mind, Greek, as Yopie Prins suggests, allows access to a foreignness or opacity within one's one language and indeed within language itself: 'The meaning,' Woolf writes of the same Aeschylian line, 'is just on the far side of language. It is the meaning which in moments of astonishing excitement and stress we perceive in our minds without words.'[109] Untranslatability isn't in Greek because Greek is so great, but because it is at the core of every language and every utterance, and Greek, almost standing for the very principle of translation as defined by Benjamin, allows us to see it. Woolf's non-translation thus becomes less about her ability or about opportunity – in fact, Greek tragedy had historically proven much more open to female translators than epic already by Woolf's time[110] – than about her desire to keep Greek's mobility, to constantly 'make room' for other future writing, taking H.D.'s definition of *palimpsest* to heart.

Yorgos Seferis's 1939 translation of Pound's first canto, itself a translation of the opening of the *Odyssey*'s eleventh book, comes from a similar impulse of resistance.[111] There were three avenues available to Seferis vis-à-vis Homer: not to translate for, after all, contemporary Greeks should be able to read and easily comprehend the language of their glorious ancestors;[112] to translate in a demotic, folk-song based idiom, a decision underwritten by the implicit ethnonationalist claim of a continuous, two-thousand-year-old oral poetic tradition; or to rewrite.[113] Seferis's contemporary Nikos Kazantzakis had painstakingly chosen the last path only a year before, his Οδύσεια an attempt not only to produce an *Odyssey* for the modern world (in line with the ambitions of other modernist epics) but to change the conceptualization of the modern Greek language itself by, for example, instituting new conventions of spelling that align with spoken pronunciation, and thus in many cases obscure etymology.[114] In the epic's opening book, Kazantzakis lays out the stakes of his approach. His Odysseus 'stoops over' the sleeping body of his father Laertes 'without compassion' and instructs his son Telemachus to rebel against *him*: 'those follow old kings best who leave them far behind', he proclaims.[115] That is, what is worth repeating from the past is the way in which the past rejected or rebelled against what had come before; 'I've done my duty as a son, surpassed my father, / now in your turn surpass me both in brain and spear', Odysseus adds.[116] Similarly, Kazantzakis the poet aims to show that *modern* Greek is capable of bearing the Homeric load, indeed of replicating the characteristics of inimitable Homer *without* relying on Homer's specific linguistic means. This *Odyssey*'s newly formed compound epithets are as evocative as their Homeric counterparts but do not translate them; new stock phrases arise (the dawn is no longer 'rosy-fingered' but a 'labourer'); a new metre is proposed, roughly isosyllabic with Homeric dactylic hexameter, but neither hexametrical nor the customary Greek folk narrative metre. Kazantzakis, like Pound or H.D., writes within the template, the space created by Homer, while at the same time overwriting Homer's specific work.

Seferis, however, did not want to choose any of these three options.[117] Instead he translates by not translating. Where Pound in his first canto had tried to create a Homer in English, using, like Kazantzakis in Greek, all the resources he thought fit for the task, Seferis translates Pound's text but not his intent.[118] The Greek poet's lumbering, ungraceful, alliterative 'Κάντο' eschews Greek metrical resources in order to faithfully record a foreign Homer. Making a point about the fruitlessness of attempting to recuperate a somehow pure or purified Greek Homer, Seferis suggests instead that taking into account other uses of Homer may illuminate Greece's own knowledge of 'its' epic poet as well as its prejudices. Through his lexical choices, moreover, Seferis consistently shows that the modern Greek language itself is richer for its borrowings and changes, for having been tested against other languages over the many years of its history. By reaching Homer through Pound, the Greek poet puts into question received ideas about the status of an original, about authenticity and purity, textual stability, and the 'degeneration' that instability or even translation might imply. Seferis thus deterritorializes Homer at a time of increased nationalist passions throughout Europe, many, including the fascist Metaxas regime ruling Greece itself, using the name or pretext of a great 'Hellenic civilization'. His act of non-translation responds to such pernicious views of the ancient Greek past and its texts as sacred or untouchable, signalling, as did Woolf, the dangers inherent in the rhetorical or actual policing of access. Survival in this case isn't about the insularity or continuity of a tradition, but as Merrill suggested in 'After Greece', also about surviving one's own personal or cultural erected systems, and about inscribing a future into both the ancient and the recent past.

Notes

1. James Merrill, *Selected Poems*, ed. J. D. McClatchy and Stephen Yenser (New York: Knopf, 2008), 25.
2. Merrill, *Selected Poems*, 24.
3. Lord Byron, 'Childe Harold's Pilgrimage', in *Byron's Poetry and Prose*, ed. Alice Levine, Norton Critical Edition (New York: Norton 2010), Canto II, stanzas 73, 85 (pp. 76, 79).
4. Merrill, *Selected Poems*, 24, 25.
5. Merrill, *Selected Poems*, 25.
6. Merrill, *Selected Poems*, 25; cf. Baudelaire's 'The Swan', whose first part ends on the swan 'stretching the hungry head on his convulsive neck, / . . . / Towards the ironic sky, the sky of cruel blue' while the second part opens on the speaker's 'dear memories . . . heavier than stone' (in *The Flowers of Evil*, trans. James McGowan [Oxford: Oxford University Press, 1998], 175).
7. Helen Vendler, 'Losing the Marbles: James Merrill on Greece', in *Imagination and Logos: Essays on C. P. Cavafy*, ed. Panagiotis Roilos (Cambridge, MA: Harvard University Press, 2010), pursues a reading consonant with mine, especially on pp. 58–63.
8. Walter Benjamin, 'Die Aufgabe des Übersetzers', in *Gesammelte Schriften*, vol. 4.1 of 7, ed. Tillman Rexroth (Frankfurt am Main: Suhrkamp, 1991), 10.
9. 'Translations that are more than transmissions of subject matter come into being when a work, in the course of its survival, has reached the age of its fame . . . such translations do not so much serve the work as owe their existence to it. In them the life of the originals attains its latest, continually renewed, and most abundant unfolding' (Benjamin, 'The Task of the Translator', in *Illuminations*, trans. Harry Zohn, ed. Hannah Arendt (London: Fontana Press, 1992), 72.
10. On the much-deployed spatial metaphor of translation, see Michael Emmerich, 'Beyond, between: Translation, Ghosts, Metaphors', in *In Translation: Translators on Their Work and What It Means*, ed. Esther Allen and Susan Bernofsky (New York: Columbia University Press, 2013), 44–57, and Matthew Reynolds, *The Poetry of Translation: From Chaucer and Petrarch to Homer and Logue* (Oxford: Oxford University Press, 2011), 3–7.
11. Benjamin, 'The Task of the Translator', 255; 'Die Aufgabe des Übersetzers', 13.
12. For a discussion of the notion of 'palimpsest' in H.D. see Susan Stanford Friedman, *Psyche Reborn: The Emergence of H.D.* (Bloomington: Indiana University Press, 1981), 29ff. Josephine Balmer has more recently taken on this trope in her work with ancient texts; see *Piecing Together the Fragments: Translating Classical Verse, Creating Contemporary Poetry* (Oxford: Oxford University Press, 2013), 183.
13. H.D., *Palimpsest* (Carbondale: Southern Illinois University Press, 1968), 1.
14. For example, *OED* 2a: 'A parchment or other writing surface on which the original text has been effaced or partially erased, and then overwritten by another; a manuscript in which later writing has been superimposed on earlier (effaced) writing'.

15 As a result, my understanding of survival here goes beyond that of Benjamin, who claims that translations cannot be further translated ('Task of the Translator', 258), a point contested most clearly by Seferis's translation of Pound's first canto.
16 See Denis Feeney, *Beyond Greek: The Beginnings of Latin Literature* (Cambridge, MA: Harvard University Press, 2016), 14–15, and ch. 2, on the 'Roman Translation Project' more broadly, with an excellent analysis of Livius. Feeney, 23–4, also briefly discusses the significance of the Septuagint translation. Richard H. Armstrong, 'Classical Translations of the Classics: The Dynamics of Literary Tradition in Retranslating Epic Poetry', in *Translation and the Classic: Identity as Change in the History of Culture*, ed. Alexandra Lanieri and Vanda Zajko (Oxford: Oxford University Press, 2008), argues that epic retranslation, such as that which occurred in Latin from Livius on, in Neo-Latin in the Renaissance, and in English since Chapman, is 'the translational scenario of maximum cultural density, rivalled only by the Bible' (p. 198).
17 'Aristeas to Philocrates', trans. Moses Hadas, in *Western Translation Theory from Herodotus to Nietzsche*, ed. Douglas Robinson (London and New York: Routledge, 2014), 5.
18 'Aristeas to Philocrates', 6.
19 Philo Judaeus, *The Life of Moses*, trans. F. H. Colson, in *Western Translation Theory*, 13, 14.
20 Judaeus, *The Life of Moses*.
21 Robert Frost, 'Conversations on the Craft of Poetry', in *Collected Poems, Prose, & Plays* (New York: Library of America, 1995), 856.
22 *The Best Kind of Orator*, trans. H. M. Hubbell, in *Western Translation Theory*, 9 (my emphasis); see also Robinson's n. 6 on the same page.
23 Jerome, 'Letter to Pammachius', trans. Paul Carroll, in *Western Translation Theory*, 25.
24 Friedrich Nietzsche, 'Translations', trans. Walter Kaufmann, in *Western Translation Theory*, 262. But, of course, every new Bible translator seems possessed of this Roman aggression to some degree; one need only look at Jerome's belligerent letter on his translation or Luther's own irate defence.
25 Quintilian, *Institutes of Oratory*, trans. John Selby Watson, in *Western Translation Theory*, 20.
26 Economics: Cicero 9 (then quoted by Jerome, 25), Dryden 174–5, Goethe 224, 225; fire: Horace 15, Pope 193; plants: Pliny 18, Dryden 174; all page numbers in *Western Translation Theory*. On the metaphorics of translation, see Reynolds, *Poetry of Translation*, and Lori Chamberlain's seminal 'Gender and the Metaphorics of Translation', in *The Translation Studies Reader*, ed. Lawrence Venuti, 2nd ed. (New York: Routledge, 2004), 306–21.
27 See, for example, the overview of mainstream translation discourses offered by Lawrence Venuti, *The Translator's Invisibility: A History of Translation* (London and New York: Routledge, 1995), esp. ch. 1 (1–42), or Douglas Robinson, 'The Ascetic Foundations of Western Translatology: Jerome and

Augustine', *Translation and Literature* 1 (1992), 3–25. Balmer, *Piecing Together the Fragments*, ch. 1 and 2, offers a concise and illuminating history of translators' statements – and thus of translation theory itself – from Roman antiquity to the present.

28 He speaks, for example, of his translation as 'my silly endeavors', and claims that 'I cannot too much diminish and deject myself' when faced with Homer; George Chapman, 'The Preface to the Reader', in *Western Translation Theory*, 138.

29 Alexander Pope, preface to the *Iliad*, in *Western Translation Theory*, 194.

30 Quoted in Maynard Mack, *Alexander Pope: A Life* (New York: Norton, 1988), 348; see p. 877 for the quotation's original sources.

31 Abraham Cowley, preface to *Pindarique Odes*, in *Western Translation Theory*, 162, 161; Robert Browning, preface to *Agamemnon*, trans. Browning (London: Smith, 1877), v.

32 Cowley, preface to *Pindarique Odes*, 162; Browning, preface to *Agamemnon*, vii.

33 For example, Homer is 'the most incomparably sacred', 'sacred Homer', in 'perpetual commerce with the divine Majesty' etc. (Chapman in *Western Translation Theory*, 135, 136). Pope follows suit: '[Homer's] style must of course bear a greater resemblance to the sacred books than that of any other writer' (ibid., 193). The trend continues: for example, William Maginn not only refers to 'these divine poems' but also calls the suggestion that multiple hands were responsible for the epics a 'great literary heresy' (in his introduction to *Homeric Ballads*, trans. Maginn [London: John W. Parker, 1850], 2, 4). 'Divine Homer' was a commonplace already in antiquity (see Barbara Graziosi, *Inventing Homer: The Early Reception of Epic* [Cambridge: Cambridge University Press, 2002], 67) but what is noteworthy here is the assimilation of this pagan context into a fully Christian one.

34 S. H. Butcher and Andrew Lang, preface to the *Odyssey*, in *The Complete Works of Homer: The 'Iliad' and the 'Odyssey'* (New York: Modern Library, n.d.), vii.

35 Butcher and Lang, preface to the *Odyssey*, viii.

36 Indeed, Richard H. Armstrong, 'Classical Translations of the Classics', has convincingly argued that the first two centuries of Homeric translation in English are the result of the Latin translation tradition's '*Nachträglichkeit* or "deferred action"' (p. 197) – that is, that Chapman and Pope were not only influenced by Latin values, but enacting Roman translation practices.

37 George Steiner, ed., *Homer in English* (London: Penguin, 1996), xxi. Steiner's assembly of Homeric translation in *Homer in English* is monumental; for a discursive overview, see both the introduction to that volume (pp. xv–xxxiv), and additionally his essay 'Homer in English Translation', in *The Cambridge Companion to Homer*, ed. Robert Fowler (Cambridge: Cambridge University Press, 2004), 363–75.

38 Butcher and Lang, preface to the Odyssey, v.

39 Christopher Logue, 'The Art of Poetry', *The Paris Review* 127 (1993), 254.

40 On, for example, the homogeneous translation of several gendered terms, see Emily Wilson, 'Translator's Note', in Homer, *The Odyssey*, trans. Wilson (New York: Norton, 2018), 89–90.
41 Richmond Lattimore, 'Translator's Note', in Lattimore, trans. *The Iliad of Homer* (Chicago: University of Chicago Press, 2011 [1951]), 68; Robert Fitzgerald, 'Postscript', in Homer, *The Odyssey*, trans. Robert Fitzgerald (New York: Farrar, Straus and Giroux, 1998), 508 (echoing F. W. Newman, *Homeric Translation in Theory and Practice*, in *Western Translation Theory*, 257: 'Those who can read the original will never care to read through any translation'); Robert Fagles, 'Translator's Postscript', in Homer, *The Odyssey* (New York: Penguin, 1996), 490.
42 Wilson, 'Translator's Note', 86, 87.
43 Lorna Hardwick, *Translating Words, Translating Cultures* (London: Duckworth, 2000), 17.
44 Matthew Arnold, *On Translating Homer*, in *Western Translation Theory*, 252 ('pedantry is of all things in the world the most un-Homeric') and 254; for other attacks on pedants, see *Western Translation Theory*, 137 (Chapman), 172 (Dryden), 195 (Pope), 208 (J. G. Herder), and 218 (A. W. Schlegel).
45 Ezra Pound, *Literary Essays* (New York: New Directions, 1968), 250.
46 See Ronald Bush, *The Genesis of Ezra Pound's 'Cantos'* (Princeton: Princeton University Press, 1976), 291–300, for the extent to which Pound's use of Homer in the early *Cantos* is indebted to his more scholarly work on Homeric translators in 1918.
47 On Joyce and Bérard, see, for example, Hugh Kenner, *Ulysses*, rev. ed. (Baltimore: Johns Hopkins University Press, 1987), 29, and Stuart Gilbert, *James Joyce's 'Ulysses'* (New York: Vintage, 1952), passim; see also Leah Flack, *James Joyce and Classical Modernism* (London: Bloomsbury, 2020).
48 See Emily Greenwood, 'Logue's Tele-Vision: Reading Homer from a Distance', in *Homer in the Twentieth Century: Between World Literature and the Western Canon*, ed. Barbara Graziosi and Emily Greenwood (Oxford: Oxford University Press, 2007), 145–76. This volume is, on the whole, an excellent resource on Homeric resonances in twentieth-century literature; see especially Lorna Hardwick, 'Singing across the Faultlines: Cultural Shifts in Twentieth-Century Receptions of Homer', 47–71.
49 Alice Oswald, *Memorial* (New York: Norton, 2011), ix. See Thomas E. Jenkins, 'The "Ultra-modern" Euripides of Verrall, H.D., and MacLeish', *Classical and Modern Literature* 27.1 (2007), 121–45, for a similar account of three very different understandings of the 'modernity' of Euripides.
50 Perhaps until Emily Wilson's *Odyssey*, who insists that 'the Homeric text grows inside my translation' (Wilson, 'Translator's Note', 86).
51 See, for example, Margaret Reynolds, ed., *The Sappho Companion* (New York: Palgrave, 2001), and Reynolds, *The Sappho History* (New York: Palgrave, 2003); Margaret Williamson, *Sappho's Immortal Daughters* (Cambridge, MA: Harvard University Press, 1995); Ellen Greene, ed., *Re-Reading Sappho: Reception and Transmission* (Berkeley: University of California Press, 1996)

and especially the essay by Yopie Prins therein (pp. 36–67); or Prins, *Victorian Sappho* (Princeton: Princeton University Press, 1999). For Sappho's wider cultural resonances in the twentieth century and beyond, see, for example, Laura Doan and Jane Garrity, eds., *Sapphic Modernities: Sexuality, Women, and Nation* (New York: Palgrave, 2007). For a transhistorical study of Sappho in France, see Joan De Jean, *Fictions of Sappho, 1546–1937* (Chicago: University of Chicago Press, 1989).

52 Josephine Balmer, trans., *Sappho: Poems & Fragments*, 2nd ed. (Hexham: Bloodaxe Books, 2018).

53 Reynolds, *Sappho Companion*, 2.

54 See, for example, the recent controversies surrounding the fragments discovered by Dirk Obbink, including the relatively lengthy 'Brothers Poem'; Brent Nongbri, 'Dirk Obbink, Scott Carroll, and Sappho', *Variant Readings* (blog), 3 August 2019, accessed 29 October 2021, https://brentnongbri.com/2019/08/03/dirk-obbink-scott-carroll-and-sappho/; Roberta Mazza, 'News on the Newest Sappho Fragments: Back to Christie's Salerooms', *Faces and Voices* (blog), 13 January 2020, accessed 29 October 2021, https://facesandvoices.wordpress.com/2020/01/13/news-on-the-newest-sappho-fragments-back-to-christies-salerooms/; and, most recently, Ariel Sabar, 'A Biblical Mystery at Oxford', *Atlantic*, June 2020, accessed 29 October 2021, www.theatlantic.com/magazine/archive/2020/06/museum-of-the-bible-obbink-gospel-of-mark/610576/.

55 Reynolds, *Sappho History*, 10.

56 Josephine Balmer, 'Finding a Place to Hide: Chasing Catullus: Poems, Translations, and Transgressions', ch. 9 in *Piecing Together the Fragments*.

57 Balmer, *Piecing Together the Fragments*, 183.

58 Ezra Pound, *The Cantos* (New York: New Directions, 1996), 58. I am here also pushing against the emphasis on nostalgia and loss in modernism's relation to Greece, seen in some recent scholarship; see, for example, Vassiliki Kolocotroni, 'Still Life: Modernism's Turn to Greece', *Journal of Modern Literature* 35.2 (2012), 1–24.

59 Ezra Pound, *Poems and Translations*, ed. Richard Sieburth (New York: Library of America, 2003), 289.

60 The title of Hugh Kenner's chapter on Pound and Sappho in *The Pound Era* (Berkeley: University of California Press, 1971), 54–75, which is still essential reading.

61 Mary Barnard, *Sappho* (Berkeley: University of California Press, 1958).

62 Though Pound initially directed Barnard to Homer – who, he noted already in 1938, had not yet been translated by a woman into English (21 March; letter in Beinecke Library, Yale University, YCAL MSS 524, Box 10) – she eventually settled on Sappho, working on her throughout the late 1930s. She returned to her translations in the early 1950s (the volume was published in 1958) and sent some to Pound but he was not engaged by them.

63 As first noted in a brief and mostly neglected note in German: Wilhelm Seelbach, 'Ezra Pound und Sappho fr. 95 L.-P.', *Antike und Abendland* 16.1 (1970), 83–4.

64 J. M. Edmonds, 'More Fragments of Sappho', *The Classical Review* 23 (1909), 156–8 (reconstruction on p. 156), and J. M. Edmonds, 'The Berlin Sappho Again', *The Classical Review* 30 (1916), 129–33 (translation on p. 130). In the original publication, Edmonds had not translated the fragmentary first three lines though he had reconstructed them identically and translated the rest of the poem. Edmonds does not reprint or translate the fragmentary lines in his 1928 Loeb edition, and these opening lines/letters are also not printed in Campbell's current Loeb (David A. Campbell, ed. and trans., *Greek Lyric I: Sappho and Alcaeus*, Loeb Classical Library [Cambridge, MA: Harvard University Press, 1982, 1990], 118), though they appear mostly without translation in Anne Carson, trans., *If Not, Winter: Fragments of Sappho* (New York: Vintage, 2003), 188.
65 Felt especially by the twenty-first-century reader, for whom the lines Pound translates have effectively disappeared from Sappho's work.
66 Pound, *Literary Essays*, 37.
67 Pound, 'A Retrospect', in *Literary Essays*, 3.
68 Canto 74, p. 464; see also Kenner's reading in *Pound Era*, 71–5.
69 That is certainly what this poem does – for one, 'rosy-fingered' is daringly applied to the moon and not the dawn – but also many others. See John J. Winkler, 'Double Consciousness in Sappho's Lyrics', in *The Lesbian and Gay Studies Reader*, ed. Henry Abelove, Michèle Aina Barale, and David M. Halperin (New York: Routledge, 1993), 577–94, and P. A. Rosenmeyer, 'Her Master's Voice: Sappho's Dialogue with Homer', *Materiali e discussioni per l'analisi dei testi clasici* 39 (1997), 123–49.
70 J. M. Edmonds, 'More Fragments of Sappho', *The Classical Review* 23 (1909), 157; Edmonds, ed. and trans., *Lyra Graeca*, vol. 1 of 3, Loeb Classical Library (London: Heinemann, 1928), 238, emphasis in the original.
71 To use a phrase coined by Emily Apter in a different context; see Apter, 'Translation with No Original: Scandals of Textual Reproduction', in *Nation, Language, and the Ethics of Translation*, ed. Sandra Bermann and Michael Wood (Princeton: Princeton University Press, 2005), 159–74.
72 In Henry Wharton's translation, and following his numeration, on which see Prins, *Victorian Sappho*, 52–73.
73 On H.D. and Sappho, see Reynolds, *The Sappho History*, ch. 8; Erika Rohrbach, 'H.D. and Sappho: "A Precious Inch of Palimpsest"', in Greene, ed., *Re-Reading Sappho*, 184–98; and for a broader perspective, Diana Collecott, *H.D. and Sapphic Modernism, 1910–1950* (Cambridge: Cambridge University Press, 1999).
74 H.D., *Notes on Thoughts and Vision & The Wise Sappho* (San Francisco: City Lights, 1982), 69.
75 H.D., *Collected Poems 1912–1944*, ed. Louis L. Martz (New York: New Directions, 1983), 170, 131, 165; information about the fragments' provenances is taken from Campbell's Loeb (see n. 64 above).
76 See Campbell, ed. and trans., *Greek Lyric*, 4–7; the second-century CE writer Aelian also reports the existence of two Sapphos, the second being a 'courtesan' (*Greek Lyric*, 7). The bibliography on Sappho, her biography, and its impact

on the poetry and its reception is vast. Mary Lefkowitz, 'Critical Stereotypes and the Poetry of Sappho', in *Reading Sappho*, ed. Ellen Greene (Berkeley: University of California Press, 1996), 26–34, and Glenn Most, 'Reflecting Sappho', in *Re-Reading Sappho*, ed. Greene, 11–36, are good starting points.

77 H.D., *Collected Poems*, 165–8, 181–4; the translation of Fr. 131 is Campbell's.
78 There are gerunds and past participles, but their function is adjectival or nominal (e.g. 'shoot / *born of* the later heat' or 'the clinging of the . . . feet'). All citations from this poem are from H.D., *Collected Poems*, 131–2.
79 One can think of Adrienne Rich's poem 'Hubble Photographs: After Sappho' (in *Telephone Ringing in the Labyrinth: Poems 2004–2006* [New York: Norton, 2007], 50–51) as working within and with Sapphic structure in a similar way.
80 Italics in the original; William Carlos Williams, *Paterson*, rev. ed. by Christopher MacGowan (New York: New Directions, 1995), 2.
81 Williams, *Paterson*.
82 Williams, *Paterson*, 222.
83 Williams, *Paterson*, 3; there is a quoted prose epigraph that precedes the lines quoted, but they are the first lines of the poem proper.
84 Williams, *Paterson*, 215.
85 I am quoting Williams's translation; *Paterson*, 215. 'Limb-loosening' eros appears in Sappho Fr. 130.
86 Williams, *Paterson*, 215.
87 By comparison, Campbell's Loeb translation comes in at 103 words, Barnard's at 87, and Carson's (in *If Not, Winter*) at 93. Though content-wise Williams leaves little out, he does eliminate what may have appeared to him as circumlocutions in the Greek (e.g. the opening and closing emphasis on 'seeming') in favour of quick and concrete depiction; of course these omitted syntactical and structural features are crucial to a full appreciation of the poem's subtleties.
88 On that feature of Sappho's poems more broadly, see Giambattista D'Alessio, 'Fiction and Pragmatics in Ancient Greek Lyric: The Case of Sappho', in *Textual Events: Performance and the Lyric in Early Greece*, ed. Felix Budelmann and Tom Phillips (Oxford: Oxford University Press, 2018), 31–62.
89 Whereas in stanzas 1 and 2 the first three lines each had three stresses and the fourth line one (replicating the similar imbalance in length in Sappho's own stanzas), the second and third line of the third stanza, as well as the second of the fourth, only have two stresses, while the first and third lines of the fourth stanza have four.
90 Williams, *Paterson*, 217, 219; cf. Baudelaire's poem 'To a Woman Passing By' (in *Flowers of Evil*, trans. McGowan, 189). On Baudelaire as crucial to the formation of the particular image of a 'decadent' Sappho, see Reynolds, *The Sappho History*, 148–68.
91 Williams, *Paterson*, 218.
92 Williams, *Paterson*, 219.
93 These resonances are everywhere evident in the corpus of Sapphic texts assembled by Reynolds in *The Sappho Companion*; for some salient examples, see chapters 4, 5, and 9.

94 Williams, *Paterson*, 221.
95 Wilhelm von Humboldt, 'The More Faithful, the More Divergent', trans. Douglas Robinson, in *Western Translation Theory*, 239.
96 Walter Benjamin, 'The Task of the Translator', 262; on Pound's *Elektra*, see Stergiopoulou, '"And a Good Job"?: Elektrifying English at St. Elizabeths', *Journal of Modern Literature* 39.1 (2015), 87–111, and Peter Liebregts, *Translations of Greek Tragedy in the Work of Ezra Pound* (London: Bloomsbury, 2019), ch. 4–6.
97 See, for example, *Brill's Companion to the Classics, Fascist Italy and Nazi Germany*, ed. Helen Roche and Kyriakos Demetriou (Leiden: Brill 2018), or Donna Zuckerberg, *Not All Dead White Men: Classics and Misogyny in the Digital Age* (Cambridge, MA: Harvard University Press, 2018). On modernism and non-translation, see the recent volume by that title, edited by Jason Harding and John Nash (Oxford: Oxford University Press, 2019).
98 Virginia Woolf, 'On Not Knowing Greek', in *The Common Reader* (New York: Harcourt, 1948), 55.
99 Virginia Woolf, *Jacob's Room*, annotated and with an introduction by Vara Neverow (New York: Harcourt, 2008) 77, 78. For a perceptive reading of the novel's figuration of Greek, as well as a brief overview of Woolf's lifelong ambivalence regarding Greek, see R. Fowler, '"On Not Knowing Greek": The Classics and the Woman of Letters', *Classical Journal* 78.4 (1983), 347–9. See also Emily Dalgarno, 'Virginia Woolf: Translation and "Iterability"', *Yearbook of English Studies* 36.1 (2006), 145–56, and Vassiliki Kolocotroni, '"This Curious Silent Unrepresented Life": Greek Lessons in Virginia Woolf's Early Fiction', *Modern Language Review* 100.2 (April 2005), 313–22.
100 Woolf, *Jacob's Room*, 158, 159.
101 Woolf, *Jacob's Room*, 156, 158, my emphasis.
102 The novel is consistently preoccupied with all the stories it is not telling while it focuses on Jacob; see, for example, pp. 73–4, 94, 98–101.
103 Narratively though not chronologically. The novelistic presentation of Jacob's death thus echoes the actual history of Thoby Stephen, Woolf's brother (whom Jacob generally resembles), who tragically died after a family trip to Greece in 1906, having contracted typhoid there; in 'reality' Jacob probably died some time after his trip, and due to the war. Such a temporal tension – between the novel's and the reader's internal or felt time and the external time of clocks – is a consistent motif in this novel and in most of Woolf's later work.
104 For a different perspective, see Shanyn Fiske, *Heretical Hellenism: Women Writers, Ancient Greece and the Victorian Popular Imagination* (Athens, OH: Ohio University Press, 2008), 191.
105 Woolf, *Jacob's Room*, 169–70.
106 Both issues much discussed in recent scholarship; see Yopie Prins, *Ladies' Greek* (Princeton: Princeton University Press, 2018), ch. 1; Nancy Worman, *Virginia Woolf's Greek Tragedy* (London: Bloomsbury, 2019); Jean Mills, *Virginia Woolf, Jane Ellen Harrison, and the Spirit of Modernist Classicism* (Columbus: Ohio State University Press, 2014); and Emily Dalgarno, *Virginia Woolf and the Visible World* (Cambridge: Cambridge University Press, 2001), ch. 2.

107 Woolf, 'On Not Knowing Greek', 55.
108 Woolf, 'On Not Knowing Greek', 39, 49.
109 Woolf, 'On Not Knowing Greek', 49. Prins, *Ladies' Greek*, 53–6.
110 The public nature of theatre permits a greater malleability and flexibility in its translation, especially when compared to the massive Homeric epics. Similarly, the multitude of available plays lend themselves to different readings and approaches and allow, say, Euripides's *Medea* to seem accessible to both an audience and a translator or adapter that may not have thought Homer equally open. Women – so unrepresented in Homeric translation until the twenty-first century (and still) – started translating tragedy much earlier on. One of the earliest examples is Lady Jane Lumley, who in the mid-1500s translated the non-choral sections of *Iphigeneia in Aulis* into English (Lady Lumley, trans. *Iphigenia at Aulis*, ed. Harold H. Child [n.p.: Malone Society Reprints, 1909]), proving an encouraging model for H.D. 350 years later, and by the nineteenth century, Anna Swanwick, Elizabeth Barrett Browning, Mary F. Robinson, and others had taken on the mantle. Recent scholarship on this topic is exceptionally rich: see, for example, Lorna Hardwick, 'Women, Translation and Empowerment', in *Women, Scholarship and Criticism: Gender and Knowledge, c. 1790–1900*, ed. Joan Bellamy, Anne Laurence, and Gill Perry (Manchester: Manchester University Press, 2000), 180–203; Fiske, *Heretical Hellenism*, esp. pp. 85–87, on the changing valences of tragedy in the nineteenth century, and pp. 24–63, on Medea's evolution on the London stage; and most recently, an entire monograph on this very question of women and tragedy by Prins, *Ladies' Greek*.
111 Seferis, trans. 'Ezra Pound: Τρία "Κάντο"', *Nea Grammata* 4–6 (1939), 193–200. See Stergiopoulou, 'Between the Lines: Seferis Anti-Writing Pound's Homer', *Comparative Literature* 66.4 (2014), 375–98, for a fuller treatment of this issue.
112 See Gonda Van Steen, '"You unleash the tempest of tragedy": The 1903 Athenian Production of Aeschylus' *Oresteia*', in *A Companion to Classical Receptions*, ed. Lorna Hardwick and Christopher Stray (Oxford: Blackwell, 2008), 360–72, on the riots incited by a production of the *Oresteia* in modern Greek; Van Steen highlights the multiple – linguistic as well as more broadly cultural – nationalist elements at play, while also briefly discussing the related 'Gospel Riots' of 1901.
113 For a cogent, transhistorical overview of intralingual translation in Greek, see Dimitris N. Maronitis, 'Intralingual Translation: Genuine and False Dilemmas,' trans. Yorgos Agoustis, in *Translation and the Classics: Identity as Change in the History of Culture*, ed. Alexandra Lianeri and Vanda Zajko (Oxford: Oxford University Press, 2008), 367–85; Maronitis, a much acclaimed Greek philologist, concludes his essay with an account of his own translation of the *Odyssey* as indebted to the language developed by modernist poetry (p. 383).
114 The luxurious first publication of this edition was not republished as such and did not find success, no doubt due to its monstrous length *and* its resistance to reading: because of its orthographical radicalness, to be easily

understood it must be spoken out loud. After Kazantzakis's death his *Odyssey* was republished with mostly regularized spelling. Kazantzakis himself offers another alternative to approaching Homer by drafting a translation of the *Odyssey* in 1942 (completed by his collaborator I. Th. Kakridis and published posthumously in 1965), following the metrical principles of his own Οδύσεια and not hesitating to coin new words. On modern Greek poets and Homer, see David Ricks, *The Shade of Homer: A Study in Modern Greek Poetry* (Cambridge: Cambridge University Press, 1989).

115 Nikos Kazantzakis, *The Odyssey: A Modern Sequel*, trans. Kimon Friar (New York: Simon & Schuster, 1958), Book 1, lines 501, 178.
116 Kazantzakis, *The Odyssey*, lines 205–6.
117 One might argue that Seferis had already tried the Kazantzakis route on a smaller scale, when composing several poems on Homeric themes, in which he negotiated his own relationship to the Homeric tradition and both its European and Greek reception: for example, 'Upon a Line of Foreign Verse' (trans. A. E. Stallings, *Poetry* 188.1 [2006], 51–3), and primarily 'Mythistorema' (in Seferis, *Collected Poems*, trans. Edmund Keeley and Philip Sherrard [Princeton: Princeton University Press, 1981], 1–59).
118 This decision does, however, mirror Pound's own to translate not directly from Greek, though he could have done so, but through a Renaissance translation into Latin; for Pound is also eager to mark the routes of Homeric reception rather than solely focus on the originary nature of the work.

CHAPTER 7

Beyond Faithfulness
Retranslating Classic Texts

Susan Bassnett

In 2011, the award-winning poet Alice Oswald published a sequence of poems entitled *Memorial*, which won both the Popescu Prize and the Warwick Writing Prize in 2013. The volume consists of a list of 215 names of ancient Greek men, followed by short poems about all those named, together with a series of similes, each of which starts with the word 'Like'. The names are of all the soldiers mentioned in Homer's *Iliad*, some of whom appear only fleetingly; the poems are little sketches of how they died, interspersed with lyrically beautiful similes that offer flashes of the natural world, a world beyond the battlefield.

Oswald is one of the growing number of contemporary writers who are turning to classic texts in what Stephen Harrison has described as a new spirit of appropriation. Harrison suggests that as great poetic figures such as Homer or Virgil are no longer read in their original languages and seen as canonical and immutable texts, so writers are emboldened 'to safely appropriate what they need for their own work and their own contemporary concerns'.[1] This new approach is linked to the central idea of contemporary reception studies, which is that the meaning of a work is shaped at the moment of its reception. Ancient works are given new life by contemporary writers in a new context.

Oswald's *Memorial* also includes a short preface, which opens with a statement: 'This is a translation of the *Iliad*'s atmosphere, not its story.'[2] She goes on to point out that from Matthew Arnold onwards, scholars have praised the 'nobility' of the *Iliad* but that 'ancient critics praised its "*enargeia*", which means something like "bright unbearable reality"'.[3] '*Enargeia*' is a word used to describe the overwhelming power of the gods when they descend to earth, the extreme made visible but overwhelmingly so, and it calls to mind the '*fulgore*' of the final lines of Dante's *Paradiso*, when he is so overcome by the vision of heaven that his imagination fails and he faints. It is, in short, a word that resists easy translation, but Oswald explains that she has made an attempt to retrieve that Homeric *enargeia* in her poem. *Memorial*, in her words, is a bipolar poem made of similes and short biographies of soldiers, both of which derive (I think) from distinct poetic sources: the similes from pastoral lyric (you can tell this because their metre is sometimes compressed as if it formed part of lyric poem); the biographies from the Greek tradition of lament poetry.[4]

Oswald refers to her poem as 'an antiphonal account of man and his world', describing it as a kind of oral cemetery. She adds a note about her relationship with the printed *Iliad*, describing her biographies as paraphrases of the Greek, her similes as translations, though she says simply that her approach to translation is 'fairly irreverent'.[5] It is an approach that she sees as compatible with the spirit of oral poetry, which she claims was never fixed and stable but endlessly adapted to new audiences. She acknowledges that she was working with a source text but explains how she uses that source text not as a fixed entity to be reproduced, but as a point of departure:

> I work closely with the Greek, but instead of carrying the words over into English, I use them as openings through which to see what Homer was looking at. I write through the Greek, not from it – aiming for translucence rather than translation.[6]

In the two brief pages of her preface, Oswald has a great deal to say about translation. She studied Classics at Oxford and so has linguistic access to the source text, but in evoking the spirit of oral poetry, she feels free to re-create her own version of the *Iliad*. That re-creation involves what she ironically terms her 'reckless dismissal of seven-eighths of the poem',[7] though this self-deprecatory remark does not adequately describe her translation strategy. The point is that Oswald is not concerned with telling a story but rather with showing the horror and pity of war. If we take just one example, the death of Antenor's two sons in Book 11, struck down by Agamemnon, in Oswald's version and compare it with Richmond Lattimore's version, we can see how Oswald zooms in on the moment when the elder brother, Coon, sees his brother Iphidamas killed and tries in vain to save him. Lattimore recounts the moment when Coon drags his dying brother back to the Trojan lines, calling on his comrades for help:

> ... Agamemnon thrust at him
> with the smoothed bronze spear underneath the knobbed shield, and unstrung him,
> then came up and hewed off his head over Iphidamas.
> There under the king, Atreus' son, the sons of Antenor
> filled out their destiny and went down to the house of the death god.[8]

Lattimore follows Homer in providing details of the weapons and the manner of the brothers' deaths, but Oswald focuses on the desperate grief of Coon:

> When a man sees his brother on the ground
> He goes mad he comes running out of nowhere
> ...
> Help for god's sake this is Iphidamas
> Someone please help but Agamemnon
> Cut off his head and that was that
> Two brothers killed on the same morning by the same man
> That was their daylight here finished
> And their long nightshift in the underworld just beginning.[9]

How do we read *Memorial*? Oswald is quite clear that she has not translated the story of the Trojan War but has sought rather to translate the atmosphere of the poem as she perceives it. For all translations are interpretations, and what readers of any translation encounter is a text that reflects the individual choices of one translator. This becomes apparent the moment that different translations of the same text are compared; every translation is different, and though sometimes the differences are minimal, at other times the differences are enormous. As Lawrence Venuti puts it in his book *Contra Instrumentalism*, no translation can ever be assumed to be providing direct or unmediated access to a source text, for 'any text is only ever available through some sort of mediation, what Jacques Derrida calls an *inscription*, which discloses that the text has always already been positioned in a network of signification'.[10]

The history of how the *Iliad* came to acquire canonical status as a foundation text of Western culture is long and complex. Rooted in an oral tradition, the poem was at some point written down and over the centuries has undergone a vast range of textual manipulations at the hands of scribes, translators, editors, commentators and scholars. What this means is that we do not have an 'authentic' original; what we have is an epic poem, divided at some stage into twenty-four books, which means that, like all the texts that have come down to us from the distant past, there are no certainties about the status of that original. There is even doubt as to whether Homer existed, and as the translator Josephine Balmer puts it, translating an ancient writer can never involve the kind of collaboration that may exist between a living writer and his or her translator; rather, it is 'the art of absence, the art of silence'.[11] Classical authors come to us from a silent, long-dead world that has to be reconstructed for each generation of readers. Balmer writes about reconstructing that world from heaps of rubble, an image reminiscent of Walter Benjamin's idea about translation as the piecing together of fragments.[12] For her, there can be no certainties when translating ancient authors, but that lack of certainty also means that the translator has the freedom to transgress, as she puts it, to experiment and to find her own way forward.

The case of Homer is further problematised by his status as the creator of two of the great foundational texts of Western culture, the *Iliad* and the *Odyssey*, both of which have had a profound influence on subsequent writers around the world. From the Renaissance onwards, as the study of Ancient Greek gained in importance, translations of Homer abounded, and the small number of educated readers of those translations would have also been able to read the original. Since George Chapman's famous translation of 1611, which so impressed the young John Keats two hundred years later, a succession of writers have produced versions of Homer in dozens of languages, with Alexander Pope's magisterial translation in heroic couplets that was completed after several years' work in 1720 being one of the most renowned in English. Many of Pope's readers, however, will have had some knowledge of Ancient Greek, but with the decline of the study of that language in the twentieth century, the ability of readers to assess translations in relation to the Greek original began to disappear, which means that almost all readers today are reliant on translations. Moreover, as the editors of a collection of essays on Homer in the twentieth century, Barbara Graziosi and Emily Greenwood, argue, there is now a tension between scholars, some of whom view Homer as the greatest ever Western writer, and those who see him as the creator of an oral epic that was fixed in writing only at a much later stage. The implication of this dispute for translators is that the status of the *Iliad* as an 'original' piece of writing has been increasingly called into doubt. This is, after all, a post-Barthesian age, and the impact of Roland Barthes's famous 1967 essay 'The Death of the Author' has been considerable.

Moreover, regardless of whether anyone has even read the *Iliad* in any of its myriad translations, the story of the Trojan War has entered into global mythology and has been the subject of countless retellings, in verse, prose, theatre, film, video games, comic books and other media. Anyone who reads the *Iliad* for the first time may have been surprised (as my students usually are) to discover that it ends before the well-known story of the wooden horse that was used by the Greeks to gain entry into Troy and so destroy the city. The assumption of new readers is that the *Iliad* tells the story of the causes of the war and of Troy's ultimate destruction, whereas what it does is to focus on the figure of Achilles and the internecine conflicts between the Olympian gods. The opening line in Lattimore's version, 'Sing, goddess, the anger of Peleus' son Achilles', makes this quite clear, as does the emphasis in the subsequent lines that this anger caused thousands of men to die violently, their bodies left to be devoured by dogs and birds of prey. Book 24, the final book, recounts how old King Priam goes to the Greek camp to beg Achilles to give him back the body of his son, Hector, whom Achilles has killed. The final scene of the poem is not the fall of Troy but Hector's funeral, his body burned on a pyre, his bones collected by his family and friends and put into a grave. Oswald's poem concludes with a string of little evocative simile poems that hint, though obscurely, at darkness and pain: 'Like leaves … Like chaff … Like thousands of water birds … Like wandering tribes of flies … Like crickets … Like strobe-lit wasps … Like tribes of summer bees … Like locusts … Like restless wolves … Like when water hits a rocky dam …' and, finally, 'Like when god throws a star / And everyone looks up / To see that whip of sparks / And then it's gone'.[13]

Oswald opens her poem not with the anger of Achilles but with a death: 'The first to die was PROTESILAUS.' The names of all the dead are always foregrounded by the use of capital letters, and here an episode from Book 2 of the *Iliad* (lines 696–703 in Lattimore) featuring the death of the first Greek fighter to leap from an incoming ship begins the series of laments for both the Greek and the Trojan dead. The image of the invading soldier killed in mid-air as he tries to jump onto dry land cannot but recall twentieth-century images of war, notably the D-Day landings of 1944 along the Normandy coast that resulted in tens of thousands of casualties. Throughout *Memorial*, there are echoes of the pain and grief of war, never explicit but implicit, as Oswald sketches the stories of the dead and creates powerful visual images drawn from nature – a poppy hammered by rain, a farm boy swept away in a flood, a hawk devouring starlings, a winter blizzard.

Memorial can therefore be read as a poem about any war, not just the conflict between Greeks and Trojans, and it can also be read as an addendum to the many narratives recounting the Trojan tragedy. Readers who know the *Iliad* will see the careful craftsmanship employed in the construction of this twenty-first-century version of Homer; readers who have never read any translation of the *Iliad* will have a strong sense of what Oswald terms the atmosphere of the Ancient Greek poem.

Oswald is not alone in being selective as to what to keep and what to discard from Homer's *Iliad*. The eighteenth-century French translator Antoine Houdar de la Motte produced a version in 1714 and explains his translatorial technique in a preface. He has retained those parts of the poem that seemed to him worth keeping, he informs his readers; he has cut out whole books, reducing the twenty-four to just twelve, changed the order of events and invented new material. His justification for this is that a great deal of Homer's poem would not interest contemporary readers:

> If you pause to reflect that repetitions make up more than one sixth of the *Iliad*, and that the anatomical details of wounds and the warriors' long speeches make up a lot more, you will be right in thinking that it has been easy for me to shorten the poem without losing any important features of the plot.[14]

De la Motte had no Greek, and his verse translation was based on a prose translation published in 1699 by Mme Anne Dacier. She too provided a preface, and if we look at both hers and de la Motte's views on Homer, what is clear is that both had immense difficulty in understanding and relating to the ancient world. Mme Dacier complains about the dreadful behaviour of the Greeks and asks how such men could be received by readers in an age when heroes are not meant to act with such brutality,[15] while de la Motte says that he has removed some of this behaviour 'since these faults would bring them down in our eyes'.[16] She also comments that Homer's fictions are too far-fetched for contemporary readers, since talking horses and golden statues that offer advice are 'too much outside the realm of verisimilitude we expect to live in'.[17] What both these translators did, therefore, was to cater for the taste of the receiving culture of their own time, an age when Shakespeare's tragedies were considered too excessive for popular consumption (think of Nahum Tate's rewriting of *King Lear* to give the play a happy ending) and even Samuel Pepys was decidedly unimpressed by the performances of other Shakespeare plays that he saw.

Oswald's version of the *Iliad* turns the poem into a lament for the pain and suffering of all those caught up in the horror of war – soldiers, families, children, animals, the very landscape itself – while the list of names is a reminder of all those war memorials that have been built in the twentieth century in the wake of two world wars. The list of names of the dead with which her poem begins recalls the lists that are still read out annually on 11 November to commemorate those who have died within living memory.

But not all versions of the *Iliad* focus on loss and pain. Eric Shanower, an American graphic artist, has taken a very different approach. He is currently producing a series of volumes of comic books, *Age of Bronze*, in which he is endeavouring not only to tell the story of the Trojan War but to bring in all the different, sometimes contradictory versions of that same event. In an essay set out in graphic format, 'Twenty-First Century Troy, or How Do You Solve a Problem Like Iphigenia and Other Matters of Grave Import', Shanower explains that he is not a classicist, just a reader and graphic artist who became fascinated by the different retellings of the Trojan War and conceived the idea of weaving them all together like a giant puzzle. His source material therefore includes not only ancient texts but all kinds of subsequent other versions, including paintings, theatre, opera and film along with archaeological reports. He decided to set his version in the Late Bronze Age, so he did some research into the period to help with his designs and also decided to remove the gods so as 'to emphasise the human motivations for the stupid and horrible things the characters do'.[18] In creating *Age of Bronze*, Shanower is seeking to shift the emphasis towards an exploration of human behaviour in a world where the power of the gods has ceased to exist.

The great Argentinian writer Jorge Luis Borges famously wrote an essay on translation entitled 'The Homeric Versions', in which he declares that translations are just a partial documentation of the changes a text undergoes over time and asks, 'Are not the many versions of the *Iliad* – from Chapman to Magnien – merely different perspectives on a mutable fact, a long experimental game of chance played with omissions and emphases?'[19] Borges's view is that there can never be a definitive 'faithful' translation of anything. We do not know what Homer thought, and 'the present state of his works is like a complex equation that represents the precise relations of unknown quantities'.[20] For Borges, then, it would have been logical to accept both *Memorial* and *Age of Bronze* as translations of Homer, each in its own way offering a twenty-first-century reading of an ancient text, and each aimed at a different readership.

In his book *What Is World Literature?* David Damrosch endeavours to define world literature, which he sees as 'writing that gains in translation'. What he means by this is that it is translation which enables readers to access works in languages other than the original, and it is through that process of transfer, which is both interlingual and intersemiotic, that new layers of meaning can be acquired.[21] Damrosch sees these new layers of meaning as heightening the creative interaction between text and readers, while the translation studies scholar Edwin Gentzler goes even further, arguing that translation has played and continues to play a major role in instituting cultural change.[22]

Sometimes, it is the time in which a translation is received that leads on to such changes, and a good example is the fate of Ezra Pound's collection of poems that came out in 1915, *Cathay*. In his introductory essay to the selected poems of Pound published in 1928, T. S. Eliot refers to *Cathay* and declares that Pound 'is the inventor of Chinese poetry for our time'. Eliot writes about the illusion that through a translation readers believe that they 'really at last get the original', when what they actually get is an impression of that original, what he terms a 'translucency'.[23] Since the appearance of *Cathay*, there has been a great deal of debate about whether the poems can be considered translations, but Pound, who also had a decidedly irreverent view of translation, chose to add the following in capital letters straight after the title of his new collection:

FOR THE MOST PART FROM THE CHINESE OF RIHAKU, FROM THE NOTES OF THE LATE ERNEST FENOLLOSA, AND THE DECIPHERINGS OF THE PROFESSORS MORI AND ARIGA.[24]

The key is in this sentence: Pound is openly acknowledging his debt to others, declaring that 'for the most part' the poems are translations of Rihaku (the Japanese form of Li Bo), but since he did not have Chinese he was reliant on the notebooks of the American scholar Ernest Fenollosa, which had been given to him by Fenollosa's widow, and reliant also on the notes provided by Mori Kainan, a Japanese poet, and Ariga Nagao, a Japanese law professor who translated for him. By using this mixed variety of sources, Pound created a sequence of poems that he defended as translations. In his biography of Pound, David Moody points out sensibly that there is no point in holding Pound to account as an 'accurate' translator since Pound did not have linguistic competence in either Chinese or Japanese and so was reliant on Fenollosa's word-for-character crib. The result, however 'was a triumph of inventive imagination and technique', as Pound found a voice 'that can speak quite naturally of a common humanity in war and love'.[25] Moody refers to the impact of some of the poems from *Cathay* that Pound sent to his friend the French artist Henri Gaudier-Brzeska, who spent the winter of 2014–15 as a soldier in the trenches. In a letter to Pound, Gaudier-Brzeska says that 'The Song of the Bowmen of Shu' and 'Lament of the Frontier Guard' depict the situation in which he found himself.[26] Lines like 'Our mind is full of sorrow, who will know of our grief?' or 'A gracious spring, turned to blood-ravenous autumn' were indeed prescient for the French sculptor trapped in the mud-filled trenches, where he would die just a few months later at the age of only twenty-four.

Cathay is an important work for our understanding of how translation works. All translations are, as already pointed out, interpretations; they are the visible signs of one individual's reading of a text originally created in another cultural and linguistic context. Writing about *Cathay*, the Mexican Nobel laureate Octavio Paz is unequivocal: 'Do Pound's poems correspond to the originals? A useless question: Pound *invented*, as Eliot said, Chinese poetry in English. The points of departure were some ancient Chinese poems, revived and changed by a great poet; the result was other poems. Others: the same.'[27]

In his essay 'How to Read' published in 1929 in the *New York Herald Tribune*, Pound sets out his theory of poetic translation. He advocates looking at what is actually going on in a poem and goes on to identify three aspects of poetry. The first, which he terms *melopoeia*, refers to the musical properties of words. This adds an additional dimension of meaning but is practically impossible to translate, 'save perhaps by divine accident or for half a line at a time'. His second aspect is *phanopoeia*, 'the casting of images upon the visual imagination', which he does see as translatable (he was an Imagist poet, after all), but his third aspect, *logopoeia*, does not translate at all. This involves the use of words beyond their direct meaning and might include wordplay, double meanings, puns, culturally specific words or allusions.[28] Pound, like Paz, recognised the impossibility of total equivalence in translation, and although he does not use the word chosen by Oswald, *enargeia*, he too reached out for something that could only be found in a text by a reader/translator able to understand that a translator needs to be able to go beyond words.

But *Cathay* also raises another interesting dimension of translation: the circumstances in which a work is received. Hugh Kenner was the first scholar to suggest that *Cathay* can be read as a collection of poems not only about exile and grief but also about the sorrow and pity of war.[29] Interestingly, Pound chose to include a translation from Anglo-Saxon in this collection, 'The Seafarer', also a poem about loss and exile and about the transience of earthly power. The fact that *Cathay* came out in 1915, when it was gradually starting to dawn on people that the war was not going to be over quickly and casualties were starting to mount, meant that there was an additional dimension to any reading. On one level, the poems could be read as being about ancient China; on another, they could be read as about the contemporary situation. *Cathay* is therefore both a collection of translations of ancient Chinese poetry and a collection of poems about the suffering of soldiers and their families in wartime.

Translation necessarily involves change. Often the discourse around translation has been negative, in that it has focused on change as undesirable, because somehow, in some way, it is assumed that a translation can be completely 'faithful' to an original. In his splendid essay on translation, the poet and translator Eliot Weinberger celebrates the fact that translation involves change. Translation, he suggests, is a liberating force, and he rejects the suggestion that not all texts are translatable. There is no text that cannot be translated; in his view, it is just that such texts have not yet found their translators, and he goes on to defend translation:

> A translation is not inferior to the original; it is only inferior to other translations, written or not yet written. There is no definitive translation because a translation always appears in the context of its contemporary literature, and the realm of the possible in any contemporary literature is in constant flux – often, it should be emphasised, altered by the translations that have entered into it. ... Poetry is that which is worth translating, and translation is what keeps literature alive. Translation is change and motion; literature dies when it stays the same, when it has no place to go.[30]

Dante's *Divine Comedy* is generally considered to be one of the greatest works of Western civilisation. It has been translated into countless languages, though it did not appear in English until the early nineteenth century. As with Homer, translators have variously rendered it in prose and different verse forms, and there is a long history of visual representations, with Gustave Doré's illustrations the most famous. Doré's illustrated *Inferno* came out in 1861 and was an immediate best-seller and the combined *Purgatorio* and *Paradiso* appeared in 1868. The impact of Doré's illustrated Dante was huge and has certainly contributed to the success of Dante in the last century and a half outside his native Italy, notably in the Anglophone world.

Another famous illustrator, the American Seymour Chwast, also produced a version of the *Divine Comedy*. He brought out his graphic novel version in black and white in 2010. Although there are occasional echoes of Doré, Chwast has produced a version for the twenty-first century, reducing the written text to a minimum so as to focus on the sequence of events that underpin Dante's great journey and the lessons he learns en route. Chwast's Dante is a figure in an overcoat and fedora, with a pipe clenched between his teeth, recalling Philip Marlowe, the detective created by Raymond Chandler in the 1930s. Virgil is a little man with a moustache, wearing a dark suit and carrying a cane – an Hercule Poirot figure – and so these images taken from detective fiction might suggest that the story which follows will be a search to resolve a mystery. Twentieth-century detectives are on the trail of a thirteenth-century mystery. Chwast develops his 1930s environment throughout. Dante and Virgil descend through a kind of subway entrance, while the feud between Guelphs and Ghibellines referred to by Ciacco in Canto VI of *Inferno* is exemplified as a shoot-out between 1930s gangsters, the crusades in Canto xv of *Paradiso* are represented by First World War soldiers and tanks, and Dante's old friend Belacqua encountered in Canto iv of *Purgatorio* is depicted as an old-time wide boy, with a striped suit, flat cap and bow tie. There are all kinds of references to 1930s cinema, and in Canto xxviii of *Paradiso*, when Dante and Beatrice see God as a point of light surrounded by nine circles of luminous angels, Chwast draws on Busby Berkeley's human waterfall sequence from the 1933 film *Footlight Parade* so that his angels are female swimmers with wings. The final page consists of the Dante/Philip Marlowe figure standing in a white space looking up at the sky, which fills two-thirds of the space, a sky drawn as black but studded with dots representing stars with a white circle in the centre and a comet in the top right-hand corner. Above the drawing are the last four lines of Dante's poem with the famous reference to the 'love that moves the sun and other stars'.

The title page credits this work as an adaptation – 'Adapted by Seymour Chwast' – which raises another question that bedevils translation studies: can we make a distinction between a translation and an adaptation, and if so, how? For my part, I find such a distinction problematic, because it returns us to the vexed question of faithfulness – that is, how far can a translation diverge from its original before it becomes an adaptation rather than a translation. André Lefevere proposed using a different term altogether, so as to refer to all versions based on a previously existing text as 'rewritings', which is a far more helpful concept.[31] This is a view shared by Venuti, who calls for recognition of the choices made by a translator so as to move beyond what he terms an instrumentalist view of translation:

> Translation is radically transformative. To develop a critical consciousness of this fact and forestall the education of a translation to its source text, different assumptions must be applied in reading translations. Readers must assume that the translator's verbal voices constitute interpretative moves, rewriting the source text with formal and semantic features that are specific to the receiving culture and its institutions.[32]

Dante has become one of the world's most translated writers, but the list of those most translated, according to the Index Translationum, contains, predictably, not only religious works such as the Bible and the Quran but also, more unpredictably, a number of books for children, and the second most translated work on the list is Carlo Collodi's *Le avventure di Pinocchio*, published in book form in 1883 after being serialised in *Il giornale per i bambini*. The book has been translated into more than three hundred languages, and sales figures are in the tens of millions. The first

English translation, by Mary Alice Murray, came out in 1892, the most recent is Geoffrey Brock's version from 2009, and the hugely influential Disney film appeared in 1940. In a useful essay, 'Does Pinocchio Have an Italian Passport?', subtitled 'What Is Specifically National and What Is International about Classics of Children's Literature', Emer O'Sullivan suggests that there is something she calls 'a world republic of childhood' populated by Pinocchios, Alices, Gullivers, Peter Pans and Pippi Longstockings whose survival depends not on actual translations of the original texts in which they first appeared but on fictions of fictions, endless retellings that have developed lives of their own in the receiving culture.[33] Such is the power of the figure of Pinocchio that cartoonists around the world often depict politicians with long, sprouting wooden noses, an international symbol of someone who tells lies.

Translations are powerful. They may have been dismissed by literary critics intent on proving that a translation is somehow an inferior creation to a work that claims to be original, but when we look at the history of all literatures, we find translations playing a significant role by introducing new ideas, new forms, new ways of thinking into the receiving culture. The ideology of national 'roots' and origins may have sought to downplay the significance of translations (attacked as foreign migrants, undesirable foreign influences), yet translations have been a continuous traffic of export and import in cycles of what today we might term global flows: Italian sources filtered through translations to Shakespeare, whose works in turn filtered through to Pushkin, whose impact on later Russian literature was immense, then Russian writers filtered back into English through translations (Constance Garnett is Tolstoy for millions of English language readers). The great familiar figures of Don Juan, Faust, Ulysses, Medea and Electra endlessly reappear in different languages across the world, travelling through translation and changing in their journeying.

No translation can ever be the same as its original, but rather than seeing this in terms of a loss, it makes far more sense to think in terms of gain, for once a translation enters the receiving culture it sets out on a new path. The *Iliad* may have begun as an oral poem, but over the ages it has become a source for writers, painters, sculptors, musicians, filmmakers, video game creators, graphic artists – in short for creative artists across the world – and has consequently acquired new life in new languages and new forms. The Trojan War in its many manifestations has become a symbol of the tragedy of war in all ages. Similarly, as Pinocchio gained global significance, the fact that he was created by an Italian writer has ceased to have any meaning, for the little puppet now belongs to everyone, everywhere.

We know that with very rare exceptions (and then only for brief periods), no literature can close itself off from other literatures, and translation enables contact between literatures, bringing about transformation. As Carlos Fuentes asks, 'Is there a fatherless book, an orphan volume in this world? A book that is not the descendant of other books? A single leaf of a book that is not an offshoot of the great genealogical tree of mankind's literary imagination?'[34] In the great interconnectedness of global textuality, the role played by translation, however we choose to define that term, is infinite.

Notes

1. Stephen J. Harrison, ed., *Living Classics: Greece and Rome in Contemporary Poetry* (Oxford: Oxford University Press, 2009), 15.
2. Alice Oswald, *Memorial* (London: Faber, 2011), 1.
3. Oswald, *Memorial*, 1.
4. Oswald, *Memorial*, 1.
5. Oswald, *Memorial*, 2.
6. Oswald, *Memorial*, 2.
7. Oswald, *Memorial*, 2.
8. Richmond Lattimore, trans., *Iliad of Homer* (Chicago: University of Chicago Press, 1951), 241.
9. Oswald, *Memorial*, 39.
10. Lawrence Venuti, *Contra Instrumentalism: A Translation Polemic* (Lincoln: University of Nebraska Press, 2019), 3.
11. Josephine Balmer, 'Jumping Their Bones: Translating, Transgressing, and Creating', in *Living Classics*, 45.
12. Walter Benjamin, 'The Task of the Translator', in *Illuminations*, trans. Harry Zohn, ed. Hannah Arendt (London: Fontana Press, 1992), 70–82.
13. Oswald, *Memorial*, 73–83.
14. Antoine Houdar de la Motte, extract from the preface to his translation of the *Iliad*, in *Translation/History/Culture: A Sourcebook*, ed. André Lefevere (London: Routledge, 1992), 29.
15. Anne Dacier, extract from the introduction to her translation of the *Iliad*, in *Translation/History/Culture: A Sourcebook*, 10–11.
16. De la Motte, extract from the preface to his translation of the *Iliad*, 30.
17. Dacier, extract from the introduction to her translation of the *Iliad*, 11.
18. Eric Shanower, 'Twenty-First Century Troy, or How Do You Solve a Problem Like Iphigenia and Other Matters of Grave Import', in *Classics and Comics*, ed. George Kovacs and C. W. Marshall (Oxford: Oxford University Press, 2011), 195.

19 Jorge Luis Borges, 'The Homeric Versions', trans. Eliot Weinberger, in *Voice-Overs: Translation and Latin American Literature*, ed. Daniel Balderston and Marcy Schwartz (Albany: State University of New York Press, 2002), 15.
20 Borges, 'The Homeric Versions', 17.
21 David Damrosch, *What Is World Literature?* (Princeton, NJ: Princeton University Press, 2003), 288.
22 Edwin Gentzler, *Translation and Rewriting in the Age of Post-Translation Studies* (New York: Routledge, 2017), 7.
23 T. S. Eliot, introduction to *Ezra Pound: Selected Poems*, in *Ezra Pound: A Critical Anthology*, ed. J. P. Sullivan (Harmonsdsworth: Penguin, 1970), 105.
24 Ezra Pound, *Cathay*, in *Ezra Pound: Translations* (New York: New Directions, 1963), 189.
25 A. David Moody, *Ezra Pound: Poet. A Portrait of the Man and His Work*, vol. 1, *The Young Genius, 1885–1920* (Oxford: Oxford University Press, 2007), 273.
26 Moody, *Ezra Pound: Poet*, vol. 1, 271.
27 Octavio Paz, further comments, in *Nineteen Ways of Looking at Wang Wei: How a Chinese Poem Is Translated*, ed. Eliot Weinberger, (Mt Kisco, NY: Moyer Bell, 1987), 46.
28 Ezra Pound, 'How to Read', in *Literary Essays*, ed. T. S. Eliot (New York: New Directions, 1968), 25.
29 Hugh Kenner, *The Pound Era* (Berkeley: University of California Press, 1971).
30 Eliot Weinberger, 'Anonymous Sources: A Talk on Translators and Translation', in *Voice-Overs*, 118.
31 André Lefevere, *Translation, Rewriting, and the Manipulation of Literary Fame* (London: Routledge, 2017).
32 Venuti, *Contra Instrumentalism*, 176.
33 Emer O'Sullivan, 'Does Pinocchio Have an Italian Passport? What Is Specifically National and What Is International about Classics of Children's Literature', in *The Translation of Children's Literature: A Reader*, ed. Gillian Lathey (Clevedon: Multilingual Matters, 2006), 146.
34 Carlos Fuentes, *How I Wrote 'Aura'* (London: Andre Deutsch, 1988), 76.

CHAPTER 8

Translation in and of Psychoanalysis
Kulturarbeit *as Transliteration*[*]

Jean-Michel Rabaté

One way of summing up the work of psychoanalysis is to say that it is a process aimed at making the unconscious conscious.[1] Could that process have to do with translation? Several eloquent scholars have pointed out the abundant use of terms similar to 'translation' in Freud's texts, and they have analysed their links with two related technical terms, 'transference' and 'interpretation'.[2] However, recently, translation has again loomed large in the domain of psychoanalytic theory. I will start with an example to introduce the subject.

Where It Was, There We Will Translate

Concluding one of his *New Introductory Lectures on Psycho-Analysis,* Freud ended with an image, an allegory almost, of the therapeutic effect of psychoanalysis, here presented in James Strachey's translation:

> Its intention is, indeed, to strengthen the ego, to make it more independent of the super-ego, to widen its field of perception and enlarge its organization, so that it can appropriate fresh portions of the id. Where id was, there ego shall be. It is a work of culture – not unlike the draining of the Zuider Zee.[3]

Freud's original text had a different layout, the last sentence beginning a new paragraph to add emphasis:

> Ihre Absicht ist ja, das Ich zu stärken, es vom Über-Ich unabhängiger zu machen, sein Wahrnehmungsfeld zu erweitern und seine Organisation auszubauen, so daß es sich neue Stücke des Es aneignen kann. Wo Es war, soll Ich werden.
>
> Es ist Kulturarbeit etwa wie die Trockenlegung der Zuydersee.[4]

I'll quote a gloss from the first page that appears on the web when one searches 'Wo Es war, soll Ich Werden':

> Freud hoped that, by bringing the contents of the unconscious into consciousness, he could minimize repression and neurosis. The English translation of the German 'Wo Es war, soll Ich werden' is 'Where It was, shall I

be'. In other words, the 'it', or 'id' (unconscious) will be replaced by the 'I', by consciousness and self-identity. Freud's goal was to strengthen the ego, the 'I' self, the conscious/rational identity, so it would be more powerful than the unconscious.[5]

This is not so bad: we learn that there is a difference between Freud's 'Ich'/'Es' and the translation by 'Ego'/'Id'. However, the shift from 'Ich/I' or 'Ich/Ego' to the 'self' and then 'consciousness' equated with 'rational identity' tends to picture the 'Ego' battling against the encroachments of the 'Id', in which the Unconscious is captured thanks to a fantastic psychomachia, the beleaguered 'Ego' struggling against a powerful Unconscious as the enemy within. What has been lost is first Freud's idea, stated a little earlier in the lecture, that the 'I' fights mostly against the 'super-ego', and then his conclusion, stating that 'I' should appropriate as much ground as possible, retaking it from an 'It', compared with inundated land that can be reclaimed from the sea. Freud gave these lectures in 1932, at a time when Dutch efforts to add tillable land to their country had succeeded. The Afsluitdijk was finished in 1932; it transformed the Zuiderzee into what was called the Ijsselmeer. Large areas of previously inundated land became available for farming and housing. The historical and geographical reference reminds us that the domain of the 'Es' can be considered as potential farmable terrain more than a dark dungeon filled with monsters.

The commentary quoted fits theories that my students find everywhere and repeat with assurance. Freud's doctrine aimed at preventing rational consciousness from being invaded by monstrous instinctual urges stemming from the 'Id'. The topology of the I, It and Super-I turns into a Walt Disney cartoon: a superegoic Jiminy Cricket helps a Pinocchio-like Ego become human by avoiding metamorphosing into a braying Id-ass. Inevitably, to introduce nuance, I send my students to the dissenting voice of Bruno Bettelheim, whose spirited refutation of the translation of 'Es' by 'Id' and of 'Ich' by 'Ego' dates from 1982.

Bettelheim renders the sentences as: 'Where it was, there should become I', and 'It is a cultural achievement somewhat like the draining of the Zuyder Zee.'[6] He explains that the sea represents the natural world more than the unconscious and definitively rejects an earlier translation in the Standard Edition of *Kulturarbeit* as 'reclamation work', a symptomatic blunder silently corrected in later editions. Bettelheim's contention is that the Standard Edition of Freud's works does 'standardize' by distorting the meaning of psychoanalysis, which turns into a dry, abstract and pseudo-scientific doctrine. Bettelheim, who came from the same Viennese culture as Freud but fifty years later, noted with dismay how current German words like *Besetzung* or *Fehlleistung* were rendered by Greek terms like 'cathexis' and 'parapraxis'. And whenever Freud mentioned *die Seele* ('the soul'), it was translated as 'the mind'.

More than twenty-five years earlier, it was in Vienna too that Jacques Lacan discussed 'Wo Es war, soll Ich werden' in 'The Freudian Thing', a lecture given in German in November 1955. Lacan insisted that Freud's sentence should not be construed as meaning 'where the id was, there the ego shall be' but keep its homely and demotic feel. Like Bettelheim, Lacan rejected the imposition of a static topology on a dynamic grammar: the subject's 'I' turns into 'the Ego', the 'it' one grapples with becomes 'the Id'. Even if these terms are capitalized by Freud (which had not been the case in the first version), one must keep the mobility of Freud's spoken syntax. Lacan also highlights the modal value of *sollen*, a verb indicating an ethical imperative. It announces a duty concerning the emergence of 'I' as a speaking subject. Punning on a French syntax distorted via a shift from *là où c'était* (where it was) to a reflexive *là où s'était* (literally: 'where it was for itself'), Lacan expands the sentence: 'Where (it) was itself, it is my duty that I come into being.'[7]

Later, Lacan proposed, 'Where it was, there must I come to be as a subject.'[8] In both cases, Freud's syntax is taken literally to render adequately the movement leading from an undefined neuter to a first-person utterance of 'I'. Meanwhile, the verb 'soll Ich' appears as a paradoxical injunction to be myself, as in: 'Be more spontaneous!' Lacan comments: 'the "must I" of Freud's formulation, which, in inverting its meaning, brings forth the paradox of an imperative that presses me to assume my own causality. // Yet I am not the cause of myself, though not because I am the creature,'[9] before comparing Freud's sentence with Descartes's foundational 'Cogito ergo sum'. In different, almost opposite manners, Lacan and Bettelheim take seriously, that is literally, Freud's explanation of his terminology, especially when he provides the rationale for words like *Es* and *Ich*:

> You will probably protest at our having chosen simple pronouns to describe our two agencies or provinces instead of giving them orotund Greek names. In psycho-analysis, however, we like to keep in contact with the popular mode of thinking and prefer to make its concepts scientifically serviceable rather than to reject them. There is no merit in this; we are obliged to take this line; for our theories must be understood by our patients, who are often very intelligent, but not always learned. The impersonal 'it' is immediately connected with certain forms of expression used by normal people. 'It shot through me,' people say; 'there was something in me at that moment that was stronger than me.' '*C'était plus fort que moi.*'[10]

To illustrate German idioms, curiously Freud ends with a French phrase: the elided 'C'...' construed as 'Ça', plus the verb. Indeed, 'le Ça' was the usual French translation for 'das Es'. While this sentence recurs in Charcot's annals of psychopathology when patients confess irrepressible urges, it evokes the strategy Freud used when he justified using sexual terms in conversations with the young hysterical woman he called Dora. Freud quoted French sayings, 'J'appelle un chat un chat' and 'Pour faire une omelette il faut casser des oeufs', testifying to his fidelity to a master who would regularly use them, and also subtly introduced sexual metaphors.[11] Moreover, Freud justifies his preference for demotic expressions by an argument of accessibility – the point is not just to convey meanings to his readers, but mostly to convince analysands of the correctness of the theory, so that they can use it and apply it to their own lives. Therapy and technique influence the choice of a simple vocabulary. The clinic should be linked with the language used to formalize the main insights of psychoanalysis: this insight was shared by Lacan and Bettelheim, both aware that Freud would hear what patients had to say before offering a theory by which their symptoms could be made sense of. Here is a double work of translation at play: first, we have a linguistic synthesis produced from data that emerge directly from the unconscious, in a first 'translation' offered by the analysand; then the psychoanalyst intervenes and chooses relevant concepts with which an interpretation will be given; it then remains to make the second translation dynamic, to have her reshape and modify the first translation. One can say that Freud would listen in order to translate, but also that he tried to remain silent in order to let analysands translate.

If Lacan and Bettelheim criticize the Standard Edition's choices, the similarities end there. Bettelheim rages against Strachey's pseudo-scientific medicalization, which as he states has transformed a supple and idiomatic German text into an ossified doctrine that has lost spontaneity; psychoanalysis should be less concerned with a scientific terminology and pay more attention to immediate engagements with affects of the 'soul' presented by patients. Lacan aims at being rigorous, which entails sounding more 'scientific' than Freud; he never avoids technical terms, often resorts to Greek and Latin terms, and punctuates his essays and seminars with his infamous algebraic 'mathemes', graphs and schemata. What Lacan rejects above all is the ideology of the 'self' or boosted ego that he saw promoted by Strachey and the first translators.

However, as all commentators agree, the Standard Edition is a monument; if one can cavil at its individual faults so easily, it is because it is consistent, robust and well organized. As Darius Gray Ornston, Patrick J.

Mahony, Alex Holder and others, including more recently Ilse Grubrich-Simitis and Mark Solms, confirm, the translation of Freud's collected psychoanalytic works remains as a huge achievement.[12] However, even those who recognize the need to respect the integrity of this quasi monument of translation have acknowledged that it needs to be revised. Newly discovered linguistic difficulties have given rise to two different attitudes with regard to the translation of Freud's works, two positions that are usually buttressed by editorial policies. Either one can treat the text as an archive in need of new, modernized and more rigorous translations, which has been the French concept at the Presses Universitaires de France or Adam Phillips's strategy when he convinced Penguin of the need to retranslate everything, or one revises and corrects a text felt to have been so 'standardized' that it has impacted our concepts and provided points of reference for further discussions, which has been Solms's position. No one would imagine changing the 'Id' into an 'It' today because the term belongs to our culture; nevertheless, a British group gathered by Adam Phillips and publishing the 'New Penguin Freud' has taken more liberties. They found a precursor in the pioneering work of Joyce Crick, a gifted Germanist who published her *Interpretation of Dreams* in 1999.[13]

Crick hit upon the idea of translating the first edition of Freud's *Traumdeutung*, which yielded a sparer text, shorn of later additions and revisions. Reading the book, one realizes that it is a both stylistic masterpiece and an autobiographical novel. Crick aims at being faithful to a fluid style, in which we sense the excitement of exploration more than the wish to build a system. One comparison will suffice. Here is Strachey's version of a passage in which Freud concludes that his notion of the Unconscious is different from all those that preceded him:

> The fact that excitations in order to reach consciousness must pass through a fixed series or hierarchy of agencies (which is revealed to us by the modifications made in them by censorship) has enabled us to construct a spatial analogy. We have described the relations of the two systems to each other and to consciousness by saying that the system *Pcs.* stands like a screen between the system *Ucs.* and consciousness. The system *Pcs.* not merely bars access to consciousness, it also controls access to the power of voluntary movement and has at its disposal for distribution a mobile cathectic energy, a part of which is familiar to us in the form of attention.[14]

In Crick's version, this becomes:

> The fact that, in order to reach consciousness, the excitations have to make their way through an immutable sequence of agencies, which we discovered from the changes imposed by the censorship they exercised, enabled

us to set up a spatial analogy. We described the relations of the two systems by saying that the *Precon.*-system stood like a partition-screen between the *Uncon.*-system and consciousness. The *Precon.*-system did not only block access to consciousness, we said, it also governed access to voluntary movement and directed the transmission of a mobile energy-charge (*Besetzungsenergie*), a part of which is familiar to us in the form of attention.[15]

Crick is both more idiomatic and more precise, rendering *Besetzungsenergie* with all its force. Indeed, we should distinguish between terms that seem untranslatable because they have no equivalent in English and terms for which a simpler or more homely equivalent can be found. The latter term echoes with the difficulty of rendering *das Unheimliche* into English. This being of one Freud's most quoted texts, one will remember that Freud takes the time to walk us though several dictionaries before concluding that the term condenses two opposite meanings, the familiar and the opposite of familiar.[16] The German etymology is *Heim*, more or less the equivalent of 'home': why not render the concept as the 'Unhomely'? David McLintock, the translator of the new Penguin version, resisted the temptation – even if he slips into it once in a while: 'we can understand why German usage allows the familiar (*das Heimliche,* the "homely") to switch to its opposite, the uncanny (*das Unheimliche,* the "unhomely").'[17] The term, meaning roughly 'uncomfortably unfamiliar', had been introduced by Ernest Jentsch in 1906, expanded and systematized by Freud so as to make sense of a variety of psychic manifestations, from the fear of dead people, ghosts and doubles, to the involuntary repetition of certain actions. It is deployed in fantastic literature, and Freud's 1919 essay, following Jentsch's prompt, moved into a famous reading of E. T. A. Hoffmann's 'Sandman' tale. However, we should resist the temptation to leave the term in German: even if it is a key concept of the younger Heidegger, for instance, a recent book by a young American philosopher shows that one can continue thinking with the concept in English.[18]

A different position from Crick's own has been adopted by Mark Solms, the editor of the new Standard edition. Solms's forthcoming *Revised Standard Edition of the Complete Psychological Works of Sigmund Freud* combines new perspectives with respect for the cumulative impact of Strachey's previous translation. His revised edition reveals a different Freud less by changing conceptual keywords, or by giving us a sense of Freud's varied styles, than by adding to an already huge corpus some letters, unpublished fragments and shorter texts that had been omitted from the canon. His decision was to keep the 'standard' version while revising terms whenever there was a critical consensus. The most important change is the decision to replace 'instinct' with 'drive' as a translation of *Trieb*, which had become a major theoretical issue. As commentators have noted since Bettelheim, Freud would use both *Instinkt* and *Trieb*, which should be sufficient ground to choose two different words in English, even if at times he seems to exchange one for the other.

We know that Freud was not so happy with some of Strachey's choices, as with 'cathexis', which he did not like, but his own choices may also have been unfortunate. His decision to render *Fehlleistung*, a term glossed by Bettelheim as meaning 'faulty achievement', and not well rendered by Strachey's Greek term of 'parapraxis',[19] as 'defective act' would not pass muster in today's English.[20] In the same short text directly written in English, Freud believes that one should replace the 'preconscious' with 'fore-conscious thinking'. He also glosses the meaning of 'daydreaming' (*Phantasieren*) as 'freely wandering or phantastic thinking', maybe not the most concise translation, but a phrase full of suggestion.

I can do little more here than mention Solms's abundant discussions about other tricky concepts like *Nachträglichkeit, Entstellung, Schaulust, Kultur, Angst* and *Verneinung*. One term stands out as offering intractable difficulties, that of *Witz*, usually rendered in English as 'joke'. *Mot d'esprit*, which has been the usual French translation, works better because it keeps *esprit* while adding *mot* to allude to those funny stories we like repeating. *Witz* links Freud to a Romantic tradition that presupposed the mechanism of the Unconscious. Like Freud's *Unbewusst*, *Witz* derives from *Wissen* ('knowledge') but alludes to a different knowledge, a knowledge that is always 'other': it is the witty knowledge demonstrated by dreams, slips of the tongue, 'defective acts' and other unconscious manifestations; this knowledge bypasses discursivity to emerge as the underside or obverse of Reason. In Romantic *Witze*, bizarre or baroque verbal forms lead to the highest knowledge, thus can reach the infinite: '*Witz* is an immediate, absolute knowing-seeing; it is sight regained at the blindspot of schematism and, consequently, sight gaining direct access to the productive capacity of works.'[21] This obliges us to explore connections between Freud and Romanticism in so far as *Witze* deploy themselves on the background of a practice of translation that should be called transliteration, as Jean Allouch has shown: it entails being aware that a given sign begs to be translated, while resisting the impulse to see it as transparent; the sign must remain an opaque signifier as long as possible, it will be deciphered as slowly as possible so as to leave a chance to the hidden suggestions contained in it whether at a material or at a semantic level. The interpreter should indeed work like Champollion, that is, by inventing a new dictionary for each new text. This slow, tentative, hesitant practice would be similar to how one attempts to render a pun or a joke in a different language. The key is often to find a prompt in an apparently random association of related signifiers and to mobilize them before seeing them related to their usual signification. In that sense, one will be both literal and creative at the same time.

Glossing Dog-Language, from Cipion to Topsy

A mixture of creativity and wordplay can be observed in Freud's correspondence with his friend Eduard Silberstein when he was between fifteen and twenty-five years old. Many parts of these letters were couched in a fanciful Spanish replete with personal allusions and grandiose schemes. Freud and Silberstein had discovered Cervantes's *Coloquio de los perros* ('The Dialogue of the Dogs') from the 1613 *Exemplary Stories* when reading a primer of Spanish literature. Their enthusiasm led them to invent a 'Spanish Academy' of which they were the only two members. Neither knew Spanish well, which did not prevent them from writing to each other in garbled but flowing Castilian. Freud chose the persona of Cipion, leaving to Silberstein the other dog, Berganza; he arranged an epistolary pact with weekly confessions,[22] an exchange meant to remain 'in the spirit of romanticism'.[23]

In these letters, Freud betrays his adherence to a German Romantic tradition marked by wit, humour, fantasy and poetic whimsy. Its predecessor was none other than E. T. A. Hoffmann, whose 'Sandman' story provided evidence for a literary definition of the Uncanny. Hoffmann had published his own sequel to Cervantes in 1814.[24] In Hoffmann's version, a first-person narrator listens to Berganza, who narrates fanciful adventures. A jocular tone dominates when Freud harps on his adolescent infatuation with a pretty young neighbour from Freiberg, his home town. Gisela Fluss metamorphoses into 'Ichthyosaura' because of obscure associations with a poem by von Scheffel that stages a lover's kiss.[25] The spirit of burlesque and satire derives from Cervantes's tale. Freud is Cipion with a more authoritative voice; Berganza spins endless yarns into which Cipion interjects witty comments. This cannot but evoke the setting of a forthcoming psychoanalytic cure, with the qualification that we have a 'writing cure' here.

Berganza appears as a *pícaro* whose adventures end in catastrophe; Cipion is a philosopher who draws meaning from them. Cipion knows Greek and gives a correct etymology for 'philosophy'. When, after a while, Silberstein mixes up identities and signs a letter by the name of Cipion, Freud rebukes him:

> Parece, que no sabeis, Señor Don Berganza, como os habeis de llamar, pues que á vestra carta del 2. Junio subscribes Cipion, lo que es usurpacion de mi nombre. Pero si quieres, que mudemos de nombre, como Jean Paul dice, que Siebenkäs y Leibgeber hicieron, consiento y espero vuestro arbitrio.
> El que hasta alli se llama Cipion.[26]

They would imitate Siebenkäs and Leibgeber, characters from three novels by Jean Paul, beginning with *Flower, Fruit and Thorn Pieces,* when they exchange their names. Siebenkäs, unhappily married, follows Leibgeber's advice. A 'body-giver', he is Siebenkäs's alter ego, his *Doppelgänger* explaining he must fake his death. Then Siebenkäs meets Natalie, falls in love and marries her 'after his death'. Freud understood his friend's role to be that of a potential *Doppelgänger.* However, his stern tone discourages any exchange of roles: he remains Cipion the cynical commentator, letting his friend roam the streets.

What stands out in Freud's letters to Silberstein is the wish that, under the aegis of the Academia Española, they should narrate to each other their day-to-day lives while using a foreign language that neither has fully mastered. Their intimate exchange will be mediated by a language in which neither is proficient. A detour via a foreign literary language provides a filter for this polyglot introspection. Freud often struggles to find adequate Spanish words when searching for nuances of thought. Thus he misremembers a passage from a play by Cervantes, quotes *cerro gordo,* which means 'fat hill' but he takes *cerro,* rather than *gordo,* to mean 'fat' and feminizes it as 'cerra', then retranslates it as 'Dicke' ('fat').[27]

The layering of languages is baffling. One sees this better in the original, as in a letter sketching several floors to be visited by Eduard. Freud sounds drunk with languages under the influence of Carlyle's *Sartor Resartus,* a book in which the English author pretends to be translating from the writings of a German philosopher. Here 'Third floor' appears in English and in a box:

> Third floor.
> Adonde Vm hallerá grande coleccion de gente Perdida, concurrida de todas las partes del mundo, come suelen habitar au troisieme etage. Sepa Vm, Señor D. Berganza, que ni del museo, ni de la, no largo tiempo ha, estincta formacion de la Greda se ha visto ó oido cosa hasta aquí; lo que facil se puede esplicar, cuando se piensa, que no se <ha> buscando á saber algo, ni de mi parte, ni de otra alguna. !Asi duerman en paz eterna! !y la tierra les sea ligera!
> Ουποτε του Ρωσανους ουτε του εταιρου αυτου πεπυσμαι τί,
> Ώστε ευ πραττοντες και ουδενοσς δεομενοι δοκουσιν.

Nec aliorum, qui in hac urbe manserunt, tibi quidquam referre possum. Solus sum, idquod nuquam antea accdit, et epistola tua prima fuit, quae tempus respondendi mihi abrogavit.

Si quieres, que te envie unos libros, que me ahí son dados á la luz, como la continuacion de Shakespeare, no ha mas que decir.

Gestern und vorgestern war ein großer Sternschuppenfall angezeigt, vielleicht daß ihn der Herrgott wegen des schlesten Wetters auf morgen verschoben hat.[28]

Freud states at the beginning of the letter that he wants to let 'other nations' speak in their own idioms, mentioning Italian, French and English.[29] This floor gathers 'lost people who have poured in from all parts of the world' – now in Spanish and underlined. Greek is used to let his friend know that he has not heard from Rosanes, Latin to state his friend's letter is the first he has received, Spanish to offer to send books by Shakespeare. He reverts to German to mention a meteor shower. Spanish is used to discuss a 'not long extinct Cretaceous', alluding to Gisela Fluss's nickname, 'Ichtyosaura', which puts her in the 'Cretaceous' period. Needless to say, in Spanish, 'la greda' does not mean 'Cretaceous' but 'clay'. In this way, Freud coins words out of mere assonances.

Freud's virtuosity with languages is amazing: he knows Greek and Latin well enough to use them correctly when giving news, as in a postcard from 1871 in which he complained about his rotten teeth;[30] his English is better than his Spanish, his French fluent and accurate, and he improved it while living in Paris. He could translate from these languages and did. Freud translated several books into German: from the English, the twelfth volume of John Stuart Mill's works and the interesting section on Samuel Butler in Israel Levine's 1923 book *The Unconscious,* a survey of the concepts of the Unconscious. From the French, he translated two books by Jean-Martin Charcot, the third volume of *Leçons sur les maladies du système nerveux* and *Leçons du mardi à la Salpêtrière,* and two books by Hippolyte Bernheim, *De la suggestion et de ses applications à la thérapeutique* and *Hypnotisme, suggestion et psychothérapie.*

At the end of this life, Freud returned to his old pastime, translation, when he helped his daughter Anna translate Marie Bonaparte's moving memoir about Topsy, Marie Bonaparte's favourite chow dog. Topsy was diagnosed with mouth cancer, given radiotherapy and survived. While Freud and his family were waiting anxiously for the visa that would allow them to leave Vienna and settle in London, and he was prevented from seeing patients because of the new race laws, he translated Bonaparte's *Topsy, chow chow au poil d'or* (1937) as *Topsy, der goldhaarige Chow* (1939). This to thank his main ally in France but also an expression of his love for pet dogs. His daughter began co-translating a manuscript given in December 1936; soon Freud took over; the translation was finished in April 1938. This beautifully crafted story begins with despair at the announcement of the fatal disease and ends with a passionate affirmation of life: 'Topsy, who has reconquered life, is for me a talisman that conjures away death.'[31] As the young Freud had understood when he let loose his enthusiastic ventriloquism of Cervantes's dogs, the same sentence might equally evoke the work of translation.

This exercise in translation is also a transferential gesture: Marie Bonaparte and Freud shared a love for their furry pets; she was thinking of Freud's own cancer of the mouth, caused by too much smoking, when she described the cancer of the jaw that almost killed Topsy. This leads us to a last question: why the proximity of terms like 'transference' and 'translation' when it comes to psychoanalytic technique as a talking cure?

The rich epistolary exchange with Silberstein anticipates insights Freud deduced via his friend Joseph Breuer from the young Viennese hysteric called 'Anna O'. Her contribution to psychoanalysis was to coin the English phrase 'talking cure' when her hysteria prevented her from using German. She spoke in a medley of four or five languages, which rendered her incomprehensible; soon English prevailed (like Freud, she read Shakespeare assiduously).[32] She developed an ability to translate any language into English almost immediately. One day, a consultant was brought in, and Breuer made her 'read a French text aloud in English'. Translating perfectly, she laughed, adding: 'That's like an examination.'[33] Under hypnosis, she was able to talk things through, thus coining two expressions for the same process, the 'talking cure' and 'chimneysweeping'.[34] One night, when her father was alive but sick, she was sat next to his bed and had a hallucination that a black snake that was coming to bite him. Her hands refused to work – her fingers turned into small snakes. Trying to pray to dissipate her terror, she found that she had no language to pray in; finally, a little English ditty came to her. She discovered that she could pray, think and speak in English, but in English only.[35]

Her 'talking cure' manifested itself as a way out of speaking in tongues, which suggests the way Freud would hystericize language by estranging it from its usual, weak, consensual function. The use of an estranged language in a cure in which words replace the hypnosis that had first done wonders for Anna O at first would become the trademark of psychoanalysis. Translation was present at the origins of psychoanalysis and it continues to puzzle us today, as we await the Revised Standard Edition. If there is a link between the activities of interpreting or translating texts and the activity of reading the unconscious as if it was a foreign language that one is learning to decipher, we can link this statement to a certain epistemology. This was Michel Foucault's thesis in 'What Is an Author?' when he explained that authors' names were necessary if one wanted to write a historiography of culture. But the concept of 'author' is even more crucial when we work with those authors he calls 'inventors of discursivity', among whom Freud and Marx figure pre-eminently. A 'return' to their foundational texts transforms the discursive practices governing their fields.[36] Foucault writes:

> In saying that Freud founded psychoanalysis, we do not simply mean that the concept of libido or the technique of dream analysis reappears in the writings of Karl Abraham or Melanie Klein, but that he made possible a certain number of differences with respect to his books, concepts and hypotheses, which all arise out of psychoanalytic discourse.[37]

Unlike scientific inventors, 'founders of discursivity' cannot be accused of factual error.[38] Their theories demand a constant reactivation, which means a practice of retranslation. However, Freud's works should be considered neither as a sacred origin, a vatic source of truth, nor as a scientific document whose accuracy can be tested by truth procedures or protocols of verification. Their textual origin cannot help being porous, full of gaps, knotted, dotted with idioms specific to one language, semantic riddles that constitute points of resistance. Returning to these texts, we accept the programme of a perpetual translation. Any return to Freud, to follow Lacan's 1950s programme, will entail not respectful imitation but a literalist reading doubling as creative rewriting. By applying the practice of reading to the obscure productions of the Unconscious made up of signs, barely legible signs on a palimpsest, psychoanalysis testifies to a need for endless literalizations that are retranslations.

Notes

* I want to thank Patricia Gherovici who read a first version of this essay and improved it with her suggestions.
1 I use the term 'transliteration' to mean a literalist rendering of an important text; see Jean Allouch's groundbreaking *Lettre pour lettre: Transcrire, traduire, translittérer* (Paris: Eres, 1984), which takes Jean-François Champollion's rosetta stone as Freud's main model.
2 See Benjamin Andrew, 'Translating Origins: Psychoanalysis and Philosophy', in *Rethinking Translation: Discourse, Subjectivity, Ideology*, ed. Lawrence Venuti (London, Routledge, 1992), 18–41; Elena Basile, 'Responding to the Enigmatic Address of the Other: A Psychoanalytical Approach to the Translator's

Labour', *New Voices in Translation Studies* 1 (2005), 12–30; Patrick Mahony, 'Towards the Understanding of Translation in Psychoanalysis', *Meta* 27, no. 1 (1982), 63–71; and Patrick Mahony, 'Freud and Translation', *Imago* 58, no. 4 (2001), 837–40.
3 Sigmund Freud, *New Introductory Lectures on Psychoanalysis*, trans. James Strachey (New York: W. W. Norton & Co., 1933), 99–100.
4 Sigmund Freud, *Neue Folge der Vorlesungen zur Einführung in die Psychoanalyse* (Vienna: Internationaler Psychoanalytischer Verlag, 1933); www.psychanalyse.lu/Freud/FreudNeueVorlesungen.pdf, accessed 4 March 2021.
5 'Wo Es war, soll Ich warden', No Subject – Encyclopedia of Psychoanalysis, last modified 20 May 2019, accessed 29 October 2021, https://nosubject.com/Wo_Es_war,_soll_Ich_werden, accessed 4 March 2021.
6 Bruno Bettelheim, *Freud and Man's Soul* (New York, Vintage Books, 1984), 61–2.
7 Jacques Lacan, *Ecrits*, trans. Bruce Fink (New York, Norton, 2006), 347–8.
8 Lacan, *Ecrits*, 734.
9 Lacan, *Ecrits*, 734.
10 Sigmund Freud, 'The Question of Lay Analysis', *Standard Edition*, vol. XX (London: The Hogarth Press, 1959), 195.
11 Sigmund Freud, *A Case of Hysteria (Dora)*, translated by Anthea Bell (Oxford: Oxford University Press, 2013), 41. In French slang, '*chat(te)*' is the woman's genitals, '*oeufs*' refers to testicles. The sayings combine sexual literalism with the inevitable breaking of word shells into substantial meaning when producing the desired *omelette* of sense.
12 See the collection edited by Darius Gray Ornston, *Translating Freud* (New Haven: Yale University Press, 1992), and Mark Solms's 'Extracts from the *Revised Standard Edition* of Freud's Complete Psychological Works', *International Journal of Psychoanalysis* 99, no. 1 (2018), 11–57.
13 Sigmund Freud, *The Interpretation of Dreams*, trans. Joyce Crick (Oxford: Oxford University Press, 1999).
14 Freud, *Interpretation of Dreams*, 653.
15 Freud, *Interpretation of Dreams*, 407.
16 See Barbara Cassin's entry in *Dictionary of Untranslatables: A Philosophical Lexicon*, ed. Barbara Cassin, Emily Apter, Jacques Lezra and Michael Wood (Princeton, Princeton University Press, 2004), 432.
17 Sigmund Freud, *The Uncanny*, trans. David McLintock (New York, Penguin, 2003), 148.
18 See Katherine Withy's excellent *Heidegger on Being Uncanny* (Cambridge, MA: Harvard University Press, 2015). Inverting the famous impossibility of rendering into English the Heideggerian couple *Sein* ('Being') and *Seiende* ('being'), her title puns on 'being' taken both as a verb and as a noun: she presents Being as such as uncanny by exploring what it means to be or feel uncanny.
19 Bettelheim, *Freud and Man's Soul*, 87.
20 Sigmund Freud, 'Introduction to J. Varendonck's *The Psychology of Day-Dreams*', *Standard Edition*, vol. XVIII (London: The Hogarth Press, 1955), 271.

21 Philippe Lacoue-Labarthe and Jean-Luc Nancy, *The Literary Absolute: The Theory of Literature in German Romanticism*, trans. Philip Barnard and Cheryl Lester (Albany, State University of New York Press, 1988), 52.
22 *The Letters of Sigmund Freud to Eduard Silberstein, 1871–1881* [henceforth *LSFES*], ed. Walter Boehlich, trans. Arnold J. Pomerans (Cambridge, MA: Harvard University Press, 1990), 57–8. I have developed this analysis in Jean-Michel Rabaté, *Cambridge Introduction to Literature and Psychoanalysis* (Cambridge: Cambridge University Press, 2014), 9–16.
23 Freud, *LSFES*, 58.
24 E. T. A. Hoffmann, *Fantasiestücke* (Frankfurt: Deutscher Klassiker Verlag, 2006), 101–77.
25 See Introduction to Freud, *LSFES*, xvii–xviii.
26 Sigmund Freud, *Jugendbriefe an Eduard Silberstein*, ed. Walter Boehlich (Frankfurt am Main: Fischer, 1989), 134; Freud, *LSFES*, 118.
27 Freud, *LSFES*, 98–9.
28 Sigmund Freud, *Jugendbriefe*, 60–61.
29 Freud, *LSFES*, 47.
30 Freud, *LSFES*, 1–2.
31 Marie Bonaparte, *Topsy: The Story of a Golden-Haired Chow* (New Brunswick: Transaction Publishers, 1994), 164. All details quoted come from Gary Genosko's excellent introduction.
32 Sigmund Freud and Joseph Breuer, *Studies in Hysteria*, trans. Nicola Luckhurst (London: Penguin, 2004), 29.
33 Freud and Breuer, *Studies in Hysteria*, 31.
34 Freud and Breuer, *Studies in Hysteria*, 34.
35 Freud and Breuer, *Studies in Hysteria*, 42.
36 Michel Foucault, 'What Is an Author?', in *Language, Counter-Memory, Practice*, trans. Donald Bouchard and Sherry Simon (Ithaca: Cornell University Press, 1977), 137–8.
37 Foucault, 'What Is an Author?', 132.
38 Foucault, 'What Is an Author?', 134.

CHAPTER 9

Translation across Brains and across Time

Christopher Honey and Janice Chen

How do we recognize our cat as the same cat, seen from behind, or side-on, or standing at the end of a passageway? How do we recognize the same idea, expressed in poetry or prose, in Russian or in English? When we examine how this commonplace mental ability arises within our brains, we find it entangled with some of the most fundamental properties of neural organization. In particular, the invariance of neural activity – the ability of neurons to generate the same responses to very different inputs – changes in a graded pattern across the systems of our brains, mapping a path along which physical signals are converted into meanings.

Both neuroscientists and literary translators aim to understand how invariance of meaning can arise across different forms. But literary translators must render experiences that are more subtle, more contextual, more complete, than a glimpse of a cat's tail. Thus, for the neuroscientist who seeks to understand invariances, the goals of literary translation match the highest levels of scientific aspiration. From a neuroscientific perspective, it is fascinating that literary translation is possible at all.

Before diving into the question of how brains are organized, and how abstract concepts might be housed within brains and conveyed between them, we should declare: this chapter does not aim to 'ground' the practice of literary translation in the neurosciences. Attempting this would be not only premature (given the state of the science) and naïve (given our limited knowledge of translation) but also unappetizing – an intellectual butchery served with a side of jargon salad. Here, we offer an assortment of ideas about 'invariance' in cognitive systems, which we hope may be enticing, perhaps stimulating, for scholars and practising translators.

Hierarchical Structure and Functional Invariance in the Human Brain

How is the human brain organized to generate invariant representations?

Consider the convoluted surface of the human brain. The sheet of neural tissue that encases the two hemispheres of the brain (cerebrum) is called the cerebral cortex (or 'brain bark'). This cortex is approximately 3 mm deep, and when flattened, it covers about the same area as three sheets of letter-size paper. The cortical tissue is spongy to the touch, and it gently and continually pulses from beige to pink as it is infused by oxygenated blood. This tissue is, in one sense, non-essential: without it we can still live and engage in basic forms of perception, learning, and even mating.[1] However, the cerebral cortex is necessary for almost all of our most cherished human abilities. Without the cerebral cortex, we would lose the more refined and flexible aspects of sight, hearing, touch, and movement. Without it, we would also lose our capacity for comprehending and producing language and our ability to reason logically. And without it, we would not be able to recall and make suppositions about the who, what, and why of the stories of our lives.

Each of the approximately 15 billion neurons in the human cerebral cortex can be assigned to one of several hundred 'regions' (Figure 9.1a). These regions of the cerebral cortex are distinguished by their anatomical characteristics, such as thickness, as well as by their functional characteristics, such as whether they respond to written words, spoken words, or neither, or both.[2] These regions are also defined by their 'connectivity': the specific subset of other brain regions with which they interact. At each moment, a typical region in the cerebral cortex is communicating directly with dozens of its partners, near and far, and this flow of information supports almost all of our higher cognitive functions.[3]

Brain organization varies systematically in a gradient which ranges from the 'periphery' to the 'interior' of the cortical network (Figure 9.1b). Regions on the periphery of the network (striped areas in Figure 9.1b) are those that are most directly connected to sensory organs such as our eyes and ears and motor organs such as our fingers; conversely, regions in the 'interior' of the network (dotted areas in Figure 9.1b) are furthest from the brain's peripheral interface with the world. The more peripheral regions are most essential for processing impinging sights and sounds, while the more interior cortical regions are involved in processing our life-memories, our desires, our suppositions.

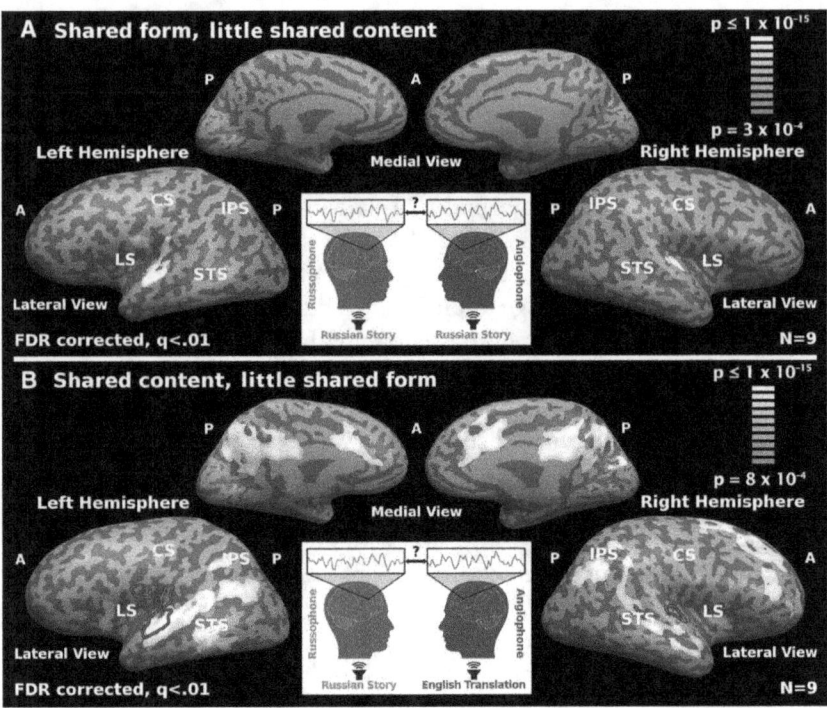

Figure 9.1 Maps of brain regions that respond in a similar manner across different listeners, some listeners hearing the same auditory narrative, and others hearing a translation of the narrative. **a)** To isolate regions primarily responsive to the form of the auditory stimulus, rather than its content, we compared cortical responses of Russophones and Anglophones listening to the Russian recording. The map shows the responses shared across Anglophones and Russophones listening to the Russian recording; areas that are coloured in white exhibited a reliable response across the two groups, with brighter white colours indicating the most similar responses. **b)** To isolate the regions responsive to the content of the narrative, we compared Russophones listening to Russian against Anglophones listening to English, after projecting out the audio amplitude envelopes. In this comparison, the two groups extracted similar content from distinct audio waveforms. The map shows the shared responses across Anglophones listening to English and Russophones listening to Russian. Outlined region denotes the areas that shared form-related responses, from A. P, Posterior; A, anterior; CS, central sulcus; LS, lateral sulcus; STS, superior temporal sulcus; IPS, intraparietal sulcus. Reproduced with permission from Figure 3 of Honey et al. (2012), which provides the colour original.

How do these communicating neurons enable us to recognize objects and entities in the world?

When a new item appears before our eyes, information about this item flows into the more peripheral regions of the cerebral cortex, and from the periphery towards the interior. As signals are conveyed, stage by stage, through the cortex, neurons appear to support distinct 'roles' or 'functions' within the broader process of visual categorization. To begin to guess at a neuron's role, neuroscientists commonly start by asking two questions. First, 'selectivity': what properties of the word does this neuron 'select' to respond to? Second, 'invariance': what properties of the world does this neuron treat as equivalent, so that changes in those properties do not change the neuron's activity?

The selectivity and invariance of neurons vary gradually and systematically across the surface of the cerebral cortex (Figure 9.1b). In particular, *neurons closer to the 'interior' of our cortical networks tend to be more selective for more abstract properties of the world, and they tend to be more invariant to changes in the basic sensory properties of the world.* A hypothetical experiment might be clarifying in unpacking this.

Imagine Esmerelda, holding a sheet of paper at arm's length, and fixing her gaze on the very centre of the paper. Suppose that she sees the letter 'O' printed near the centre of the page and suppose that we are observing the activity of neurons in her brain as she maintains her steady gaze. Light reflects from around the letter 'O' and the photons are detected at her retina. From there, the signals describing the visual image are conveyed in less than 30 milliseconds to the earliest stages of visual processing in the most peripheral regions of her cerebral cortex. What kinds of neuronal responses will we observe as this visual image is transmitted, stage by stage, from the periphery of her cerebral cortex towards its inner reaches?

Neurons in the outermost stages of cortical processing – the neurons which respond earliest to visual and auditory signals from the world – are usually selective for basic sensory features. For example, consider a neuron at the first or second stage of visual processing (the back of the brain, shown in stripes at right of Figure 9.1b). This neuron might be selective for a 'crescent curve' of just the size and orientation that composes the top-left of the letter 'O'. In that case, the neuron will respond to the letter 'O' with vigorous 'spiking' bursts of electrochemical activity. Importantly, this hypothetical visual neuron does not care whether its preferred crescent curve is part of a particular letter: it would respond vigorously to the letters 'C' and 'Q', it would respond feebly to a tilted '*O*' in which the crescent-curve was distorted, and it would not respond at all to the letters 'X' or 'P', which do not possess the crescent curve. All in all, our hypothetical experiment would reveal that this neuron, in the earliest stages of visual processing, is *selective* for the angle and location of a curving line in the world, and this neuron is *invariant* to whether that line composes part of any letter. In a sense then, the neuron is selective for a 'low-level' feature in the world (a curving line segment) and it is invariant to a more 'abstract' property of the world (letter).

Now, if we continue our hypothetical experiment, and observe the activity of neurons closer to the interior reaches of our brains (and further from its sensory-motor periphery), we will observe an opposite pattern: we begin to find neurons that are selective for abstract features, and invariant to low-level features. For example, such neurons may respond not only to our letter 'O', but also to other closed-loop forms such as '*O*' or 'o' or 'o' or the image of a loose-looped lasso. The neurons in this stage of visual processing are able to respond to such a wide variety of forms because they are combining ('pooling') signals that they receive from multiple different neurons in the earlier states of processing. A group of (say) a dozen neurons at earlier stages of visual processing may be selective for a dozen different locations and orientations of line segments – but at the later stages of processing, a single neuron will receive input signals from all twelve, and it can generate a combined response. As a result, neurons deeper inside our brains can respond in a way that is invariant to changes across those twelve different features, and instead corresponds to a more abstract notion 'of something visually O-like', unshackled from the specific 'O' of a single shape or size.

Now if our hypothetical experiment were to proceed yet further towards the interior of the cortex (towards the darkest-dots regions in Figure 9.1b), we would observe this pattern becoming more and more pronounced: neurons further inward become more selective to more abstract properties of the world, and more invariant to its sensory features. For example, we may find a neuron that responds not only when Esmerelda sees a letter 'O' in print, but also when she hears the sound of breathy spoken '*oh*!' We may find a neuron with a more conceptual flavour:[4] a neuron that fires a vigorous electrochemical burst in response to the word 'nought'; and also to the mathematical equation '2 minus 2'; and to a worn-out road sign declaring 'Welc_me t_ Minnes_ta'; and also to the image of a magazine with Oprah Winfrey on the cover. Such neurons could be invariant to very profound changes in the physical properties of the signals we receive from the world.[5] Of course, such neurons would still be selective in their own way: they might respond (to varying degrees) to many conceptual variants of 'O', and yet they would remain silent when Esmerelda lays her eyes on the symbol '1'; or when she detects the scent of coffee; or when her arm starts to ache from standing statue-still, holding the sheet of paper up before her eyes.

These observations about Esmerelda and the 'O' illustrate (in caricature) one of the most important ideas in neuroscience research in the past half-century: *with respect to the brain, as we move from the sensory world inward, stage by stage, we find more and more neurons whose activity is selective for abstract properties of the world and invariant to sensory changes.* Importantly, this phenomenon is not limited to the visual pathway – it is also observed in the cortical pathways for processing sound and touch, for example. Therefore, it is common to say that the cerebral cortex possesses a 'hierarchical' organization. In a mixture of spatial metaphors, the regions closer to the outside of our brain networks are traditionally said to be at 'lower' stages of processing, and these signals proceed up a conceptual ladder towards the 'higher' stages, which are more cloistered from the sensory world. This hierarchical principle has its exceptions, but it stands as one of the fundamental principles of brain organization: the lower stages are more responsive to a fixed set of features in a particular channel of sensation and action, while the higher stages of processing are more flexible and more 'associative' across senses, and across meanings. The stages of the hierarchy are the pathway along which signals are converted into meanings.

We are not surprised that our brains can respond in a flexible manner, invariant to sensory specifics: we experience it every day, recognizing the same cat, or the sound of a friend's voice, under diverse conditions. However, when we understand how this invariant function arises in the stage-wise, hierarchical, organization of our brains, we can begin to ask new questions, with some relevance to the art of translation. First: can some neurons generate responses that are invariant across languages? Second: if meaning is abstracted in a hierarchical manner, stage by stage across the cortex, then what kinds of information are represented at the 'apex' of the cortical hierarchy? Third: at which levels of the cortical hierarchy do we find the processes for conceiving and remembering narratives? As we sketch some answers to these questions, perhaps we will learn something about the kinds of information that are necessarily lost in translation between languages, and which kinds of information can cross the divide.

Translation across Brains and Languages

In 2009, we began studying how listeners respond to the same story presented in two different languages. One of our colleagues, Yulia Lerner, a native speaker of Russian, provided us with a story from her life in the form of about eleven minutes of spoken Russian. Yulia also provided us with her own written English translation of the story. Yulia was not (and is not) a professional translator, but her approach was basically 'interlinear': she attempted to translate word for word, but without violating the grammar of the target language. Then, after Yulia's translation had been recorded by a male speaker of American English, we possessed two spoken versions of the 'same' real-life narrative: one in English and one in Russian. To study brain responses to these stories, we recruited Anglophones and Russophones who lived around Princeton, New Jersey. In the end, we managed to scan the brains of nine Anglophones (who did not speak Russian) and nine Russophones (who spoke Russian with native proficiency, and English to varying degrees).

Our methodological choices might appear arbitrary and amateur to students of language and translation, but this basic set-up enabled us to ask a very simple question: *which parts of our brains respond based on how a story sounds (independent of its inferred meaning), and which parts of our brains respond based on what a story means (independent of its sound)?*

As the brain is organized in a hierarchical structure, with 'lower' levels being concerned with sensory properties of the input and not with meaning, we can expect that brain regions at these lower levels will generate very different responses to the different-sounding Russian and English speech: in one case, the sound arriving at our ears is Russian spoken by a woman, and in the other case they hear English spoken by a man. As we look higher up in the hierarchy, brain regions at each level become increasingly selective for conceptual properties and invariant to sensory properties. Thus, we might expect that somewhere along the way, 'higher'-level brain regions will begin to respond similarly across the two translations. If we do locate such common responses, the discovery tells us in which brain regions, and at what level of the hierarchy, input from the world has been processed and abstracted to such a degree that the meaning of the language matters while the sound of the language matters not.

How could we identify brain regions that responded primarily to the sound of the story (rather than its meaning)? The answer is illustrated in Figure 9.2. To identify regions that responded to the sound, we compared the brain responses of Anglophones listening to the Russian story against the brain responses of Russophones listening to the Russian story (AR vs. RR). For these two groups, the acoustics arriving at their ears are the same, but the meaning that they derive from them is very different. Thus, if a brain region produces similar responses in both groups, then it very likely reflects a response to the acoustics.

And how could we identify the regions that responded primarily to the meaning (broadly construed) of the story (rather than its sound)? In this case, we compared the brain responses of Anglophones listening to the English translation against the brain responses of Russophones listening to the Russian original (AE vs. RR). Here, the sound arriving at the ears is very different but the meaning was (we hoped) quite similar, and so there could be brain regions that would respond in common despite all the superficial differences.

How did we measure brain responses? While the participants were listening to each of the stories, we recorded the activity levels of populations of neurons in different brain regions via snapshots of changes in blood oxygenation. These snapshots were captured once every 1.5 seconds and each provided an image of the activity levels in a 3D grid about 60,000 'voxels' (3D pixels) of the brain. This brain imaging method (functional magnetic resonance imaging, fMRI) thus enabled us to measure an approximate brain 'state' as people were experiencing each moment in the auditory narrative.

What did we find? We observed a relatively small patch of the cerebral cortex that responded to the acoustics (Figure 9.2a): unsurprisingly, it was located in areas of the brain that are generally thought to process sound, within and around the middle Sylvian fissure in the left and right hemispheres. Neurons in these areas respond in a way that depends on the pitch and amplitude of sound, as well as on whether sound is rising or falling.[6] However, in addition to this sound-responsive patch of cortex, we observed a very large swathe of cortex responsive to the meaning of the language, independent of the sound (Figure 9.2b). In terms of the hierarchy, invariance across languages began just above the lowest levels of sensory processing. Responses were shared across Russian and English versions of the story in multiple stages of processing in the lateral temporal cortex (the speech processing pathway), as well as in networks of higher-order regions including the temporoparietal junction and the anterior and posterior medial cortex. In these higher-order regions, Russophones and Anglophones (each hearing their preferred language) responded very similarly. In fact, the match between Russophone and Anglophone brains (responding to very different sounds) was almost as good as the match between Anglophone and Anglophone brains (responding to identical sounds).

The widespread invariance we observed suggests that, despite all the nuance, the cultural specificity, the awareness of difference in literary and artistic traditions, and the sensitivity to the ways in which language shapes and performs identity, there may be a reason why metaphors of invariability remain so prevalent in the way that translators speak about their craft.[7] If there is a fundamental similarity in how brains perceive two different linguistic instantiations of a story, then there might also be something that

A Cortical Network Structure 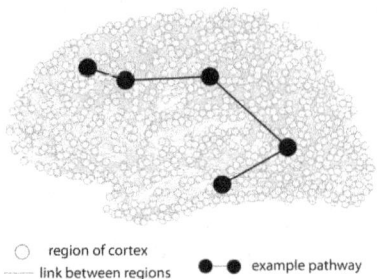 **B** Cerebral Cortex Gradient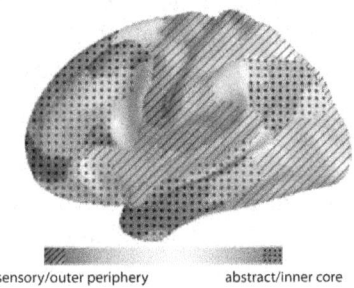

Figure 9.2 (**a**) Illustration of the network structure of the human cerebral cortex. Regions of the cerebral cortex are linked by a dense of network of pathways, mostly short-range, but some long-range, which permit signal flow from the periphery inward towards the core, and also from the core outwards to the periphery. The example pathway in this figure includes flows in both directions. Figure adapted from Bertha Vázquez-Rodríguez et al., 'Signal Propagation via Cortical Hierarchies', *Network Neuroscience* 4, no. 4 (November 2020), 1072–90. (**b**) Illustration of the primary gradient across the human cerebral cortex, spanning from more sensory regions to more abstracted regions of the cerebral cortex. The peripheral regions (striped, darker to lighter = outer to inner) are closer to our sense and action organs (e.g. our eyes, our muscles, and our receptors for touch). The abstracted regions (dotted, lighter to darker = outer to inner) are closer to the 'inner core' of our brain network. For a more comprehensive visualization, we strongly recommend viewing Figure 1 of Daniel S. Margulies et al., 'Situating the Default-Mode Network along a Principal Gradient of Macroscale Cortical Organization', *Proceedings of the National Academy of Sciences of the United States of America* 113, no. 44 (November 2016), 12574–9.[8]

does not change in translation: an element of translation that is all transmission and no transmutation. Of course, while neuroscience can currently tell us that such a thing exists, it cannot tell us precisely what it is: the tone, the cultural associations, the lexical properties, the literal meanings, a combination of all of these. Nonetheless, we can dive deeper into this question about 'language-invariant' brain representations by considering the other (non-linguistic) cognitive functions and processes in which these 'language-invariant' regions are involved.

Towards Language-Invariant Information?

Given that there are brain regions whose responses to a story are (nearly) invariant to the language of expression, what else do we know about the function of these brain regions? The brain regions exhibiting the most clearly language-invariant narrative responses were found in a 'network' of regions that is known as the 'default mode network' (DMN).[9] The name 'default mode' may sound authoritative, as though scientists know exactly what purpose and function these brain regions serve: this is very far from the reality. This set of regions has a number of befuddling and absorbing properties; it has only been studied intensely in the past fifteen years, and there is no consensus regarding its raison d'être.

DMN regions are located at the innermost interior of the cerebral cortical network. If we accept that the cerebral cortex is a networked structure (Figure 9.1) with a periphery (close to the sensory world) and an interior (far from the sensory world), then DMN regions are deep in the interior of our brains.[10] And if we accept that there is a functional hierarchy – with 'higher' stages of processing corresponding to steps inward from the periphery – then the DMN regions sit at or near the *apex* of this functional hierarchy.[11] Thus, if the hierarchy in our brains is a ladder of abstraction, leading away from the sensory world and towards language-invariant representations, then perhaps DMN regions represent the most abstracted level of all.

Another property of DMN regions, perhaps more relevant to thinking about translation, even literary translation, is that DMN regions appear to extract and generate the skeletons of narratives:[12] these regions process information related to the 'who', the 'what', the 'where', and the 'why' of a scenario. Subsets of DMN regions are thought to be especially important for the representation of spatial layouts, social interactions, schematic and thematic norms, as well as our own goals in a situation, and the goals of others. Altogether, the interactions between these high-level regions are thought to enable us to perceive and conceive 'what is happening in this scenario and why'.

Can psychology and neuroscience identify essential features of a narrative 'event', a coordinate system for defining its deep structure? Unsurprisingly, this has turned out to be a difficult and complex question. It is very challenging to decompose ostensibly simple scenarios (e.g. having a picnic with friends) into a set of 'dimensions' which can be independently manipulated and empirically tested. Intense effort over the past quarter-century has generated theories of 'scene construction',[13] 'self-projection',[14] 'episodic simulation',[15] as well as psychological theories of 'discourse representation',[16] and the elements of imagination in discourse.[17] Keeping in mind the somewhat ill-defined status of these ideas, let us survey these neural and psychological theories of the 'deep structure' of situations and narratives.

Spatial Theories: First in our survey of theories of event representation are those that emphasize the role of a coherent spatial context in 'scene construction'.[18] Here the idea is that, when we mentally represent a 'situation' or 'scene', our minds employ a 'spatial scaffold'.[19] This scaffold is, according to the theory, especially important for imagining complex and detailed episodes. Generating and maintaining this spatial scaffold requires interactions between DMN regions (at the apex of the cortical hierarchy) and the hippocampus (a subcortical region famous for its role in memory). Both the hippocampus and posterior DMN regions are also clearly involved in spatial navigation and spatial reasoning, and so these more ancient spatial functions are proposed to be co-opted for scaffolding our situation representations. A 1972 study by John Bransford et al. provided an early demonstration of the importance of spatial relations in situation-imagery.[20] They ran an experiment in which participants read sentences and answered questions about them; for example, each participant would read exactly one of the two sentences below:[21]

(1) Three turtles rested on a floating log and a fish swam beneath it.
(2) Three turtles rested beside a floating log and a fish swam beneath it.

Later in the experiment, participants were asked whether they had already seen either of the following two (new) sentences:

(1′) Three turtles rested on a floating log and a fish swam beneath them.
(2′) Three turtles rested beside a floating log and a fish swam beneath them.

The experiment found that participants who had previously read Sentence (1) would often (mistakenly) agree that they had already seen Sentence (1′), but participants who had previously read Sentence (2) were more inclined to say that Sentence (2′) was new to them. Thus, Sentence (1) was confusable with (1′), but (2) was not confusable with (2′). What accounts for this phenomenon? Although these sentences are all superficially similar, they imply different spatial configurations: the relative position of the turtles and the fish is consistent between (1) and (1′), but inconsistent between (2) and (2′). Thus, these data provide empirical evidence for a familiar mental phenomenon: readers generate internal representations of the spatial layout of scenes, and they retrieve these spatial images as part of their memory of what they have read. Going even further, Gordon Bower and Daniel Morrow argued that spatial properties are automatically invoked in our minds as we read narrative text.[22] They showed that, when readers read about characters moving through a building, they were automatically 'reloading' information about objects that were in the same room, and also, to a lesser extent, information about objects in other rooms nearby. Altogether, these psychological findings are consistent with the idea that one of the language-invariant features being represented in our brains is a kind of 'spatial scaffold' for the situations and episodes in a narrative.

Script and Schema Theories: A second set of ideas about 'scenario representation' gives less emphasis to the spatial scaffold, and instead emphasizes stereotyped sequences of actions and goals. In particular, the literature on 'scripts' and 'schemas' highlights the fact that life repeatedly presents situations involving sets of actions in reliable sequence.[23] For example, the schema for eating a meal at a restaurant might correspond to a kind of canonical narrative: first, being seated, then looking at a menu, then conversation, ordering the meal, and so forth. Similarly, the schema for flying from an airport is a familiar narrative of checking in, checking luggage, passing through security, and so forth. Authors and translators, of course, commonly use such schemas to exploit and manipulate a reader's expectations about what actions characters are likely to take next. In this respect, it is interesting that some aspects of schema representation *generalize* within the DMN: these regions appear to track which 'stage' of the schema or script we are currently engaged with regardless of (for example) the specific people at the meal or the specific layout of the restaurant.[24] Thus, a part of our brain is tracking 'Have they ordered their food yet?' and it does so in a similar manner across different settings: generalizing, perhaps, across Rowan Atkinson's Mr Bean enjoying some *Fine Dining* and Samuel L. Jackson's Jules Winnfield philosophizing in a diner in *Pulp Fiction*.

Social Thinking Theories: A third set of ideas about 'event representation' emphasizes the role of 'mentalizing': the fact that understanding narratives requires understanding what other people (fictional or real) desire, and what they believe about the world. A canonical experiment here examines the neural (and psychological) systems that enable us to perform a 'false belief task': making inferences about what another person believes to be true, even in the cases when that is different from what we know to be true. This disconnect between what we know and what characters know has been explored in the dramatic arts since at least the time of Sophocles. Today, when we image people's brains while they perform inferences about the beliefs of other characters, we find that DMN regions are robustly involved.[25] A current direction of research aims to understand how different subsets of high-level regions are involved in different aspects of mental inferences. For example, it has been suggested that more frontal neural systems track a protagonist's emotions, and more posterior regions track the reasons for a certain belief.[26]

Emotion Theories: Finally, in contrast to spatial and schema theories noted above – theories which traditionally are aimed toward a rational organization of situation representations – there are also theories of situation representation that emphasize the role of emotions. The connection between emotional processing and high-level 'scene representation' has roots in so-called 'appraisal' theories of emotion, which indicate that our emotions, rather than reflecting simple approach/avoid drives, arise out of an evaluation of the situations around us, and in particular the 'deep structure' of those situations.[27] This is a relatively new area of neuroscientific investigation, but it is now clear that activity in DMN regions co-varies with the emotional parameters of our experience,[28] and that the emotional appraisals associated with DMN activity represent abstracted situational and moral properties of what we read.[29]

Altogether, it seems that 'language-invariant' DMN regions are involved in an overlapping clusters of mental functions, including: tracking the spatial relations between entities in a scene; representing and predicting the stages of stereotyped narrative sequences; representing the mental states of other people and agents; and representing the emotional content of a scene.

Do the processes and representations in DMN regions provide us with a universal language (an inter-lingua? a unified tongue? a Benjaminian 'pure language'?), hidden deep in the recesses of our cortical networks and unbound from any one human language or culture? A 2020 study by Steven M. Frankland and Joshua Greene proposes that the abstract representations in DMN regions may provide the elements of what Jerry Fodor called a 'language of thought'.[30] However, it is not clear to what extent the mental processes supported by DMN systems constitute a 'language'. Moreover, if a 'language of thought' did exist, this would not imply that such a language could or would provide an inter-lingua between the languages that we speak and write and sign. We may conceive of the representations in DMN regions as providing 'channels of thought', common pathways of neural activity, shared because they are shaped by a common evolutionary history, anchoring our thinking near meanings that can be shared across people. These inter-personally shared neural processes do not necessarily take the form of a language (with syntax), but may still reliably follow a schematic structure, anchored around a set of shared default elements that we use to perceive and imagine situations. The various theories of situation representations summarized earlier all emphasize different dimensions (space-based, schema-based, social, emotional), and so perhaps these will eventually be understood as the 'default elements' for any situation representation we generate in our minds. Of course, the brain and mind do not have a habit of decomposing neatly along our preferred theoretical distinctions. Still, in the meantime, we can have some confidence that we have identified a set of dimensions, facets, features, which are important for the neural activity in the DMN, those most interior regions of our brains.

Translation between the Past and the Present

We noted above that DMN regions, which exhibit some of the most translation-invariant responses in our brains, are located in the inner reaches of our cortical networks, and that they are implicated in the representation of 'scenes' and 'scenarios' and 'minds' and 'emotions' as variously understood. But in fact, this same set of brain regions is also known to be intimately involved in yet another aspect of brain function: *memory*. Brains are not used only for perceiving the events in the world around us. They are also repositories of memory, which we continuously retrieve, conceive, and generate. This recursive process of memory encoding and retrieval is one of recursive translation: when we retrieve a memory, we translate from the past into the present; when we store a memory, we encode our present understanding into an interior format that can be later re-read. Moreover, the recollection of past events and the imagination of future events may rely on a common situational code.[31]

In a study from 2017,[32] we investigated how brain responses are translated between the experience (past) and the recollection (present) of a narrative. This experiment had two phases: first, seventeen people (mostly undergraduate students) came one at a time to the laboratory and watched fifty minutes of the first episode of the BBC's television series *Sherlock*, while reclining in the brain scanner. Second, immediately after watching the show, each person spoke aloud what they remembered of the narrative, attempting to retell the story in detail from start to end. In Table 9.1, you can see some examples of what eight different people recalled, verbally, from a single scene in the show; they generated these recollections about half an hour after their original viewing experience.

Similar to the approach used in the Russian-English translation study described above, we used fMRI to measure neural responses associated with the understanding of a narrative. However, in this experiment we recorded neural activity both during the act of perception (watching the video) and the act of remembering (recounting aloud) as pertaining to the same material. Therefore, we could ask a new set of questions about the translation

Table 9.1 *Transcripts of eight different people's spoken recollections of the same one-minute scene in BBC's* Sherlock, *Season 1, Episode 1: 'A Study in Pink'.*

1: We see Sherlock Holmes in the morgue, and there is – , he's examining one of the bodies of this string of suicides that they think maybe they are just unrelated. But, he asks for a riding crop and just starts beating the body, hoping for bruising because that will tell whether the death is recent or not. And, he sort of bluntly – , he bluntly remarks on how the mortician is like flirting with him because she's put on make-up and then later she takes it off. She's asked him out to coffee, but he just interprets that as, 'Would you like me to get you a cup of coffee?'

2: And so this person brings him to Sherlock, who's in the lab, and is kind of analysing, um, certain things. And I think before this scene where Sherlock is in a lab, he's in a mortuary. He wants to figure out how a body will bruise if he like hits it with a riding crop. So, he's sort of doing that, and then this girl is there and like wants to, wants him to ask her out or something. So, she puts on make-up and asks him if he wants coffee? But he said yes, but he like just wants the coffee. And yeah, but not necessarily he's not interested.

3: Next they show Sherlock for the first time, and he's like at this place where there's a dead person and a, what do they call it, a body bag. And there's this young girl who has her hair in a ponytail, she's like wearing a lab coat, and she like kinda tells him about the guy in the body bag. And then I remember Sherlock like starts like whipping the guy, it seems like he was whipping him, I don't know exactly what he was doing. And then for some reason the girl had gone out of the room, but she comes back and Sherlock notes that she's wearing lipstick, so apparently like she likes Sherlock and she's like trying to get his attention and then … Oh yeah, she asks him if he wants coffee, but like obviously she's trying to ask him out on a date, and he's like yeah I'll take coffee, black, two sugars, and bring it upstairs. And so, then the next part I remember, I guess he went upstairs and he's in this lab.

4: And then it switches to the morgue. So, either that scene happened before this or after. But basically, there's a body of this woman and like we see these shots from the perspective of the corpse. Look at it, and she's like oh what happened? And like the lab tech-assistant, oh I just got in, like 62 possible causes of death or something. Next thing you know, Sherlock's getting at it, hitting the corpse with a riding whip and the woman comes back, Sherlock asks, oh you have lipstick on? And she's clearly trying to ask him out, and he hardcore rejects her. And she asks if he wants to get coffee later, and he's like oh yes, black one sugar. And so he tells her please note down what bruises come down in 20 minutes, it's imperative to his alibi.

5: Actually, the first scene in the lab, I think, is the first time we see Sherlock. And he's talking in the morgue with the morgue scientist, I guess, and she, uh what would you call it? I can't remember, I'm drawing a blank on the name of a doctor in a morgue. And she, I guess he's supplying him with a body so he can do some experiments with how a body looks bruised with some sort of like horse whip, like a caddy whip. And she leaves, and then comes back, and then she's wearing lipstick, and then he notices that she's put on lipstick, so and uh she asks him out to get coffee and he sort of fly-ly remarks you know, yes, I'll have a coffee now, you know, sort of refusing to acknowledge that she just asked him out on a date, so she clearly put on the lipstick to, cuz she liked him.

Table 9.1 (*cont.*)

6: And this is where we first get introduced to Sherlock. The fat guy brings Watson to Sherlock's laboratory. However, I should say before that, sorry, he's at the morgue. So, Sherlock is in the morgue whipping corpses, as a joke. He is ... We get a sense of his sort of removal from normal life, as the morgue assistant asks if he would like coffee, meaning if he would like to go on a date and get coffee. However, Sherlock misreads this and asks for, or he says yes please, black with two sugars. Quite a comedic moment I must say.

7: Then the scene shifts to Sherlock Holmes, he's looking at a corpse in a morgue. He's talking to the lady, the lady, he starts beating the corpse with like a stick and asks about bruises. The lady comes back, he asks her why she's suddenly wearing lipstick and gives her a kind of a sideways glance, and she responds that she asks him if he would like to get coffee, and he basically tells her that I would like black with sugar, which is kind of rude.

8: And then I believe that that's when they go to, or that's when we see a picture of Sherlock opening up a bodybag. And then this woman comes in. He says like How fresh or something and the woman says some number of hours, I guess it was a recent kill or something and then Sherlock says Shame, I knew him? or something. And then we see him whipping something, like a lot, really hard, and the woman comes in and says Did you have a hard day or something? And he notices that she had put lipstick on so mentions it. She like, or that she hadn't had it before, and then she gets a little embarrassed and says, 'Yeah I was just retouching it', and then she tries to ask him on a coffee date, but basically says, 'I think Can I get you coffee or something', and he says 'yeah, black two sugars'. But that's obviously not what she meant.

between past and present: when we recall a past experience, to what extent are we re-instantiating the original physical state of the brain? Do our brains attempt to 'replay' the states they were in during the original experience, as though living them for a second time? And if so, is the entire brain doing this re-living, or only some levels of the hierarchy?

How did we practically investigate the mapping between the perception and memory of a real-world narrative? In recalling the fifty-minute show, people spoke for between ten and forty-five minutes (depending on their loquaciousness), which typically consisted of a fairly literal account in roughly correct chronological order from beginning to end of the narrative. Thus, for a typical person we had about 2,000 snapshots of brain states during television-viewing, and about 400–1,800 snapshots of brain states during recollection of the show's events. We then broke the show timeline into fifty 'scenes' of one minute on average (breaking at major director's cuts); and for every person's recall, we grouped their spoken sentences according to the same fifty scenes. This meant that we could, for any given Scene X in the movie, compare between: 1) brain states occurring at the time a person was watching Scene X; and 2) brain states occurring at the time a person was remembering and talking about Scene X. We measured how similar the brain states were between watching Scene X and remembering Scene X.

Importantly, we could measure the similarity separately within hundreds of brain 'parcels' that covered the entire cortex. The brain 'state' in each parcel was a spatial distribution of activity: a fingerprint describing which sub-volumes inside the parcel were most and least active in response to a particular event. These fingerprints were distinct – there was one pattern for the scene where Sherlock met Watson for the first time; another pattern for the scene in which Watson dreamed of gunfire on the battlefield; yet another pattern for the tense police press conference interrupted by Sherlock's texting. So (where in the brain) were these fingerprints accurately re-instantiated (translated) from the original experience to the recall?

We found that brain fingerprints from watching the show were re-instantiated within default mode network (DMN) regions of people's brains as they spoke, in a way that was selective for individual scenes. In other words, in DMN regions, the fingerprints of activity were substantially similar between the original television-watching experience and the subsequent remembering of it, and also unique from one scene to the next. This re-instatement was strongest in the DMN and extended a bit below it in the hierarchy, to the most abstract (highest) level of the brain regions which support visual processing; this hints at some non-very-detailed visual imagery occurring during recall. If there were any brain states being 're-lived' in lower levels of the hierarchy, these were not clear enough for us to detect.

The neural fingerprints in the DMN were not only invariant across perception and memory – they also exhibited some invariance across people. To examine this, we compared the neural fingerprints associated with a specific scene across different viewers of the show, and we found that they were very similar to one another, not only during the viewing, but also during recollection. Thus, two people might recall a particular scene in different ways, emphasizing different details, but there was enough shared representation of the 'situation structure' – who, what, where, and why (see Table 1 for examples of these elements in people's memory reports) – so that one person's brain activity while remembering a scene could be used a template to predict the memory-activity of another person remembering that same scene from the show.[33]

What can we derive from the two properties of DMN regions described above? These are the regions that 'return' to the state they inhabited during a narrative experience when we re-live that experience in memory, and these are the regions that sit atop the cortical hierarchy. With a spoonful of interpretive licence, and consistent with the work described above regarding spatial, social, schematic, and emotional information represented in these regions, let's state the claim: *the cerebral cortex abstracts away the features of momentary sensation, step by step, until, at the end of this process, it derives a representation of a moment in a narrative.* Much of the time the narrative that is represented in DMN regions is the narrative of our lives, or an alternative narrative we might live if we make a certain choice. But some stimuli in the world, especially narrative artworks, have the ability to co-opt this innermost system of our cerebral cortices, and to involve that system in the representation and propagation of imagined scenarios.

The case for an evolutionary benefit to narrative abilities is easily made: if one ape can tell another the thrilling tale of how crossing the river *here* and avoiding a jungle cat *there* will lead one to a delicious and nutrient-laden fruit tree, then both apes are more likely to survive and pass on their genes. The fruit-tree narrative does not require subtlety to accomplish its function: the basic who, what, where, and why will suffice. Indeed, brains may find it efficient to discard the sensory details of experiences, if the goal is to convey practical information to another mind. In a second 2017 experiment,[34] we demonstrated this act of 'memory transmission' between brains: people who had never seen the BBC's *Sherlock* lay in the brain scanner and *listened* to another person's spoken recollection of the events of the show.[35] In the brains of these 'naïve listeners', we observed DMN activity fingerprints very similar to those in the brains of the people who had actually watched the show. In other words: someone watched the TV show, then spoke about it, and the people who listened then achieved nearly the same brain representations (unique to each scene) as if they were watching it themselves. In this way, the original experiencer had (in a sense) translated their experience into a story; they became a storyteller and their listening audience became experiencers-by-proxy. Note that the listeners did not have to the same work of 'abstracting away from sensory details' that was done by the storyteller; after this filtering and compression work had been done by the brain of the storyteller, the teller was able to deliver a 'pre-digested' narrative for consumption by hungry new ears.

Today, equipped with neural machinery that is hungry for stories told by other apes, we find ourselves in a world with ever-expanding technologies for delivering stories. A brain system that (perhaps) evolved to comprehend spoken, goal-specific narratives, then developed on a diet of more entertaining and moralistic stories, told around nomadic fires;[36] later came the expansiveness, complexity, and depth of written forms; then the multi-sensory firehose of movies and television; and their mutated cousins, interactive fiction and video games. Humans have a seemingly insatiable hunger for the translated experiences of others, and for re-digesting these into our own DMN fingerprint banks.

Conclusions

Why do some regions of our brains generate the same responses to very different sounds and sights and odours? At a superficial level the answer is simple: one of the purposes of our brains is in helping us to recognize desirable objects (e.g. a safe and delicious plum), but plums do not always look and smell the same, so some systems within our brains establish a system for quickly recognizing a delicious ripe plum across a wide variety of circumstances.[37]. However, our human purposes do sometimes extend beyond the consumption of fruit. Our brains also serve other purposes – the pursuit of beauty, truth and goodness; the pursuit of love and mates; the pursuit of an understanding of what is likely to happen in the next minute, and what is likely to happen in the next year of our lives. But even at this level it is crucial that we are able to categorize events via their abstract meaning and import,[38] and thereby to extract a skeleton of meaning. Most generally, being able to perceive the similarity of superficially dissimilar items is an elemental process in human thinking,[39] and in brain function.[40]

From the sensory information arriving at our eyes and ears and fingertips, our brains translate, stage by stage by stage, across a series of increasingly subjective formats, towards a representation in the innermost regions of the cerebral cortex, a representation of events in the form of who-and-what and where-and-why and what-it-means-to-me. We use this common format to represent and recollect the events of literary narratives and, also, the stories of our lives. Right now, neuroscience has only a rough sense of how these stage-by-stage transformations occur, and our understanding of these most-interior representations is little more than a collection of speculative theories. Will these theories of brain and mind flower to reveal a more precise picture of the narrative mind, a map useful to literary translators? For now, we have only glimpsed the cat's tail, and we continue in search of the cat.

Notes

1 I. Q. Whishaw, 'The Decorticate Rat', in *The Cerebral Cortex of the Rat* (Cambridge, MA: MIT Press, 1990), 239–67.
2 Matthew F. Glasser et al., 'A Multi-Modal Parcellation of Human Cerebral Cortex', *Nature* 536, no. 7615 (August 2016), 171–78.
3 See Patric Hagmann et al., 'Mapping the Structural Core of Human Cerebral Cortex', *PLoS biology* 6, no. 7 (July 2008), e159; Ed Bullmore and Olaf Sporns, 'Complex Brain Networks: Graph Theoretical Analysis of Structural and Functional Systems', *Nature Reviews: Neuroscience* 10, no. 3 (March 2009), 186–98; as well as Richard Passingham et al., 'The Anatomical Basis of Functional Localization in the Cortex'. *Nature Reviews: Neuroscience* 3, no. 8 (August 2002), 606–16.
4 R. Quian Quiroga et al., 'Invariant Visual Representation by Single Neurons in the Human Brain', *Nature* 435, no. 7045 (June 2005), 1102–7.
5 There is no one-to-one relationship between neurons and concepts, even at the innermost levels of neural representation. Even if a neuron responds in an invariant manner to an abstract concept (e.g. thinking of a specific person), that neuron will also respond to other concepts. Altogether, a single abstract concept (e.g. the notion of a specific person) is, conservatively, linked to hundreds of thousands of 'abstract' neurons. See Stephen Waydo et al., 'Sparse Representation in the Human Medial Temporal Lobe', *The Journal of Neuroscience: The Official Journal of the Society for Neuroscience* 26, no. 40 (October 2006), 10232–4.
6 See, for instance, Lawrence Venuti, *Theses on Translation: An Organon for the Current Moment* (Pittsburgh and New York: Flugschriften, 2019), 7, https://flugschriftencom.files.wordpress.com/2019/09/flugschriften-5-lawrence-venuti-theses-on-translation.pdf, accessed October 29, 2021.
7 See Christopher J. Honey et al., 'Not Lost in Translation: Neural Responses Shared across Languages', *The Journal of Neuroscience: The Official Journal of the Society for Neuroscience* 32, no. 44 (October 2012), 15277–83.
8 See, for example, Mark Chevillet et al., 'Functional Correlates of the Anterolateral Processing Hierarchy in Human Auditory Cortex', *The Journal of Neuroscience: The Official Journal of the Society for Neuroscience* 31, no. 25 (June 2011), 9345–52.
9 For examples of how these regions seem to represent language in a way that is shared across English, Mandarin, and Farsi, see Benjamin D. Zinszer et al., 'Semantic Structural Alignment of Neural Representational Spaces Enables Translation between English and Chinese Words', *Journal of Cognitive Neuroscience* 28, no. 11 (November 2016), 1749–59; and Morteza Dehghani et al., 'Decoding the Neural Representation of Story Meanings across Languages', *Human Brain Mapping* 38, no. 12 (December 2017), 6096–6106.
10 See Margulies et al., 'Situating the Default-Mode Network along a Principal Gradient of Macroscale Cortical Organization', 12574–9.

11 The abstraction performed in cortical circuits is not a purely logical abstraction of the kind we find in mathematics. Instead, it is a process by which our brains gradually translate information from an objective format (the physics of the world) to a subjective format (representations of that are relevant for our personal thinking, understanding, and deciding).
12 Raymond A. Mar, 'The Neural Bases of Social Cognition and Story Comprehension', *Annual Review of Psychology* 62 (2011), 103–34.
13 Demis Hassabis and Eleanor A. Maguire, 'The Construction System of the Brain', *Philosophical Transactions of the Royal Society of London. Series B, Biological Sciences* 364, no. 1521 (May 2009), 1263–71.
14 Randy L. Buckner and Daniel C. Carroll, 'Self-Projection and the Brain', *Trends in Cognitive Sciences* 11, no. 2 (February 2007), 49–57.
15 Donna Rose Addis et al., 'Remembering the Past and Imagining the Future: Common and Distinct Neural Substrates during Event Construction and Elaboration', *Neuropsychologia* 45, no. 7 (April 2007), 1363–77.
16 Arthur C. Graesser et al., 'Discourse Comprehension', *Annual Review of Psychology* 48 (1997), 163–89.
17 Herbert H. Clark and Mija M. Van der Wege, 'Imagination in Discourse', in *The Handbook of Discourse Analysis*, ed. Deborah Schiffrin, Deborah Tannen, and Heidi E. Hamilton (Oxford: Blackwell, 2001), 772–86.
18 Hassabis and Maguire, 'The Construction System of the Brain'.
19 Jessica Robin et al., 'The Spatial Scaffold: The Effects of Spatial Context on Memory for Events', *Journal of Experimental Psychology: Learning, Memory, and Cognition* 42, no. 2 (2016), 308–15.
20 John D. Bransford, J. Richard Barclay, and Jeffery J. Franks. 'Sentence Memory: A Constructive versus Interpretive Approach', *Cognitive Psychology* 3, no. 2 (1972), 193–209.
21 Underlines are shown to emphasize the key differences, but these were not shown in the experiment.
22 Gordon H. Bower and Daniel G. Morrow, 'Mental Models in Narrative Comprehension', *Science* 247 no. 4938 (1990), 44–8.
23 Roger C. Schank and Robert P. Abelson, 'Scripts, Plans, and Knowledge', in *Proceedings of the 4th International Joint Conference on Artificial Intelligence* 1 (San Francisco: Morgan Kaufmann Publishers Inc., 1975), 151–7.
24 Christopher Baldassano et al., 'Representation of Real-World Event Schemas during Narrative Perception', *The Journal of Neuroscience: The Official Journal of the Society for Neuroscience* 38, no. 45 (Sep 2018), 9689–99.
25 Rebecca Saxe and Nancy Kanwisher, 'People Thinking about Thinking People: The Role of the Temporo-Parietal Junction in "Theory of Mind"', *NeuroImage* 19, no. 4 (August 2003), 1835–42; and Yaara Yeshurun et al., 'Same Story, Different Story', *Psychological Science* 28, no. 3 (March 2017), 307–19.
26 Jorie Koster-Hale et al., 'Mentalizing Regions Represent Distributed, Continuous, and Abstract Dimensions of Others' Beliefs', *NeuroImage* 161 (November 2017), 9–18.

27 Gerald L. Clore and Andrew Ortony, 'Appraisal Theories: How Cognition Shapes Affect into Emotion' in *Handbook of Emotions*, ed. Lisa Feldman Barrett et al. (New York: The Guilford Press, 2008), 628–42; and Richard S. Lazarus, 'Progress on a Cognitive-Motivational-Relational Theory of Emotion', *The American Psychologist* 46, no. 8 (August 1991), 819–34.
28 Kristen A. Lindquist et al., 'The Brain Basis of Emotion: A Meta-Analytic Review', *The Behavioral and Brain Sciences* 35, no. 3 (2012), 121–43.
29 See Amy E. Skerry and Rebecca Saxe, 'Neural Representations of Emotion Are Organized around Abstract Event Features', *Current Biology* 25, no. 15 (August 2015), 1945–54; and Ajay B. Satpute and Kristen A. Lindquist, 'The Default Mode Network's Role in Discrete Emotion', *Trends in Cognitive Sciences* 23, no. 10 (August 2019), 851–64.
30 Steven M. Frankland and Joshua D. Greene, 'Concepts and Compositionality: In Search of the Brain's Language of Thought', *Annual Review of Psychology* 71 (2020), 273–303; see also Jerry A. Fodor, *The Language of Thought* (Boston, MA: Harvard University Press, 1975).
31 Addis et al., 'Remembering the Past'.
32 Janice Chen et al., 'Shared Memories Reveal Shared Structure in Neural Activity across Individuals', *Nature Neuroscience* 20, no. 1 (2017), 115–25.
33 Importantly, the signals in DMN are not *only* reflecting basic structural features that are shared in everyone's memory. If two groups of individuals have different interpretations of a scene or story, it is also possible to 'decode' which interpretation they had using the signals in DMN regions. See Yeshurun et al., 'Same Story, Different Story'; and Mai Nguyen et al., 'Shared Understanding of Narratives Is Correlated with Shared Neural Responses', *NeuroImage* 184 (January 2019), 161–70.
34 Asieh Zadbood et al., 'How We Transmit Memories to Other Brains: Constructing Shared Neural Representations via Communication', *Cerebral Cortex* 27, no. 10 (October 2017), 4988–5000.
35 This raconteur was originally a participant in the first *Sherlock* experiment described above.
36 See Polly W. Wiessner, 'Embers of Society: Firelight Talk among the Ju/'hoansi Bushmen', *Proceedings of the National Academy of Sciences of the United States of America* 111, no. 39 (September 2014), 14027–35; Daniel Smith et al., 'Cooperation and the Evolution of Hunter-Gatherer Storytelling', *Nature Communications* 8, no. 1 (December 2017), 1853; and Lucas M. Bietti et al., 'Storytelling as Adaptive Collective Sensemaking', *Topics in Cognitive Science* 11, no. 4 (October 2019), 710–32.
37 Roger N. Shephard, 'Toward a Universal Law of Generalization for Psychological Science.' *Science* 237, no. 4820 (1987), 1317–23.
38 Jerome S. Bruner, *Study of Thinking* (New York: John Wiley & Sons, Inc., 1956).
39 Douglas R. Hofstadter, 'Analogy as the Core of Cognition', in *The Analogical Mind: Perspectives from Cognitive Science*, ed. Dedre Gentner, Keith J. Holyoak and Boicho N. Kokinov (Cambridge MA: MIT Press, 2001), 499–538.
40 Carol A. Seger and Earl K. Miller, 'Category Learning in the Brain', *Annual Review of Neuroscience* 33 (2010), 203–19.

CHAPTER 10

Covalent Effect
Literary Translation Practice and the Pedagogy of the Multilingual Workshop

Aron Aji

Almost all literary translation workshops taught in US colleges and universities are multilingual in composition, involving students who translate into English from different source languages and an instructor who almost never possesses proficiency in all the languages present in the workshop. The obvious question we are frequently asked is, 'How does it work?' The honest answer, to a large extent, is 'by necessity', but we also invoke 'literariness', arguing that our primary focus in literary translation workshop is the creation of *literary* works of consummate aesthetics in the target language, works that reflect both the distinctness of the original and the immediacy of contemporary language. We expect the students, even the most adventurous and avant-garde among them, to affirm linguistic fidelity unequivocally since it is so central to the ethics and discipline of literary translation.

At the University of Iowa, we also invoke 'tradition'. The first multilingual literary translation workshop in a US university was offered at Iowa fifty-five years ago, to support the international writers who held long-term residency at the University's famed Writers Workshop; with the formal inauguration of the International Writing Program (IWP) three years later, the translation workshop became a staple of IWP, pairing students and international writers in residence to translate the latter's work collaboratively. The creative energy built around the translation workshop also provided the spark – and for some time the motor – for *Modern Poetry in Translation*, the renowned journal that was started by the then new director of the translation workshop at Iowa, Daniel Weissbort, and the British poet Ted Hughes. Iowa's MFA program in Literary Translation, too, is an offshoot of the translation workshop, founded by Weissbort and Gayatri Chakravorty Spivak, who was a faculty member in UI's Comparative Literature program. True to its roots in creative writing and comparative literature, our MFA program still combines creative practice and international literature in-the-making, requiring students to take several multilingual translation workshops as well as the IWP Translation workshop, where they still collaborate with some of the IWP residents each fall.

Unsurprisingly, 'How does it work?' was also the first question I asked when invited to facilitate the translation workshop at Iowa about ten years ago. My early experiences were pleasantly reassuring. The high-calibre students were proficient in their source languages as much as they were in reading literature; our workshop felt like a balanced mix of literary studies classroom and creative writing workshop, and we were able to identify and interrogate translation issues by staying focused on the literary dimension of the manuscripts. We would ask the translator to rework an inelegant sentence in English by walking us through the syntax in the original, or to resist rendering a sonnet in free verse by analysing more patiently the metre and rhyme in the original, and how these elements contribute to the overall effect of the poem. As rewarding – even epiphanic – as these discussions were for both the translator and the rest of us, they remained, for the most part, discrete interlinguistic exchanges in a multilingual setting. To be sure, resolving, say, an Italian>English translation challenge frequently triggered a healthy perspectival shift, and even a new creative strategy, in, say, a Korean>English translator. Inveterate linguaphiles that translators are, we delighted in experiencing vicariously the subtleties and aesthetic range of each other's source languages. However, to reposition multilingualism from a circumstantial aspect of the classroom to the pedagogical core of the course would require a systematic re-articulation of not only the mechanics of the workshop but, to some extent, also the theoretical and craft-centred assumptions about translation.

Multilingualism and Translation

Such re-articulation strikes me as especially worthwhile given that emerging translators today practise their craft in the pervasively multilingual global environment where international literature is produced and circulates.

In the contemporary context of globalization, translation is not merely a functional tool for inter-lingual transaction, but it also becomes what scholars like Michael Cronin call the *new epistemology* – how we know the others, ourselves, and the dynamic diversity that surrounds and shapes us.[1] Most countries across the globe include, in ever-increasing numbers, professionals, artists, academics, and learned readers who function in more than one language, proficient not only in their vernacular ('mother tongue') and national languages but also, in regional cosmopolitan languages and the global lingua franca, those languages that facilitate communication across national borders. In this fluid context, we come to recognize that languages are eminently un-static, polyvalent, and open to reciprocal influences. Written texts, too, whether imaginative, expository, or digital, often emerge and are experienced as moving across actual or imagined 'borders'. Lydia Liu, scholar of Chinese linguistics and translation, in 1995 diagnosed this multilingual condition as 'translingual practice', which has only obtained greater and wider relevance since.[2] Translingual practice, as Liu describes, is:

> the process by which new words, meanings, discourses, and modes of representation arise, circulate, and acquire legitimacy within the host language due to, or in spite of, the latter's *contact/collision* with the guest language. Meanings ... are not so much 'transformed' when concepts pass from the guest language to the host language as invented within the local environment of the latter ... [Translingual exchanges] ... account for the process of *adaptation, translation, introduction, and domestication of words, categories, discourses, and modes of representation from one language to another.*[3]

It is important to note that global writing does not connote homogenization, even if the risk is most certainly present given the formidable influence of English and a few other major languages. Rather, the dynamic networks of exchange can and actually do encourage new syntheses, resulting from the interface of increasingly diverse writing forms and modalities that come into contact with each other. Especially in light of the digital revolution that has left no world region untouched, we find it increasingly difficult to make once conventional distinctions between national literatures, between the source and target languages, while many texts are in effect 'translated', as Rebecca Walkowitz in her book *Born Translated* argues, *while they are being conceived and composed.*[4]

Perhaps a hypothetical question such as the following encapsulates the condition of global writing most vividly: how do we read, say, a Syrian novel written in Arabic by a refugee author who cites the Japanese novelist Murakami as her main influence, whom she had read in English translation while living in Germany?

Functioning as they will be in this dynamic reality of multilingualism, literary translation students need to reflect directly and deliberately on the nature of both literary production and the attendant forms of translation practice in the context of globalization. To begin with, there are theoretical questions: how do international languages (regional cosmopolitan or global lingua franca) adapt to their global use? What are the currents of translingual exchange particular to a given multilingual zone (or region)? How do national languages change or preserve their character in the process of international, translingual exchanges? What kinds of power dynamics determine the extent to which a language resists or adapts to change? How does translingual exchange provoke assimilation or transgression? There are also questions about translation practice: how do we translate a world/global author who writes with awareness and influence of other languages and literatures? Or multilingual authors – heritage speakers, refugees, expatriates – who write in more than one language, and who at times come into literature in their second or third language? How do we translate them into English since, for many world writers, English is almost always a constituent influence? How does an English translation do justice to rather than disequilibrate the presence of Anglophone diction and culture in, say, a Murakami or a Shafak novel, given that the very style of these authors depends on multilingual hybridity? (To wit, consider Antoine Berman's famous list of deformations, included in his 'Translation and the Trials of the Foreign',[5] that arise in the process of translation, when these deformations, as a matter of creative practice, permeate the very language of the literary work being translated.)

Likewise, some of our long-held assumptions about the scope and process of translation are put to test by this multilingual reality. For instance, self-translations or author–translator collaborations – modes of translation that have gained currency – entail multiple subjectivities (real or imagined), negotiated agencies, by involving the translator in the very process of creating the original work. As Karen Emmerich argues most persuasively in her *Literary Translation and the Making of the Originals*,[6] these modes of translation inevitably challenge the assumption of the fixed and discrete original work as a reliable gauge to validate a translation; they blur further the already hazy line between creative authorship and the translator's subordinate craft, and they foreground the fact that translation is a generative rather than derivative iteration.

Equally noteworthy is the growing number of second-language translators into English (or into French, Russian, or any other regional cosmopolitan language with historical claims to power). Pragmatically speaking, second-language translators have become indispensable for widening the multilingual range of international literature circulation; they compensate for the insufficiency of first-language translators with proficiency in less commonly translated languages, a condition further aggravated in the case of English by the steady decline in foreign language education in the USA. (and Britain? And Australia? And Canada? And India? And New Zealand? And South Africa? And ….?). But second-language translators also can (and in best instances do) broaden the scope of translation practice itself by capitalizing on the generative confluence of multivalent stylistic conventions (lexical, phonetic, graphemic, etc.) rooted in each language and those hybrid strategies invented across languages during the translation process.

Obviously, the translingual currents feeding into the original text, or, for that matter, into its translation, are rhizomatic and not easily traceable. Whereas an author or translator might readily recognize a few of the currents, at least some of the currents probably remain intuitive and elusive in the process of the original composition or, later, its translation. This may explain why the subject of writing or translating in our multilingual contemporaneity has lent itself to diagnostic scholarship more than it has, at least so far, to discussion of method or theory. Several recent studies, chief among them Yasemin Yıldız's *Beyond the Mother Tongue*,[7] David Gramling's *Invention of Monolingualism*,[8] and Rebecca Walkowitz's *Born Translated*, amply challenge our long-held nation-centred or monolingualist assumptions (or, for that matter, the very stability of the literary work) and they present compelling analysis of world writers and literary works with tangles of linguistic and cultural roots. The relative paucity of methodological or theoretical approaches to multilingual texts – how they are produced or how they might be translated – can be explained by their intrinsic complexity and the wide-ranging diversity they present. Be that as it may, the fact and consequences of their multilingual character nevertheless ought to be among the crucial concerns of translation practice and pedagogy.

This essay, then, presents my reflections on *a single* method and *a single* pedagogy, based on my own experiences in practising and teaching literary translation. My discussion is necessarily personal, descriptive, and hypothetical, intended to illustrate how the fact of multilingualism has shaped my own approaches in these two areas.

My Multilingualism

Born, raised, and educated through college in Turkey, I functioned in several languages at once – in my early years, almost daily. The vernacular languages spoken in my family were Ladino, the Spanish of the Sephardic Jews, and Turkish. It is very likely that Ladino was my mother tongue since it wasn't until elementary school that Turkish became my primary language. Two other languages were constantly present: the Hebrew of my grandfather with rabbinical training; and French, the cosmopolitan language that connected my family to our overseas relatives and to Levantine communities in Turkey. I received private lessons in French to gain, in my family's thinking, proficiency in more than one global lingua franca. At my secondary school and college, English was the primary language of instruction. Actually, my multilingual upbringing was unexceptional. While language sets varied, most of my generation in Turkey, both in urban centres and in the provinces, functioned in one or more languages besides Turkish – Kurdish, Arabic, Greek, Italian, Armenian, Bosnian, Zaza, and so on – depending on their ethnicity, the multi-ethnic communities in which they lived, and the extent to which their local reality was connected to the exterior, whether the nation, the region, or the globe. The situation is no different in most parts of the world, even if our multilingual condition is often overlooked because of the strong hold our national languages have on our immediate reality.

Traversing multiple languages, the multilingual mind holds more than one language active at any given time, as if operating (or perhaps acting by a survival reflex) to combine strengths in one's languages in order to obtain the widest expressive capacity possible. Such coactivity of languages is often observed by psycholinguists studying cognition among bilingual or polyglot individuals. Even when one language dominates, as English eventually did in my case, the other languages organize themselves in relation to each other, with one's dominant language obtaining the greatest benefit from these relationships. But certain relationships privilege themselves, depending on the context. My English and Spanish mostly co-act as languages of socialization and affinity; or my English taps Turkish when I experience heightened emotions, probably because the grammar and vocabulary of my emotions developed most fully in Turkish. Given the sustained synergy among the coactive languages, the best word that describes the multilingual cognitive processes is 'translational'.

Covalent Effect

I translate literature in this cognitive space where languages are coactive and act on/with each other synergistically. Mining the dynamic interstices of languages, I am interested in what happens not only *in* but also *to* English when it enters into this very intimate relationship with a particular Turkish text, when English translates as much as it is translated by the Turkish text. When successful, my translations seek something more than, or different from, equivalence – what I would like to call instead, a covalent effect.

Equivalence privileges the target language, aiming to convey the source text mainly according to the linguistic codes and aesthetic conventions of the target language. The source text is a guide, an arbiter, even at times a stern one, but, as translators from Etienne Dolet through Friedrich Schleiermacher to Gideon Toury have long argued, ultimately translation is mainly concerned with the target language. Even the most foreignizing translation often ends up valorizing the primacy of the target language as it enacts its transgressions self-consciously and conspicuously. The foreign is recognizable expressly in relation to the target language conventions that are perhaps disturbed but that nonetheless prevail.

When translating for covalent effect, I aim to privilege the language of the source text at least as much as the target language, keeping the language of the source text – with its linguistic codes and aesthetic conventions – co-active throughout the translation process. This language functions as the principal determinant of each translational move I make while carrying the source text into the target language. I say 'at least as much' also because the language of the source text is the principal medium of invention that I need to recreate. My goal is to make English assimilate as much as possible the imbricated layers of style, meaning, and affect created in and through the language *particular* to the source text. The final translation attempts to produce a 'third text', as it were, a result of closest possible synergy of the linguistic codes of the source text and expressive capacity of the target language. Although my ideal reader would be a bilingual person who can detect where, how, and why the target language is transformed for covalent effect, I am no less concerned with producing a literary translation in English that can be experienced and hopefully enjoyed in terms of its intrinsic merits.

To reiterate, my aim is not to propose a theory of covalence but to describe a method, specifically, my own, that is sensitive to the multilingual condition in which literary texts are produced and translated. However, my method does derive from a general discontent I have felt concerning translation theories in the West which have long held a strong monolingualist bias, perceiving the target language as the principal site of cause or consequence concerning translational operations. This is evident in most of the classical statements in the West, from Goethe and Schleiermacher to Berman and Steiner. (Alas, all men, fully invested in the power dynamics of their culture.) As Maria Tymoczko observes,[9] even the more recent, post-structuralist, post-colonial, theories – by Sherry Simon, Homi K. Bhabha, Gayatri Chakravorty Spivak, and others – end up pointing to a 'romantic' 'elsewhere', an implausible 'in-between' space. Since translation by definition involves 'movement from one system of language to another', the 'in-between' space, according to Tymoczko, is a useful metaphor to 'reflect dissatisfaction with dominant discourse in dominant cultures', however, it imagines a lookout point within the confining enclosures of the very same discourse it aims to challenge.[10]

The target language is of course where the translation materializes. But to address what happens during translation, how and to what end, mainly in the target language, carries a serious risk of subordinating the source text, reducing it to a merely instrumental role, as if the primary reason of its existence were to be translated – and to the degree of perfection that only a translator with excellent command in his/her native language can achieve! In proposing covalent effect as an alternative method, I am seeking to privilege the language of the source text to the extent that other methods of equivalence have usually not. My not so inconspicuous repetition of the phrase 'the language of the source text' should make clear that I consider this language as something different from the so-called mother tongue or native language of the cultural context in which the source text is produced. As the first and primary medium of invention along the translation artery, this language is itself 'made', it is a literary artifice complete with surface and deep structures – its lexicon and syntax, metaphoric layers, inner rhythms, sounds, and emotional code. In striving for covalent effect, I want the language of the source text, with its complete and startling otherness, to somehow compel the target language to assimilate to the former's intrinsic logic and characteristics as well as possible.

To illustrate the covalent effect, I turn to Bilge Karasu, the late Turkish post-modernist author whose works I have periodically translated, works that have crucially shaped my approach to translation. A linguistic philosopher at Hacettepe University, Karasu could read in seven languages and translated from four (including works by T. S. Eliot, Lorca, Simenon, Yourcenar, and Calvino). Arguably the most cosmopolitan writer of his generation, Karasu was at the same time a leading architect of New ('Pure') Turkish, keenly interested in developing it into a language capable of producing great literature. In other words, language, for Karasu, was both a medium and the object of literary invention – if you will, the instrument and the music of his writing. Karasu's language emerges in the nexus of several languages, including old Turkish (which he tried to purge of its Arabic and Persian influences) and the world languages in which he read and from which he translated literary works, a rich network of signification that, in turn, helped him shape the form and style of his own writing. For these reasons, translating Karasu has required that I make his language covalent with English – not standing alongside but bonding with it – by crafting a translation language that, while recognizably English, could reflect as palpably as possible the linguistic code of Karasu's texts.

The following is an excerpt from Bilge Karasu's *Uzun Sürmüş Bir Günün Akşamı*,[11] which I translated as *A Long Day's Evening*.[12] The book is his most critically acclaimed in Turkey and epitomizes his aesthetics. The two-part narrative consists of internal monologues by two eighth-century Byzantine monks, Andronikos and Ioakim, who reflect on the crisis of faith they each endure during the period of iconoclasm. The speaker of the excerpt below is Ioakim, an elderly monk nearing death, during one of his daily walks while in exile, in Ravenna. I offer the excerpt in Turkish, followed by my English translation.

> Havanın yumuşaklığından doğan, gelişen bir şey var. Yürümeye başladığında hava güneşliydi ama yavaş yavaş bir serinlik yayılıyordu ortalığa. Şimdi, yürüdüğü, etlerini, ekmeklerini, hafif bir yorgunluk esrikliği bastığı, basmaya başladığı için, bütün çabasını bacaklarıyla kollarına yüklediği için, dışarılardan içine doğru bir sıcaklık akmağa başlaması, şaşılacak bir şey değil. İçinden dışına doğru çıtırtılı birtakım kıvılcımlar gibi sıçrayan ürperti de uzun zamandır bildiği bir duygu. Ama güneş Aventinus'un ardına çekildikçe, yürüdüğü yolda gölge koyulaştıkça, ileridekı ağaçlığın biraz seyrelmiş ama hala yemyeşil duran dalları arasında, yaprakları arasında, hışırtı artıp sertleştikçe, dağılan ışığın yumuşaklığı katmerleşiyor, kabarıyor. Koyulan bir serbet düşünüyor İoakim, gül yapraklarının, rengini yitirdiği halde, incelip saydamlastigi halde, o şerbetin içerisinde güllükten, yapraklıktan, salt tatlılıktan öte bir nesne oluvermelerini düşünüyor. Koyulan, olgunlaşan – aradığı söz bu – bir
>
> Olgunlaşan. Yemişler düşünüyor şimdi, olgunlaşan, derileri incelen, çatlayan, içlerindekinyumusakligi, tatlılığı, artık kapalı, örtülü tutamazmış gibi çatlayan yemişler ... Bu deri çatlaklarının kıyıları, kenarları, çabuk kararır. Birkaç gün, birkaç saat ötesi, ölümün bu başlangıcını çürük diye, küf diye, kararma diye ilerletir. Gul yapraklarını koruyan sey, onları güllüğün, yapraklığın, tatlılığın ötesine götüren şey, o koyu şerbetin içinde yarı yarıya erimeleri değil mi?[13]

Something is born, it grows out of the air's softness. When he started his walk, there was sunlight, but also a cool breeze beginning to make itself felt. Now, after walking for some time, after experiencing the light drunkenness of exhaustion in his joints, his flesh, after bearing all the burden of exertion in his arms, his legs, he isn't surprised that a wave of heat begins to seep through his skin, to the interior of his body. The inner chill shooting outward like crackling sparks is also a sensation he has known for a long time. But as the sun retreats behind Mount Aventius, the shadows deepen along the path he's been walking, the rustling grows louder, sharper, among the leaves, among the branches – somewhat sparse yet still green – in the woods ahead of him, as the soft, diffuse lights swells then redoubles. Ioakim thinks of a thick nectar, how suspended in that liquid, the faded, translucent petals of a rose suddenly become something beyond roseness, beyond petalness, beyond pure sweetness. Dense, ripening – this, the word he's been looking for –

Ripening. He is thinking of fruit now, ripening fruits, their skin growing thinner, breaking open, as if they can no longer remain hidden, covered, no longer contain the softness, the sweetness teeming inside of them ... The edges of the split skin blacken quickly. Within days, within hours, the onset of death – call it rot, call it mold, call it blackness. Is it not also true that what protects the rose petals, what carries them beyond roseness, petalness, sweetness, is exactly their half-dissolution in the nectar?[14]

The interplay of key themes (ripening/dissolution) unfolds from start to finish, originating in the initial sensory observation and moving through meditation/introspection, culminating in epiphany. Richly sonic, the two paragraphs mimic each other's rhythm and movement, with the second functioning as a reprise, giving the entire passage a sonata-like quality. The noticeably crafted language and form demand that we pay attention to the figures of sound, syntax, the pattern of pauses and stops, in other words, the composite acoustic experience that complements as well as amplifies the interplay of themes. We experience several things at once intellectually and acoustically: the setting of the walk (a trail covered with dried pine needles and cones by a river); the time of the year (autumn); the rhythm of Ioakim's meditation (casual observation widening and deepening along the tendrils of memory, leading to an epiphany, a grand metaphor about life and death). The acoustics of the passage also reflects the pace of Ioakim's walk, the duration of our reading closely approximating the duration of this stretch of Ioakim's walk. Quite remarkably, the entire narrative of *A Long Day's Evening* sustains the same effect: the book itself follows the sonata form, and our reading of it lasts approximately as long as the narrative chronology, that is, the combined duration of the walks taken by the monks.

In translating this passage, I attempt to make English assimilate as much as possible the acoustic properties present in the Turkish. My translation, comprising 269 words and 1,330 characters, remains close to the Turkish version, which comprises 183 words and 1,299 characters – that is, as close as I could get, given Turkish texts usually become 20 per cent longer in English translation. The sonic characteristics are crucial: the tone, the mood, but also the acoustic experience of the Turkish text. Of the 1,299 characters, 231 are high vowels (two thirds of which are 'i's and 'e's) and 100 are plosives/fricatives (including 44 't's, 22 'ç's, 25 'k's, 9 'p's); as I interpret it, the combination of high vowels and plosives/fricatives parallels the movement of introspection or 'ripening'. The 303 low vowels (two thirds of which are 'a's and 'ı's) and 154 elongators (half of which are 'y's and 'ğ's) evoke tones of lament (fittingly, the Turkish word is 'ağıt'), consistent with the theme of dissolution. Finally, as I see them, the patterns of pauses and stops in the passage reflect the rhythm of Ioakim's own slow introspection/meditation while they also indicate the measure of our reading experience. For the sake of brevity, here is a shorter segment (third, fourth, and fifth sentences) to illustrate my approximations:

> Şimdi, / yürüdüğü, /etlerini, /eklemlerini, hafif bir yorgunluk esrikliği bastığı, /basmaya başladığı **için**, /dışarılardan içine doğru bir sıcaklık akmağa başlaması, şaşılacak bir şey değil.// İçinden dışına doğru çıtırtılı birtakım kıvılcımlar gibi sıçrayan ürperti de uzun zamandır bildiği bir duygu. // Ama güneş Aventinus'un ardına çekildikçe, /yürüdüğü yolda gölge koyulaştıkça,/ ilerideki ağaçlığın biraz seyrelmiş ama hala yemyeşil duran dalları arasında, / yaprakları arasında, /hışırtı artıp sertleştikçe, /dağılan ışığın yumuşaklığı katmerleşiyor, /kabarıyor.//

— 73 words, 532 characters
— pauses: [/-/-/–/–/—] [//————//] [–/–/–/—/-/-/-] (note the near-symmetry)
— consonances

> Now, /after walking for some time, /after experiencing exhaustion/—its light drunkenness—in his joints,/ his flesh, /the burden of exertion in his arms, /his legs,/ /he isn't surprised by a wave of heat seeping through his skin, /to the interior of his body. //The flash of inner chill, /like crackling sparks, /is also a familiar sensation.// But as the sun descends Aventius, / the shadows deepen along the path he's been walking, /the rustling grows louder, /sharper among the leaves, /among the branches/—somewhat sparse yet still green—in the woods ahead of him, /as the soft, /diffuse light swells /then redoubles.//

— 102 words, 505 characters
— pauses: [/-/-/-/-/—/——] [//- - –//] [——/—/-/-/—/-/-/-]
— consonances

In the longer excerpt above, two additional translation strategies might be noticeable (although, hopefully, not to the extent of disrupting the reading experience). The first is the abundant use of comma splices to accentuate, on the one hand, the pause and stops in the Turkish, and, on the other hand, Ioakim's internal monologue and associative thinking.

The second strategy concerns the conjunction 'and', which is absent in this passage as it is throughout the 180-page-long text. In Turkish, the word for 'and' is the originally Arabic 've'. Along with accentuating further the staccato rhythm, the omission is meant to mimic Karasu's own omission of 've', committed as he was to the new, purer Turkish, free of Arabic and Persian influences. His elimination of 've' results in rendering the relationships between the conjoined objects more precise and pronounced. The elimination of 'and' (over 500 of them, to be precise) in the English translation obtains the same effect. For instance, the phrase 'sunrise between the earth and the sky', when recast as 'the earth, the sky, the sunrise in between', foregrounds the speaker's camera-like visualization.

Lastly, my emphasizing of acoustic patterns for covalent effect has much to do with the complex cognitive operations of hearing, in general, and their significant function in Turkish as a richly oral/aural language, in particular. Hearing is arguably the most reflexive, persistent, autonomous of our senses. It is, on the one hand, evocative, un-administered, and *im*mediate, and, on the other hand, highly associative, mnemonic, and interpretive. Sound experience entails intellectual as well as visceral processes, evoking, often at once, cognitive, intuitive, neural, and emotional reactions. Our most regulated and trained experiences of sound are epistemic: the critical, interpretative coding and recall of sound as signifiers of stored information. However, sounds also stimulate our senses, provoking visual images, smells, tastes, tactile memories that we experience or intuit through simultaneous sensory associations. This is why I approach the acoustic composition of a text (or for that matter, of a language), the sounds, rhythms, pitch, accents, pauses, stops, etc. that make up this composition, as the material imprint of how the text wants to be read or, more holistically, experienced. In Turkish, acoustic experience is quite crucial to communication, whether written or oral. Morphemic structure of words, flexible syntax, vowel harmony, and the system of agglutinating suffixes combine to make Turkish richly allusive, naturally musical and emotionally evocative; even literary texts often reflect the traditionally oral and recitative character of the language, in which the semantic and the affective are tightly interfused. English, of course, is a very different language: rational, empirical in impulse, buttressed by a vast and exacting vocabulary, a systematic and imposing grammar, a widely codified prosody and literary conventions, and so on. In my translation process, I engage directly and deliberately with these incommensurable characteristics of the two language systems. Translating for covalent effect means bonding English as closely as possible to the linguistic and affective codes of the source text; it means making the idiosyncrasies of the Turkish text breathe through the language of my translation as much as possible.

Some Thoughts on the Pedagogy of the Multilingual Workshop

I hope my discussion of method already suggests some of the elements of my pedagogy, such as: making the language of the source text central to the entire translation process; emphasizing the linguistic code of the source text rather than one's proficiency in the source language; going beyond lexical comprehension, and treating the source text as a document of acoustic and formal notations; developing attentive listening skills to approach the source text not only intellectually but also aurally, to experience its affective qualities; and so on. Here I will point out some of the particular characteristics and practices we foster in our multilingual workshop environment, in order to address the question with which I began, 'How does it work?'

What we do and how well we do it, of course, depend largely on the composition of the workshop. Any given semester, students translate from six to eight different languages, most translated by one student each, except for the 'major' languages – Spanish, French, German, and Italian. In recent years, we have sought to accept students who work with less commonly translated languages, such as Gujarati, Bulgarian, Romanian, Sinhala, Kurdish, Turkish, Ukrainian, and Macedonian. These students are often native or heritage speakers of those languages, and they possess native or near-native fluency in English, having studied it often from elementary or secondary school through college. As translators into English, we are keenly aware of the power dynamics at play when international literature circulates primarily in English. The presence of less commonly translated languages in the workshop therefore enables us to interrogate, in real terms, the position and capacity of English within a wide range of languages.

Two other characteristics of the workshop are important to mention. First, we actively encourage participation by students from other MFA writing programmes – namely, poetry, fiction, creative non-fiction, playwriting. Their first-hand knowledge of the creative process and how writing style or voice or narrative structure is crafted, proves invaluable while we analyse how those same elements operate in the source text and might be re-created in English. Second, students typically enrol in translation theory or critical reading seminars concurrently with the translation workshop. The combination enables us to temper the lure of, on the one hand, meta-discourse in the theory courses and, on the other hand, what Lawrence Venuti famously called at his 2010 American Literary Translator's Association keynote address the 'belletristic practice' of translating texts without method or broader cultural context.[15] Our foundation theory course, Issues in Translation, is expressly designed to complement the first workshop the students take, featuring, as we shall see, exercises that address translation for covalent effect.

As an introductory assignment, each student submits a two-part essay; the first part describes the distinctive characteristics of his/her source language, while the second part focuses on a short passage from the student's source text, to discuss its key stylistic features. Shared in advance with the class, these documents at first generate an encompassing conversation about the multilingual context of contemporary translation, and later, they serve as reference guides for manuscript workshops. Each manuscript submission is also accompanied by a page-long reflection on the specific linguistic and translational challenges the translator wishes the workshop to address. To help us focus on process and resist evaluating the manuscript mainly for readability in English, the translator freely underlines passages and provides footnotes throughout. To be sure, these practices encourage rigorous critical and reflective habits of reading and translating. At the same time, they are intended to privilege the language of the source text, to keep it coactive throughout the translation process. Lastly, from each manuscript, we choose a passage for the kind of acoustic analysis I illustrated above when describing my own translation method. The passage can be either problematic or highly accomplished in the English (in fact, it is best not to focus on only one kind) since our goal in conducting the comparative analysis of the passage in the source and target language is to become conscious of where the texts converge as well as diverge, in order to illustrate both the instances of covalent effect and the strategies to bring the two languages to bond closely. In practice, the acoustic analysis is not merely about identifying sonic markers (assonance, alliteration, punctuation, etc.) printed on the page. We also ask the translator to read the source passage and its translation out loud, always more than once or twice, often three or more times, while the rest of the participants take notes without looking at the printed text. The rounds of readings are meant to encourage us to 'quiet down' our critical, analytic mind (accustomed to interpreting) in order to 'hear' the passage and its translation as acoustic experience.

During one semester, we typically workshop two discrete manuscripts per student, and a revision of a previously workshopped manuscript. This schedule is aligned with our work in Issues in Translation which features a set of assignments particularly designed to synchronize with the second and third rounds of workshop. The set is called TUI, or Translating Under the Influence, a name that appropriately connotes disinhibition and risk-taking. Once every three weeks, students choose a short passage they have previously translated to re-translate under the influence of a theory or method discussed in the course. Besides generating lively discussions, these exercises prove highly revealing for students, as they discover the limits they may have been intuitively imposing on their translations, the de facto authority of the English language, or the compromises we make often all too readily when favouring 'readability' over valid translation. In one instance, a student, who translated under Nabokov's influence,[16] found, in the course of producing her 'footnotes reaching up like skyscrapers', that the close succession of named landmarks in her passage actually provided a series of intertextual references to literary works commonly known in the source culture, and they had to be retained in the translation, as clues at least for the diligent reader who could trace them back to their sources. Another student, who retranslated under the influence of Carol Maier,[17] could identify those aspects of the source text that he had resisted while translating. Or the student who translated under Berman's influence could not only see the various deformations in her translation, but at least as importantly, she could identify the unorthodox inventions employed by the original author. Or the student who had been struggling with the rhythm and pacing of a paragraph-long sentence in the original decided to apply – with uncharacteristic abandon – Clive Scott's avant-garde techniques, colour-coding adjectives to identify tonal texture, visualizing the setting details, mapping out the sonic patterns with different fonts, and so on.[18] None of these exercises is meant to yield a perfect translation. Rather, they are meant to strengthen the translator's grasp of the linguistic code of the source text, to help them arrive at valid translation decisions through reflective and creative practices carried out across both languages, and, not the least, to better appreciate the relationship between theory and praxis as they begin to articulate their own methods.

In the final analysis, the aim of these practices is not to recruit converts into one common method of translation, whether mine or somebody else's. As the core of workshop pedagogy, translating for covalent effect is a useful means to capitalize on the rich possibilities of the multilingual workshop; to keep the multilingual condition of contemporary translation environment in the forefront of our thinking and doing. Even the most domesticating translators have much to gain from critically reflecting on the interplay of languages both in their own translation and in the environment where their translation will circulate. Translation, by its very scope, aims to resist, even overcome, the monolingualist self-privileging of any language. In Paul Ricoeur's words, 'Translation carries the ambition of de-provincializing the mother tongue, which is invited to think of itself as one language among others, ultimately to see itself as the foreign.'[19] Moreover, translation is not a purely interlingual transaction in search of lexical or formal equivalencies. Rather, it involves one language experiencing itself in relation to another language, shaping itself according to the demands of the other; often the target language confronts its expressive limits to gain new capacity to recreate the foreign forms, visions, and voices that the source text engendered – by forcing the expressive limits of its native language.

Notes

1 Michael Cronin, *Translation and Globalisation* (London: Routledge, 2003).
2 Lydia Liu, *Translingual Practice: Literature, National Culture, and Translated Modernity – China 1900–1937* (Stanford, CA: Stanford University Press, 1995).
3 Liu, *Translingual Practice*, 26, my emphases.
4 Rebecca Walkowitz, *Born Translated: The Contemporary Novel in an Age of World Literature* (New York: Columbia University Press, 2015).
5 Antoine Berman, 'Translation and the Trials of the Foreign', *The Translation Studies Reader*, 3rd ed., ed. Lawrence Venuti (New York and London: Routledge, 2021), 240–53.
6 Karen Emmerich, *Literary Translation and the Making of Originals* (London: Bloomsbury, 2017).
7 Yasemin Yildiz, *Beyond the Mother Tongue: The Postmonolingual Condition* (New York: Fordham University Press, 2012).
8 David Gramling, *The Invention of Monolingualism* (London: Bloomsbury, 2016).
9 Maria Tymoczko, 'Ideology and the Position of the Translator: In What Sense Is a Translator "In Between"', in *Apropos of Ideology: Translation Studies on Ideology, Ideologies in Translation Studies*, ed. Maria Calzada Perez (New York and London: Routledge, 2003), 181–201.
10 Tymoczko, 'Ideology and the Position of the Translator', 200.
11 Bilge Karasu, *Uzun Sürmüş Bir Günün Akşamı* (Istanbul: Metis Publishing, 1971).
12 Bilge Karasu, *A Long Day's Evening*, trans. Aron Aji (San Francisco: City Lights, 2013).
13 Karasu, *Uzun Sürmüş Bir Günün*, 68.
14 Karasu, *A Long Day's Evening*, 80–81.

15 See Venuti's keynote address at the 2010 Convention of the American Literary Translators Association in Philadelphia is available, along with a response by Tim Parks, at https://mdash-ahb.org/the-translation-forum/1-towards-a-translation-culture/, accessed 29 October 2021.
16 Vladimir Nabokov, 'Problems of Translation: *Onegin* in English', *The Translation Studies Reader*, 113–25.
17 Carol Maier, 'A Woman in Translation, Reflecting', *Translation Review* 17, no. 1 (1985), 4–8.
18 Clive Scott, *Literary Translation and the Rediscovery of Reading* (Cambridge: Cambridge University Press, 2015).
19 Paul Ricoeur, *On Translation*, trans. Eileen Brennan (New York and London: Routledge, 2006), 9.

CHAPTER 11

Notes on the Translator's Space/The Editor's Place

Dan Gunn

As the conclusion to a three-day conference on 'Translation and Space', held in May 2019 at the University of Modena in Italy, the plenary speakers were invited back onto the dais in order to sum up what they would be taking away from the proceedings. My fellow panellists gave eloquent speeches to support their ideas: that *space* was indeed a crucial aspect of translation and translation theory, implicating everything from migration to digitisation; that *space* was, on the contrary and along with *borders* and *border-crossing*, a trope that had outlived its usefulness, not least in that it had tended to elide the critical importance of *time*, and time's relation to the passage of words and objects across languages and cultures; and abundant views situated between these two poles of space-endorsement and space-proscription.

Many of the theories expounded over the three days had appeared persuasive to me, and the broad arguments often seemed relevant, even urgent. Yet, when listening, my heart had raced only when hearing of particulars – examples. So I hope it was more than mere weariness, or the prospect of an excellent meal to follow, that reduced my own summary to a single sentence: 'What I take away from the conference', I announced, 'is that it's all in the detail.'

*

Another single sentence, this one from the tens of thousands uncovered, transcribed, translated, annotated, selected, and then published in the four-volume *Letters of Samuel Beckett* of which I was an editor: 'This vitaccia is terne beyond all belief.'[1]

Beckett writes this in the midst of a letter in English, on 24 February 1931, from Paris, to his great friend and predecessor at the Ecole Normale Supérieure, Tom MacGreevy, who was then back in Dublin. It is a fascinating statement in itself, of course, summing up the fatigue Beckett felt as a young man who still had to make his way in Paris, his anomie, everything

179

that contributed to making Dante's Belacqua so central to his worldview, slouched as this figure is at the base of the mountain of Purgatory, lacking the impetus even to begin to make the climb. But the statement also focuses the challenge to the editor I was (and am): what on earth to do – if anything – with such a sentence?

Any answer I found myself offering seemed to demonstrate just how thin the line was between scholarly editing and translating, this when the popular view of scholarly editing remains in arrears of the current view of translation; where in recent decades we have come to realise that, as the title of Lawrence Venuti's influential 2012 book has it, *Translation Changes Everything*,[2] the ideal of scholarly editing persists as one of achieving a transparency that allows the original to appear in its most lucid, unimpeachable, and indeed *original* form. To take a single example, Neil Fraistat and Julia Flanders begin their introduction to *The Cambridge Companion to Textual Scholarship* with the following caution, seeing their volume as being a corrective to precisely such a view: 'The role of the scholarly editor is too often assumed to be best performed when least visible: when the editorial work has produced a seamless artifact from which its own traces have been effaced.'[3] The neutrality to which textual editing may once have laid claim was one which, over twenty-five years, was stripped from me, as I attempted to edit the letters of the master-translator who was Beckett. I was left feeling as if, in editing, I were performing practically the same gestures that were habitually mine when working as a translator.

*

In 2014 I read and was greatly taken by a book on translation by one of the contributors to the present volume – *La malinconia del traduttore*, by Franco Nasi.[4] The idea occurred to me to ask of the author permission to attempt a translation of it for inclusion in the collection of chapbooks I run, the Cahiers Series. Only, before making this request, I had to contemplate the violence implicit in what I would be asking – and, when doing this, draw courage from my mentor in all matters editorial, Catharine Carver, one of the *éminences grises* of editorial practice in the latter half of the twentieth century.

It was through Catharine, who had become a friend years previously, that I was introduced to the Beckett letters project, she having been consulted by the editors named by Beckett himself, Martha Fehsenfeld and Lois Overbeck, who had been told that Catharine was the person best placed to give them advice on their project. (Catharine had been the editor of more celebrated writers than I ever fully understood, from Flannery

O'Connor to Leonard Cohen to Saul Bellow to Iris Murdoch to Richard Ellmann – and on; to her incomparable talent for editing fiction she added an expertise in the editing of biography and their invaluable support, letters.) Though not given to the confessional mode, one day during a pause in our work Catharine told me that of all the editorial jobs she had undertaken over the course of her long life, one that had given her particular satisfaction was the abridgement of Leon Edel's five-volume biography of Henry James to a single volume. What had afforded her special, almost mischievous pleasure, she explained, was the act of creating without adding a single word, as she cut and spliced sentences, paragraphs, pages, in a way that allowed her to make the book entirely her own while remaining quite as evanescent – as *grise* – as she believed a literary editor should be.[5]

All the issues of the Cahiers Series are roughly the same length, and this length cannot vary much because of the constraints of the form as well as of the binding. What this meant was that I would be obliged to ablate approximately three-quarters of Franco Nasi's book, while still trying somehow to give it a coherence. Before I started, I obviously had to ask permission of the author and sense his reaction to the prospect of major amputation being performed on a text which he had obviously laboured over for months if not years; my choice of medical metaphor is not random, as I did indeed feel rather like a surgeon who must announce both good and bad news.

*

Any catalogue of Beckett's statements in his letters about translating is likely to make for grim reading. Here is a brief sampling, all from 1957 and bearing on his attempt to translate *Fin de partie*: 'how sick and tired I am of translations and what a losing battle it is always'; 'I feel more and more strongly that it is a hopeless undertaking'; 'The French is at least 20% undecantable into English and will forfeit that much of whatever edge and tension it may have'; 'It is a hopeless undertaking'; 'excruciating results'; 'Heartbreaking work'. Then, the work done: 'I find it dreadful in English, all the sharpness gone, and the rhythms. If I were not bound by contract to the Royal Court Theatre, I wouldn't allow it in English at all.'[6]

In lodging his complaints to his friends, Beckett signals that the very term *translation* is tendentious, when what he is attempting is a 'decanting', what he calls 'englishing or anglo-irishing'.[7] Yet even as he points towards the abyss between two languages, and the pain involved in having to descend into that abyss, Beckett is indeed finding expressions in English that do service. And when *Endgame* comes to be staged in London, he is so attached to certain words – English words – that he is willing to forgo the entire production if he cannot have them present: when the Lord Chamberlain takes exception to God's being called 'the bastard', Beckett reluctantly offers as a substitute 'the swine'; and when that goes down no better with the public censor, he refuses further compromise, leaving the play to be presented, at its London premiere, in French.

*

The groans over *Fin de partie* are as nothing compared to what Beckett emits when he is goaded by his French publisher Jérôme Lindon to release, more than twenty years after writing them, the story *Premier amour* and the novel *Mercier et Camier*. 'Lindon dug up Premier Amour I know not where,' he writes to his friend and lover the translator Barbara Bray. 'He wants to publish limited with Mercier & Camier. Couldn't bring myself to reread either.'[8] When he is subsequently pushed by his British publisher John Calder to put these texts into English, he resists at first, before averring: 'I capitulate.' But then he adds, almost menacingly: 'I hope you don't realize what this will involve for me.'[9]

The resourcefulness Beckett deploys in 'Englishing' *First Love* has been much commented upon, not least by Christopher Ricks in his wonderful *Beckett's Dying Words*.[10] To take an example from the story's opening page, the unremarkable 'Personellement je n'ai rien contre les cimetières' becomes, more than twenty-five years later, 'Personally I have no bone to pick with graveyards' – a few extra macabre drops squeezed from the avowal.[11] Still more noteworthy is the following, when the protagonist-narrator admits to being so infatuated with Lulu (or Anne, as he later renames her) that he has to ask himself the precise nature of this love, wondering if it is of the intellectual variety, and concluding: 'Je ne peux pas le croire. Car, si je l'avais aimée de cette manière, est-ce que je me serais amusé à tracer le mot Anne sur d'immémoriaux excréments de bovin. A arracher à plein main les orties.'[12] This translates into English: 'For had my love been of this kind would I have stopped to inscribe the letters of Anna in time's forgotten cowpats? To divellicate urtica *plenis manibus*.'[13] Something funnier and stranger has emerged, certainly – Beckett is often funnier in English than in French. But is it really a translation? Indeed, is it even *legitimate*?

Any answer to these questions is likely to have to appeal to the proper name of the author and arbiter of the two texts, in a gesture that appears quaintly old-fashioned or wildly inappropriate in the context of Beckett's work, which so ruthlessly deconstructs the proper name and the notion of the originary authorial subject. Should one postulate at least two Becketts: Beckett-translator who here has morphed into Beckett-editor?

What is surely the case is that I am being misleading in suggesting that his translation of this last sentence is 'into English', since it is into something more like *Latin-in-English*. Ricks educes a rationale to the Latinism: 'Within Beckett, it will often be a dead language which will strike the right note and a chill.'[14] And Ricks is surely right to sense that in his opting for the foreigner – the dead foreigner – Beckett is putting into relief the imaginary nature of the gap between original and copy, in which gap I espy the editor, floundering:

> The antithesis of translation and creation is both indispensable and inadequate, and the same goes for texture and context in the very writing. In all of these cases, we shall need, not to settle for, but not to be unsettled by, the conviction that the terms antithesized are distinguishable even though they are not distinct.[15]

*

It is no coincidence, presumably, that most of Beckett's major correspondents were linguists, able to cope with such sentences as the one with which I opened ('This vitaccia …'). When addressing Tom MacGreevy, Beckett would occasionally write in French, particularly when broaching a subject he judged to be private. To his Dutch translator Jacoba van Velde he would write in French, but occasionally in English. His letters to Barbara Bray are scattered with languages other than the dominant one, English, and when in Tunisia he even sometimes dates his missives using the Hejira calendar. With the great friend of his later years, Avigdor Arikha, he would commonly converse in German, though he wrote to him mostly in French; Arikha may have been the only one fluent in even more languages than Beckett – 'Seven, on a good day', he told me one year before his death.

The temptation is to think of Beckett's friends and correspondents as great movers across countries and languages. But they were also something like the contrary: the interlocutors for whom he did not have to *move across*, for whom he could stay in the language which best expressed whatever notion had come into his head at that particular moment. For us transcribers of Beckett's infamously impenetrable handwriting, this repudiation of translation proved a nightmare. Long hours our team would pore over a letter in French to Arikha, for example, in which Beckett recounts how inert he is feeling. 'Oui, trop de main nuit', he writes, 'trop de tête aussi, trop de trop peu sans doute aussi, mais c'est par là la seule chance qui nous reste.' Not the easiest of formulations, but at least we were confident of our reading. The sentence that follows was straightforward enough: 'Je ne fais rien.'[16] But what followed defied and almost defeated us, even though we collectively had several score years of experience in decrypting Beckett's 'foul fist' (as he himself described his hand). What followed was – as one of us transcribers suddenly spotted – 'Drift about, la tête à mille lieues'.

*

When trying to follow Beckett on his excursions through the languages of Europe, I was often made to think of a novel – or *autofiction* as we might call it these days – whose force derives in no small order from a similar excursion. Curzio Malaparte's *The Skin* is a work which formulates an ideal of Europe and its languages in and from the ashes left by its conflagration in World War II. There is one scene in particular that would habitually focus my fascination with the tension between translation and the resistance to translation, a scene which makes it unavoidably clear that the decisions – to translate or not to translate; to elide geographical and linguistic specificity or to respect it – are always in some sense bound up with realities of power as well as with fantasies of belonging.

The scene is one where the narrator-protagonist, named Malaparte, shares a lunch of couscous with some French and American officers as they overlook Rome, which they are about to enter after the German withdrawal from the city in June 1944; the couscous may or may not contain the boiled hand of a *goumier* who has recently stepped on a mine. What the novel has up to here presented is an extraordinary series of grotesques, hyperboles, and paradoxes; outrageous scenes of abjection and debauchery that have accompanied the allies since their arrival in Naples on their advance north through the Italian peninsula. The officers speak with Malaparte in French or Italian, indifferently, as they upbraid him for all the snobbery and exaggeration they find in his earlier account of the war, published shortly before as *Kaputt*; their dialogue, in both the Italian original (*La Pelle*) and in the English translation, is recorded in French, Italian, and English, into which regularly obtrude words from several other European languages, German notably. Malaparte is taunted by Pierre Lyautey, who claims, 'Judging from *Kaputt* ... one would say that Malaparte eats nothing but nightingales' hearts, served on plates of old Meissen and Nymphenburg porcelain at the tables of Royal Highnesses, Duchesses and Ambassadors.'[17] Malaparte's rejoinder is a remarkable encomium on the qualities of the fare they have just ingested – which may or may not have included the *goumier*'s hand but which in any case is, for him, the glorious product of the geographical and historical diversity that constitutes Europe. The supra-national linguistic space that he is trying to carve out – an ideal European home to which they might all belong – depends upon the untranslated and untranslatable nature of the dialogue that has preceded his speech, as well as upon the absolute particularity of proper names and localities, upon which he expands:

> Do you remember the Liri trout – slim and silvery, with delicate fins that diffuse a faint green radiance and have a faint green radiance and have a darker, mellower silveriness? The miniature trout from the Liri are like those found in the Black Forest; they are like the Blauforellen of the Neckar – the poets' river, the river of Hölderling – and of the Titisee; they resemble the Blauforellen found in the Danube at Donaueschingen, where the Danube has its source. That regal river rises in the park of the castle of the Princes of Fürstenburg, in a white marble basin that looks like a cradle and is adorned with neoclassical statues.[18]

And so it goes on, for another page and more, concatenating geography and history in a European microcosm where the proliferation of proper names asserts an absolute particularity that turns at the same time mythically pervasive and ubiquitous: Europe is in this dish, here, now, always – not least in the laughter the homily is intended to evoke, the laugh of a Europe defeated and dismembered.

Malaparte's motive for eroding the symbiotic bond between nations and languages derives from a politics, and a personality, the polar opposite of Beckett's. But the assertion that it is possible to recognise the languages of Europe in their differences while also intimating that they share some common source, or more importantly that they can *create* a sodality of speakers and readers who are united not by nation but by a rejection of monolingualism – and thereby of translation as narrowly conceived, with its traditional assumed hierarchies of source and target – is one I came to believe that they shared.

*

Given how often Beckett apologises for his handwriting, and is obliged to supply words that proved illegible in previous letters, he must have been aware that only a portion of any of his handwritten missives would in fact be read. Could MacGreevy decipher 'vitaccia' or 'terne' – or Arikha 'Drift about'? Yet that he was capable of writing clearly is attested to by the fact that a vast number of his letters did arrive at their destination (and were kept).

When Beckett felt cornered or coerced, especially into an intimacy or confederacy he was resisting – the case of Barbara Bray after she moved from London to Paris in 1961 may be the clearest example – there appears a deterioration in his handwriting not attributable solely to his cataracts or to the Dupuytren's contracture affecting his hand. Yet, rather in the manner of translators who turn what may be nonsensical or incomprehensible into sense – rather as if we had sat *Godot*'s Lucky down and enjoined him to speak to us in *complete plain words* – we editors transformed all the hesitations and concealments his handwriting could contain into uniformly legible type.

*

Beckett himself could use translation as a means to achieve a merciless sort of revision. Once he – reluctantly – gets going on *Mercier et Camier*, he reports, in a letter to Bray, 'Advance slowly with M.&C. Much left unsolved such as 'petite reine' (bicycle).'[19] Three days later, things are only worse, as he again explains to Bray: 'Come to a stop for the moment with M. & C. Too depressing and in no mood to give particular satisfaction in Brewer St.' – Brewer Street being the home of the prospective publisher of his translation, Calder and Boyars.[20] He subsequently applauds Bray's suggestion of 'Raleigh' for 'petite reine' but admits, 'stuck at end of Chap. 1 in translation. Even worse in English.'[21] Nineteen months later he can report to the American academic Ruby Cohn: 'My translation abandoned for the moment.'[22] And six months after this, to Cohn again: 'Misspent 10 days at Ussy, among the missel thrushes madly breeding, typing out what I'd translated of M. & C.', adding wryly, 'Gastric trouble ever since'.[23] Until, more than one year later, he can write to his close friend Jocelyn Herbert: 'Nothing of interest with me. Potter along among what feel like the last odds & ends. Finished translating Mercier & Camier, that old ghost, rough draft, months of revision & retyping left to do.'[24]

More than three years on the job, and what does Beckett have to show for it? A novel in English entitled *Mercier and Camier*, as it states on the frontispiece, 'Translated from the original by the author'. Does the novel deserve to bear the same name when it is at least 12 per cent shorter, many passages having been left out entirely – including the one that speaks of the 'petite reine'?[25]

Beckett *could* not translate certain passages, or *would* not? The distinction is hardly sustainable. Only later, near the end of his career, does he decide that a text, *Worstward Ho*, is irremediably untranslatable: 'I find Worstward Ho untranslatable & shall not try', he writes – because he had tried, and failed; 'Personally I cannot translate Worstward Ho & it will not appear in French.'²⁶ (It *did* appear in French, years later, in a translation by Edith Fournier, with the title *Cap au pire*.)

*

If the graphic surface of any Beckett letter may be radically simplified when transcribed, then the same holds for the writing's material support, which is likely either to disappear or be reduced to a gnomic notation. So much in the human exchange that is – or was – correspondence gets lost in the passage into print, not least the life of the letter after it was sent – the *afterlife*. This, when the question of how much of a text – *after* its author has released it or given up on it or lost it – should be retained is one that will of course have confronted every experienced translator. To translate the editorial amendments or not, the variants, the authorial *pentimenti*? And what to do with a text of which several versions compete for attention?

Such questions returned to me when, in 2016, I was helping to catalogue a collection of Beckett letters, and I noticed that several envelopes, and more surprisingly postcards, had holes in them where their stamps had been cut or torn out. The son of Beckett's friends to whom the missives had been sent and whose collection I was cataloguing explained to me that the arrival of a letter from abroad was quite an event, for postman and concierge, through whom the teenage philatelist on the stair would be alerted, who would turn up shortly after at the family flat, hopeful. Given how precious Beckett's friendship was to both parents, the sacrifice involved in excision of a stamp must have been considerable. One such wounded card had been sent from Taroudant in Morocco depicting a 'Mehariste Saharien' – a 'Warrior of the Sahara', who sits astride a camel whose nose has just been spared by scissors that have cut a generous margin around the stamp.

*

Even though Beckett was an intensely visually alert writer, few of his picture postcards made it into our heavily text-dominant four volumes. Two cards, amongst many others, failed to be selected because their texts alone were of limited interest; yet they come alive when combined with their image.

One was sent to his childhood friend, later lover, Mary Manning, whose husband Mark Howe had recently died. The message of condolence is not exceptional; but the image is entirely surprising, being of a tall, statuesque member of the British aristocracy, depicted by Thomas Gainsborough in all her eighteenth-century finery – a style of dress, and of painting, entirely at odds with Beckett's characteristic aesthetic. An enigmatic choice, until the name of the painter's subject is known: Lady Mary Howe – a visual joke, then, leavening the message of condolence.

Or a card sent to a young admirer, André Bernold, in which the text is mostly an apology for not being well enough to meet up in person. But the image: of a painting from 1942 entitled *The Two Travellers* by one of the few painters, Jack B. Yeats, whose work Beckett, that least acquisitive of men, actively sought to collect. Two men on a road leading nowhere, both hatted, turning to one another; one of them is holding a bag or small case – quite as if they were demanding speech bubbles from *En attendant Godot/Waiting for Godot*.

The single word that appears most commonly when Beckett talks of translation is 'loss'. To translate is to lose, in at least two senses of this word, and to commit to the act of mourning that must accompany loss if loss is not to become overwhelming. (There may be ways that the open-ended nature of digital media can attenuate the comparable feeling of loss that is likely to beset the literary editor who is obliged constantly to make choices that imply exclusions and sacrifices. However, my suspicion is that the fantasy of completeness that digital editions may foster, with no page limit or terminal date-stamp, is likely to find a comparable loss in an awareness that the plethora of material can never find the ideal reader to whom it is directed – that the reader's limits soon come to substitute for the book's or the volume's or the publisher's.)

*

Any dream we editors might have nurtured of *completeness* was undone from the outset, not only by the fact that our edition was to appear shortly after Beckett's death, with many letters still in private hands and only gradually emerging into the light of day, but also and above all by Beckett's vague instructions as to the remit of the edition, which ended up lending undue importance to one statement he had made, restricting permission to 'those passages only having bearing on my work'.[27] However this statement was to be interpreted – and every single individual interpreted it differently – it was clearly not a blanket endorsement. Loss was built into our project from the outset. Yet despite this, each of our four volumes, for a reason so obvious that it took me some time to see it, has since come to feel to me plethoric, jam-packed, almost embarrassingly profligate.

I have often been asked the reason why his most trusted publisher, Jérôme Lindon of Les Editions de Minuit, who after Beckett's death became his literary executor, was so adamantly opposed to his most cherished author's letters appearing in print – an opposition that delayed our publication by many years. The first reason, I surmised, was a highly principled one that had guided the editorial policy of Minuit – originally a clandestine press established during the Occupation – from the time Lindon had taken it over, which determined that as little information as possible should be given about the house's writers, ensuring all the emphasis should be on the work. (The covers of Minuit books were traditionally blank but for titles and names; Lindon had chosen not to publish in French Beckett's biography by James Knowlson even though it had been authorised.) The second reason, I felt almost sure after discussions with Lindon, was that the letters that he was reading, almost all from the 1930s, when Beckett's writing was its most obscure – the letters to Nuala Costello, for example, are hermetic – were not comprehensible to him; even my co-editor George Craig, who had followed in Beckett's footsteps at Trinity College Dublin and the Ecole Normal Supérieure twenty-five years later, often struggled to understand him. Rather than give the benefit of the doubt, Lindon preferred to err on the side of caution. But it was the third, and what I judged to be most compelling reason, that bears upon the sort of translation that we were effecting in turning letters into books – a reason that can be summed up in a single word: *jealousy.*

At every step of our editorial process our endeavours were impeded by the shock Beckett's correspondents experienced when they realised just how many close companions, friends, lovers, correspondents, Beckett had; this when, almost without exception, they had judged themselves to have been singled out as special, even unique.

The sense of having been chosen for particular attention, of having been anointed even, speaks volumes of Beckett's ability to home in on the other's interests and to offer his undivided attention – either when physically present or through letters. However, it also speaks of how effective he was at compartmentalising his companions and colleagues, keeping them blithely unaware of one other: he had his theatre friends, his drinking buddies, his painters, his family members, his musicians, his translators; he had his wife, his principal lover (Bray), his several other lovers ... There were overlaps, of course, but to take one example, the novelist Robert Pinget, who kept a journal of his friendship with Beckett, broke off this journal in despondency when he realised that he was not quite so special or privileged as he had imagined himself to be.[28]

Yet, in our edition of Beckett's letters, the regime is one of uncritical promiscuity, where the individuals he sought to avoid assembling are compressed together within covers that turn a lifetime of scrupulousness into – as in my own more despondent moments I feared it had become – something approaching a *partouze*.

The violence is not to be underestimated: witness the play entitled *Play*, from 1962–1963, written not long after Barbara Bray left London to join Beckett in Paris, with its depiction of a hellish lovers' triangle, and what may be its most memorable line: 'Adulterers, take warning, never admit.'[29]

*

In stating his opposition to bilingual editions of his work, Beckett wrote the following (in a letter to his editor at Faber and Faber): 'I am not keen on bilingual edition of the novels or the plays … It suggests an invitation to consider the work as a linguistic curiosity, or an adventure in self-translation, which does not appeal to me.'[30]

What follows, in conclusion to the present notes, comes therefore with apologies to the one whom we chose to contract to 'SB', and whose letters in their several languages feature, in our edition, a translation into English directly beneath them …

The French, German, and Italian versions of Beckett's letters (published by Gallimard, Suhrkamp, and Adelphi respectively) print the letters only in their own language. I continue to ask myself if this editorial policy constitutes a display of respect for one of the great translators of the twentieth century, or the exact contrary; both seem, rather as in the rabbit-duck illusion, intermittently, flickeringly, to be plausible.

The French version of that sentence with which I opened, as offered by André Topia (where the word *version*, in this context, carries something of the French word signifying *translation* – into French – as opposed to *thème* – out of French), reads: 'Cette vitaccia est incroyablement *terne* (*…* intending 'in French in the original').[31] The German, by Chris Hirte, reads: 'Diese vitaccia ist terne wie nur was'; the underline is Beckett's, but the French intruder goes un-signalled in the text, receiving a translation – 'öde' – in a footnote.[32] The Italian, by Massimo Bocchiola and Leonardo Marcello Pignataro, reads: 'Questa *vitaccia* è plumbea da non credere', where the underline becomes italics, obliging a footnote which signals that 'vitaccia' is 'in italiano nel testo', and where 'terne' turns Italian.[33]

Sad to admit, our own attempt to do justice to the master-translator-who-so-mistrusted-translation turned into a pusillanimous footnote, satisfactory only in that it reflects the flatness that Beckett himself is evincing: '"vitaccia" (It., miserable life, wretched existence); "terne" (dull, colourless)'.[34]

*

As I was busy amputating limbs and ablating organs from *La Malinconia del traduttore*, I understood better the origin of Franco Nasi's fascination with the colour blue, as well as how it was informed by his time spent in the music clubs of Chicago. As I performed my gruesome operation, I even came to know the book's author. And I was therefore able to salve my conscience somewhat when, *viva voce*, I witnessed his delight at my proposal that the title for the cahier that his book was about to become should be: *Translator's Blues*.[35]

It was as if, after all the surgery, the Italian had been waiting for this moment of English-language homecoming.

*

The dinner to which the speakers at the Modena conference on 'Translation and Space' were invited at the end of the three days' proceedings proved to be as excellent as I had anticipated. As my appetite subsided, I started almost to regret that I had been so terse in my response to the question about what I had learned from the conference.

And then I noticed the menu on the table next to mine, my eyes alighting on one of its entries: 'Tagliatelle al ragù' had become, in translation (in italics) directly beneath it, '*Tagliatelle with a Bolognese sauce*'.

Notes

1 Samuel Beckett, *The Letters of Samuel Beckett* [henceforth *LSB*] *I: 1929–1940*, ed. Martha Dow Fehsenfeld and Lois More Overbeck, with George Craig and Dan Gunn (Cambridge: Cambridge University Press, 2009), 68.
2 Lawrence Venuti, *Translation Changes Everything* (London and New York: Routledge, 2012).
3 Neil Fraistat and Julia Flanders, 'Introduction: Textual Scholarship in the Age of Media Consciousness', in *The Cambridge Companion to Textual Scholarship*, ed. Neil Fraistat and Julia Flanders (Cambridge: Cambridge University Press, 2013), 1.
4 Franco Nasi, *La Melancolia del traduttore* (Milan: Medusa Edizioni, 2008).
5 See Lyall H. Powers, 'Leon Edel: The Life of a Biographer', *The American Scholar* 66, no. 4 (Fall 1997), 598.
6 Letters of 30 January 1957 to Thomas MacGreevy, Trinity College Dublin, MacGreevy collection; 16 February 1957 to George Devine, Harry Ransom Center, University of Texas in Austin, Beckett Collection; 6 April 1957 to Barney Rosset in Samuel Beckett, *LSB III: 1957–1966*, ed. George Craig, Martha Fehsenfeld, Dan Gunn, and Lois More Overbeck (Cambridge University Press, 2014), 38; 7 May 1957 to Donald McWhinnie, *LSB III*, 46; 18 May 1957 to Barney Rossett, Grove Press Records, The George Arents Research

Center, Syracuse University Libraries; 23 May 1957 to Jake Schwartz, Harry Ransom Center, University of Texas in Austin, Beckett Collection; 3 July 1957 to Thomas MacGreevy, Trinity College Dublin, MacGreevy collection.
7 25 January 1957 to Jack Lambert, Bodleian Library, University of Oxford, J. W. Lambert papers.
8 7 January 1969, *LSB IV: 1967–1989*, ed. George Craig, Martha Fehsenfeld, Dan Gunn, and Lois More Overbeck (Cambridge University Press, 2016), 144.
9 31 January 1970, *LSB IV*, 222.
10 Christopher Ricks, *Beckett's Dying Words* (Oxford: Oxford University Press, 1993).
11 Samuel Beckett, *Premier amour* (Paris: Les Editions de Minuit, 1970), 8; Samuel Beckett, *First Love*, in *The Complete Shorter Prose, 1929–1989*, ed. S. E. Gontarski (New York: Grove Press, 1995), 25.
12 *Premier amour*, 30–31.
13 *First Love*, 35.
14 *Beckett's Dying Words*, 98.
15 *Beckett's Dying Words*, 98.
16 Letter of 25 April 1963, *LSB III*, 540. In George Craig's translation, this becomes: 'Yes, too much hand does harm, too much head as well, no doubt too much too little does as well – but it's our one remaining chance. I am doing nothing.'
17 Curzio Malaparte, *The Skin*, trans. David Moore (Evanston, IL: Northwestern University Press, 1997), 283.
18 Malaparte, *The Skin*, 285–6.
19 Letter of 12 May 1970, *LSB IV*, 230.
20 Letter of 15 May 1970, *LSB IV*, 232.
21 Letter of 1 June 1970, *LSB IV*, 234.
22 Letter of 10 January 1972, *LSB IV*, 280.
23 Letter of 16 June 1972, *LSB IV*, 299.
24 Letter of 20 August 1973, *LSB IV*, 341–2.
25 See Steven Connor, 'Traduttore, Traditore: Samuel Beckett's Translation of *Mercier and Camier*', *Journal of Beckett Studies* 11/12 (1989), 27–46.
26 Letter to Charles Krance of 1 July 1985, *LSB IV*, 657; on Beckett's draft of a short section of *Worstward Ho*, see letter to Jérôme Lindon of 7 May 1985, *LSB IV*, 565–7; and letter to András Barkóczi of 17 June 1986, *LSB IV*, 678. In his Translator's Preface to *LSB IV*, George Craig educes reasons why this text in particular may have thwarted Beckett-the-translator.
27 See General Introduction to *LSB* I, xxi.
28 Entry dated 16 June 1961 in 'Notre ami Samuel Beckett', unclassified in the Bibliothèque littéraire Jacques Doucet.
29 Samuel Beckett, *Play*, in *The Complete Dramatic Works* (London: Faber and Faber, 2006), 310.
30 Letter to Peter du Sautoy of 17 April 1965, *LSB IV*, 665.
31 Samuel Beckett, *Lettres I, 1929–1940*, ed. Martha Dow Fehsenfeld and Lois More Overbeck, with George Craig and Dan Gunn, trans. André Topia (Paris: Gallimard, 2014), 160.

32 Samuel Beckett, *Weitermachen ist mehr, als ich tun kann, Briefe 1929–1940*, ed. Martha Dow Fehsenfeld and Lois More Overbeck, with George Craig and Dan Gunn, trans. Chris Hirte (Berlin: Suhrkamp Verlag, 2013), 140.
33 Samuel Beckett, *Lettere Volume I: 1929–1940*, ed. Martha Dow Fehsenfeld and Lois More Overbeck, with George Craig and Dan Gunn, trans. Massimo Bocchiola and Leonardo Marcello Pignataro (Milan: Adelphi, 2017), 45.
34 Beckett, *LSB I*, 70.
35 Franco Nasi, *Translator's Blues*, trans. Dan Gunn (London: Sylph Editions and The American University of Paris, 2015).

CHAPTER 12

The State of Things

Chad Post

To the casual observer living in an anglophone country (I'll be focusing exclusively on the situation in the United States in this essay), the past decade has ushered in a new golden age of literature in translation. This rise in the number of works being translated into English, and the attention they receive, has roughly corresponded with my career in publishing, first as associate director at Dalkey Archive Press, then as publisher of Open Letter Books at the University of Rochester, where I also maintain the Three Percent website and its associated projects.

Using the Translation Database – which I maintain for *Publishers Weekly* – we can see that the number of translated works of fiction and poetry published in the USA on an annual basis has increased from ~360 in 2008 to over 600 (2016–18). In addition to the Best Translated Book Award (founded on the Three Percent website in 2008), the National Book Foundation launched a National Book Award for Translation. Attendance at the American Literary Translators Association (ALTA) annual conference has almost doubled over this same period. The number of institutions of higher learning in the USA offering courses or degrees in literary translation continues to grow. *My Brilliant Friend*, the first book in Elena Ferrante's Neapolitan Quartet, was a hit HBO show. (And a best-selling book – something that's incredibly rare for a work in translation.)

These successes have created a belief in the possibility of literature in translation being profitable. Publishing houses – like most content producers – have a tendency to chase after trends, to try and replicate what has already worked in the marketplace. This can happen on a macro level (publishing more international writers overall in hopes of discovering the next worldwide phenomenon) or on a more micro level (looking for Italian titles about female friendship similar to Ferrante's works).

One result of the commercial success of authors such as Roberto Bolaño or Elena Ferrante is the significant growth in the number of publishers who produce literature in translation. AmazonCrossing started publishing works in translation in 2010 and consistently does more than anyone else in America. (They brought out 61 titles in 2016.) Transit Books, Two Lines, Open Letter (the press I run at the University of Rochester), New Vessel, Deep Vellum, and Restless Books are all recent entrants to the world of international literature, joining more established presses like Archipelago, Dalkey Archive Press, Europa Editions, and New Directions, who have continued to expand the number of translations they publish every year. And in early 2019, HarperVia – a new imprint of HarperCollins – was launched with the goal of publishing around twenty-four titles in translation a year.

That's not even taking into consideration all the literary journals that are now accepting and publishing more translated pieces. From online-only venues like *Words Without Borders* (the grandmother of online magazines dedicated to international literature) and *Asymptote*, to places like *Gulf Coast* and *The Massachusetts Review* and *Two Lines* and *Arkansas International*.

Beyond that though, there's a sense that at least some foreign authors are now household names. Well, maybe not exactly 'household', but it's hard to imagine even a quarter of knowledgeable readers being able to name a single contemporary foreign writer back in 2004, whereas sixteen years later it's hard to imagine that any serious reader *hasn't* heard of Knausgaard or Ferrante or Sebald or Bolaño.

And according to a March 6, 2019, article in the *Guardian*, sales of translated books in the UK were up 5.5 per cent in 2018, part of a 'steady' rise in sales. Translation into English is having a moment!

But if that's the case, then why aren't the numbers *bigger*? It's definitely encouraging that the number of translated works of fiction and poetry published in the USA has 'skyrocketed' to over 600, but it feels a bit blusterous when you remember that some 50,000 literary titles originally written in English also came out last year. Although attendance at the ALTA conference has doubled, that means that only around 500 translators come every year. Compare that with the 16,000 attendees of the American Writing Programs conference in Portland in March 2019 and you will be reminded that for all the seemingly good news about the publishing of international literature, the overall figures are still relatively *small*.

Even that *Guardian* article is a bit of a bummer. Sure, sales are up 5.5 per cent, but what's missing from the article is the increase in the overall number of translated books published in 2018. What if the total number of translations increased by 10 per cent, but the sales only by 5.5 per cent? That's definitely *not* the article that would spark additional interest in the Man Booker International longlist, which was announced just a few days later. Besides, translations have been belittled for so long, with pieces like 'America Yawns at Foreign Fiction' and 'Why Americans Don't Read Foreign Fiction' appearing regularly at places like the *New York Times* and *Daily Beast*. Given that, who can fault the *Guardian* for being a bit overly optimistic?

However, if you look at the *Guardian*'s list of the ten best-selling translations of 2018, you might be surprised to find out that the number one title, *The Thirst*, by Jo Nesbø (who also holds down the second place slot with his novel *Macbeth*), only sold 123,066 copies. That puts it at number sixty on the list of overall 2018 best-sellers (with *Macbeth* not placing in the top 100), behind such classics as *Gangsta Granny*, *The Wonky Donkey*, *12 Rules for Life: An Antidote to Chaos*, and *5 Ingredients – Quick & Easy Food*. Also worth noting: the best-selling title in the UK in 2018 was *Eleanor Oliphant Is Completely Fine*, which sold 806,469 copies – almost seven times more copies than Nesbø's thriller.

And to put *that* in context: around 15 *million* people saw *Captain Marvel* on opening weekend. Which is almost twenty times the number of people who bought *Eleanor Oliphant Is Completely Fine* over the entire course of 2018.

Aspirational Publishing Don't Need No Data

Over the years, the general lack of broad, reliable data has made the publishing industry tough to accurately assess and analyse. Let's start with Nielsen BookScan. Launched in 2001, BookScan collects point of sale data from a number of book retailers, providing publishers with details on how many copies of a particular book were actually sold to customers over a given period.

At the time, BookScan was revolutionary for a couple different reasons. First off, until then, publishers had only a vague sense how many copies of their books were actually sold to readers. They could gather data on how many copies they had shipped to bookstores, wholesalers, and direct to readers, but had no idea how many of those copies shipped to stores were still sitting on shelves, soon to be returned due to lack of interest.

A word for the uninitiated: returns have been the bane of publishing for decades. During the heyday of the expansion of the superstores (especially Barnes & Noble), it wasn't unusual to 'sell' a significant number of copies of a particular book to a chain store, only to have 50 per cent or more of those come back six months later. 'Sales' were always best guesses, and publishers lived in fear of finding out that the 'sell-through' rate for their books was much smaller than they had anticipated.

BookScan remedied that. Sort of. Now publishers can know, more or less, how many of the copies advanced to stores end up in the hands of customers. The problem is that it doesn't track *all* the bookstores. Not all stores participate, and direct sales from the publisher to the consumer aren't counted either. The conventional wisdom is that BookScan captures, at best, about 75 per cent of all sales. It's still impossible to know how accurate (or inaccurate) these numbers are, since it's in the best interest of publishers to downplay what percentage of total sales are tracked. (The history of publishing is a series of exaggerations.) And there's no easy way for journalists to get honest figures from publishers because, again, it's not in their best interest to be honest, especially if benevolent dishonesty can generate more buzz. (I've always been told that it's OK to multiply your print run by four. So, when we print a lead title at Open Letter, we obviously have an initial print run of 20,000. Which is a lie, and also a pretty lame one, since 20,000 isn't a very large number in the cultural sphere. See, again, *Captain Marvel* or the number of listeners to your favourite podcast.)

This isn't meant to undercut the overall value of BookScan, because it is, for better or worse, the best source of data that we have. Even when it's incomplete, it's consistently incomplete: you can measure titles against one another and see how titles are doing in a relative sense. And, prior to BookScan, the *New York Times* best-seller list was based on a survey – not even on actual sales.

Let that sink in for a minute. It's an ill-kept industry secret that, even today, the *New York Times* best-seller list isn't 100 per cent objective, but is created out of BookScan data plus a bit of editorial intervention.

Given its primacy in discussions of which books to publish, which authors to invest in, and how to allocate marketing budgets, sales ought to be the *most* reliable data set for publishers. But given that even sales numbers are a bit slippery, the question becomes: are there any numbers that are more certain?

Well ... not really. Publishers live and die by aspiration. They don't do market research, there are no focus groups (like there was for, say, *Captain Marvel*), the profit and loss sheets they put together for titles they want to publish are loaded with hope – especially given that at least 50 per cent of a book's success is based on luck.

Luck driven by availability bias. The success stories mentioned above are the ones that readily come to mind when thinking about literature in English translation; the success of these authors and books feels both significant and inevitable in retrospect. But what I didn't list above were the hundreds and hundreds of authors whose books sold fewer than 500 copies, the presses that do two books in translation a year, the fact that the increase in the number of translations published annually has *stalled*. We have no counterfactuals at hand, so it's easy for publishing – an industry wedded to imitation and trend chasing – to believe its own narrative of success. It's human nature to look for explanations, for causality, and to frame ending results in a more mechanistic, logical way. By coming up with plausible, replicable explanations for why something sold really well, publishers take credit for breakout books, and blame bad luck for the titles that didn't reach their audience.

The point of this essay isn't to poke fun at the flawed thinking of publishing employees, but to try and step back for a second and seriously assess the translation field circa 2020 and contemplate what issues are holding us back, and what the future might look like.

Three Problems for Translation

(1) *For the past decade, the focus on the total number of books published in translation annually has helped 'normalize' international literature, but sales haven't kept pace, causing smaller presses to struggle under extreme financial pressures.*

In 2005, when the PEN World Voices Festival was relaunched, translator/academic Esther Allen convinced Bowker – the purveyor of ISBN numbers, the 13-digit numbers that distinguish one book from another – to figure out how many books published in the USA were in translation. Her hope was to get a bit of information that would entice various publications to write about the festival. Instead, she got a number that redefined the conversation for years to come.

Bowker wasn't the first entity to state that around 3 per cent of all books published here in the USA were translated into English – the National Endowment for the Arts had said as much, although their methodology was too quirky for them to stand behind it. And translator/translation theorist Lawrence Venuti in *The Translator's Invisibility* produced some rough charts showing that, no matter what decade you choose, only 2–4 per cent of all publications that came out during that period were translations into English.[1]

What happened when Bowker came out with their figure – which, to be honest, was a bit ill-defined, since it lacked granularity and specificity – was a doubling-down by non-profit organizations on *producing* more works in translation.

The general argument was that the asymmetrical flow of literary culture – English-language titles are translated and published throughout the world, but next to nothing comes back from those countries into English – is bad for American culture. Put in the best light, because of this imbalance, readers are being deprived of important literary voices from around the world, but to many, this insularity reflects the cultural arrogance of perceived American superiority.

As a result, the presses named above (Deep Vellum, Restless, New Vessel, Transit, AmazonCrossing, etc.) came into existence. Universities invested in translation programs. The creation of global literary citizens – through schooling, the publication of more books, the professionalization of the field of translation – became a particular focus among translation advocates. And yet, the philanthropic money needed to transform this aspect of book culture has yet to materialize, and the 3 per cent argument devolved into a lamentation about costs instead of opportunities.

It costs a normal independent press around $35,000 to publish a translated book. That includes staff salaries, printing, marketing, operational costs, rights to the book, and payment to the translator. If you use the $100/1,000 word standard (or £95/1,000 in the UK), it generally costs $7,500 to translate a 300-page novel – 20 per cent of the total costs of publication.

That would be fine if books sold more than 5,500 copies, on average. (Quick information dump: the average book is $16, and the publisher gets 30 per cent of that after bookstore discounts and distribution fees, which is around $4.80/copy sold against that $35,000 outlay.) But, for worse, that's not the case.

A 2016 article in the *Guardian* makes the argument that translated fiction is 'punching above its weight'.[2] The basic argument goes as such: if 3.5 per cent of the books produced were in translation, and if translations sold as well, on average, as books written in English, they would account for 3.5 per cent of sales. But they don't – they accounted for 7 per cent of all sales dollars in 2015. Which begs an explanation. What are some reasons for why translations would sell better – on average – than fiction originally written in English?

One possible reason: readers are hungry for international literature.

As much as I want to believe this is true, it's also highly unlikely. There is anecdotal evidence, for sure, but listicles, best-seller lists, Twitter mentions, staff recommendations in bookstores, water-cooler conversations, etc., still revolve around authors writing in English. There's a reason why most international authors, given the choice (as was recently the case with

Valeria Luiselli), choose to write in English instead of waiting for their books to be translated.

Using BookScan – and incorporating its incompleteness into my methodology – I estimated the sales of all books in translation published in January 2018. Only four of the translated titles published that month yielded sales projections of more than 1,000 copies over the course of 2018. Once more, with context: 90 per cent of the translated books published in January 2018 will create less than $6,400 in revenue for their publishers. This is not an industry, it's a charity.

Which would be fine – if only there were donors. Not only is there no national private foundation in the United States willing to support publishers doing translations (although the government does support them through the National Endowment for the Arts), but the richest companies in the USA – Apple and Amazon – give a combined $1 million dollars a year to literary organizations. That's about 1/153rd of the money *Captain Marvel* earned over four days. Days!

Because the 3 per cent figure is so shocking and tangible, publishers, foreign governments, ~~the Silicon Valley nouveau riche~~, all focused on how *many* books in translation were published annually – at the expense of all other possible evaluative measures. For years – and yes, I am very much partially responsible for this – the industry focus was solely on bringing more translations to market. No one cared about how many people read these publications, about the intrinsic value of books – it was all about creating more options.

Which isn't bad! The more options available, the easier it is to figure out which titles resonate. And if a percentage – 2 per cent? 5 per cent? – really hit, sold 10,000 copies, then you have some encouraging data to work with.

Not to mention, a significant increase in the number of translations being published would be a huge boon for translators. They would have a lot more work available to them, and the best of the best could charge much higher per-word fees. But, if the average sales for translations start to slip – even by only a couple of hundred units – the budgetary pressure on non-corporate presses (the ones producing around 85 per cent of all translations) would likely be too much to bear. There is very little room for error in publishing in general, but this is especially true when it comes to translations. One mistake – a 600-page book that only sells 600 copies – can ruin a small house.

So, should our primary focus still be on counting translations? If 100,000 translation units are sold every year, regardless of the number of titles published, should it really matter if these sales are spread out over 300 books or 600? Or is the 100,000 number the one to try to alter? Back in the days of 360 translations a year, the latent audience for international literature was sufficient. Everyone's books sold *well*. Then the field started to try to expand, even though most presses were undercapitalized and, as a result, with rare exceptions, average sales of translations declined.

The '3 per cent problem' has dominated the conversation among translation professionals for a couple of decades, and it may be time to set it aside. It's not necessarily a problem that needs to be fixed, or rather, the way to fix it isn't necessarily by focusing on the production side of things, but on how to continue growing audiences.

We never tried to build an audience; we tried to build a library.

(2) *The financial incentives for the different agents in the industry (publishers, translators, distributors) are not aligned, with most players' gross revenue tied to a title's overall sales, but translators being paid by the word, as if they were day labourers.*

Remember that thing about aspiration and publishing? Well, most salaries can be tracked as a percentage of total sales. The CEO of Penguin Random House has a salary, but the bigger payout comes from the success of the house and their acquisitions. Stumbling into a best-seller is how most editors move up the ladder. No one asks you how well *read* you are when you interview; they ask how many best-sellers you've produced.

This is one of the reasons that most payments in publishing are sales-dependent. You sell 1 million copies, you get $1,000,000. Makes sense!

But if you're a translator? You get paid based on your labour. You work hours, you translate words, you do a service. That deserves a payment, obviously, but how much? And how should this be determined?

If we accept the old-school model of publishing (aka the 80-20 rule, aka one success allows for a majority of failures), this is a bit complicated. Traditionally, the majority of books a press brings out in a given year will lose money. And a select few will be mega-hits. Those mega-hits will lead to the press making an annual profit, thus allocating funding for future books that are unlikely to break even. It's a tough game that, historically, has relied on a handful of surprise mega-successes, a few more break-even titles, and a lot of stuff that doesn't end up finding its audience.

In today's MBA- and quants-driven environment, that situation – of a few successes underwriting all the books that lose money – seems rather quaint. In Andre Schiffrin's *The Business of Books*, he references how, when Pantheon was acquired by Random House, the message from the top down was that *every* book had to turn a profit.³ This might not actually happen – if for no other reason than how sales are distributed – but it obviously plays a role in deciding what makes it to the marketplace.

Knowing that the vast majority of translated books won't sell enough copies to justify their publication, should translators be paid based on their work, or on the success of their work? For the uninitiated, here's a quick rundown of author payments: a publisher offers an 'advance against royalties' for the rights to a particular title. The amount of the advance is (theoretically at least) determined by market forces: expected sales, cultural capital accrued by publishing that book, perceived interest among competing presses, etc. But the core principle is that the advance will 'earn out' through sales of the book and the subsidiary rights. If you offer $10,000 for the rights to a book, you expect to sell enough copies so that [List Price] × [Royalty Rate] × [Net Copies Sold] + [Proceeds from Subsidiary Rights Sales] => $10,000.

This is all pretty self-explanatory, and is why Stephen King's advances are magnitudes of times larger than a random debut author.

But how should this capitalist quirk work with regard to translators? Should they – and all their works – be treated equally? If a publisher is doing a translation out of love and for the benefit of culture, knowing that breaking even is the best possible scenario (even *with* additional revenue from donations and grants), should that translator be paid the same as the translator who works on a book that is highly likely to sell ten to twenty times more copies? Reversing this: should King and the debut author be paid, not according to sales potential and licensing opportunities, but according to the number of words they write?

An immediate reaction to the idea of tying a translator's fee to the sales of the book they translate is: 'Hell no'. The work a translator does to render a very challenging title (aka book that won't sell well) into English is just as labour-intensive, if not more so, than that done by a translator translating a potboiler that will sell extremely well because *Girl with a Dragon Tattoo* did.

The fixed cost of translation puts the publisher in a bit of a bind. If the expenses are the same, why publish the book that might be better, yet won't sell as well? For the benefit to their reputation for being brave enough to have published a really challenging – yet important – author? Publishing critically acclaimed books that the marketplace can't support is standard operating procedure for non-profit publishing houses, but even so, the long-term calculus gets a little wobbly if you take into consideration that the authors providing the most to non-corporate presses – either by reputation or sales – are likely to be co-opted by commercial houses with much larger marketing resources.

This might seem like a small point, but the way that translators get paid – by the word, regardless of the size of the press they're working for – results in a scheme wherein smaller presses are forced to take on a lot of the risk and early expenses bringing an author to the English-reading audience and then, if they're successful (winning a major prize or selling a significant number of copies), that author leaves for a larger press capable of offering a higher advance, spending more money on marketing, and, almost always, reaching a lot more readers. And the press that paid those initial fees, that shouldered the risk and laid the groundwork for the author's future success, will be left with good karma. From this perspective, the idea of paying translators a fixed rate regardless of the press's budget works as a disincentive for smaller publishers.

The flipside is where this 'problem with translation publishing' becomes really clear: when a translator translates a book that does enormously well, they are credited with being a 'great translator' and can command a higher rate. Which I, as someone who is *always* on the side of labour, believe is great news for the translator! But it's still a bit illogical, since the book's success is just as likely tied to luck, timing, marketing, the book itself, or other factors that have little to do with the quality of the translation.

This mixture of systems – one tied to sales success, the other based on a different set of labour calculations – creates a sort of tension which, from an accounting perspective, makes English-language titles much more appealing. You pay the same set of fixed costs across all titles, and your variable costs (author advance, printing expenses, even marketing) are tied to the revenue a book generates. Adding on an additional expense – the cost of the translation – that varies based on the length of the book (instead of its viability in the marketplace) can seem like bad business.

Let's see how this dynamic plays out in another scenario: distribution and sales reps.

Again, for the benefit of anyone not already in the publishing business: sales reps for given presses bring their catalogues and offerings to bookstores, online retailers, libraries, academics, wholesalers, and specialty markets (like Target and Hallmark), so that these outlets can order copies three to six months in advance of the book's publication. Outlets need a steady stream of product to sell; publishers need to know what's going to be going where, so that they know how many copies to print.

If you're a Big Five press or subsidiary (Penguin Random House [PRH], HarperCollins, Macmillan, Simon & Schuster, Houghton Mifflin

Harcourt), your sales reps represent *only* your titles. A PRH rep talks up PRH books. Makes sense.

If you're not a big press, and you're publishing books in the USA, you're probably represented by Ingram Publishing Services (IPS). That's a bit facetious, since there are another one or two distribution options out there, but the vast majority of indie/non-profit presses are part of Consortium, IPS, or Publishers Group West – all of which are owned by Ingram, the largest book wholesaler in the USA, which has now expanded into the distribution game.

Even if Ingram didn't own all of these formerly independent distributors, the same situation holds: the sales reps for Consortium (for instance) are independently contracted and represent titles from several dozen different publishing groups in addition to the 120+ presses (and 1,000+ unique titles) in any given Consortium catalogue. And a significant portion of their income is on commission. If a bookstore orders 500 copies of a book, they get a cut; if a bookstore orders two copies, they get a much smaller cut.

What is the incentive for a sales rep? To push the best translations that have lasting cultural value, but have a low ceiling sales-wise, or to ignore all those books, and push the few dozen titles of the many thousands of the new titles they represent every year that will actually shift a significant number of units? And what happens if everyone believes that the financial success of a non-translated title is ten times more likely than that of a translated one?

At least in this situation, the publisher of literary translations only has to pay a percentage of *actual sales* to the distributor rather than a fixed cost. But at the same time, they're working from a significant disadvantage if, *if,* the best-selling titles are overwhelmingly being written in English. (Which is very much the case. See above.)

(3) *Obsession with quantifiable, trackable data tends to devalue literature in translation.*

As a culture, we are obsessed with things that are trackable. Putting aside all of the above discussion about verifiable sales, actual expenses, etc., a healthy proportion of Americans wear some sort of device that tracks their number of steps, calories, or heart rate. Our phones inform us, weekly, of our usage rate. One of the most popular websites online is FiveThirtyEight, which filters all of its stories about sports and culture through data analysis. Newspapers, websites, listicle machines all track the number of visits and various other readership metrics to determine the importance and value of writers, topics, and the like. Authors check bestseller lists weekly – and Amazon lists every hour. Baseball nerds love WAR (Wins Above Replacement), because it's a way of quantifying what you see on the field.

Going back to those *Captain Marvel* numbers for a minute – what seems more important to culture, a blockbuster superhero movie or a literary translation from the Indonesian that sells 350 copies? Well, from a purely investment perspective, the Marvel movie makes more sense. Much larger audience, more potential for profit, merchandising and future spin-offs, and obviously, bigger is better. Thankfully, non-profit publishing offers a possible alternative – funding sources that offset the losses that theoretical Indonesian book would accrue.

One problem though: over the past twenty years, fundraising for non-profit publishing has worked itself into a rather static position. Back in the 1980s and 1990s, Jim Sitter helped get the Mellon Foundation and Lila Wallace-Readers' Digest Fund to support non-profit publishing houses. He helped make the Minneapolis non-profit scene a thing by convincing a number of large local foundations to support literature along with the other arts. (The Loft – a literary arts centre in Minneapolis – received over $500,000 from foundations and corporations in 2018. That doesn't include the $200,000 in government funding and almost $330,000 from individuals. A large part of this is thanks to Jim Sitter.) His vision and work helped create a scene that would keep Minneapolis loaded with non-profit literary arts ventures for decades to come – organizations that could make ends meet because they had a way of offsetting the distressing *quantifiable* data from their actual work.

If you're not in Minneapolis? There aren't any major family foundations you can apply to for support. The private donations from the richest philanthropists have been redirected from arts funding (think Guggenheim and Rockefeller and museums and libraries) to STEM research so that, grain of salt and bitterness here, rich people can figure out how best to live forever on their Seasteader nation-state with their guns and cryptocurrency.

The more we value quantitative analysis, the harder it will be for literary arts to make a case for itself. It's a small artistic subset. Full stop. Although virtually everyone in the United States can read (and has a Twitter account), there's much more money that will be donated to museums next year than to organizations producing books. This is somewhat logical – museums can't survive on entrance fees alone – unless those entrance fees are astronomical, thus cutting out a huge portion of the population that could benefit most from visiting a museum – and most literary organizations are for-profit, and are making ends meet, which makes you wonder about those smaller ones that are asking for donations ... This reinforces a set of values that prefers the immediately popular, the financially successful, the timely, to works of art that accrue meaning over generations, over successive readings, over value based in longevity and intangibles instead of box office take or best-seller lists.

Reader, the news from the USA is predictably dire: as a culture, we pay attention to large numbers. Whether it's the Nielsen ratings for CNN vs. Fox News or the BookScan numbers for a Macedonian collection of stories, we have conflated the countable with success. It's a capitalist impulse, one that is fuelled by technology capable of counting, well, basically, anything.

It's also incredibly logical. For a publishing company to stay in business, it must pay attention to the numbers. The potential danger – in terms of the diversity and health of literary culture as a whole – is conflating numbers with a book's true value or meaningfulness. There are no metrics to determine the overall 'impact' of a piece of art on its audience.

This is where there's a bit of a divergence between corporate presses (the so-called Big Five, or Big Four, depending on future mergers) and independent (especially non-profit) publishers. The Big Five are motivated solely by profit, and the best CEOs will do whatever they can to continue growing the bottom line. Non-profits strive to balance profitability against fulfilling their mission. In a very basic sense, non-profits should exist to add diversity to the literary landscape. Instead of focusing only on titles with healthy profit and loss sheets (it's common among large publishers to generate these on a book-by-book basic, using the potential profit as a guide in deciding which books to publish), these presses should also be publishing titles that may not find their audience for several years or more.

Divorced from quantitative metrics, the intent to publish books that aren't immediately profitable – such as literature in translation from lesser-read languages – is admirable, something that can garner moral support and, theoretically, philanthropic funding. The difficulty in taking this approach lies in the increase in overall costs, due in part to the recent, relative success of international literature. Because of increased competition, agents have more power than ever, and can command larger advances for their authors. Translators, as professionalized and knowledgeable about the business side of things as ever, can increase their fees. Booksellers, especially Amazon, continue to negotiate for better discounts, reducing the amount of money a publisher receives per unit sold. Distributors for independent presses take – in the form of distribution costs, marketing fees, and warehousing – over 50 per cent of a press's net profits. All of these are disincentives to publishing books for the 'good of culture', instead of using the numbers available – as scant as they might be – to predict and influence success.

It's a publisher's job to figure out how to raise the necessary funds (through sales, donations, investments) to achieve their overall goal as a cultural organization. And, unfortunately, as society becomes more aware of, and/or obsessed with, quantifiable numbers, with relating to cultural products in this way (such as paying extra attention to the day's 'Top 10' on Netflix), the arguments made by the traditional liberal arts crowd about the intrinsic value of consuming more specialized art don't resonate the way they used to. Publishers need to develop a new vocabulary for discussing the long-term impact of books.

Great, interesting books will always be published, and many classics of tomorrow will be the flops of today. But as publishing becomes more of a 'winner-take-all game',[4] we're approaching a crucial juncture for small press publishing – and, by extension, for literature in translation – a situation that was only exacerbated by the impact of the global pandemic brought on by COVID-19.

As best-selling titles morph into mega-best-selling titles, with the overall percentage of sales becoming even more concentrated in a select few books, we run the risk of completely burying these other, slow-but-steady works that need time to find their audience. If the gap between best-selling, profitable books and sales for 'midlist', 'cult', or translated titles increases, and as the costs of doing business continue to rise, it's less likely that a small press will be able to afford to take the risks that they used to. Instead of trying to introduce someone like Aliocha Coll (a very unknown, deceased Spanish author Open Letter will be publishing in 2022), it will be even more common to chase after books that are more likely to sell or are already attached to significant funding.

Diversity is key to a thriving, vibrant culture, and this extends beyond race, sexual orientation, or identity politics into the aesthetic realm as well. There should be both mega-hits like *Captain Marvel* and books like Coll's *Attila*, which is unlikely to sell more than 1,000 copies. The potential of Coll's work to impact – in a social or artistic sense – a small percentage of those readers in an outsized way, is worthwhile, is meaningful, is a problem worth solving. Every subset deserves the art that speaks to them.

General Conclusion

Publishing is always in a 'crisis'. If it's not the closure of hundreds of bookstores, it's the rise of Amazon. If it's not absurd advances that will never be earned out, it's a paper shortage. It's library budgets collapsing and the shift in disposable income and leisure time allocation to streaming services and iPhone apps.

Much of this is an identity problem: in an age of screens and big data, it's hard not just to sell the idea of spending fifteen hours alone in your head, reading a book, but to demonstrate that your business is still valuable, even if only 700 people spend those fifteen hours with one of your books.

As we move away from the 3 per cent problem and start to address new, more complex elements of translation and commerce, we need to find new terms to discuss what we do, new business practices that are born from non-cutthroat capitalist strategies, and new forms of revenue that will allow all of us to achieve what we really want: more readers for more books from more voices from around the world.

Notes

1. Lawrence Venuti, *The Translator's Invisibility* (New York: Routledge, 1995), 12–14.
2. Alison Flood, 'Translated Fiction Sells Better in the UK than English Fiction, Research Finds', *Guardian*, May 9, 2016.
3. André Schiffrin, *The Business of Books* (New York: Verso, 2001).
4. The phrase is used, for instance, by Alexandra Alter in 'Best Sellers Sell Best Because They're Best Sellers', *New York Times*, September 19, 2020.

CHAPTER 13

Translating into a Minor Language

Rumena Bužarovska

Undoubtedly, the words 'small' or 'minor' harbour negative overtones. Pair 'small', 'new', or 'minor' with anything related to the history or culture of what is now known as The Republic of North Macedonia, and you are likely to spark the wrath of those claiming that *Macedonian* collocates with the old, the grand, the original. But the fact remains that the Macedonian language was only codified in 1945, after Macedonia became a sovereign state within Yugoslavia – for the first time in its history. The language into which I translate, and in which write, is thus not only minor in the sense that it is spoken by a relatively small number of people: it is also quite new.

Bearing in mind the difficulties arising from working with scant resources and a relatively poor written tradition, translating into Macedonian has been – and to some extent still is – a path wrought with challenges. There are several issues to consider, such as historical and political factors in Yugoslav Macedonia that preferred Serbian and Croatian translations. The lack of translation policies and the absence of a market for literature during this time allowed individual scholars and literary magazines to shape translation trends, and hence the literary output published in this newly codified language. An international poetry festival, attractive at the time because of the position of Yugoslavia as a middle ground between the East and the West, had a surprising effect on what became translated and popular, not just locally but also regionally. And finally, the transitional period from socialism to capitalism after the break-up of Yugoslavia brought new trends in translation. New government cultural policies favouring the funding of specific publishing houses coupled with high unemployment rates enabled the exploitation of translators, ultimately resulting in not just a decline in the quality but also a colossal and sudden increase in the quantity of translations.

Historical Background

Macedonian is a South Slavic language spoken in the territory of what is today officially North Macedonia and by a diaspora and minorities outside its borders. To avoid perhaps erroneous estimates of the number of people who speak the language, it suffices to consider the population living in North Macedonia: according to the 2002 census – and yes, a census has successfully been avoided by the governing political parties ever since – this is a little over 2 million inhabitants,[1] a quarter of whom belong to the ethnic Albanian minority and are presumed to have knowledge of Macedonian, the official language of the state.

The Macedonian alphabet – Cyrillic, like that of the neighbouring Bulgaria and Serbia – was proposed in 1944 at the Anti-Fascist Assembly for the National Liberation of Macedonia and adopted the following year, along with the Macedonian orthography. With this, the language was codified and pronounced as the official language of the country, by which Macedonian became a recognized language alongside those of the other republics in the Yugoslav federation, with Serbo-Croatian as the official language.

The standardization of Macedonian is largely owed to the scholar, writer, and translator Blaže Koneski, who wrote the *Grammar of Literary Macedonian language* in 1952 and 1954,[2] and subsequently edited a three-volume dictionary of the Macedonian language with Serbo-Croatian definitions. To the contemporary translator, these are books of the utmost importance, owing to the fact that, even after Yugoslavia fell apart and Macedonia gained independence in 1991, few attempts were made by other lexicographers.[3] To this day, the only other significant resource for translators is the new *Dictionary of the Macedonian Language*, whose final volume was published in 2014.[4] Regardless of the existence of a National Institute for Macedonian Language, the contemporary translator still frequently has to resort to using dictionaries from the region and scouring texts from the late nineteenth and early twentieth century for manuscripts in unstandardized Macedonian in search of new words, as we will later see in the case of the translator Ognen Čemerski.

Translating in Yugoslav Macedonia

Very little information is available about the state of translation before independence in 1991. The main source is 'World Literature in Macedonian (1945–1990)',[5] together with a few other articles chronicling and evaluating the work of individual translators. The Association of Literary Translators (Друштво на книжевни преведувачи) publishes a magazine, as well as a collection of a few relevant articles presented at the Symposia of the International Encounters of Literary Translators, which has taken place regularly since 1971. Many of these collections are nearly impossible to find due to irresponsible archiving, though those available mostly feature impressionistic essays and are dominated by a few individuals and their personal views on translation. As a result, to gain deeper insight into how a body of translated literature is built, to find out whether it is the state or the individual translator who plays a more important role in the choice of translated works and how much translation is related to the social and political context, I interviewed four prominent translators who have built the foundations of translation from three different languages: Bogomil Gjuzel from English,[6] Vlada Urošević from French, and Tanja Urošević from Russian.[7] I additionally interviewed Zoran Ančevski,[8] a translator from English into Macedonian whose work extends over the pre- and post-independence periods.

But let us begin by looking at Anastasija Gjurčinova and Sonja Stojmenska-Elzeser's research into 'World Literature in Macedonian (1945–1990)' and the body of translated work during the first stage of independence, within the Yugoslav federation, where Serbo-Croatian was the official language. To provide additional context, it is important to note that Serbo-Croatian translations enjoyed status and prominence (they still do, nowadays, as Serbian and Croatian translations, stemming from yet another inferiority complex of the smallest, youngest state in the federation). As an official language of Yugoslavia, Serbo-Croatian was present on television and radio; it was a mandatory language in school and was considered a language with a higher and more sophisticated status than Macedonian. Born in 1981, I probably belong to the last generation to have been exposed to Serbo-Croatian translations and am thus able to speak the language now technically separated into Serbian, Croatian, Bosnian and Montenegrin. The lack of Macedonian educational institutions also meant that Macedonian intellectuals were educated in Serbo-Croatian, or by Yugoslav experts (in my interview with Bogomil Gjuzel, he testifies that in the early 1960s they had a visiting assistant professor in English literature from Zagreb). Thus, Serbo-Croatian and Russian, due to the socialist affiliation of the Yugoslav state, were the main foreign languages spoken in post-war Macedonia. This explains the dominant body of Russian literature translated in the first post-war decades, as well as the use of Serbo-Croatian as a bridge language for translation.

A total of 950 books were translated into Macedonian from 1945 to 1990.[9] There are at least two factors to be taken into account when considering the low number of translations: first and foremost, the wide availability of Serbo-Croatian translations, but also the population of the country, which according to the census of 1953 was a little over 1.3 million, seeing a steady rise to a little over 2 million by 1991.[10] Gjurčinova and Stojmenska-Elzeser further delve into the analysis of the percentage of representation of various literatures, showing that Russian literature occupies the primary position (289 translated works), with translations reaching a peak in the 1960s, but experiencing a drop in the '70s. The most translated authors are Maxim Gorky, Leo Tolstoy, Fyodor Dostoyevsky, Anton Chekhov and Nikolai Gogol.

To find out more about translation choices and policies after World War II, in 2019 I interviewed the late Tanja Urošević (1936–2020), a prominent translator from Russian from the first generations of translators in Macedonia, and second on the list of translators with the most translated works from the Russian – with fifteen.[11] She claims that in postwar Macedonia translating the Russian classics was an easy way of earning money because they had already been translated into Serbian. She states that as someone who worked in the National Radio, she witnessed translators asking typists to come into work an hour early, when they would 'hold the Serbian text and dictate out loud'. She also claims that translating the Russian classics was 'safe': she found that she was not in favour with the state because of her personal choice to translate dissident writers such as Bulgakov, Pasternak, and Tsvetaeva. For instance, she notes that, though many Macedonian translators enjoyed summer fellowships in Sochi, she herself was never sent to the Soviet Union, despite her significant body of work.

French literature – from France, as opposed to 'francophone' – is the second most translated into Macedonian, with 158 published works, mostly during the 1960s and 1970s. Jules Verne, Honoré de Balzac, and Victor Hugo are at the top of the list, indicating that writers of classics and children's literature were most frequently translated during this period, as these works would have been – and in some cases, still are – parts of the mandatory reading lists of the elementary and high school curricula. Vlada Urošević (b. 1934), one of the most prolific and prominent Macedonian writers, translators, and scholars, is listed as the most prolific translator of French literature. In my interview with him, he pointed out the difference between translation practices in the past and now by highlighting the existence of literary magazines in the past – namely *Razgledi, Sovremenost*, and *Stremež* – featuring translations by upcoming translators and serving as a sort of 'exercise room' for them. Translators were usually writers, he points out, and they would produce books only after making a name for themselves in those literary magazines. Following the break-up of Yugoslavia in 1991 and the creation of an independent state, 'The Ministry of Culture, unfortunately, cancelled those magazines as obsolete', thereby ending this practice. Vlada Urošević points out that publishing houses commissioned works from him – Baudelaire, Apollinaire, Rimbaud – but as a result of his previous translations and interests in those magazines. Stipends for young scholars during the late 1960s provided by the French government played an indirect role in forming the body of translated literature. In 1968, Urošević was a scholar at the Sorbonne: 'This stay in France was a great introduction into French literature which instilled in me a desire to translate as much as possible the works that I liked. I did not pay much attention to what was in demand here so I managed to impose my understanding of French literature.' This indicates that literature in Macedonian translation, as well as the body of scholarly work related to Macedonian language and literature, was built around the interests and desires of highly motivated individuals.

Although American literature was completely absent from Macedonian translation in the 1940s and featured only a few publications in the '50s, its rising popularity starting from the 1970s brings it to the third position according to Gjurčinova and Stojmenska-Elzeser's research. Here, too, the most translated authors are those included in school curricula: Jack London, Pearl Buck, Ernest Hemingway, and Mark Twain. Both Vlada Urošević and translator, professor, and poet Zoran Ančevski (b. 1954) testify to the lack of English-speakers during the 1940s and '50s, with Ančevski claiming that his generation is the 'first generation of translators who summoned up the courage to translate directly from the source language'.[12] Hence, it is possible that the most prolific translator of American literature, Sveto Serafimov, also translated from the Serbian. Evidence of this can be seen in Ognen Čemerski's study of the translation of maritime terminology in *Moby Dick*, where he compares Sveto Serafimov's 1982 translation with Milan S. Nedić's Serbian translation of 1962: 'Hence, if Serafimov translated directly from the English, almost all the sentences, formulations, idioms, syntax along with Milan S. Nedić's descriptive solutions have magically, more or less telepathically transported themselves into the work of the Macedonian translator. It is with equal magic that the Serbian and Macedonian texts mirror each other in the transfer of Biblical names.'[13] I noticed this myself when analysing Sveto Serafimov's 1992 translation of Raymond Carver's 'Cathedral' in the collection *What We Talk About When We Talk About Love* ('Cathedral' is not originally part of this collection, yet finds its way into the Macedonian version). There were many aberrations from the original text, including non-existent and rather irrelevant, and as such, absurd, additions: 'He dunked his bread into his peas', Serafimov adds to the dinner scene.[14]

A surprising fact is that British literature in Macedonian translation comes after American literature – surprising, because the official university curriculum at the English Department of the oldest and largest state university is based on English (UK) language and literature, merely offering elective courses for American literature. This, in turn, is mirrored in the way English is taught in schools: with an emphasis on British culture, and a rather dismissive attitude towards American culture and pronunciation. What is not surprising, though, is that Shakespeare and Dickens are the most translated authors, while Sveto Serafimov yet again is the most prolific translator into Macedonian.[15]

The theory that driven individuals shaped trends in language, literature, and translation – such as the cases of Blaže Koneski and Vlada Urošević – is supported by the prevalence of multiple translations of Shakespeare's work. The first Macedonian translator and scholar of Shakespeare, and professor at the English Department, Ivanka Kovilovska Poposka, has noted three stages in the translation of Shakespeare in Macedonia: the first stage is the indirect phase where the translation was done through a bridge language. This is followed by the collaborative stage, where translators worked from a literal English translation. The third phase is the translation from the original.[16] Ivanka Koviloska Poposka and Bogomil Gjuzel were the first to translate directly from the original; Dragi Mihajlovski published his translation of the complete works of Shakespeare in 2013.

Why was Shakespeare retranslated so early on in the development of Macedonian literacy? Bogomil Gjuzel (b. 1939) testifies that his Shakespeare translations were either done by commission, as an employee of the Macedonian theatre, or as a continuing legacy of Ivanka Koviloska's work. It seems that because she taught Shakespeare at the University, Ivanka Koviloska instilled a passion among her students and a lasting legacy of two-semester mandatory courses on Shakespeare's works. Dragi Mihajlovski, hence, in his seminal study on translation, *Under Babylon: The Task of the Translator*,[17] devotes a chapter on the retranslation of Shakespeare's sonnets, taking the poet Aco Šopov's indirect 1976 translation as a starting point for analysis, continuing the tradition of Shakespeare scholars in Macedonia that was instilled by Koviloska – just like Vlada Urošević, who employed his influence as translator, writer, and professor to create a lasting scholarly debate on French Surrealism.

Such is the case with the translations of Spanish-language poets, mostly introduced by the poet and translator Mateja Matevski (1929–2018), who introduced Lorca to the Macedonian readership, in addition to Pablo Neruda, Rafael Alberti, Juan Ramón Jiménez, Octavio Paz and Justo Jorge

Padrón.[18] Gjurčinova notes that the particular choice of writers during the Yugoslav era was political, connected to the anti-fascist affiliations of Lorca and Neruda.[19]

Other world literatures – German, Czechoslovakian (listed as such at the time), Italian, Romanian, Spanish, etc. – also note translations during the pre-independence era, following a similar pattern: the most translated writers are either authors of classics or of children's literature that was to be included in the mandatory reading lists of the school curricula.

Though merely 17.16 per cent of translated books are poetry,[20] it seems that the Struga Poetry Evenings festival played a seminal role in the introduction of international poets not only to Macedonian literature but to audiences in Yugoslavia. Established in 1966, the Golden Wreath has been awarded to internationally renowned authors (such as Ginsberg, Auden, Hughes, Neruda, Brodsky, Atwood, and Amichai). Gjuzel claims that Auden, winner of the prize in 1971, was virtually unknown in Yugoslavia, but it was Gjuzel in fact who introduced him to our audiences through his translations.[21] ZoranAnčevski attests to the role of the festival in promoting world literature in translation: 'I believe that the Struga Poetry Evenings were pioneers in the translation of many worldly renowned authors when one couldn't even find translations of those authors in Yugoslav literary magazines.'[22] Although Gjurčinova and Stojmenska-Elzeser's research does not go into the details of how many of the translated works of poetry are editions of the Struga Poetry Evenings festival, they point out that the publishing of poetry collections by the laureates (though they fail to mention the festival also published collections by other poets in their Pleiades edition) accounts for many of the published translations within this period.[23] The festival seems to have been particularly attractive before the 1990s, as it was a safe meeting point for many poets on opposites sides of the Iron Curtain, keeping in mind Yugoslavia's non-affiliation with the Soviet bloc but its existence as a socialist country with close ties to the East. The festival still takes place annually and continues to account for a number of poetry translations published within various festival editions.

Independence

With independence and the shift of the political system, translation into Macedonian changed greatly, due to the new cultural strategies of the government, as well as the vacuum created once people stopped reading Serbian and Croatian translations, either because they were more difficult to attain or because the population was no longer exposed to Serbo-Croatian and consequently lost the ability to comprehend the language.

Though the newly established Ministry of Culture cut off funding for the literary magazines where literary translators and writers originally made their reputations, they established a strategy of so-called national interests, thereby funding publishing houses that apply for the publication of translated books. This, in turn, allowed the development of a new publishing market, and new publishing houses. However, due to the high unemployment rate – currently 17.8 per cent, according to statistics[24] – translation fees dropped and created room for the exploitation of translators, which in turn resulted in poor-quality translations.

I dare to share some of my first experiences in publishing translations. At the time, I simply walked up to a publishing house that I thought would not double-cross me and asked them if they would like to publish my translation of *Life & Times of Michael K*, by J. M. Coetzee, whose *Waiting for the Barbarians* had already been published in Macedonian, perhaps having taken a hint from its popularity in neighbouring Serbia. Though Coetzee had recently won the Nobel Prize, it had not occurred to anyone to publish any of his novels in Macedonian. My publisher agreed, and we applied for support from the Ministry of Culture and received it. At the time I was translating – 2005 – the Internet was a novelty, so I was able to use it for resources and tried to find a speaker of Afrikaans to explain certain cultural concepts and the transcription of names to me. It was by chance that I stumbled upon an email address from someone at Stellenbosch University who turned out to be a phonology professor who generously transcribed Afrikaans expressions for me, also helping me with the cultural nuances in the text. (I unfortunately lost this correspondence after someone hacked into my email account.) When the book came out, the editor hadn't checked the final draft, so the book was published with all the tracked changes actually printed on the pages. This was, for me, a disappointing initiation into the world of translation.

I had similar absurd experiences with my next translation. This project – which I admit was very ambitious – came in 2008 and it was Lewis Carroll's *Through the Looking Glass*. This time, it was the publishing house who approached me and asked if I would be interested in translating this book. Having a fascination with Alice, I agreed, knowing that I had ample time and a normal translating fee for our standards, in fact a fee that was prescribed by the Ministry of Culture but that translators never actually received. The publishing house had applied for a project with the Cultural Programme of the European Union. As I was young and inexperienced, I did not understand that the publishing house expected me to hand over half of my translation payment to them once I had received the funds, as in fact the translating fee prescribed by the project was twice the sum they had offered. Hence, when the money was wired, I had to go to the bank, withdraw half of the funds and take it to the publishing house in an envelope. At the time, I wasn't aware that not only was I being exploited, but I was also probably aiding them in committing a crime, a crime that has become standard practice in Macedonian publishing houses, who use poor sales as an excuse to exploit translators who are in high supply due to the high unemployment rate. When I later translated *The Colour of a Dog Running Away*, by the contemporary Welsh author Richard Gwyn, a book supported by a similar European fund, having knowledge and experience of what was going on, I was surprised to see that my publisher transferred the entire sum to me – but he was an exception. Going back to *Through the Looking Glass*, my next shock was to find out, after the book was published, that ZoranAnčevski had mistakenly been credited for translating the poems in the text.

My translation of *Life & Times of Michael K* brings me to a phenomenon that bridges the periods pre- and post-Macedonian independence: the idiosyncratic role of prizes. The Association of Literary Translators, which has been holding annual conferences since 1971 and awarding prizes to prominent – and less prominent – translators for their work, gives an annual Golden Quill award, honouring a new translator for an outstanding first translation. Watching the news on television, I heard that I had won this award: the Association never bothered to let me know personally, or to actually present me with the award – which is in fact no more than a piece of paper. My negative experience with this Association, which has been otherwise dormant in discussing national matters regarding translation policies and/or providing constructive criticism and analysis of existing translations, is hardly unique and was attested to by my interview subjects (ZoranAnčevski and Tanja Urošević).

Though translation research in Macedonia is scant, it is Dragi Mihajlovski, known for his translation of the complete works of Shakespeare, who set out translation theories regarding translating classic works into Macedonian – *Beowulf*, Milton, Eliot, Shakespeare, English ballads, Keats.[25] A proponent of domestication in translation, Mihajlovski applied this principle to the translations of *The Importance of Being Earnest* and *Charlotte's Web*. His manner of translating Shakespeare's blank verse has sparked debate – with the scholar Rajna Koška siding with Mihajlovski's view that the metre and verse of the original need not be reflected in the translation, and that trochaic and dactylic feet are more natural for the rhythm of the Macedonian language.[26] The only other such study on the principles of translation into Macedonian is by Ognen Čemerski, who described his journey in transferring maritime terminology into the language of a landlocked country.[27] Čemerski's research is of particular interest to translators struggling to find words and phrases in a language that has been newly codified and is apparently devoid of terminology found in the original: he shows us how, through scouring manuscripts from the turn of the century, interviewing fishermen from the Lake Ohrid area as well as employing the terminology of architecture, one can translate the seemingly untranslatable maritime terms in *Moby Dick*.

Apart from Mihajlovski and Čemerski, few have ventured to enrich the otherwise poor pool of translation research. There is the 2017 study *On Literary Translation*, by the scholar Vladimir Cvetkoski, which includes portraits of six prominent Macedonian translators (Mihail D. Petruševski, Venko Markovski, Blaže Koneski, Georgi Stalev, Bogomil Gjuzel, and Dragi Mihajlovski) and further aims to provide a chronological overview of published works in the field of literary translation. Furthermore, the magazine *Kulturen život* has a tradition of publishing texts regarding translation research (for example, Elka Jačeva Ulčar on the most common grammar mistakes in translation, Rajna Koška with two articles on translating Shakespeare, Zvonko Taneski on Slovak translations into Macedonian, Simona Madžoska on the state of translation in Macedonia), but alas, some of these articles cannot be found at all because the National Library has either not catalogued them (such is the case with my own article on the translations of *Catcher in the Rye*), or has lost the relevant issues (as in the case with Elka Jačeva Ulčar and Simona Madžoska's articles). In order to access these works, I had to call the editor and some of the writers and ask them to personally send me the articles. Similarly, I found out through Madžoska's article that the annual Seminar for Macedonian Language, Literature and Culture (part of the Ss. Cyril and Methodius University) themed its 2006 linguistics session on issues in translation. However, the seminar proceedings can only be found in the Ohrid city library (allegedly – as frequently they exist in catalogues, but the books are simply not there). Through word of mouth, I found out who had edited the volume: I contacted the editor and she informed me that the proceedings had been uploaded on to the University website, and that she did not own a physical copy of the volume. I went to the University website only to find that the link for the download – alas, for all of the proceedings – had been removed. I then managed to find an existing link with a list of all the participants and the papers they had presented, to here discover that the papers mostly concerned linguistic issues in translation and did not involve evaluations of translations or analysing works through applying theories of translation. The only scholar who continues to catalogue and comment on the process of translation into Macedonian is Anastasija Gjurčinova, who was kind enough to send me her articles or either direct me to people who might have them – as even the university or the library has lost copies of these works. Gjurčinova, for example, has also catalogued and evaluated the translation of works from Italian into Macedonian (Gjurčinova 2015),[28] something that our culture is in dire need of, specifically after the Gargantuan translation project the like of which I have yet to hear has occurred elsewhere.

When Translation Mirrors Architecture

In 2010, the right-wing government of the then Republic of Macedonia uncovered their plans for the reconstruction of the capital, a project known as Skopje 2014. I remember watching the video and laughing at the preposterous nature of the project, thinking it would never come to fruition. And yet it did. Soon, Skopje had been transformed into what *The Guardian* dubbed 'Europe's New Capital of Kitsch'.[29] The city centre became unrecognisable: a wall of narrow white buildings with neo-classical façades and towering yet flimsy hollow columns suddenly lined the river that runs through the city, blocking the view of its Modernist and Islamic architectural legacy. An 80-foot statue of Alexander the Great on a horse above a multicoloured fountain playing music dominates the main square. Alexander – known as 'Equestrian Warrior' in a childishly sly move to hinder the Greeks from formally complaining – faces a slightly smaller statue of his father, Philip, on the other side of the river, perched atop a pedestal underneath another colourful fountain. Olympias, Alexander's mother, is in the space between them. She also sits upon a pedestal soaked in a fountain, but is presented in four stages of motherhood, completing the image of the pagan holy trinity. These grotesque statues are the work of until then a relatively unknown sculptor, Valentina Stevanovska, who turned out to be the most commissioned artist in the project, in which hundreds of badly sculpted sculptures and statues pepper the city centre. Skopje 2014 is deeply disturbing: it is hollow, flashy, tasteless, and horribly expensive, costing more than 684 million euros,[30] enabling crime and corruption that are able to go unpunished in a highly dysfunctional country such as mine.

Ultimately, it was a national inferiority complex coupled with the questioning of Macedonian identity by its neighbours that provided room for megalomaniac projects focused on presenting Macedonian heritage as splendid, grand, and ancient – in other words, a heritage that guarantees a national identity. Skopje 2014 is the most visible form of this nationalistic frenzy, but it was at the same time that a series of equally grandiose sister projects emerged – in the field of literary translation.

In an essay on the twenty years since the independence of the Republic of Macedonia, 'After Twenty Years', Mitko Madžunkov, a member of the Macedonian Academy of Arts and Sciences, writes about Macedonian identity and language: 'The identity of a nation above all lies in its language, the gatekeeper of its memory.'[31] He further criticizes the decaying state of the Macedonian language, as well as the government's focus on the process of so-called 'antiquization', rather than the Slavic heritage of the language and the richness of its southern dialects. Claiming that all these years after the codification of Macedonian, people have yet to learn to love their literary language, he praises the efforts of the government and Ministry of Culture 'to finance capital projects important for the promotion of our language. … When the main works of world literature are translated into a clean and mature literary language, then nothing in the world can challenge either the language or the people and culture to whom it belongs'.[32]

Thus spoke Madžunkov of the first Gargantuan project commissioned by the government of the former prime minister Nikola Gruevski (now a refugee with political asylum in Hungary, wanted by Interpol after fleeing Macedonia when he was given a prison sentence). The project – unimaginatively named Stars of World Literature – encompassed 560 volumes of classics of world literature, though for some reason it also includes Henry Kissinger's *The White House Years* and Konrad Adenauer's *Memoirs*. Mitko Madžunkov became chief editor of the editorial board who selected the books, edited the translations, and proposed guidelines for the translations and the afterword essays of the works. Apart from Mitko Madžunkov, there were five other men on the editorial board – writers, translators, professors, and/or members of the Macedonian Academy of Arts and Sciences: Luan Starova, Taško Širilov, Dragi Mihajlovski (the translator of the complete works of Shakespeare, mentioned above), Venko Andonovski, and Ratko Duev. All of the volumes in the project were translated within four years, with several publishing houses getting tenders for the translations and allowing ample room for the exploitation of translators.

To my great regret, I participated in this project, having one day met Dragi Mihajlovski at work, in the English Department where we both taught. He said he had put me down for the translation of Capote's *In Cold Blood*, as well as three novels by Coetzee, to be published in one volume: *Boyhood, Youth*, and *Disgrace*. It felt odd that *Summertime* was not in the selection, but I was young and felt privileged that an important figure such as Mihajlovski had asked me to translate these works I deeply admired, so I agreed. I was then approached by the publishing house and given a very low translation fee, which I foolishly accepted, thinking that if I did not, I would perhaps lose the opportunity to translate such great works.

In his essay 'Stars of World Literature',[33] Madžunkov points out that specific guidelines would be provided to the translators and writers of the afterwords to ensure that these works retained high standards. As a translator, I was subjected to one such set of guidelines: it was a document called 'Glossary of Incorrections – Version 2', and was essentially a list of words or phrases that were not to be used in any of the translated books, as well as a list of their equivalent variants. This is, in fact, a list of exclusions that disallows the use of words used in Serbian, for instance, or words that would be used in colloquial speech. There are absurd examples where certain words that exist in the dictionary are excluded and replaced with variants of the south Macedonian dialect (such as the verb *vdžaši* – to be stunned, awestruck – to be replaced with *vdžasi*, or the word for governess *dadilka* to be replaced with the dialectal *dadijarka*). The document ends with the following comment: 'All words in this *Glossary of Incorrections* have been taken from the revised translations of the *Stars of World Literature* project. We are convinced that the best way to learn is from one's mistakes!'

Once a translator submitted his or her work to the publishing house, they would send it off to the editorial board for revision. The editorial board would then play 'find/replace' with the words in the glossary – and if there were words from the list that were still being used, they would send it back to the publishing house for revision. I remember that Ognen Čemerski, having coined words and used non-standard language in his translation of *Moby Dick*, found a way to convince them that this was founded on research and was in the spirit of the original; I also wrote explanatory notes to the board, clarifying that the translation of Perry Smith's father's letters in Capote's *In Cold Blood* were intentionally illiterate. I emphasized that they should leave the direct speech alone since it was deliberately colloquial. I was lucky that my novels survived the revisions, with a few edits from the glossary that I reluctantly had to let go. But other works were not so fortunate.

This was the case with *The Adventures of Huckleberry Finn*, translated by the writer and translator Kalina Maleska. After submitting her translation, she received it back with a message from the editorial board saying that the language in the novel needed to be standardized, upon which she sent them an explanation regarding the importance of colloquial language in the novel. She writes: 'But I was caught by surprise several days ago when I saw the printed version of the novel and found that this spoken, colloquial, non-standardized language of the uneducated fourteen-year-old boy had turned into Macedonian standard language abiding by all the rules of written literary language.'[34] Maleska distances herself from this translation, claiming that the changes made on 'literally ever page' of the novel without her permission are 'unprofessional and unethical'.

There are further examples of how the editorial board comprised of six male academics dealt with selecting and reviewing 560 volumes of translations. There are instances where literary works were translated by more than one translator, such as Tolstoy's *War and Peace*, whose first three volumes have been translated by one translator (Ana Neverova Hristova) and the fourth by another (Emil Nijami). There was also the occasion when the board commissioned a translation of a poetry anthology entitled *Poets of the Beat Generation* and included Ginsberg, Burroughs, and Bukowski in it. I was to translate Bukowski. The translator of Ginsberg, Zoran Ančevski, informed the board that Bukowski was not part of the Beat generation, so they reluctantly changed the title of book to *American Avant-Garde Poets*. Also, once they had tried to buy the rights for *Boyhood*, *Youth*, and *Disgrace* by Coetzee, they had been informed that *Boyhood* and *Youth* were part of a trilogy, and that separate rights to the novels would not be sold. So, they decided to only go with *Disgrace*, which I translated as part of the project,[35] again for a ridiculously low fee.

Not much criticism has been generated about these translations, perhaps because all the translators were busy translating. Living in a small country makes it very difficult to criticize objectively, because the bad translator might be your friend, neighbour, relative, or at least a friend of a friend, and the laissez-faire editor was probably your professor. But the damage done to Macedonian literature in translation and to the Macedonian language did not end here. Several new editions were proposed and carried out by the government in the following years, privileging recipients of renowned prizes such as the Pulitzer and Booker. By 2017, there were 316 volumes translated and edited by the same editorial board, excluding Dragi Mihajlovski.[36] This period also marks the emergence of the Nobel Prize Edition, consisting of 146 published books,[37] edited by three members: again Mitko Madžunkov, Ratko Duev, and Taško Širilov. The Catalogue of the Ministry of Culture published in 2015 also notes the emergence of yet another project that proposes the publication of 366 books: Heights of World Philosophy, History, Psychology, and Psychoanalysis, though according to the database of the National Library, it seems that only about half of the projected books were published, probably due to the change of government in 2017. Other translation projects were commissioned by the Ministry of Culture too: 135 Volumes of Macedonian Literature – translated into English, as well as the ridiculous-sounding project Translation of 1000 Scholarly and Scientific Books and Textbooks Used at the Best, Most Prominent and Most Renowned Universities in the USA, England, and for Studies of Law in France and Germany. According to a recent news report, tens of thousands of these books are stuck in the National Library and other institutions, taking up space, with the new government not wanting to take on the responsibility of dealing with them.[38]

In 2015, I wrote an article in the magazine *Kulturen život* analysing the various translations of *Catcher in the Rye*. As this book is on the reading list in high schools, publishers will publish the book (it is questionable whether they have actually acquired the rights) to lucrative ends. A similar situation occurs with the five existing translations of *Alice in Wonderland*, each of them worse than the first one published in 1957 and translated indirectly from what I found was a combination of two Serbian versions.[39] The last translator of *Catcher in the Rye* is Ivana Ilkovska in 2015, as part of the Stars of World Literature project. Ilkovska's translation, it seems, translates the novel's name correctly (unlike all the others, which thus destroy the symbolism in the title), but remains rigid in its language, missing out on the colloquial *skaz* of the original.[40] The name of this translator stood out to me because she had been my student and her name appeared to crop up frequently. I then made a list of all the works she'd been credited as a translator of, the years when those books were published, the series, and the publishing house. Most of these books were published under the auspices of government projects, with one newly established publishing house which had been given the tender for the publication – Ars Studio. The number of years – four. The number of works translated in those four years? Forty-three. Forty-three books in four years – a fact which speaks for itself. *Tom Jones, To the Lighthouse, Dubliners, The Collected Stories of Cheever, Interpreter of Maladies, No One Writes to the Colonel, The Narrow Road to the Deep North, The Magician of Lublin* – these are just some of the forty-three books translated in these four years.

But the translator is the least of those who should bear the blame for leaving behind a shabby legacy. Many of the translators were in their twenties and thought they had been given a chance they should not miss. But there are also those who were working in the publishing houses that won the tenders for the government projects. These publishing houses decided how much to pay their employees, and word has it that, in fact, just to keep their jobs, employees were made to slave away translating books they did not choose, and all as part of their regular salary. What was the editorial board doing when all of this was happening? How did the translators and professors in the editorial board protect their own former students from violent exploitation? They kept their mouths shut, got paid, and attended the book launches hosted by the fugitive criminal former prime minister. No one looked into the four publishing houses which miraculously received all the tenders for the projects. No one was asked to account for the monstrous body of bad work that has not only impoverished the regular taxpayer: it has impoverished the language and literacy of the country as a whole.

Conclusion

I see translation as a political act inseparable from its social context that has lasting consequences for the development of a country's cultural legacy. As a translator in a small country that has been transitioning from socialism into capitalism for more than two decades, I find that the political climate is crucial for the choices a translator makes. Hence, the challenges of translating into a minor language are not only conditioned by the unavailability of resources and, in the case of Macedonian, also the lack of a written tradition: they are strongly related to government policies and economic instability, which in the case of independent Macedonia has created ample room for corruption through the exploitation of translators and a preference for quantity over quality.

Notes

1 *Statistical Yearbook of the Republic of Macedonia* (2013), www.stat.gov.mk/Publikacii/PDFGodisnik2013/03-Naselenie-Population.pdf.
2 Blaže Koneski, *Gramatika na makedonskiot jazik, del 1*. (Skopje: Prosvetno delo, 1952); Blaže Koneski, *Gramatika na makedonskiot jazik, del 2*. (Skopje: Prosvetno delo, 1954).
3 Simona Gruevska-Madžoska, 'Dali sme izgubeni vo prevodot', *Kulturen život* 3–4 (July-November, 2006), 33.

4 Kiril Koneski, ed., *Tolkoven rečnik na makedonskiot jazik T-Š*. (Skopje: Institut za makedonski jazik 'Krste Misirkov', 2014)
5 Anastasija Gjurčinova and Sonja Stojmenska-Elzeser, 'Svetskata kniževnost vo prevod na makedonski jazik (1945–1990)', *Spektar, God.* X, no 19 (June 1992), 93–107.
6 Bogomil Gjuzel (translator from English into Macedonian), in discussion with the author, 7 May 2019.
7 Vlada Urošević (translator from French into Macedonian) and Tanja Urošević (translator from Russian into Macedonian), in discussion with the author, 20 June 2019.
8 Zoran Ančevski (translator from English into Macedonian), in discussion with the author, 20 May 2019.
9 Gjurčinova and Stojmenska-Elzeser, 'Svetskata kniževnost', 95.
10 *Statistical Yearbook of the Republic of Macedonia* (2013).
11 Gjurčinova and Stojmenska-Elzeser, 'Svetskata kniževnost', 97.
12 Ančevski, discussion.
13 Ognen Čemerski, *Trista vetrila! Ili za preveduvanjeto i prebroduvanjeto* (Skopje: Blesok, 2015), 105.
14 Rejmond Karver [Raymond Carver], 'Katedrala', in *Za što zboruvame koga zboruvame za ljubovta*, trans. Sveto Serafimov (Skopje: Kultura, 1990), 45.
15 Gjurčinova and Stojmenska-Elzeser, 'Svetskata kniževnost', 100.
16 Rajna Koška-Hot, 'Čekajki go vistinskiot zbor', *Kulturen život* 57, no. 3/4 (July–November 2012), 19.
17 Dragi Mihajlovski, *Pod Vavilon: Zadačata na preveduvačot* (Skopje: Kaprikornus, 2002).
18 Anastasija Gjurčinova, 'Spanish Poetry in Macedonian Translations (after 1945)', in *IberoSlavica: A Peer Reviewed Yearbook of the International Society for Iberian-Slavonic Studies*, ed. Beata Elzbieta Cieszynska (Lisbon: CompaRes 2011), 85.
19 Gjurčinova, 'Spanish Poetry', 87.
20 Gjurčinova and Stojmenska-Elzeser, 'Svetskata kniževnost', 103.
21 Gjuzel, discussion.
22 Ančevski, discussion.
23 Gjurčinova and Stojmenska-Elzeser, 'Svetskata kniževnost', 106.
24 Republic of North Macedonia State Statistical Office, *Labor Market News Release* (7 June 2019), www.stat.gov.mk/pdf/2019/2.1.19.20_mk.pdf.
25 Mihajlovski, *Pod Vavilon*.
26 Koška-Hot, 'Čekajki go vistinskiot zbor', 18.
27 Čemerski, Ognen *Trista vetrila! Ili za preveduvanjeto i prebroduvanjeto* (Skopje: Blesok 2015).
28 Anastasija Gjurčinova, 'Prevodite od italijanskata kniževnost na makedonski jazik', in *Makedonsko-romanitsički jazični, književni i preveduvački relacii (2000–2015)*, ed. Irina Babamova (Skopje: Blaže Koneski Faculty of Philology, 2015), 199–210.

29 Kit Gillet, 'How Skopje Became Europe's New Capital of Kitsch', *The Guardian* (11 April 2015), www.theguardian.com/travel/2015/apr/11/skopje-macedonia-architecture-2014-project-building, accessed 29 October 2021.
30 'Skopje 2014 Uncovered', Project for Investigative Journalism and Cooperation Between Media and Civil Society – USAID Program for Strengthening Independent Media in Macedonia, last modified 1 May 2018, http://skopje2014.prizma.birn.eu.com/en, accessed 30 June 2020.
31 Mitko Madžunkov, 'Po dvaeset godini', *Naše pismo* 18, no. 73/74 (2012), 6.
32 Madžunkov, 'Po dvaeset godini', 6.
33 Mitko Madžunkov, 'Dzvezdi na svetskata kniževnost: voved kon edicijata', *Naše pismo* 18, no. 73/74 (2012), 2–5.
34 Kalina Maleska, 'Zošto strav od kolokvijalniot jazik?', *Okno* (1 December 2014), https://okno.mk/node/42715, accessed 29 October 2021.
35 For help with terms in Afrikaans or other locally specific words this time round I used social media to search for people in Macedonia who are from South Africa, which is how I met Jacob Laubscher, a South African man married to a Macedonian woman living and working in the south of the country. Jacob helped me immensely with the translation.
36 Government of the Republic of North Macedonia, 'Promovirani 53 naslovi od novata edicija, "Svetsko kniževno bogatstvo"' (11 October 2016), https://vlada.mk/node/12460?ln=en-gb, accessed 30 June 2020.
37 Biljana Kjulavkovska, *Katalog: Kapitalni knigoizdatelski proekti* (Skopje: Ministry of Culture of the Republic of Macedonia, 2015).
38 Sotir Trajkov, 'Knigite od kapitalnite proekti koi ležat po magacini' Vladata kje gi distribuira po magacini od septemvri, https://arhiva.telma.com.mk/knigite-od-kapitalnite-proekti-koi-lezhat-po-magatsini-vladata-ke-gi-distribuira-po-institutsii-od-septemvri/, accessed 7 March 2021.
39 Rumena Bužarovska, 'On the Macedonian Translations of Alice', in *Alice in A World Of Wonderlands*, vol. I, ed. Jon Lindseth (Delaware: Oak Knoll Press, 2015), 358.
40 Rumena Bužarovska, 'Igri so lovcite vo 'ržta', *Kulturen život* 1, no. 2 (2015), 53.

CHAPTER 14

An Other Language
Translation and Internationality
Naoki Sakai

It may go without saying that an encounter with a foreign language, a language different from one's own, allows one to reflectively recognize the language of one's self. In this instance, one may observe a routine dialectic procedure of self-consciousness or self-recognition through a reflective negativity. Before proceeding to the typical formula of self-postulation, however, we should pay more attention to the terms in which the dialectic of self-knowledge is played out. How do we know that we are somewhat dependent upon our language, that we are predetermined by what is called "our own language" or "native language," which is supposedly handed down to us from our mothers, our families, our ancestors, our nation, or our tradition?

In logical sequencing, the recognition of one's own language seems preceded by that of a foreign language. A foreign language is, always, another and one more language, or *an other language*, that is other than one's own, posterior to one's own, even though it is anterior to one's own in the temporal sequence of cognition. Thereupon one of the most elementary questions about translation, which is also among the most difficult to answer, is this: most often, translation is apprehended as an event that takes place involving two entities, each of which is recognized as a unified and self-enclosed entity; it is most often taken for granted that translation takes place between two individuated languages.

Historicity of Language as a Concept

Rather than confronting the task of elucidating the individuation of language head-on, let me begin this chapter with a short autobiographical account of how I encountered this problematic for the first time.

It was when I was involved in my dissertation research, in the late 1970s and early '80s. The field I chose to enter as a graduate student was the intellectual history of early modern Japan, from the seventeenth century through to the Meiji Restoration (1868), a period roughly stretching from the inauguration of the Tokugawa Shogunate around 1600 until a sort of revolution in 1868, when Japanese society began to be rapidly modernized. This is why today the Meiji Restoration is regarded as a milestone that marks the end of the early modern era – usually called the Tokugawa or Edo period in conventional chronology – and the beginning of the modern era in Japanese national history.

The early modern era witnessed the rapid development of linguistic studies in Japan, and, in due course, I began to read old studies on languages published in the seventeenth and eighteenth centuries in northeast Asia. As a matter of fact, as I read some books and essays on languages and related matters of the Tokugawa period, I became interested in the subject matter commented on, analyzed, and interpreted by the Tokugawa scholars from a variety of intellectual backgrounds – some Confucian scholars, some Buddhist monks studying the sutra in Sanskrit and Pali, some specialists of Chinese rituals, and yet others early pioneers of Japanese mythology. Many of their treatises were actually written in classical Chinese, and some other narratives, encyclopedia articles, commentaries, historiographies, government ordinances, and personal letters written in a variety of styles, pseudo-classical Japanese (*gikobun*), a peculiar composite of classical Chinese and academic Japanese (*yomikudashi bun*), epistolary Japanese (a different composite of Chinese and Japanese words, *sôrôbun*), styles of theatrical and recital narrative (*katari*), and so on. Let me highlight this extraordinary diversity of graphic and textual modes in contrast to the relative homogeneity of narrative styles in modern Japan; I will later return to the issues of this diversity of language uses that characterized the societies of the Tokugawa or the Edo period in the Japanese archipelago. In examining the variety of published texts – not only academic treatises, but also vernacular literature which began to be mass-produced through the introduction of commercial printing technology and the new literary device of the direct citation of colloquial speech – I was struck by one conspicuous absence in spite of the abundance of discussions, analyses, commentaries, and interpretations of many aspects of linguistic activities. The linguists and philologists of the Tokugawa period argued extensively about speech patterns, etymology, morphologies according to which words were classified and their grammatical functions recognized; conjugation patterns of verbs, adjectivals and adverbials were identified, and phonetic diversity – synchronic as well as diachronic – was studied in Confucianism, Buddhism, Shintoism, and Japanese mythology, collections of local folk tales, and so on. I was puzzled, however, that, despite this amazing wealth and breadth of scholarship, it was almost impossible to find a word signifying the concept of "language" in the sense of a national or ethnic language.

The Tokugawa philologists and linguists paid meticulous attention to many aspects of linguistic activities such as speaking, listening, writing, reading, composing, drawing, and so on. Yet they did not seem to have a concept that summarily signified what we today call "language" in the sense of the English, German, French, Chinese, or Japanese language that is supposed to designate one that is commonly spoken, written, comprehended, and read by the members of a community that shares the same ethnicity or nationality delimited by definite geographic boundaries. Accordingly, they did not have a clear awareness of *foreign* languages, of *other* languages. It follows that there seemed to exist no clear recognition of their *own language* or *languages* among the scholars of the Tokugawa Japan.

Logically speaking, it is almost impossible to prove that there was no concept or word for a specific referent in the entirety of one society or geographic realm of discourse for a given period, whereas its presence can easily be demonstrated by mentioning one exemplary case. The topic of "language" in Tokugawa Japan was no exception. However, I was fortunate enough to avoid being caught in an endless pursuit of the impossible task of proving a negative since, later in the eighteenth century, a small number of philologists began to challenge the conventional academic practices of Tokugawa Japan; they argued for something like "language" by introducing a particular way of viewing speaking, writing, hearing, and reading in a certain discourse on linguistic activities. A small number of philologists began to talk about a "foreign" language that contaminated what should have been authentically their own. As the discursive formation underwent a radical change, there emerged, perhaps for the first time, a new *historical a priori* of discourse, which, with certain reservations indeed, we can approximate to the modern notion of "language." I was able to contrast a discursive formation in which "language" was absent to another formation where it was evident. But their own "language" which they referred to was not existent in its presence in their contemporary world. Instead, they began to talk about their own in its absence or in its loss. What they first recognized was the predominance of another "foreign" language, by which their own "language" must have been conquered, oppressed, or annihilated. In their historical mythology, their own language must have existed before the arrival of foreign language, but in their sequencing of recognition, the knowledge of an "other" foreign language preceded it. In my dissertation,[1] I called this event of disruption, this sudden emergence of "their language," the "stillbirth of the Japanese as a language and as an ethnos."[2]

Indeed I was bewildered that the national or ethnic language of the Japanese people had not been recognized until around the eighteenth century. I had never been told that multitudes inhabiting the Japanese archipelago did not recognize the presence of their own national or ethnic language, which they must have spoken, read, written, and listened to in everyday life in premodern Japan. The modern disciplines of national history and linguistics – the study of the Japanese language (*kokugo*) was specially marked as a discipline distinct from other branches of linguistics[3] – were imported from European and American academia and established as academic disciplines at newly formed universities in the late nineteenth century; as a rule, these disciplines projected the presence of the Japanese nation (or Japanese ethnicity) and the Japanese language back into a past prior to the modernization of Japanese society. The founders of modern linguistics were particularly uncritical of the presumptions they projected onto the past, precisely because they were wittingly committed to the missions of nation-building in the late nineteenth and early twentieth centuries.

It is worthwhile noting, however, that the discovery of the Japanese language – prompting the establishment of the school of National Studies (*Kokugaku*) – occurred much earlier, in the eighteenth century, more than one century before the introduction of national disciplines of Japanese history, linguistics, and literature in Japanese education. But the Japanese language as their mythological imago was entirely different from the image of the national language of Japan promoted in the late nineteenth and early twentieth centuries. Only through an acknowledgement that multitudes inhabiting the Japanese archipelago *must have been* speaking and listening to a language entirely foreign to Chinese languages, as well as living in an entirely different linguistic milieu prior to the contamination in antiquity of the originary Japanese nation by Chinese writing, could the scholars of National Studies recognize, perhaps for the first time, that the Chinese classical language and Chinese ideographic characters were foreign to the Japanese.[4] The acknowledgement of Chinese language(s) as foreign made it possible for them to value their own native language as an imaginary figure or a mytheme around which their academic inquiries of National Studies were organized. Simultaneously it became possible for them to talk about their own ethnic community which *must have shared* the same language and which had nonetheless ceased to exist under the contamination of Chinese civilization. Having discovered that, in premodern Japan, there had hardly been a recognition of language as such, or the national language in general, and that the very concept of language could emerge only after certain intellectual disruption or revolution, I began to inquire into the very discursive formation – still dominant in the early twenty-first century – in which the presence of a nation or ethnic language is taken for granted. This is to say that the Japanese language serves as a *historical a priori*.

Let me draw the reader's attention to two points. In the first place, the discovery of a Japanese language and ethnos was never based on the acknowledgement of verifiable empirical facts; it was prior to any factual corroboration in terms of empirical experience; it belonged to the register in which the very possibility of empirical experience was preliminarily constituted. It was prompted by the introduction of a certain imaginary; certain images of the speech community and language could be projected into the distant past, of which no written history existed. In this respect, the arrangement of images concerning native language and community was deliberate in the sense that the scholars of National Studies always sought for the ancient times when people did not know how to write and read; they postulated a history of illiteracy before writing.

In the second place, the discovery of language in general, and of the Japanese language in particular, was accomplished by the postulation of an other foreign language in the schematism of co-figuration. It was facilitated by the introduction of the dialectic of the other and the self, of a foreign language and one's own language. It is by means of a new representation of translation that a foreign language was postulated as an other language in contradistinction to which one's own language was asserted. Only when Chinese writing was recognized as "foreign" did it become possible to imagine the existence of a Japanese language as an individual one that *must have preceded* the civilizational contamination by Chinese literacy. The new regime of translation was introduced, whereby it was rendered appropriate to imagine Chinese writing and Japanese speech as separate, as external and antagonistic to one another. Two distinct unities of language, Chinese and Japanese, were thus associated with the cartographic configuration of the ocean, the continent, and islands, even though neither the subjects of the Qing dynasty nor those of the Tokugawa Feudal Confederacy had acquired the modern notion of territory. To this extent, the spatial configuration of co-figuration was somewhat anticipated in the discursive revolution of the eighteenth century. But, it is important to note, this geographic figuration of Japan and China took place outside the international world, prior to the inclusion of Japan in the reign of internationality in the modern world.

In order to further elucidate what is suggested by the emergence of language, we must be concerned with two problematics. One is the individuation or the individuality of language. The other is the modern regime of translation, a certain institutional arrangement, by means of which the practices of translation are represented, regulated, and integrated into a disciplinary formation in the production of knowledge.

The Individuation of Language

In elucidating what is meant by the individuation of language, I first want to express my gratitude to Morio Tagai, who wrote a brilliant book entitled *Ferdinand de Saussure – Solitude of <Linguistics> and the Dream of [General Linguistics]*.[5] I came to know the issues surrounding the concept of language mainly through Tagai's meticulous analysis of the body of writings left behind by Saussure and his students.

It is well known that the first published version of Ferdinand de Saussure's *Cours de linguistique générale* (edited and published by Charles Bally and Albert Sechehaye in 1922[6]) contains many additions and interpretations by the editors that seem to betray some arguments presented at the lectures on general linguistics (1907–1911) at the University of Geneva by Saussure; it is hard to say to what extent the publication of this version can be ascertained to be attributable to the original lecturer. So, today, one relies on transcriptions and/or commentaries taken by some other students who attended the famous linguist's lectures at the University of Geneva. Saussure gave three term-long courses on general linguistics from 1907 to 1911, and it is known that several students took notes on them. In reading some transcripts and commentaries left behind from his last course (the third course on general linguistics, 28 October 1910–4 July 1911), an enigmatic statement appears that one of the enrolled students, Émile Constantine, attributed to Saussure. According to Constantine, Saussure argued: "The result: we can map boundaries clearly for dialectal features, but mapping boundaries of a dialect is impossible."[7]

The major themes addressed in the third-year course (1910–1911) on general linguistics included the problem of comparison concerning historical (temporal) and geographic (spatial) diversity in linguistics. Here, let us keep in mind that, in discussing dialectal diversity, Saussure sustains throughout a rigorous distinction between dialect and the dialectal features (*caractères dialectaux*). To elucidate this point, he appeals to an episode of a traveler who journeys from one place to another and encounters different dialectal features. As he travels, he has to adjust his use of words, pronunciation, and expressions in general. He is forced to compare one set of features to another as he moves along. As he travels from one locality to another, he crosses new frontiers that indicate new features. It is therefore feasible to draw a map of dialectal features by drawing these lines that mark the transition in dialectal features. In showing the transition in features but not the circumference of a geographic enclosure, the lines on this map of dialectal features have been called "isogloss lines" or "lines of isoglosses" (*isogloss* deriving perhaps from *isotherm*, meaning localities with the same temperature). However, these isogloss lines, each separating one area from another, never fit together. "If the areas fitted together after this fashion, then what people imagine a dialect to be would be correct. Because a given dialect would then differ at all locations, in all features, from the neighbouring dialect. But that never happens."[8] Certainly one cannot deny the existence of different dialectal features between one place and another, between one group of speakers and another. Again: "We can map boundaries clearly for dialectal features, but mapping boundaries of a dialect is impossible."

Let me construe the issues being addressed in the notebooks recorded by Émile Constantine. The traveler notices that a feature of language spoken locally changes as he moves from one locality to another; this change is recognized as a difference in dialectal feature and mapped as one instance of border crossing from one region to another. But *a* dialect – please allow me to treat a dialect as if it were an individual – has many features. Therefore, it is reasonable to expect that, as the traveler continues, he will draw many different maps of dialectal features. But there is no guarantee whatsoever that those maps of these multiple features will all coincide with or converge into the same circumference so as to form an enclosure. From this schematic presentation, Saussure draws two conclusions:

(1) Supposing there were a (uniform) language A and an equally uniform language B, the presence of a transition zone would be surprising. But language A is an aggregate of dialects internally related, while language B is likewise an aggregate of dialects. Everything is transitional from one end of the area to the other.[9]

Difference in dialectal feature can be mapped as a line separating one region, where a particular dialectal feature is homogeneously shared, from another region where a distinct feature is homogeneously shared; in a similar manner, difference in another sort of dialectal feature can be mapped as a line separating one region from another.

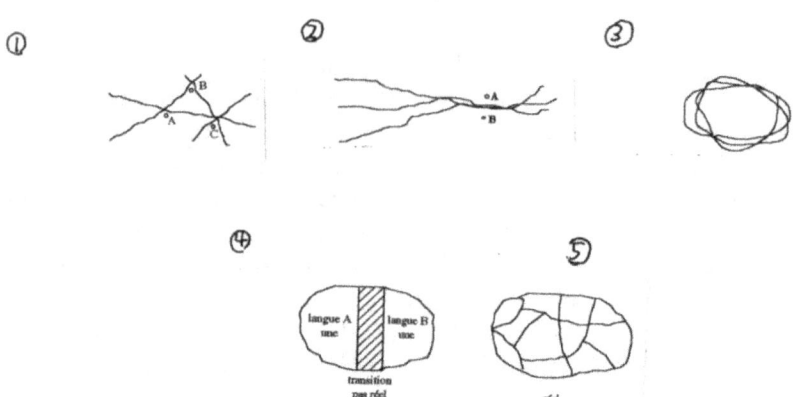

Figure 14.1   Illustrations of dialectal features (Saussure, *Troisième cours*: figures are on p. 26, p. 27, p. 28, p. 31, and p. 31 respectively).

In some rare cases, a line of difference in one dialectal feature may overlap with another line of difference in another dialectal feature. But there is no guarantee that this will happen repeatedly.

Many lines of differences in multiple dialectal features all converge to form an enclosure. This *cannot* be expected to happen.

If such a convergence should happen, a circumscribed language would be separated from another circumscribed one. And language A can be separated from language B by a boundary. But this never happens.

Lines of difference in dialectal features do not converge, and they never form a circumscribed enclosure of one language.

(2) In the schema I have just presented, I assume dialects to be closed, but ultimately there are only dialects open to all sides, formed by the succession of waves in which they participate. We must not imagine there are boundaries between language A and language B.[10]

Dialects cannot be understood as a series of closed, determinate, circumscribed linguistic types. Thus, Saussure denies that one can deduce from these differentiated dialectal features the segregation of one dialect from another or the plurality of dialects. The traveler can compare one dialectal feature with another, but he cannot conclude from the perceived actuality of dialectic diversity, a plurality of dialects. Dialectal diversity cannot be construed in terms of a plurality of enumerable units. It may be possible to represent dialectal features in terms of borders, but it is almost impossible to map a dialect as an enclosed or unified region encircled by a coherent border because the dialect is not an individual; it cannot be individuated. From this it immediately follows that a similar operation can be conducted not only about dialects but also about languages. An exactly identical deductive reasoning can be applied to languages in general. Therefore, it is not hard to conclude that languages as individual unities do not exist. Just as dialects cannot be enumerated, languages cannot be enumerated either. We cannot talk about the plurality of languages as if they could be counted as one, two, three, just like apples and oranges.

What is called into question by Ferdinand de Saussure is a set of presumptions that one relies upon in order to compare, count, and distinguish languages. These must be presumptions or the rules of operations that we require in order to carry on the business of internationality as usual, since one does not know in what modalities and under what conditions languages can possibly be enumerable, distinguishable, or comparable as required in the modern international world. Regardless of whether or not we are assured by what measure something like water can be counted, through what procedure one mountain range is distinguished from another, or in what aspect apples can be compared with oranges, we make preliminary judgements, namely presumptions, asserting or presuming that languages are in fact enumerable, distinguishable and comparable from the outset. In order to count time, for example, one is likely to appeal to counting units such as seconds, minutes, and hours; days, months, and years; or periodical units such as centuries and names of eras; in order to compare one society with another, one could focus on the types of polity such as representative parliamentarianism, monarchy, or one-party dictatorship. Yet, when we deal with languages (or dialects), we *presume* that languages are unproblematically individual unities whose enumerability is somewhat given; they are distinguished from one another as circumscribed enclosures, which can be compared with one another as if, from the outset, they were given as indivisible entities.

Thus, it is *presumed* that languages are countable, distinguishable and comparable prior to the determination of the measure, of the manner of distinction, and of the terms of comparison. Consequently, we take for granted that languages are entities that can be treated by the formula of logical classification, the hierarchical ordering in terms of *individual, species,* and *genus* a logical procedure traditionally attributed to Aristotle.[11]

Accordingly, in our conventional treatment of languages, each one is recognized as a particular individual case subsumed under the general class of languages; each language is distinguished from another by its species difference or *diaphora*. In other words, it is taken for granted that at the same time each language is an individual and a member of a set or *species* of languages. Yet it is necessary to note that the application of classical formula cannot be done coherently even in this instance. For, within each language, there are dialects, so that a language encompasses a wide variety of dialectal features and is composed of an ensemble of such dialectal diversity. In this respect, insofar as each language consists of dialectal diversity, a language is not an *individual*, that is, it is not an indivisible unity that cannot be further divided. On the contrary, we never deny that any language contains regional diversities and is already a composite of dialects, even if we overlook diachronic diversity. As long as we regard dialect as appropriate to the classification formula of *individual, species,* and *genus*, a language must be registered, not at the level of the indivisible unit, but at the level of *species*, a set consisting of dialects. Inevitably all these logical inconsistencies derive from the presumption that a language is an individual, and that the plurality of languages should be construed in terms of international juxtaposition.

Why are we so accustomed to treating languages as individuals, each of which forms an indivisible whole, unambiguously distinguished from other languages, and compared with other unities in a homogeneous space? The world in which these presumptions are incontestably endorsed is constituted as the *international world* where many different languages, such as German, English, Chinese, Spanish, Korean, and so forth, are supposed to coexist side by side. It is supposedly a space of commensurability in which languages are enumerable, distinguishable, and comparable. Just as scientific cartography invented by people like Gerardus Mercator in the early modern period projects the vision of the world, these presumptions sustain the world of internationality where the necessary conditions for the possibility of the modern world are endorsed. Just as modern cartography was called *fabrica mundi* – the fabrication of the world, meaning "'the proportion,' the 'order' or 'texture' of the world the map is supposed to represent," according to Sandro Mezzadra and Brett Neilson[12] – the international world thus fabricated is an embodiment of the modernity in which each territory of state sovereignty is expected to be unambiguously distinguished by a national border, and juxtaposed to other comparable national territories. An equivalent to *fabrica mundi*, what regulates the imaginary of the modern international world in translation is what I have called "the schematism of co-figuration," operating in the representation of translation according to the modern regime of translation.[13]

Thus it is no surprise that I could hardly find the concept of "language" in the discourse on linguistic activities in northeast Asia prior to the eighteenth century when I conducted my dissertation research. The inhabitants of the Japanese archipelago, for instance, did not apprehend everyday activities of speaking, listening, writing, reading, drawing, inscribing, and so forth in terms of internationality. Neither did they attempt to translate "foreign" texts written in Chinese characters into a "language of their own" according to the modern regime of translation.

The internationality of the world is nothing but an arrangement of biopower sustained by a set of presumptions according to which languages are postulated preliminarily as indivisible unities that are enumerable, unambiguously distinguished, and mutually comparable. Just as the modern international world indicates a political organization of global space in which sovereign states are juxtaposed to one another, each endowed with its subject population as well as its own territory clearly circumscribed by its national border, internationality means the reign of rules, summarily conventionalized in International Law (*Jus Publicum Europaeum*); every square meter of land surface on the earth must be subjugated to a sovereign state. Furthermore, the internationality of the modern world demands that languages are individuals, each associated with a national population. Hence, each language thus postulated is named after its nation, German, Japanese, French, Korean, Italian, and so forth.

Now the set of presumptions that sustain the internationality of the modern world must be investigated with a view to the very process by which the diversity of language is transformed into multiplicity, and reduced to an international plurality.

Representing Translation

At stake in our discussion on the individuality of language are the postulates of operation – norms, criteria, and rules of conduct – according to which a language is distinguished, compared, and identified as a countable unity that is juxtaposed to other similar and comparable unities of language. These postulates are most effectual when translation is represented. However, let me issue a disclaimer in my use of the term "representation." As far as the modern regime of translation is concerned, the representation of translation is not a constative statement that is descriptive of an experience empirically given. It is similar to *fabrica mundi* in its function, for this representation fabricates rather than reproduces or reiterates; it projects what is yet to come rather than constates or ascertains what has been objectively established. It is before the reality is proven valid, acceptable, or truthful, or prior to the procedure of corroboration or substantiation that the postulates are demanded. No matter whether or not they are empirically verifiable, these postulates must be accepted. Therefore, they are called "*pre*sumptions," and precede empirical verification. These presumptions are necessary because a certain operation, which is also characterized as a pro-ject, cannot be undertaken without them. Therefore, let me tentatively call this operation or project, for which these postulates are required, "translation" of a sort – not translation in the actuality of the present perfect but a "prescriptive translation" to come in the future anterior.

Retrospectively I can see that what I found in premodern Japan was a situation in which the conception of language was yet to be regulated by the presumptions of the international world; until the eighteenth century, the inhabitants of the Japanese archipelago did not know how to operate according to the modern regime of translation. In due course it was natural or unsurprising that they did not know the concept of language as an individual accommodated in the system of the modern international world.

The Modern Regime of Translation

Translation is commonly used metaphorically, to such an extent that it is not easily distinguishable from a metaphor or a figurative expression in general; all too often it serves as a trope by which, for instance, a medical doctor's diagnosis is *translated* into everyday parlance for ordinary folks, or the literary script of a novelistic work is *translated* into the cinematic medium. Might translation be a metaphor in its etymology, so that, strictly speaking, there is no way to prevent translation from being used as a substitute for a metaphor? Given a wide range of tropic uses of the word "translation," it is no surprise that some scholars search for the definition of what translation ought to be in its propriety, for a definition of translation that serves effectively to distinguish translation as a trope or metaphor from translation proper, or translation in and of itself. So, what is translation proper, after all?

In our conventional apprehension of translation, the conduct of translating or the act of translation is presumed unnecessary unless *different* languages are at issue. In the last few centuries – at least, since the inauguration of the universal system of national education – the dominant apprehension of translation has assumed that it occurs between two different languages or a pair of languages, such as German and French or Hebrew and Greek. (For the time being, let us evade the possible question about whether or not translation is able to involve more than two languages. As becomes immediately obvious, this question itself depends upon how we are possibly able to count languages, on the modality of a language's enumerability.) In most cases, each of the paired languages between which the act of translation is performed is regarded as an individual marked by a clear-cut border that divides its inside from its outside, as an internally consistent entity that sustains an indivisible unity. Accordingly, it is further assumed that two *different* languages between which translation is conducted are different from one another, both in terms of individuality as well as indivisibility. Once again, it seems that we are drawn back to the initial question: what allows us to regard language as an individual, that can be symbolically, figuratively, and spatially represented as an enclosure with a clear border that divides its interior from its exterior?

Roman Jakobson is one linguist who has responded to these queries about the indivisible individuality of a language in translation as well as the difference of languages in translation at the same time. According to him, the non-tropic or proper use of translation is given in contrast to those apparently tropic or metaphoric uses of the word;[14] the propriety or the archetype of translation must be reserved for the type performed between two natural languages. He argues that translation in the proper sense must be distinguished both from *intralingual* translation – translation within the same language, not involving another one – and *intersemiotic* translation – translation involving non-linguistic sign systems – and that in the proper sense of the word it means an *interlingual* translation, a translation between one language and another, between two different languages external to one another.

The formulation Jakobson deploys in classifying translation types seems to be based upon an uncritical endorsement of the set of presumptions I have impugned. Conceding that the three types of translation he puts forth are operational hypotheses, whose truth values are to be judged by how well they serve to illuminate the workings of translation, I can hardly repress the suspicion that he guilelessly replicates conventional notions about the event of translation, the definition of translation, and the figures or schemata of languages in terms of which this dialogic event called translation is represented, imagined, or figured in the space of internationality.

Under these circumstances, let me reiterate my initial question concerning different languages: what kind of difference is at stake when we problematize the conventional view of translation? It is supposed that the difference of and in languages prompts translation, but the conduct of translation is also a response to this difference because it is usually believed that this sort of difference gives rise to a difficulty in understanding between interlocutors. For, whenever translation is mentioned, a certain scenario is presupposed by which some difficulty in comprehension or conversation naturally arises when different languages are involved. In our conventional apprehension of translation, therefore, difference in and of languages is often equated to the cause for some difficulty or impediment in apprehension between a speaker and a listener in dialogue, whereas, when no difference is involved, we do not normally expect such obstacles to arise. Accordingly, translation is supposedly a natural response to this dialogic barrier or hindrance that happens between interlocutors.

First of all, it is important to note that the conventional presumption about the difference between languages is misleading. Even though I should concede to the uses of such terms as difference, identity, the identity, and the individuality/indivisibility of language, and so forth, it is simply impossible to espouse the general thesis that difference in language is a cause of failure in communication or understanding. Heterogeneity in languages may well give rise to difficulty in comprehension among interlocutors, but the identity or homogeneity of language does not guarantee communicative success in understanding at all.

In this regard, let me further expound what kind of difference is expected or demanded in our apprehension of translation. How do we conceptualize this difference that supposedly accompanies or gives rise to the occasion of translation, insofar as translation is a response or reply to this situation marked by language difference? Is it a difference upheld in classical logic[15] – what is referred to as specific difference (*diaphora*) – that exists between two substances or individuals each of which cannot be further divided (*atomos* or *adiairetos*), and both of which share some common property by virtue of belonging to the same class, namely the *species* of languages in our case?[16]

The two languages A and B are separated from one another, and they are specifically different. At the same time, they can be subsumed under the same category since they both belong to the same class, that is, the species of languages. Thus the difference at issue is represented in terms of an interstice between two unified individual things, two individual languages, as if they were represented spatially as two figures or territories external to one another and marked by their respective circumscribing borders. Indeed, difference cannot be of a specific kind when either a "category mistake" or catachresis is committed. In addition to "category mistake" and catachresis, could there be some other kind of difference beyond a specific one, to remove the need to postulate two substantive or unified individuals between which there is an interstice?

While Jakobson sees no problem in subsuming the difference in languages to which translation is a response under the general category of difference between individuals, our discussion of translation may well take an alternative approach, since we entertain a different conception of difference, precisely because our discussion of it does not start with the premise that translation proper is an *interlingual* one, or as a response to difference subsumed in the classical concept of specific difference or *diaphora*. What if we assume that the difference of languages cannot be subsumed under specific difference, under the general category of difference between individuals both of which belong to the class of languages?

We cannot preclude the possibility that the difference involved in translation can be something else that is not subsumed under the general category of specific difference or *diaphora*; it can be a difference that does not require the postulation of languages as individuals. The difference at issue indicates not a space in which two different languages are linked together by communication but rather a locale of address where one interlocutor addresses her- or himself to another interlocutor. This difference is represented in the modality not of the present perfect but of the future anterior; it is not represented as a gap or cut that is bridged or spanned as a *fait accompli* but instead as a task to be worked on, a task that will have been accomplished in the future. While the representation of difference in communication is descriptive and constative in the modality of the present perfect, it is prescriptive in the modality of the future anterior. Tentatively I call this difference "discontinuity."

We now must call into question the historical conditions thanks to which the very classification of these types of translation – interlingual, intralingual, and intersemiotic translations – appears indisputable. These historical conditions are, most often, summarily referred to by "internationality" in the modern world, by the fact of our imaginary of the world that it is given to us, already predetermined as a juxtaposition of territories, nations, and languages. Henceforth, let me situate the problematic of translation in the modern international world.

It is implicitly assumed – and rarely thematically problematized – that, while there is one common world, the world accommodates many languages. Even though humanity is one, it contains a plurality of languages. It is generally upheld that, precisely because of this plurality, we are never able to evade translation. Thus, our conception of translation is almost always premised upon a specific way of conceiving the plurality of languages. Not surprisingly, we are often obliged to resort to a certain interpretation of the fable of the Tower of Babel when trying to think through the issues of the unity of humanity and translation. Assumed behind this fable is a certain vision of the international world, by which the entirety of humanity is divided into units of languages, and each constitutes an individual unity that cannot be mixed or conflated with other such units. The internationality of the international world thus represented consists in the imaginary formula thanks to which individual languages are juxtaposed in an homogeneous and continual space. Hence each is external to any other. It follows that the link between any two languages is necessarily of an interlingual kind, so that the representation of the international world coincides with the Babelic vision of the world that is fragmented by the individuality of languages and unified only through interlingual translation. Interestingly enough, the inter- of interlingual translation somewhat resonates with the inter- of the modern international world.

How do we recognize the identity of each language, or, to put it more broadly, how do we justify presuming that the diversity of a language or languages can be categorized in terms of one and many or of an *interlingual* plurality? For example, is it not possible to think of language in terms of those grammars in which the distinction of the singular and the plural is irrelevant? What I am challenging is the notion of the individual unity of language, a certain "positivity of discourse" or "historical *a priori*" in terms of which we understand what is at issue whenever a different language or a difference in language is at stake. My question is: how do we allow ourselves to tell one language from others? What allows us to represent difference in and of languages in terms of specific difference?

I stated my answer to this question some thirty years ago, and I still believe it is valid.[17] My answer is: the individual unity of language is like a *regulative idea*. It organizes knowledge, but it is not empirically verifiable. Immanuel Kant introduced the term "regulative idea" in his *Critique of Pure Reason*. The regulative idea does not concern itself with the possibility of experience; it is no more than a rule by which a search in the series of empirical data is prescribed. What it guarantees is not the empirically verifiable truth; on the contrary, it forbids the search for truth "to bring it[self] to a close by treating anything at which it may arrive as absolutely unconditioned."[18]

Unlike some religious convictions, the regulative idea never confirms truth absolutely or unconditionally. Therefore, it only gives an *object in idea*; it only means "a *schema* for which no object, not even a hypothetical one, is directly given."[19] The individual unity of language cannot be given in empirical experience because it is nothing but a regulative idea that enables us to comprehend other related data about languages "in an indirect manner, in their systematic unity, by means of their relation to this idea."[20] It is not possible to know whether a particular language exists as a unity or not. The reverse is true: by prescribing to the idea of the individual unity of language, it becomes possible for us to systematically organize knowledge about languages in a modern, scientific manner. It follows then that the existence of a national or ethnic language cannot be empirically verifiable. In this respect, it is a construct of schematism, figuration, and imagination. Just as a nation is in the imaginary register, so is a national or ethnic language.

To the extent that the unity of a national language ultimately serves as a *schema* for nationality and offers the sense of national integration,[21] the idea of the individual unity of language opens up a discourse in which not only the naturalized origin of an ethnic community but also the entire imaginary associated with "national" language and culture are sought after, debated, and refuted. What is of decisive importance is that such a language is represented in a schema or an image of national or ethnic totality. Regardless of whether or not it is somewhat proven to exist, first of all, it must be projected and postulated as an image. Only through an integrated image of a language can a vast variety of traditional heritages, bundles of familial lineages, and a wide range of fragmented customs be synthesized and unified into the figure of national culture. In short, it is in this arrangement of biopower that the imaginary of an ethnic community, whose members are supposed to share the same language, common tradition, or set of collective customs, comes into being; but it does not necessarily follow from this postulate of ethnic community in imagination that an ethnic community or a prototype of national community can be shown to be present factually or empirically. On the contrary, one could argue that an ethnic community ought to be brought into existence, whereas actually it is totally absent. An argument about the absence of national language, or, by implication, of an ethnic community, can equally serve to endorse a sort of discourse in which the individual unity of language is postulated. As was the case in the birth, or more precisely stillbirth, of the Japanese nation, the imaginary of an ethnic community becomes available in its absence, in the modality that it is absent where it should be present.[22] What is at stake in the discourse of national language is not the actual existence of a national or ethnic language, but rather the very possibility of imagining it as a topic. Such a discourse opens up the theme of a national language as a possible topic in such a way that it becomes possible to discuss many of its aspects, including its absence. Regardless of whether it is affirmative or negative, adorable or deplorable, present or absent, the very possibility of imagining such a language as some shared medium that must have once been shared is postulated there. This is to say that, in such a discourse, the very figure of a proto-national language is introduced for the first time as "a historical *a priori*."[23]

The language that is debated over may be pure, authentic, hybridized, polluted, or corrupt, yet regardless of its particular assessment, the very possibility of praising, authenticating, complaining about, or deploring it is offered by the unity of that language as a regulative idea. It is rarely challenged that the English language is a national matter, and that the wellbeing or soundness of the language is intimately related to the welfare of the nation. Moreover, by focusing exclusively on the language of the majority, it seems that little attention is paid to the fact that many other languages, heterogeneous or even foreign to what is assumed to be "good English," are spoken in the population coextensive to the territory of the United States of America, the United Kingdom, Australia, New Zealand, or many other English-speaking countries.

Regardless of how unscientific and capricious popular discussions on "good and beautiful English" may be, the strategic principle of national language is scarcely challenged. It is precisely because of this strategic aspect of the *schema* of national language that the discussion of good and proper language has never failed to be oppressive toward minorities who are perceived as deviating from the "standard," thereby rendering it possible to mark the authentic from the inauthentic in terms of nationality. Nationality is not merely a matter of the inside and outside of the national community; it is also a matter of prescription and manipulation. It demands and prescribes how one should conduct oneself in order to participate in the feeling of nationality,[24] rather than whether one is or is not in the national community in an exclusively descriptive way.

For Kant, as I have so far argued, a regulative idea is explicated primarily with regard to the production of scientific knowledge; it ensures that the empirical inquiry of some scientific discipline never reaches any absolute truth, and is therefore endless. Furthermore, Kant qualifies the regulative idea as a *schema* that is not exclusively in the order of ideas, but also in the order of the sensational. Hence, the regulative idea works in the realm of imagination, of the faculty of the human mind that synthesizes the ideational and the sensational.

Kant's critical philosophy was contemporaneous with the emergence of a new form and image of community called "nation;" he witnessed the revolutions which helped to establish a new state sovereignty based on the nation. In this regard too, the institution of the nation-state is no older than German idealism. In due course, we are led to suspect that the idea of the unity of language as the *schema* for ethnic and national communality must also be a recent invention. The regulative idea thus serves to organize the modern international world as well as the imaginary formation of national or ethnic language in that world regulated by the *inter*-lingual schematism of *inter*-nationality.

By now this much is evident. From the insight that the unity of national language is a regulative idea, it follows directly that we do not and cannot know whether a national language, such as English or Japanese, exists as an empirical object unless it is sustained by the institutionalized rules of aesthetic technologies. The unity of national language enables us to organize various empirical data in a systematic manner so as to allow us to continue to seek knowledge about that language. At the same time, moreover, the regulative idea offers not an object in experience but an *objective* in praxis toward which we aspire to regulate our uses of language. It is not only an epistemic principle but also a strategic one. Hence, it works in a double register: on the one hand, determining propaedeutically what is to be included or excluded in the very database of a language, what is linguistic or extra-linguistic, and what is proper to a particular language or not; on the other, it indicates and projects what we must seek as our proper language, what we must avoid as heterogeneous to it and reject as improper for it; the unity of a national language as a schema guides us on what is just or wrong for our language, what is in accord or discord with its propriety.

In this respect, it is worth noting that invariably the modern discussion of national language assumes itself to be situated "after Babel," so to speak, in a world marked by "many in one," in a characteristically particular manner. Walter Benjamin is among those authors who rely upon the mythology of Babel, but it is noteworthy that he deliberately adopts a particular tropic strategy that highlights the fragmentary nature of languages while also purposefully obliterating the very distinguishability of interlingual and intralingual translations.[25] He emphasizes languages as fragments and splinters that retain the shapes and contours of the original unity, and thereby he very judiciously evades postulating languages as individuals and indivisibles, each of which is internally coherent or organically intact. By "pure language," he designates one that can never be an individual or indivisible. If we follow Benjamin's tropics strictly, it would have been extremely difficult or almost impossible either to equate translation proper to an interlingual translation, or to represent it to ourselves as a transaction taking place in the interstice between two individuated figures of languages. In this respect, he illustrates an entirely different orientation from that of Roman Jakobson. Inopportunely, nevertheless, we must admit that Jakobson represents the overwhelming majority, as a consequence of which very few scholars in translation studies today appreciate Benjamin's discussion on translation.

By virtue of the fact that we take the model of interlingual translation as translation proper, we are obliged to acknowledge that we live in a world "after Babel," but this post-Babelic world is ordered by internationality. In the *modern* era, an inquiry into language begins with the acknowledgement that universal language has been lost, so that humanity is inevitably fragmented into many languages. None of us can occupy the position of totality from which the oneness of humanity is immediately apprehended. Every one of us is necessarily situated within one or some languages; our apprehension of humanity is destined to be partial because it is no longer possible for any of us to have access to an aerial view from which the entirety can be grasped instantaneously. Instead, the apprehension of oneness requires tedious processes in the interstices of many autonomous and individuated languages. Accordingly, I have tentatively called these processes *translations as they are represented according to the modern regime of translation*.

Of course, translation serves as a metaphorical term with much broader connotations than an operation of the transfer of meaning from one national or ethnic language to another, but in this context I am specifically concerned with the delimitation of translation according to "the modern regime of translation," by means of which the idea of the national language is practiced and thus concretized. Thus, what I want to suggest is that the representation of translation in terms of "the modern regime of translation" is facilitated as a *schema of co-figuration*: it helps to project a paired *schemata* of individual languages between which interlingual translation is supposed to take place.

Precisely because this difference is predetermined as a specific kind between two individuated languages, the representation of interlingual translation necessarily requires a pair of *schemata*, a pair of two figures. It partakes in the figure of two, a dialectic duality of the other and the self. To the extent that the representation of interlingual translation is projected by means of a pair of *schemata*, it is a process of a *co-figuration*.

The paired *schemata* work as if they are one synthetic schema, so that only when translation is represented by the schematism of co-figuration does the putative unity of one national language as a regulative idea ensue. The *schema of co-figuration* is an apparatus that allows us to *imagine* or *represent* what goes on in translation; it allows us to give to ourselves an *image* or *representation* of translation as a set of prescriptive presumptions.

A corollary immediately follows: unless some language other than itself is represented, a language would never be figured. A language is identified only through the schematism of co-figuration, so that the image of one's own language is dependent upon how an other language partnered with it is represented. Put another way, only when an apparatus is available by which to recognize and imagine a different language into which a topic, theme, or message is translated from this language can a language be figured out as an autonomous and individuated language independent of the other. This is to say that, unless a foreign language is recognized, one's own would never be recognized as such. This is why a national language becomes representable and recognizable only in an international world, even though the internationality of this world may not be immediately ascribed to the one instituted by the Eurocentric international law, *Jus Publicum Europæum*.

Thus imagined, the representation of translation is no longer a movement in potentiality. This image or representation always contains *two* figures, and, in due course, is necessarily accompanied by a spatial interstice in terms of "border." Hence, the image of translation is given by the schematism (the putting into practice of schema) of co-figuration in the modern regime of translation. In other words, the unity of a national or ethnic language as a schema is already accompanied by another one for the unity of a different language. This is how the unity of a language is possible, only in the element of "many in one," of internationality.

Translation may well take various forms and processes insofar as it is a political labor to overcome the points of incommensurability in the social. It need not be confined to the particular regime of translation; it may well be outside its modern regime. In the context of our discussion of translation, the "modern" is marked by the introduction of the schema of co-figuration; without this it is difficult to *imagine* a nation or ethnicity as a homogeneous sphere. Thus the economy of the foreign, that is, how the foreign must be allocated in the production of the domestic language, has played a decisive role in the *poietic* – and poetic – identification of the national language. Without exception, the formation of modern national language involves certain institutionalizations of translation, according to what we have referred to as the modern regime of translation.

Conclusion

This chapter is not designed to give a comprehensible vision of what translation can be. Instead it is designed to historicize what we take to be "translation proper" – provided that not only the peoples in the West but also in the Rest are designated by "we" in this case – and to show that the modern regime of translation, a bio-political technology in terms of which we conduct, apprehend, evaluate, and judge "translation," is a rather recent invention. Yet, undeniably, this modern regime of translation is viable only in the modern international world, a particular order of inter-state politics, which originated in Europe around the seventeenth century and subsequently spread all over the globe, through modern colonial rule and capitalist commodification. In other words, our apprehension of translation is under the auspices of the international order in which the world supposedly consists of a horizontal juxtaposition of national languages, and each of these national languages is assumed to be an individual, indivisible unity. Prior to the modern international world, a plurality of languages existed, but this plurality was not one of individuated languages. Yet the modern regime of translation drastically changed our ways of apprehending the plurality of languages and their differences. Since the eighteenth century, step by step, we have been obliged to accept the legitimacy of an imaginary order according to which one's belonging to the newly constructed community of "nation" is most decisively and deterministically marked by one's own "national language."

I do not believe that the modern international world will disappear in the near future, even though for the majority of humanity on this planet, the basic unit – the nation-state – of this international world is rather new – less than one century old, as a matter of fact – and appears temporary and artificial. Nevertheless, I have no doubt that the very structure of the international world is in transition. As Sandro Mezzadra and Brett Neilson argued in *Border as Method, or, the Multiplication of Labor*, the borders of the modern international world are less and less effective in regulating the global distribution of labor power, capital, population, knowledge, and commodities. What we conventionally call "globalization" is eroding the regularities of the international world. Far from giving rise to a "borderless" world, globalization generates more and more borders and new regimens of discrimination which do not necessarily follow the regularities of the modern international world.

Notes

1. The dissertation was later published as Naoki Sakai, *Voices of the Past: The Status of Language in Eighteenth-Century Japanese Discourse* (Ithaca: Cornell University Press, 1991).
2. Naoki Sakai, 『死産される日本語・日本人』 [The Stillbirth of Japanese as a Language and as an Ethnos] (Tokyo: Shinyô-sha, 1996; pocketbook version, Tokyo: Kôdansha, 2015).
3. The study of Japanese language was recognized as a distinct branch of language studies and was called kokugogaku (国語学) in contrast to linguistics in general (言語学).
4. The segregation of the native from the foreign took place in multiple registers: the spoken versus the written, the phonetic versus the ideographic, the emotive-sentimental versus the conniving-intellectual, and so on. These dichotomies cannot be simply reduced to the cartographic configuration of Japanese islands versus the Chinese continent. For more details, see Sakai, *Voices of the Past*.
5. Morio Tagai, (互　盛央)、『フェルディナン・ド・ソシュール：＜言語学＞の孤独、「一般言語学」の夢』 [Ferdinand de Saussure: The Solitude of <Linguistics> and the Dream of (General Linguistics)] (Tokyo: Sakuhinsha, 2009).
6. Ferdinand de Saussure, *Cours de linguistique générale*, 5th ed., ed. Charles Bally and Albert Sechehaye (Paris: Payot, 1955).
7. Ferdinand de Saussure, *Troisième cours de linguistique générale (1910–1911): d'après les cahiers d'Emile Constantin,* ed. Eisuke Komatsu, trans. Roy Harris (Oxford: Pergamon Press, 1993), 26a.
8. Saussure, *Troisième cours,* 28a.
9. Saussure, *Troisième cours,* 31a.
10. Saussure, *Troisième cours,* 31a.
11. I rely upon the traditional terminology established in Aristotle's *Metaphysics*, Book X, trans. C. D. C Reeve (Indianapolis: Hackett Publishing Company, 2016), 158–74 (1052a14–1059a16).
12. Sandro Mezzadra and Brett Neilson, *Border as Method, or, the Multiplication of Labor* (Durham, NC: Duke University Press, 2013), 31.
13. For further explication of the schematism of co-figuration and the regime of translation, see Naoki Sakai, *Translation and Subjectivity: On 'Japan' and Cultural Nationalism* (Minneapolis: University of Minnesota Press, 1997).
14. Roman Jakobson, 'On Linguistic Aspects of Translation', in *Selected Writings*, vol. 2 (The Hague and Paris: Mouton, 1971), 261.
15. Aristotle, *Metaphysics*.
16. Here let me outline the preliminary procedure involved in the classification according to classical logic. In order for difference between two individuals A and B to be specific, A and B must both belong to the same group. It would be tantamount to sheer meaninglessness if A and B are a desk and a family. A desk can be an individual just as a family can be an individual. A desk and a

family cannot be comparable to one another unless the common denominator is specified. For instance, as two words or nouns, they can be compared, yet the referents these words refer to remain incomparable. The minimal condition for comparison is that A and B share some common quality. Expressed in propositional form, the two propositions, for example, 'A is C' and 'B is C', are upheld where C signifies some quality or predicate that A and B share. In the absence of such a shared predicate, a specific difference between two individuals is unthinkable.

17 Sakai, *Voices of the Past*, 326.
18 Immanuel Kant, *Critique of Pure Reason*, trans. Norman Kemp Smith (New York: St. Martin's Press, 1929), 450 [A 509; B 537].
19 Kant, *Critique of Pure Reason*, 550 [A 670; B 698] (emphasis added).
20 Kant, *Critique of Pure Reason*, 550.
21 Fukuzawa Yukichi translated the English term 'nationality' into *kokutai* ('national body'), in the 1870s in Japan. Later *kokutai* was used to express the sovereignty of the Japanese Emperor system. By *kokutai*, Fukuzawa reiterated what John Stuart Mill said of nationality consisting of 'a portion of mankind' that 'are united among themselves by common sympathies which do not exist between them and any others – which make them co-operate with each other more willingly than with other people, desire to be under the same government, and desire that it should be government by themselves or a portion of themselves exclusively. This feeling of nationality may have been generated by various causes. Sometimes it is the effect of identity of race and descent. Community of language, and community of religion greatly contribute to it. Geographical limits are one of its causes. But the strongest of all is identity of political antecedents; the possession of a national history, and consequent community of recollections; collective pride and humiliation, pleasure and regret, connected with the same incidents in the past.' See John Stuart Mill, *Utilitarianism, On Liberty, Considerations on Representative Government*, ed. H. B. Acton (London: J. M. Dent & Sons, 1972), 391. Fukuzawa includes what is above almost verbatim in his exposition of *kokutai*. See Yukichi Fukuzawa, *Outline of the Theory of Civilization* (New York: Columbia University Press, 2009), 30.
22 In *Voices of the Past* I discussed the formation of discourse in which the Japanese language was invented for the first time in the eighteenth century (pp. 311–17). Later I returned to this topic in 『死産される日本語・日本人 [The Stillbirth of Japanese as an Ethnos and as a Language].
23 Michel Foucault, *The Archaeology of Knowledge & The Discourse on Language*, trans. A. M. Sheridan Smith (New York: Harper & Row, 1972), 126–31.
24 See *Voices of the Past*, 209–319.
25 Walter Benjamin, 'The Task of the Translator', in *Walter Benjamin: Illuminations*, trans. Harry Zohn, ed. Hannah Arendt (London: Fontana Press, 1992), 70–82.

CHAPTER 15

Five Entries on Translation and Loss
Michael Cronin

1.

1943. Sándor Márai has spent three months in bed recovering from a viral illness in wartime Hungary. As the writer makes his slow recovery, he receives a copy in the post of the Czech translation of his novel *Csutora* (1932). He is aghast. Márai is unable to read or understand Czech, but his attention focuses on the cover of the book. It features a drawing that is supposed to represent the subject of the novel, his dog Csutora, which the Hungarian writer describes as a 'horror born out of the imagination of the Czech illustrator who has drawn a kind of cross between a short-haired fox terrier and a toilet brush. Csutora, my dog, was a puli whom I had faithfully described from both the inside and the outside.' The canine confusion makes him doubt the ability of translators to get anything right: 'In the hands of a translator what remains in the imagination of others of what we write and think? What terrible misunderstanding is contained in every word that one human uses to address another?'[1]

Although Márai generalises the fickleness of translation to all human communication, it is clear translators are the immediate culprits, front-line defenders of the indefensible. Márai's doubts were hardly new, even then, and the tagline of loss has been endlessly recycled in the rhetoric of translation commentary. If poetry is allegedly what gets lost in translation, the topic of loss and translation is rarely, if ever, lost. Each time, it is announced as if it is an unforgettable, incontrovertible truth. Translators variously respond to these after-dinner platitudes with an eye-roll, a shoulder shrug, mild irritation or silent fury. Titles such as *Gained in Translation* (2000) or *Found in Translation* (2018) constellate publications on translation as if wrong-footing the expectation is enough to debunk it.[2] But what if we were to take loss seriously? What would come out of not losing sight of what loss involves? What have we to lose in finding out what different kinds of losses – linguistic, cultural, ecological –

have in common? And what if being a loser were not so much a label to be rejected as a condition to be explored?

2.

'Being alive means experiencing loss'. Judith Schalansky's terse assertion in the preface to *An Inventory of Losses* (2020) follows on from her discussion of a cemetery that was situated at the heart, not the periphery, of a remote Danish fishing village.[3] It is generally assumed in modernity that we do not like to be reminded of our losses. Our cemeteries are not found in our central plazas but on the outskirts of our cities, the forgotten suburbs of the afterlife. The German writer asks the question: who is closer to life, 'someone who is constantly reminded of their own mortality or someone who manages to suppress all thought of it'?[4] By way of answer, she draws up her own inventory of losses, ranging from lost islands and extinct species to the lost poems of Sappho, the incinerated scribblings of an eccentric and the lost biography of an amateur astronomer. *An Inventory of Losses* uses the fine detail of what no longer is in order to explore the world of what might have been. Loss clarifies. We never cease finding out how much we have lost, in what is arguably the most common experience of bereavement. Schalansky, however, in describing the purpose of her book, sees her writing not as an elaborate threnody for the vanished grandeur of lost worlds but as an urgent invitation to value the present:

> This book, like all others, springs from the desire to have something survive, to bring the past into the present, to call to mind the forgotten, to give voice to the silenced and to mourn the lost. Writing cannot bring anything back, but it can enable everything to be experienced. Hence this volume is as much about seeking as finding, as much about losing as gaining, and gives a sense that the difference between presence and absence is perhaps marginal, as long as there is memory.[5]

It is memory that links large-scale stories of historical shift and destitution to microhistories of individual loss. What gives these microhistories their specific identity and contour is not so much what individuals have gone on to – the story the obituaries tell us – but what they have left behind. Childhood, parents, homes, first loves, teeth, toys, favourite sweaters. What constitutes a life (provisionally) is what remains when all the rest is lost. Losses, as much as our gains, define us. The French novelist and philosopher Vincent Delecroix points out that the experience of loss cannot be reduced to the fey cameos of nostalgia but is integral to what makes our experience of the world intelligible:

> Ce qui est perdu n'est pas au bord ou à la marge de notre expérience du monde, mais en son centre et partout, parce qu'il la rend possible. Il faut alors se représenter ce qui est perdu non comme un contenu de la conscience nostalgique de la simple mémoire, mais comme une *condition* de l'expérience, tandis que l'absence de cette condition, l'impossibilité de se rapporter au réel à partir et au travers de ce qui est perdu, atteste la réduction voire la perte de l'expérience.⁶

Loss is foundational and additive, not marginal and subtractive. Jorge Luis Borges senses this in an essay he wrote in 1931 on the subject of Gustave Flaubert's style. He was not persuaded by the French master's claim that perfection of style made his prose immortal. In fact, he believed only that that which could be lost could be retrieved. Trying to stave off loss only made loss inevitable:

> The perfect page, the page on which no word could be altered without harm is the most precarious of all. Changes in language erase shades of meaning, and the 'perfect' page is precisely the one that consists of those delicate shades of meaning that are so easily worn away. On the contrary, the page that becomes immortal can traverse the fire of typographical errors, approximate translations, and inattentive or erroneous readings without losing its soul in the process.⁷

Borges puts loss at the heart of Flaubert's stake on posterity. If loss is constitutive of our experience, if life cannot be imagined without loss, then it follows that part of what makes a text live in translation is what it loses. If poetry does not get lost somewhere in the translation, then it is in trouble – the poetry, that is, not the translation. For the page to become 'immortal' in translation, the question is not one of accepting with pained patience the entropic falling away of substance in moving from one language to another. Rather, embracing loss is a precondition of a translation that is alive in its partiality rather than stillborn in its completeness.

Writing in his journal in 1849, Søren Kierkegaard indeed saw the immortal, or more modestly the future posterity of his writing, as dependent on two preconditions, translation and loss: 'O, some day after I am dead, *Fear and Trembling* alone will be enough to immortalize my name as an author. Then it will be read and translated into foreign languages. People will practically shudder at the frightful emotion in the book.'⁸ The Danish theologian and philosopher cannot see any viable notion of the future without loss (unless one embraces faith in a divinity; we will return to this). It is the 'approximate translations' that will ensure the posthumous fame of the frightful emotion; the loss of his other works will ensure that this one is not lost. His reputation entails loss, and it is the books that do not get translated (that are, literally, lost without translation) that define how or for what he will be remembered. Thus, loss is less a lack that needs to be remedied, a criticism that needs to be endlessly refuted in a defensive or elegiac mode, than a dimension of translation that makes the practice integral to the business of leading a meaningful life.

3.

Returning to Ireland from Germany, the Irish writer Hugo Hamilton wonders about the significance of borders. His ruminations are both the idle musings of a visa-friendly passport holder and a manifesto of unease that details contemporary loss:

> Does anyone need to have a fixed identity any more, or is that an old concept now which applies only to those people who have lost something. Or have we all lost something in the transformation to a more mobile, more 'liquid' world. We are more connected, more virtually together in one community, but also more dislocated and less warm-hearted.[9]

There are no question marks for the first two questions in the text, as if the interrogations are so common, so widespread, that they hardly require typographical punctuation. The questions persist because loss is not an abstraction but rather, as noted above, the precondition of lived experience, the sculpting agency of identity formation. When the Indian American writer Madhu H. Kaza reflects on her own passage from India, she sees translation shadowing experiences of loss:

> At some point I began to understand that my discomfort with translation was connected to the trauma of immigration. Something went quiet in me when I was brought to the U.S. from India as a child. Although I assimilated and lost my accent, a vital part of me got stopped at the border. My inner life remained untranslated, its contours beyond what the receiving culture wanted to or could comprehend. As an immigrant child I felt an aura of illegitimacy about my claim to be an American. At times I lived with radical insecurity. As an adult, when I translated from Telugu, my first language (which I'd learned in college), I experienced a repetition of the loss I'd felt as a child. I not only worried about my own distance from the language but also wondered how the text I was translating would be received in the U.S., whether and on what terms it would belong.[10]

Translation is bringing into play much more than words on a page. The 'radical insecurity' of the migrant is often acute for those in possession of words on a page – the documented – but can be fatal for who those who do not – the undocumented.

According to the International Organization for Migration (IOM), deaths recorded on the three main Mediterranean Sea routes in the nine months to the end of September 2019 were 1,071 individuals. The figure for the same period in 2018 was 1,930 deaths.[11] This is a 'repetition of loss' that plays out along many different borders, maritime and terrestrial. It may be useful to consider these particular kinds of disappearance within the framework of an economy of loss that points to a specific role for translation. Vincent Delecroix reminds us in *Apprendre à perdre* (2019) that central to orthodox understandings of economic activity is the phantom of loss:

> Dans ce sens désormais commun qui désigne l'échange des marchandises et les créations de richesses, la logique économique semble se présenter d'abord comme l'acte simple *d'économiser*, justement, c'est-à-dire de limiter les pertes, la dépense, de la soumettre à une utilité stricte – ce qui peut éventuellement en faire, comme dans l'investissement, la source d'un gain. Prise dans toutes les logiques de l'utilité, la perte est *comprise*.[12]

Silas Marner, as the despairing archetype of the emerging Victorian middle class in George Eliot's eponymous novel, is obsessed with loss. He is terrified of losing his money, and the grim accountancy of his days is given over to making sure that not a penny goes amiss. Similarly, Charles Dickens's Scrooge in *A Christmas Carol* (1843) is haunted from the outset not so much by the ghosts of Christmas as by the spectre of dispossession. For much of the novel, losing his money is of far greater concern than losing his soul. However, as Delecroix argues above, loss is contained within the ethic of bourgeois miserliness. The scrupulous watchfulness makes sense only if the losses are real. This is integral to the notion of the business cycle, where losses in one period are cancelled out in another, economic 'recovery' obliterating the losses of the recession in the circular boom-bust cycle of the capitalist economy:

> La *hantise* de la perte s'y dessine, par l'effet conjugué de la crainte obsessionnelle de la perte (ou de la dépense inutile) et de sa dénégation (dans le rendement ou la rentabilisation). Hantise du négatif.[13]

Loss is both dreaded (attacks on public spending, fears of fiscal profligacy) and denied (never let a good crisis go to waste, the invisible hand of the market setting all things to right). Loss is to be avoided at all costs, but it is unavoidable, often at great cost. What needs to be hidden from view is an economic order that allows migrants to perish in the 'liquid modernity' of the Mediterranean. This year Oxfam reported that the world's 2,153 billionaires have more wealth than the 4.6 billion people who make up the poorest 60 per cent of the planet's population.[14] Such disparities and their spatial distribution, predominantly in the Global North, make economic migration an inescapable feature of the contemporary world. In this scenario, it is clear who are the winners and who are the 'losers', and indeed one of the arguments advanced by both liberal and progressive economists who advocate for migration is that it turns losers into winners.[15]

If the negative haunting of loss drives economic orthodoxy, then translation is potentially unsettling in ways we often forget. Unsettling because it is translation that potentially gives voice to the lost lives of migrants told by those who survive and get their stories out. Migrants such as Behrouz Boochani, a Kurdish Iranian, who won Australia's richest literary prize in 2019 for *No Friend but the Mountains* (2018). In this work, he describes his own migrant journey and the inhuman conditions in the Australian detention centre on Manus Island. His text transmitted one text message at a time from the detention centre, was written in Farsi and translated into English by Omid Tofighian working with interpreter Moones Mansoubi.[16] What Tofighian and Mansoubi did was to make obvious what was lost, what was left out in lurid accounts in the populist press on migrant threats and in official narratives on conditions of migrant detention. If they had not translated Boochani's text, his voice and experience would have been lost to the Australian public and the wider Anglophone world that directed attention to his plight.

Translation, however, not only unsettles the parable of perpetual gain; it can also become a party to the economic fiction of cyclical restitution. In a white paper entitled *How to Win in the Indian Market with Localization*, Lionbridge, one of the world's leading translation service providers, makes the case that an English-only policy for a country with twenty-two official languages is outdated and misguided. Companies that want to capitalise on the tech-savvy burgeoning middle class in India need to factor in linguistically diverse and culturally appropriate translation: 'Indian Internet users conversing in local languages on the web will total 536 million by 2021, dwarfing the nation's English-first user base. And with digitally-influenced consumption projected to double in India by 2030 – encompassing 40 per cent of all purchases – the stakes are very high indeed.'[17] The nature of these stakes is also spelled out in simple terms, 'because these consumers are so particular, they force you to ask a fundamental question: if they can't count on your company to give them product and service information in their local language, will they then turn to a competitor who can?'[18] What the absence of translation entails is loss. Loss of customers. Loss of business. Loss of reputation. What gets lost in (the absence of) translation is revenue. Providing goods and services through the medium of translation in local languages means making good those losses. If the economy is 'un ensemble de logiques visant à réagir à la perte, opérations de neutralisation, de compensation ou d'annulation',[19] then the translation logic of the localisation industry is quintessentially economic in its logic and not just in the banal sense of striving after markets. Pragmatic translation promises the operations of neutralisation, compensation (a well-worn translation term) and annulment (of difference) to counteract the clawback of loss. The notion of potential interlingual or intercultural loss must be instantly repressed, as acknowledging this loss would mean disrupting the cycle of endless profitability. In the international translation industry, loss is both brandished as a threat (missed opportunities) and discounted as a possibility (we have the solutions).

4.

What happens when there is no boom after the bust or when the cycle begins to flatline, permanently? Standing outside his school on a cold February day holding two placards, Dara McAnulty, a young teenager from Northern Ireland, wonders why people passing by the climate protest keep asking him about 'me' and 'how I felt'. Nobody seemed interested in the science or the facts or why

> young people around the globe have been forced to act, young people who value education profoundly but are nevertheless compelled to act against the inaction. I'm not a doomsday prophet, though. I can't be like that because I see so much beauty every day, and this is a huge privilege. I would never question their grief, their fear, because these are real things too. Millions are already facing an ever more precarious existence in the climate catastrophe that is manifesting.[20]

Sentimental soundbites are preferred over climate realities. What the young naturalist and reluctant activist acknowledges is that if precariousness is a way of life under late modern capitalism, then conditions are set to dramatically worsen as a consequence of global warming. If loss is the dirty secret of orthodox economics, fossil fuels become the ultimate dirty secret. The fiction of the cycle driven forever onwards and upwards by carbon resources discounted the losses to the environment as 'externalities' that did not count because they were not counted. As McAnulty's generation knows only too well, it is no longer possible to postulate an anthropocentric, hierarchical order where the non-human world is passively subject to the interventions and manipulations of the human subject. The non-human is striking back. The twenty warmest years since records began in 1850 have been in the past twenty-two years, with the four years between 2015 and 2019 being the warmest ever recorded. Vertebrate populations on the planet have fallen by an average of 60 per cent since the 1970s. Extinction rates for all species have increased to between 100 and 1,000 times the 'background rate' of extinction. At this stage, more than 75 per cent of the Earth's land is substantially degraded. Topsoil is now being lost ten to forty times faster than it is being replenished by natural processes; since the mid-twentieth century, 30 per cent of the world's arable land has become unproductive due to erosion; and 95 per cent of the Earth's land areas could become degraded by 2050.[21] The limits to the earth's carrying capacity means that the logic of indefinite gain that sustains the cycle's capacity to deny loss breaks down. In the words of Vincent Delecroix, 'si la planète s'épuise, une limite infranchissable vient clore l'illimitation nécessaire au dépassement de la perte temporaire'.[22] Pretending the cycle can continue means the gains are achieved at an ever higher cost. The eventual loss, as the planet warms to unacceptable levels, is catastrophic and generalised. Plastic waste symbolises the losses that are never lost, the losses that accumulate like bad debts no one wants to pay. Paradoxically, an economic system haunted by the spectre of loss is set to lose everything.

One response to these mounting losses is grief. We mourn the destruction of the planet we inhabit, paralysed by the scale of the damage to the environment and inconsolable at the magnitude of the task of reparation. As the poet Kathryn Kirkpatrick asks in her poem 'Mother, Ireland', 'How shall I write / redemption as the weather shifts?'[23] Redemption, if that is the right word, does not come, however, through the denial of loss. Julian Barnes in *Levels of Life* (2013), the book written after the death of his wife, noted that the loss of a loved one in contemporary society is often seen as a temporary behavioural disadvantage that needs to be frogmarched through the therapeutic tick boxes of ritual recovery.[24] 'Working' through grief enters the productive cycle where the loss can eventually be made good through the gain of a restorative return to a life beyond mourning. Céline Lafontaine sees this inability to take the loss of death seriously, in what she calls the 'post-mortal society' of the West, as a fundamental anthropological stumbling block to individual and societal wellbeing.[25] Pandemics bring the register of death and loss to the fore but usually under the rubric of terror. Death in the post-mortal society is above all a matter of private hygiene and public sanitation. Out of sight, out of mind.

The economic phobia around (financial) loss in modernity coexists alongside a social phobia around (psychic) loss, vital energies seen to be consumed by the death cults of institutional religions or ancestor worship. However, accounts of personal loss remind us that mourning, like pregnancy, is not a sickness for which there is a cure. It is an objective condition and state of mind, not a physical ailment. When Roland Barthes grieves for his deceased mother in *Journal de deuil* (2009), what becomes obvious is how present she becomes in her absence: 'L'étonnant de ces notes, c'est un sujet dévasté en proie à la présence d'esprit.'[26] In other words, loss becomes an instrument, a means of exploring the significance of what his mother means or has meant for him. As Judith Schalansky observes, 'like a hollow mould, the experience of loss renders visible the contours of the thing mourned, and it is not uncommon for it to be transformed by the figurative light of sorrow into an object of desire'.[27] Measuring the extent of what has been lost, you become aware of the complex potential of what might have been realised – if the person had lived differently or lived longer. Future possibility lives in past potentiality. This is why Aeneas in Book VI of the *Aeneid* travels into the underworld to meet the shades of the past, including his dead father, Anchises. He goes there not to dwell in the past but to explore the future through the vision of his illustrious descendants. In effect, loss itself, and the longing produced by loss, is the true golden bough guaranteeing Aeneas a safe passage into the future. What the French critic, the German writer and the Latin author are all intimating is that a mode of enquiry that situates loss at its centre and not at its margins is infinitely more productive than modes that seek to disenfranchise loss in the name of perpetual gain. Aeneas's bright branch, Schalansky's hollow mould and McAnulty's placards are instruments in this new regime of enquiry. So, I would argue, is translation.

The title of one of Bohumil Hrabal's novels in English is *Dancing Lessons for the Advanced in Age* (1964). The British novelist Adam Thirlwell wonders about that title and claims:

> The history of translation is the history of mistakes. Hrabal's title in Czech is *Tanecní hodiny pro starsí a pokrocilé*, which is more like 'Dancing Lessons for the Older and More Advanced'. And I prefer this more ambiguous, sadder title. Because there is no reason – that is what the little *a*, meaning *and*, is saying – that the older should be the same as the more advanced. Everyone is always immature, and inexperienced. Even the mature, and experienced.[28]

Thirlwell's 'mistake' is more a matter of a loss of nuance, the foreclosure of the possibility of another reading. His perception of loss in the title of the published translation in English causes him to reflect on the potentiality of the Czech. The translation, like the hollow mould, 'renders visible the contours of the thing mourned', which suggests the productivity of the 'mistake'. The French translator Mireille Gansel describes how she initially translated *Sensible Wege*, the title of a poem by Reiner Kunze, as 'Fragile Paths' and then thirty years later retranslated it as 'Sensitive

Paths'. A change in one word reflected three decades of reading and experience, and she notes that at the moment of making the change she 'understood translation both as risk taking and continual re-examination, of even a single word – a delicate seismograph at the heart of time'.²⁹ As Delecroix puts it, 'le possible perdu, la perte le condense, le coalise, le détermine'.³⁰ When Gansel realised something was missing, something was lost in her translation, it was not as if she had lost something she had always had. The intimation of loss brought a new possibility, a new meaning to the fore. Loss in translation is again not so much restorative as generative; in Jacques Derrida's language, the lack becomes a supplement.

For Thirlwell, the fundamental challenge posed by any translation is how to minimise loss. Any translation genealogy is basically a matter of conjuring loss (the word Thirlwell prefers, freighted with the schoolroom torture of correction, is 'mistake'). When Joseph-Pierre Frénais, the first French translator of Laurence Sterne, tried to find an equivalent to Sterne's English word 'hobby-horse', 'Frénais invented the French word *dada* – and a century and a half later this word would be picked up at random from a French dictionary by Richard Huelsenbeck, Hugo Ball and Tristan Tzara as they tried to christen their polyglot, international movement obsessed with bad reproductions, with playfulness and flaws.'³¹ The French translator wants to avoid the loss of this crucial word in English, and it is this potential loss that leads him to invent or create. If the English text of Sterne is a past that already exists, Frénais's translational exploration of that past opens up future possibilities not only for the French language but for French literature in the ludic explosiveness of Dada. Loss is inseparable from translation, not as some unfortunate residue or telltale sign of incompetence or carelessness (it can be these things) but as constitutive of the specific mode of enquiry that is translation. When we sit down to a translation or when we discuss the merits of a translation in scholarly or classroom settings, we are haunted by the economist's 'négatif'. I think, however, that we need to move loss in translation into a different register – not so much from the prescriptive to the descriptive, as argued by the polysystem theorists in the last century, but into a different kind of ontological space that frees it up to dialogue with other issues and practices.

5.

Kathryn Schulz, a staff writer with the *New Yorker*, has written about the human tendency to lose things:

Passwords, passports, umbrellas, scarves, earrings, earbuds, musical instruments, W-2s, that letter you meant to answer, the permission slip for your daughter's field trip, the can of paint you scrupulously set aside three years ago for the touch-up job you knew you'd someday need: the range of things we lose and the readiness with which we do are staggering. Data from one insurance company suggests that the average person misplaces up to nine objects a day, which means that, by the time we turn sixty, we will have lost up to two hundred thousand things.[32]

In the course of a life, she estimates, we will spend 'roughly six solid months looking for missing objects'.[33] Trying to remember where we lost something not only involves trying to remember where we put it but what it looks like. What kind of memory key was it exactly? Was there any stitching on the outside of the wallet? Anyone who has lost luggage in transit will know the difficulty of distinguishing one black suitcase from another. Losing then calls for a special form of attention. We have to work hard to call to mind the precise nature of what has gone missing; the taken-for-granted demands precision in recollection. Marcel in *À la recherche du temps perdu* (1913) remembers the lost bedrooms of his childhood with an exactness of detail that would have been lost on his younger self.

Loss involves not just attention, however, but status. What is the status of the missing object? Ontologically, it occupies a strange space. In one sense, it is of course absent. That is why we go looking for it. It is present to our minds, we cannot forget it, hence our irritation. Its absence is always a potential present, so it is neither wholly absent nor obviously wholly present. Oscar Wilde once quipped that the only way to achieve immortality was to never pay your debts. Nobody ever forgets someone who owes them money. The memory of the loss rankles and with it the hope, however forlorn, of recovery. Losing things not only troubles our daily routine but also disrupts a particular way of viewing events that is central to Western ontology. I am sitting or I am standing, but I cannot be doing both at the same time. Otherwise, I am in the realm of the paradoxical. The work of *logos* is to determine. The more the object is determined, the greater the sensation of the object's existence. As Hegel notes, as long as pure Being is indeterminate, it is indistinguishable from pure nothingness. It is a pure void. There is nothing to see and still less to say.[34] Hence, the great movement in Western art in the early and late Renaissance, as E. H. Gombrich has pointed out, to give weight, heft and substance to the world through the determinations of the artist's brush.[35] The more vivid the sense of the world on canvas, the more it could be said to properly exist.

The difficulty is what to do with or how to think about transitional states, that position between one condition of being and another. Is the missing object present or absent or both at the same time? Aristotle in his *Physics* tries to offer a definition of the colour grey and claims that it is black with respect to white, and white with respect to black.[36] There is a distinct uneasiness here about what is neither black nor white but something in between. The ontological fixation makes thinking about certain phenomena difficult or problematic. Can we say there is an exact moment when people fall out of love? Is there a precise minute or hour or day when I begin to grow old? Can we specify the hour, the day, the year when the Soviet Union entered irreversible decline? What is the ontological status of that book that must be somewhere on my shelf? Is it present or absent or both? The troubled ontological status of the missing object does easily accommodate loss in cultures that cherish ontological certainty. Nor does it bode well for what happens to translation if it is conventionally associated with forms of loss. But as Schulz points out, loss is everywhere: 'our problem is not that we put too many things into the category of loss but that we leave too many out.'[37] She argues that loss can often feel like an anomaly, a disruption in the usual order of things:

> In fact, though, it *is* the usual order of things. Entropy, mortality, extinction: the entire plan of the universe consists of losing, and life amounts to a reverse savings account in which we are eventually robbed of everything. Our dreams and plans and jobs and knees and backs and memories, the childhood friend, the husband of fifty years, the father of forever, the keys to the house, the keys to the car, the keys to the kingdom itself: sooner or later, all of it drifts into the Valley of Lost Things.[38]

Translation is *not* anomalous in its association with loss. This *is* part of the usual order of things. Translation, however, is in a very basic sense always bound up with loss because it is only by losing the text in the original language that you can produce a text in a target language. One must normally give way to the other – with the exception of multilingual editions, and they are generally exceptions – because the target reader demands to read in a language they understand. However, the absent text is present in the translation insofar as the content and structure of the source text generally constrain what can be done in the target text. The fact of Charles Baudelaire having an albatross as the central image in his famous poem means that, as a translator, I would usually be expected to make this image present in 'my' language. The translation theorist Kobus Marais, drawing on the work of Terrence W. Deacon, makes a case for the power of what is absent. Deacon points out that the hole is one factor that makes a wheel turn. The hole – materially absent – has a causative effect on the wheel – which is materially present. Absential things, things that do not exist materially, have a causal effect on things that do exist materially. Absential things can also be meanings or values or intentions.[39] Marais gives the example of a farmer who buys five acres of land. If she decides to plant strawberries, then she is constrained by what she can do next. For example, not planting corn means that she is constrained to the extent that she cannot keep cattle. Not only does the notion of the absential link mind and matter, but it also shows that unrealised or lost possibilities have an explicit causative effect on what can happen. Culture illustrates this process in its coming into being:

> In the emergence of cultural forms or habits, work is done to constrain the chaotic stream or web of semiosis to a particular form, which then accrues meaning, because of the causative effect of semiotic possibilities that have not been realized. In a movie, for instance, the camera angles obtain and give meaning, among others, by virtues of the angles that have not been taken, and in drawing, negative space is a well-known concept. In music orchestration, the meaning of particular instrumentation is determined by instruments that could have been chosen, but were not.[40]

For Marais, translation is a 'semiotic process of performing work on meaning by effecting constraints ... on the possibilities of meaning'.[41] The implication here is that getting exercised about what is 'lost' in translation is fundamentally wrong-headed as it is only loss – the absential, the decision not to activate or realise certain possibilities – that makes translation, the work of constraint, effective and meaningful. Things go missing all the time. If they did not, forms could not emerge nor habits be formed. Schulz suggests that 'disappearance reminds us to notice, transience to cherish, fragility to defend. Loss is a kind of external conscience, urging us to make better use of our finite days.'[42] What emerges in the act of translation as central to the construction of culture is that loss is not only an 'external conscience' to make us value what we already have but that it is inseparable from what it means to have anything in the first place.

Notes

1 Sándor Márai, *Journal: Les années hongroises, 1943–1948*, trans. Catherine Fay (Paris: Albin Michel, 2019), 18.
2 Kathleen Shields, *Gained in Translation: Language, Poetry and Identity in Twentieth-Century Ireland* (Berlin: Peter Lang, 2000); Frank Wynne, ed., *Found in Translation* (London: Apollo, 2018).

3 Judith Schalansky, *An Inventory of Losses* (London: MacLehose, 2020), 14.
4 Schalansky, *Inventory of Losses*, 13.
5 Schalansky, *Inventory of Losses*, 25–6.
6 Vincent Delecroix, *Apprendre à perdre* (Paris: Payot, 2019), 111; italics in the original. What is lost is not at the edge or on the margins of our experience of the world but is central to it and is everywhere, because it is what makes it possible. What is lost needs to be represented not as the object of the nostalgic awareness of ordinary memory but as a *condition* of experience, while the absence of this condition, the impossibility of relating to the real from and through what has been lost attests to the diminution or even the loss of experience.
7 Jorge Luis Borges, *The Total Library: Non-Fiction, 1922–1986*, ed. Eliot Weinberger, trans. Esther Allen, Suzanne Jill Levine and Eliot Weinberger (Harmondsworth: Penguin, 2001), 54.
8 Quoted in Joakim Garff, *Søren Kierkegaard: A Biography*, trans. Bruce H. Kirmmse (Princeton, NJ: Princeton University Press, 2005), 251.
9 Hugo Hamilton, 'The Island of Talking', *Irish Pages* 4, no. 2 (2007), 23–4.
10 Madhu H. Kaza, editor's note, in *Kitchen Table Translation: An Aster(ix) Anthology*, ed. Madhu H. Kaza (Pittsburgh: Blue Sketch Press, 2017), 13.
11 IOM, 'Mediterranean Migrant Arrivals Reach 76,558 in 2019; Deaths Reach 1,071', 11 October 2019, accessed 21 April 2020, www.iom.int/news/mediterranean-migrant-arrivals-reach-76558-2019-deaths-reach-1071.
12 Delecroix, *Apprendre à perdre*, 49; italics in the original. In the common understanding of economic logic as involving trade and wealth creation, it would seem to primarily concern the basic act of *economising*, in other words, limiting losses and controlling expenditure, making it subject to strict utilitarian outcomes – which can eventually result, as in the case of investment, in the making of gains. Bound up with different forms of utilitarian logic, loss is *included*.
13 Delecroix, *Apprendre à perdre*, 50. The spectre of loss emerges, through the combined effects of an obsessional fear of loss (or needless expenditure) and its denial (through turnover or profits). The haunting of the negative.
14 Oxfam International, 'World's Billionaires Have More Wealth than 4.6 Billion People', 20 January 2020, accessed 21 April 2020, www.oxfam.org/en/press-releases/worlds-billionaires-have-more-wealth-46-billion-people.
15 Kimberly Clausing, *Open: The Progressive Case for Free Trade, Immigration, and Global Capital* (Cambridge MA: Harvard University Press, 2019).
16 Calla Wahlquist, 'Behrouz Boochani: Detained Asylum Seeker Wins Australia's Richest Literary Prize', *Guardian*, 31 January 2019, accessed 21 April 2019, www.theguardian.com/world/2019/jan/31/behrouz-boochani-asylum-seeker-manus-island-detained-wins-victorian-literary-prize-australias-richest.
17 Lionbridge, *How to Win in the Indian Market with Localization* (2019), 3, accessed 21 April 2020, www.lionbridge.com/content/dam/lionbridge/legacy/2019/10/Lionbridge-Indian-Market-Whitepaper-090519-FINAL.pdf.
18 Lionbridge, *How to Win in the Indian Market*, 4.

19 Delecroix, *Apprendre à perdre*, 49. A set of logics aiming to respond to loss, operations of neutralisation, compensation and annulment.
20 Dara McAnulty, *Diary of a Young Naturalist* (Beaminster, UK: Little Toller Books, 2020), 198.
21 Laurie Laybourn-Langton, Lesley Rankin and Darren Baxter, *This Is a Crisis: Facing Up to the Age of Environmental Breakdown* (London: Institute for Public Policy Research, 2019), 6–7.
22 Delecroix, *Apprendre à perdre*, 59. If the planet is exhausted, an absolute limit then puts an end to the absence of limits required to go beyond temporary losses.
23 Kathryn Kirkpatrick, 'Mother, Ireland', *Canadian Journal of Irish Studies*, no. 40 (2017), 223–4.
24 Julian Barnes, *Levels of Life* (London: Vintage, 2013).
25 Céline Lafontaine, *La société postmortelle* (Paris: Seuil, 2008).
26 Roland Barthes, *Journal de deuil* (Paris: Seuil, 2009), 40. What is astonishing about these notes is we have a devastated subject prey to the presence of mind.
27 Schalansky, *Inventory of Losses*, 13–14.
28 Adam Thirlwell, *The Delighted States* (London: Picador, 2007), 209.
29 Mireille Gansel, *Translation as Transhumance*, trans. Ros Schwartz (London: Les Fugitives, 2018), 36.
30 Delecroix, *Apprendre à perdre*, 120. Loss condenses, brings together, determines lost possibilities.
31 Thirlwell, *Delighted States*, 373–4.
32 Kathryn Schulz, 'Losing Streak: Reflections on Two Seasons of Loss', *New Yorker*, 13 February 2017, 68.
33 Schulz, 'Losing Streak', 68.
34 Georg Wilhelm Friedrich Hegel, *The Science of Logic*, trans. and ed. George di Giovanni (Cambridge: Cambridge University Press, 2010), 60.
35 Ernst H. Gombrich, *Art and Illusion: A Study in the Psychology of Pictorial Representation* (Princeton, NJ: Princeton University Press, 2000).
36 Aristotle, *The Physics Books 5–8*, trans. Philip H. Wicksteed and Francis M. Cornford (Cambridge, MA: Harvard University Press, 1934), 77.
37 Schulz, 'Losing Streak', 75.
38 Schulz, 'Losing Streak', 75; italics in the original.
39 Terrence W. Deacon, *Incomplete Nature: How Mind Emerged from Matter* (New York: W. W. Norton, 2013).
40 Kobus Marais, *A (Bio)Semiotic Theory of Translation: The Emergence of Social-Cultural Reality* (New York: Routledge, 2019), 136.
41 Marais, *(Bio)Semiotic Theory of Translation*, 137.
42 Schulz, 'Losing Streak', 75.

CHAPTER 16

'A Kind of Radical Positivity'
Reflections on the Craft, Contexts, and Consequences of Writing Translations

Kate Briggs, Jen Calleja, Sophie Collins, Katrina Dodson, and Natasha Soobramanien

This written exchange took place in several phases. Early in 2019, I invited Sophie Collins, Jen Calleja, Katrina Dodson, and Natasha Soobramanien to respond 'live' online to a set of questions relating to the themes of the present volume. We did this in a shared document. Some of us had met before, some of us live within the same time zone; some of us hadn't and don't. And yet, as far as possible, we wrote and responded spontaneously to one another, as if we were in the same room. The document grew; questions shifted in emphasis and multiplied. I then made and shared a first edit of our exchanges, giving us all an opportunity to add to, or to rephrase, our contributions. In this more considered phase, the document grew further, and again new questions, concerns, and enthusiasms emerged. Our responses have been written and edited for clarity, but I wanted them to retain some of that initial liveness: what follows is the transcript of four practitioners thinking more or less in the moment, reading and reacting to each other's experiences and positions, and falling in and out of agreement. It is a conversation without consensus and clearly without end – but powered by an ongoing investment in thinking, reading, and writing translations.

– Kate Briggs

'There was a certain amount of unlearning I had to do ...': on unlearning and confidence

KATE BRIGGS: When I was translating very actively – every day and moving from project to project over a number of years – I noticed that I seemed to be getting better at it: a bit faster, building up a familiarity with the ways a certain kind of sentence structure could be rendered in English and so on. When I started out, I would rarely break up long sentences, for example.

But then, as I became more experienced, I learned some common, plausible, well-tested methods for rendering certain French constructions into English, methods that I would now be in a position to share with a beginner translator. I wonder: is this what people mean when they talk about the *craft* of translation?

JEN CALLEJA: Having translated almost constantly for the last seven years, I can definitely relate to being able to work faster. More than anything, I think this corresponds to a certain amount of unlearning I had to do around what I believed translation to be, to do with linguistic exactitude and reverence. I had to learn to trust myself and my way of expressing German literature in English. When it comes to learning 'go to' ways of solving certain problems, I still find this useful in the early drafting stage, but as there isn't one way of translating anything, I constantly keep in mind that these could also be forged anew or are still changeable depending on context. When it comes to doing things that some would consider daring (!) like breaking up sentences, that came from a certain permission granted by other translators – you do learn from those who have come before you what the parameters and boundaries are; you have to spend time thinking about what your own practice is, what it could be. This is a kind of legacy to the craft of translation.

KATE BRIGGS: I like this: craft defined as a process of coming to a slow and probably very personal understanding of one's own practice, which might well involve undoing or unlearning certain received ideas around what is permissible. And doing this in response to the work of others, whether this means responding positively, finding an approach you might want to adopt for yourself or – and probably just as usefully – negatively. I find Emily Wilson's ongoing updates on her translation process very inspiring in relation to this.[1] She seems to be constantly reflecting on how existing translations of Homer have responded to, or ignored, certain problems. And so to be actively thinking with the translation labour of and precedents set by others, even if it's to then propose an entirely different way of doing things.

You write about this too, Katrina, in your essay 'Understanding is the Proof of Error':[2] your sense of having Giovanni Pontiero – one of [Clarice] Lispector's previous English-language translators – in the room *with you* as you worked. But despite, or maybe because of all this, I remain suspicious of any effort to generalize translation activity. As Jen notes, we have to be constantly alert to the possibility that what might have worked once, in another scenario, may well not work here.

SOPHIE COLLINS: I too feel very suspicious of 'rules' or (inflexible) principles when it comes to translating, in much the same way that I tend to reject 'writing tips' as a poet – they are often institutionally generated, homogenizing. At least in poetry, or perhaps in poetry in particular, 'craft' tends to be deployed as a euphemism for a set of so-called universal aesthetic standards.

In translation, my sense is that an insistence on, or adherence to notions of, 'craft' impacts not only on how texts are translated but also on what gets translated: if source texts don't lend themselves to easy solutions (or indeed support our Anglophone perception of a particular culture and its literary culture, whether formally or thematically) they might be rejected (by translators, editors, publishers) and therefore remain untranslated.

On the other hand, there are of course patterns of expression in any language, and a lot of source texts – whether poetry or prose – will replicate these. In such cases, it seems useful – maybe inevitable – to have templates for translating. So perhaps it's simply about recognizing when you encounter a source text that confounds such patterns, one that requires you to slow down and avoid 'naturalising' it in a bad way. I'm thinking here of poet and critic Veronica Forrest-Thomson's notion of 'bad naturalisation', coined in her book-length study *Poetic Artifice*.[3] It describes an approach to poetry analysis in which the reader and/or critic attempts to reduce the strangeness of the poem in question by converting it into an 'intelligible', collective 'statement about the non-verbal world' – a kind of superficial, thematic reading of the text. What is avoided here is the opportunity to dwell in the poem, to get to the heart of its use of language or 'artifice', as Forrest-Thomson has it, and to evaluate it on its own terms or 'levels'. When it comes to literary translation, I fear that, often, if a text cannot be easily 'naturalised', it is dismissed. Another side of this coin is that when a so-called strange text *is* translated into English, idiosyncrasies in the translation are frequently attributed to a failure in comprehension or expression on the part of the translator.

NATASHA SOOBRAMANIEN: I did an MA in Creative Writing. Such programmes, in the UK at least, have historically been committed to a very particular idea of craft: it was the argument for establishing them in the first place, in fact, at a time when there was a great deal of snobbery about the process of studying creative writing, this idea that writing was not something that could be 'taught'. But of course it is – in the same way that art practice is taught, by virtue of creating a pedagogical community and structures within which a guided exploration of technique, process, theory and so on can occur. But those who argued that writing could not be taught were themselves figures with a great deal of cultural capital that helped sustain their own sense of entitlement to the position of being a writer and/or deciding who else got to be one. I understand that traditional ideas of craft can be really problematic in developing a writing or translation practice. But they can also be helpful in opening access to these spaces of privilege. What's tricky is the feeling that there are no discernible rules – and that's when more unspoken *norms* come into play, which are harder to negotiate from a position of non-privilege and can enforce exclusion at entry level, I think.

What getting on the MA did for me was in some way validate my desire to write and to be published. I was lucky enough to be taught by W. G. Sebald (someone who had very close involvement with the translations of his own work into languages he spoke – I often wondered how his translators felt about this). And lucky that he felt so personally uncomfortable with the idea of 'craft', which I think also, in terms of pedagogy, relates to a speaking for, or on behalf of, something or someone other than yourself: the tradition, for example. When it came to writing, Sebald felt able only to pass on the learning that he had accrued himself over the years, or that of the writers he had studied closely (and taught), as a way of modelling the kind of deep thinking and feeling of one's own way through the writing process: the very kind of individualized concept of craft being discussed here.

JEN CALLEJA: When I hear the word 'craft' with regard to translation and writing in general, it does bring to mind a singular thing, a 'serious' practice that only certain people will reach the heights of, a certain way of working and a specific working dynamic. It makes me feel uncomfortable and excluded, which means that there's the possibility others feel that way too. I've always been unnerved when I heard people uphold that one needs to have X experience or qualifications and behave in a Y way, as these are often patriarchal, sexist, classist. My 'craft', my 'practice', is, first, personal and unique to me (though shared either in part or wholly with other literary translators); second, it has come about from devouring the multitude ways of approaching translations and figuring out what sits well with me; and, third, from gaining confidence in what I am doing. I think I reached this point mainly from realizing that translation itself is all about multitudes and endless possibilities, as well as about you as an individual: it's also about what you want to achieve with it.

KATRINA DODSON: Kate, I had a very similar experience to the one you describe, over the course of translating Clarice Lispector's *Complete Stories* for two years.[4] It felt like an apprenticeship in many ways, learning about manipulating language to convey an overall effect that could transcend the specifics of language (in its force of image, feeling, and relations) and developing a precision of style by translating four decades of writing by someone with an incredibly assured sense of self and voice – and then to undergo a very intense editing process. For me, the idea of translation as both craft and art goes hand in hand with the development of a personal translation philosophy. It constantly evolves through 'devouring the multitude ways of approaching translations', as Jen says, and keeping the parts I believe in as I grow more conscious of my affinities and tendencies. I didn't fully trust my own voice layered over Lispector's until after I turned in the entire manuscript and had to revisit it in edits. I had a visceral response to my editor's suggestions, knowing instinctively what felt like a fitting revision, what choices I had to defend, and, most frequently, what required yet another solution.

I don't want the idea of translation as a craft to be exclusionary, but I do think it signals a certain devotion necessary to produce really good work, that it requires time, attention, and a deep attunement to multiple languages and to another writer's sensibility. The experience we gain in recognizing certain patterns between languages (the nuts and bolts of handling common turns of phrase, standard punctuation, and syntax) lets us work faster to produce a translation that's more consistent and self-coherent. Having a foundational practice in place also lets the translator devote more energy to the thornier obstacles that require deeper resources of creativity, such as so-called 'untranslatables' like idioms, puns, rhyme, colloquial language, and culturally specific terms.

It's in this necessity of inventing original solutions that I think translation is more an art. The art also exists in that ambiguous realm of 'confidence': this trusting in your own voice and ability to create a distinct whole and to make risky choices and carry them off. By 'risky', I mean places where the translator is forced to move conspicuously past the original due to a break in the relation between languages and contexts, and for the sake of making the translation sing on its own. Here, the reader might be jolted into noticing the translatedness of a text, because of a certain stylistic flourish or idiomatic quality. Take Emily Wilson's surprising choices in *The Odyssey*,[5] like her anachronistic 'canapé', for example. Some have been suspicious of those decisions, but for me, Wilson created such a distinct and coherent voice, tone, and rhythm from the start, that their cumulative effect produced a certain *rightness* that I might normally have raised an eyebrow at.

KATE BRIGGS: Yes: what I like about craft – what, of craft, I'd want to hold onto – has exactly to do with the slow process of what you call attunement. In other words, with the sense of translation as a *practice*, with all that comes with the term (ongoingness, revision, rethinking, and investment). I have written in favour of amateur translation: I wanted to invite more reader–writers into this specialized sphere of literary translation regardless of their level of linguistic or cultural expertise. But I made this invitation for very specific reasons, one of them being to alleviate some of the gatekeeping that Sophie and Jen spoke of earlier: these received notions of the sort of knowledge that you need to have in place before translation can even begin. The other being an insistence on translation as process of knowledge-acquisition: we learn through the doing of it. I'd like more people to be given, or to find for themselves, that vital sense of permission: I can try this, I can start worrying over how this could possibly be written again in another language, and get fascinated, and frustrated, and excited by the possibilities. But trying and getting excited is just the beginning. Then comes the work, the learning, the great intellectual and creative adventure. The confidence we are all speaking of is hard won – and it *should* be hard won, because it only comes from doing the work, which means the reading, the thinking, the revising, the feeling your way. Hard won as well as always precarious. This is important, too: never assured once and for all.

JEN CALLEJA: I mentor emerging literary translators who work from a range of different languages, and one of the main things I focus on in mentorships is giving them confidence, giving them 'permission' to be translators. I show them the multiple approaches, and try to make the translation scene and industry more accessible. I'm often approached by postgraduate students who know a lot about theory and who have excellent linguistic skills, but who don't know how you would even start to translate a work of literary fiction or a poem in collaboration with an author and/or editor, or how you pitch or get commissioned. In other words, how you find the work or how you 'do the job' in real life. This is also part of the 'craft' of being a literary translator, but that isn't spoken about all that often. Probably because things like who gets a foot in the door and money are seen as irrelevant, or vulgar – not part of 'craft'.

'Who can afford the time and focus required to pour their soul into this kind of work?': on privilege and precariousness

KATE BRIGGS: Yes, absolutely. And this suggests to me that the question of 'craft' must also, always, be linked to questions of context. By which I mean: the methods or principles we uphold in our work, the 'norms' we adhere to, consciously or unconsciously, are surely all always situated, linked to the education we've received, the experiences we've had, the spaces in which we are able to work. In *This Little Art* I wrote of the 'lady translator' – a terrible phrase, really![6] But I wanted to claim it as a way of skewering my own white, middle-class privilege. I was drawn to translation in part because it was challenging, interesting work that I knew I could do from home with young children. I did not have a teaching job at the time of beginning my longest translation projects, but I had a sense – I guess I made a calculation – that doing the translations might lead to teaching work. In other words, I had an expectation that I could probably end up earn a living via teaching in higher education. So my translation work has always been supplementary to my other work in these rarefied environments. This has meant that to a great extent I have been able to choose my translation projects, or at least prioritize the ones that really interested me, rhythm-ing them in the earlier days with translating articles/website copy/press releases which interested me less. The general point I wanted to make is that because translation is so labour-intensive, still for such relatively low pay, it tends to be an activity of the privileged: either those who have another way of earning income or – and this is crucial too – those who can run the risk of choosing to earn relatively little, to live precariously, because they are supported in other ways. And this, clearly, is a problem.

JEN CALLEJA: Being in a position where I predominantly make a living from being a literary translator, I haven't always been able to pick and choose my projects, and pitching can be a long and sometimes unrewarding process. I started translating while I had a full-time job. I felt motivated enough to translate in lunch breaks, after work, on the weekends. Both bits that I liked and bits I was asked to translate. I've always had at least a part-time job – as a freelance editor, as a translator in residence, as an anti-harassment workshop leader – to supplement my work as a translator.

Many people I come across think of translation, literary or otherwise, as a very prestigious job, which in turn makes me feel very good about having it as a profession. Then there are still others I come across or who propose work to me that clearly don't rate it as a skilled job, and those times I find it quite demotivating. The rates for translators – relatively low per word (though I've heard UK publishers claim it is fair compared to other countries) – really almost sets you up not to want to have it as a job or to feel like you're a fool for doing it. But literary translators aren't the only creative practitioners to feel that way.

KATRINA DODSON: Literary translation is similar to other creative and intellectual endeavours in that it requires slow, intensive labour that doesn't correspond to the capitalist value system. If I tallied up the hours worked and divided them by how much I get paid directly from the translations I produce, my hourly wage would be a joke. I think a lot of writers, especially poets, as well as artists, musicians, and filmmakers could say the same, though, perhaps with the exception of poets, they all have a bigger potential pay-off than translators could ever hope for (unless you translated the Marie Kondo book or another mega-bestseller). And academics produce dense works of scholarship that require the support of institutions, never expecting their books to turn a profit in a free-market sense.

I know other translators who supplement their literary translation work with legal, business, and academic translation or by working in adjacent areas of publishing, but relatively few can live solely from literary translation without other forms of income or support. And it's true, this severely limits who can afford the time and focus required to pour their soul into this kind of work.

KATE BRIGGS: To come back to Natasha's experience of creative writing pedagogy, the idea of craft would seem to imply a set of skills that *are* teachable, so I'm very interested to hear more about your approaches to teaching.

KATRINA DODSON: When I teach translation, I try to emphasize ways for students to start developing their own philosophies of translation, studying translator statements and comparing approaches. I've seen many beginning translators treat the text with what Italian translator Anita Raja calls 'an ill-conceived sacralization of the original',[7] reluctant to rearrange syntax or lose the least bit of cultural specificity. But just as frequent is a tendency to explain away deliberate ambiguity, radically change diction and punctuation, or turn an extended delirium or emotional rant into a clipped series of grammatically compliant clauses due to a fear of following the original too closely or lack of trust in the author. When workshopping with students, I emphasize close reading of an author's style and the effect of their choices. I think translators should always be attuned to whether the original language is *marked* in some way, that is, if it is doing something unusual. If so, then our translation should try to match that *marked* quality in a convincing way, to move the reader with the thrill of whatever's happening in the language rather than merely sounding awkward. This is similar to what Sophie was saying about noting when a writer is confounding established patterns of expression and slowing down the reading, rather than automatically 'naturalising' or domesticating the writing into familiar linguistic structures that flatten that author's idiosyncrasies.

I also like discussing how much context a reader of the translated text will need in order to appreciate it on a level that approaches the way readers have embraced the original. This is especially relevant when translating literature from a country like Brazil, whose history and culture are still not well known to Anglophone audiences. I want students to consider the possible ways in which additional framing *can* be a valid part of a translation, and that there's an art to determining when these kinds of interventions enrich the text instead of sabotaging it, and what form and scope they should take, elements such as prefaces, afterwords, footnotes, endnotes, and stealth glosses, all dependent on what kind of reader relationship the translator imagines.

'Translation as the record of a human interaction': on 'intimacy' and 'affinity' in translation practice

SOPHIE COLLINS: I feel very strongly that dominant modes of literary analysis – primarily, this need for the text to be understood in terms of an essential message, and, when it comes to style, for it to either conform to dominant literary standards in the receiving culture or, if it is to deviate from these, to do so in an immediately intelligible way (a regular, trackable way) – are linked to the way we translate and to perceptions of literary translation and readers' expectations of translation(s) more generally. Our continuing preoccupation with 'fidelity' is both the cause and symptom of this in that it indicates that a single, 'correct' interpretation can be made of a source text – this is of course a fallacy.

I am interested in developing a conceptual alternative to 'fidelity': 'intimacy'. I recently wrote about this in *The Poetry Review*.[8] It's still a term I'm thinking about and feeling out, but I guess, at this stage, I can safely say that 'intimacy', in terms of a translation practice, is intended to promote a direct, sustained, concerted engagement with the source text. I'm increasingly suspicious of the term 'bridge translation' and the way it is being deployed in the context of contemporary UK poetry as a stand-in for 'literal translation'. 'It's related to Gayatri Chakravorty Spivak's notion of 'critical intimacy' and her rejection of so-called objectivity or 'critical distance' as a perspective that will provide the most 'accurate' reading of a text.[9]

NATASHA SOOBRAMANIEN: When Nathacha Appanah, the Mauritian novelist, translated my novel into French,[10] it really did feel like a very intimate experience to have her translate the work. More so than if the translator had been, say, a white French man. There were perhaps obvious reasons why Nathacha was drawn to translate it: her novels and mine share similar themes – of dispossession, displacement, the trauma of exile, of colonial history and its legacies – but also, my book was a 'cannibalistic translation' of *Paul et Virginie*, by Bernadin de Saint-Pierre, a work she too was familiar with and, as a writer of Mauritian origin, had similarly complicated feelings towards.

JEN CALLEJA: I consciously sought to translate Michelle Steinbeck because she was a woman of a similar age who wrote in a way that felt familiar to my own writing. There was no guarantee that we could have a good working relationship, but we are now very close, and have spent a lot of time together. I love gossiping with my authors, hanging out with them; I invite them to my shows, we share music and talk on WhatsApp. I admit – to myself – that perhaps my intentions for intimacy with authors isn't necessarily 'pure'. After all, there is a certain cultural capital enjoyed by the translator of a well-regarded author, and at the base of it you have a 'working' relationship that means that forming a friendliness could be a defence mechanism to avoid fraught disagreement or conflict. But I genuinely enjoy making friends in all collaborative creative processes, very much including translation. I do often joke that sometimes the translation is a trace and remainder of a period of hanging out with a new friend. Being considered an equal collaborator and peer has always been personally important to me when translating an author. I've only translated living authors so far. It's not always possible to have the depth of correspondence or interaction due to an author's availability. But I do always make an effort to break down that traditional author–translator dynamic before it's begun. I can't handle hierarchies! This has always been true across every job I've had, and from all creative collaboration. I think it probably comes down to the treatment of women and working-class people in all spheres of life.

SOPHIE COLLINS: Translation as the record of an interaction – a timed interaction, even. I find this so interesting, and it certainly speaks to my experience of translating Lieke Marsman's work from the Dutch.[11] I decided to write my translator's note in the form of a series of letters which charted our interactions throughout the translation process.

Of course, one thing I am aware of is that if you start figuring translation in terms of 'intimacy', as well as laying the ground for some positive relationships and reflections, you open the door to potentially 'unhealthy' relationships between source texts and authors. When I first wrote about 'intimacy' in translation (holding up Don Mee Choi and Kim Hyesoon's work as a kind of prototype for 'intimate' translation[12]), I also wrote/thought about 'possessive' translation – named and first encountered by me in Gonzalo Aguilar's piece, 'Augusto de Campos: The Translation of a Name.'[13] Aguilar is talking about a very different situation, but I had been reading and rereading Michael Hofmann's review of Alissa Valles's translations of Zbigniew Herbert, 'A Dead Necktie',[14] and saw there (and, later, elsewhere, in relation to other authors/translators) a kind of 'possessiveness' over the source text/author.

NATASHA SOOBRAMANIEN: I'm not a literary translator but I do think of myself as a writer who translates: both for myself – in my head, when I read (Kreol and French), and as part of my writing process – in the translation of source material used in research, or the embedding of passages from other writers in my own writing, as extended quotes. In the case of some of these writers, English translations already exist (for example, Jeffrey Zuckerman's translation of Ananda Devi's *Eve de ses décombres*[15]), but for thematic purposes and for affective reasons, it is important to me that these translated fragments be produced by a writer of Mauritian origin, and/or a woman of colour. Since the translations I need do not yet exist (for all the usual reasons), I must produce them myself. While I loved Jeffrey Zuckerman's translation of *Eve*, because of its setting, because of its subject matter, because of Devi's eponymous protagonist and what she lives – I think I would have preferred to have read a translation by a woman, a woman of colour. Who knows, perhaps the Anglophone daughter of Mauritian immigrants to the UK, Australia, New Zealand, Canada …? Where is *her* translation of this book, I wonder? I am wondering whether, sometimes, translators should consider that, however much they might want to translate a work, it is perhaps not for them. This seems an analogue of Sophie's idea of intimacy, I think: a kind of delicacy or sensitivity around who gets to translate what.

KATE BRIGGS: I wonder whether the considered standing aside you describe, which might also include the active support of another translator, could be part of engaging more meaningfully with the collaborative, knowledge-sharing force of translation? But your point also makes me want to learn more about your relationships to the languages you work in.

KATRINA DODSON: I learned Portuguese at twenty-three, when I moved to Rio de Janeiro and taught English and later studied Brazilian literature as part of my PhD in comparative literature. I'm not Brazilian, but I feel at home there in part since being mixed-race is the norm. My mother came to the USA in 1975 as a refugee from Vietnam, as did my half-brother and half-sister – my American father served in the Foreign

Service. There was a lot of racism against Vietnamese after the war, and my mother wanted her kids to be perfect Americans, so she hardly spoke to us in Vietnamese. I didn't really learn it until college and while studying abroad in Hanoi. It's something of a mystery to me, and a source of anguish, that I ended up as a fake Brazilian, whereas I speak Vietnamese like a child and am much more tentative with it – every mistake throws my identity into question.

JEN CALLEJA: I'm British-Maltese. My dad decided that it would be too confusing for my brother and me to be brought up bilingually, so I can't speak Maltese. Being 'around' it made me curious about languages, and I did French and German (badly) at school (my dad says German is a 'proper', 'useful' foreign language, which I think about all the time). I moved solo to Munich when I was eighteen and lived there for a year, which improved my German but not to a significant level of fluency. I studied literature at Goldsmiths and started very slowly reading German-language novels in my spare time, which is how I taught myself advanced German, or specifically, how German is used to write novels. I did an MA in German Studies, where I studied and specialized in translation theory. That's where I 'discovered' that translating literature was a thing.

NATASHA SOOBRAMANIEN: I was born in London to Mauritian parents and spoke only Mauritian Kreol until I was five, but when I started school and spoke no English, my parents were told by the school to stop speaking Creole with me. Being young immigrants with little formal education, they did not challenge this and so I lost my first language. I've had to acquire it again as an adult. It feels damaged.

SOPHIE COLLINS: My parents are both English, but I grew up in North Holland from the age of four, only moving back to the UK to study English Literature when I was eighteen. My Dutch is more or less fluent, but I've always had an anxiety around speaking it aloud (as opposed to reading or writing it), which is due to my education and home environment having been rooted primarily in English (I went to a European school); I never quite got the chance to 'find my voice' in Dutch and am therefore dogged by an impostor syndrome whenever I speak it. This increased year on year once I'd moved back to the UK as my connection to the Netherlands became increasingly tenuous – despite the fact that I spent most of my life there.

KATE BRIGGS: Are you able to describe how these experiences inform your approach to – or desire for – translation?

SOPHIE COLLINS: Translating is both cathartic – restitutive – and a source of shame for me: on the one hand, translating Dutch literature allows me to encounter and learn a literary Dutch that I never had the opportunity to when I was younger, and to re-establish a connection with a culture I left behind as a young adult; on the other, it forces me to face my own insufficiencies in this language that I have an at once strangely close, strangely distant relationship with. Given the commonalities in all of our language histories, I wonder if turning to translation is for many a kind of measure of reclamation.

KATRINA DODSON: I keep coming back to questions of mastery and authenticity in relation to being bilingual or multilingual, mixed-race, and having a conflicted relationship to one's national identity, particularly in the context of translation. After I finish my current translation project (it'll be three years on a complicated Brazilian modernist novel, *Macunaíma, the Hero With No Character*, by Mário de Andrade), I want to turn to writing about my mother's life in Vietnam and to reclaim my relationship to Vietnamese, as incomplete and imperfect as it feels.

KATE BRIGGS: How does 'authenticity' relate to, or ground, this notion of 'intimacy', I wonder? It seems vital that publishers seek out translators who share affinities and understandings and experiences with regard to the works to be translated, and again I really take on Natasha's point that the degree of affinity and shared experience and understanding is a question that translators should always consider when taking on a project. But I'm also interested in the productive potential – the force and necessity – of antagonistic, or apparently uncomplementary relationships too: relationships founded on marked difference, total incompatibility ... I suppose my question is: who is in a position to be intimate with whom? What are the conditions for intimacy? And what of the value of the incompatible, unlikely, mismatched translator? For affinities that are not grounded in shared lived experience, but in difference?

'You will not misrepresent the book': on the distribution of responsibility

KATE BRIGGS: I value how intimacy and friendship – the kind of collaborative experiences that Jen and Sophie have enjoyed with their authors – offer an alternative to the traditionally hierarchical writer–translator dynamic, reinforced by the concept of 'fidelity'. But somehow I get stuck. It seems to me that there is something very distinctive about that relationship which can't be straightforwardly evened out. It has to do with the distribution of responsibility, and care. In my own translation experience, I did indeed feel like I knew the work I was translating very well. But in my case the intimacy only worked one way: I know and feel close to Barthes's work, but he doesn't know mine. Likewise, I accept responsibility for representing Barthes's work in English, as his translator, but he doesn't – it would be impossible for him to – accept responsibility for mine. My situation is extreme because Barthes is dead, of course. But I think this distribution of responsibility is crucial to understanding what is at stake in the work of translating (rather than rewriting, adapting, paraphrasing) anyone else's work, however intimately you know them or don't know them, however close or distanced you feel. As a translator I accept the responsibility of representation in a new language and context. This is what the task involves, and it doesn't work in both directions at the same time. If we collapse this particular distribution of responsibility, which *isn't* evenly shared, I worry that we then risk missing what is actually at stake, politically, aesthetically, in every translation project.

JEN CALLEJA: It definitely is a large and unique responsibility to speak for someone who can't 'speak for themselves'. I always think of the line in the translator's contract where it specifically says you will not misrepresent the book. It can be a terrifying, almost paralysing thought. As a translator, you have to make a claim that you're the right person to be given the task to speak for a great writer – sometimes someone that people class as a genius.

I repress this anxiety of translating a book by figuring out my priorities and what the expectations are placed on me by the publisher and the author. They will be expecting, for instance, a work of literary fiction that matches what they have been told about the book and that everything in the book appears in the translation. My priority is often first and foremost: tell the story. Am I telling the story? Does this feel like a story, or a string of perfectly OK sentences? Another is: am I recreating how it makes me feel? Am I sticking too close to the words? I have John Berger's urge to go to the pre-verbal. I am thinking of his line that 'true translation demands a return to the pre-verbal' in *Confabulations*[16] – to go behind the words and to return with what you find there as a kind of mantra in my mind. There's also: am I keeping the detail, the ambiguity, the sense of familiarity or unfamiliarity the original reader would have? This is how I show care for the work and the author, by challenging myself to do the best I can with certain considerations.

Like you say, this is a one-sided responsibility. But then again, an author can choose to be actively supportive of you, either to you in person or in correspondence or in public, and I think this is their way of recognizing what translators have to put themselves through and lightening this burden. Incidentally, my author Michelle Steinbeck has now translated one of my poems – something tiny compared to a novel, she admits. I understood the happiness she expresses as a sense of relief that she had in some way 'returned the favour' and had made a concrete gesture to engage with my work as I had hers.

KATRINA DODSON: I think translators are always negotiating this space of distance and intimacy with a text – on one hand always a total stranger to us and on the other an animated object with a subjectivity we think we know better than most living people.

SOPHIE COLLINS: Rather than claiming to collapse those distinctions altogether, what is valuable about 'intimacy' is how it challenges the ways we *evaluate the translated text*. Certainly, my prizing 'intimacy' over 'fidelity' in translations is an attempt to undermine the cult of the author, of the individual, and to promote more equitable, collaborative approaches to translation. More fundamental than that, however, is the need I see to challenge our perception of the source text as something whose own meaning is fixed, immutable. If we fail to do this we not only risk reducing the role of the translator to something robotic, unrelated to interpretation, but we continue to support a literary culture that is built on essentialism, that only admits texts which are perceived as non-threatening.

KATE BRIGGS: I think that's absolutely right – it makes me think of Karen Emmerich's recent essential work on how translations 'make' or stabilize unstable, mobile originals, and not only the other way round.[17] But in addition to this, what I value most about translation is the way it offers a model of distributed authorship (if not exactly, or only very rarely, even-handed collaboration). In our literary culture, the model for what counts as creative production (and a creative life) still seems to be so much based on some fantasy of the unattached individual, working in solitude, unencumbered and uninterrupted by responsibilities to others. The taking on of responsibility and the fundamental together-ness of translation – in the sense that a translation cannot be written by an author working on her own, solely invested in her own self-expression – looks far more like my approach to writing, and my life, than any other model I've encountered.

But with responsibility comes the question (and your experiences) of the 'consequences' of *publishing* translations.

'Equivalence between languages simply doesn't exist in the way we would like to think it does': on mistakes, shame, and false polarities

KATRINA DODSON: I've never been more terrified of consequences than when I was translating a lifetime of work by a dead, beloved Brazilian icon, famously known for the difficulty and strangeness of her language and widely hailed as a 'genius'. Who the hell was I to speak for her? I quintuple checked every possible language query, and then checked some more, underwent a rigorous editing process, had heart palpitations on the eve of publication – I was ecstatic to be done with the whole ordeal but also sick to my stomach with anxiety over how it would be received and what I got wrong. And I did find mistakes in the translation, which I corrected for the paperback edition. I'm sure I'll find more if I can ever stand to read all 645 pages again.

KATE BRIGGS: I can completely identify with this: I felt positively serene when I published my book on translation compared to publishing the translations themselves. And my anxieties were definitely related to this sense of imposture, I would even say something like embarrassment at my own presumptuousness ('Who on earth did I think I was?'). Which is a curious thing, because translation is so often figured as the *least* presumptuous of literary activities: the *most* helpful, discreet, selfless.

SOPHIE COLLINS: I think translation is a process which inevitably generates a sense of shame in the translator, due the way 'fidelity' forces us to compare our translation to a notional ideal.

When we police translations by strenuously enforcing 'fidelity', we engineer shame in the translator by forcing her to measure her translation, which is an extension of herself, against an imagined or notional translation that is flawless – perfect in its equivalency. Judged in this way, the translator will almost definitely fail in her task, just as vulnerable humans fail when they measure themselves against imagined, idealized, and non-existent selves, because equivalence between languages simply doesn't exist in the way we would like to think it does – theorists like Kwame Anthony Appiah have shown this time and time again.[18]

KATRINA DODSON: But when it comes to translation errors, I think we have a responsibility to be as thorough as possible in our linguistic and literary research, to intimately retrace the steps of an author and their relationship to language as we learn as much as we can about at least two languages side by side. Yet beyond the due diligence aspect of translation, what matters most is how we're able to convey the force and idiosyncratic sensibility and pleasure of the original, casting it in our own personal idiom even as we perform another literary persona.

JEN CALLEJA: I've actually just written some poems about the negative comments I've received about my translations – from a review, a comment online, an unsolicited email. It's cathartic. It's typically seen as embarrassing not to be ashamed of 'errors' and not to apologize.

KATRINA DODSON: I think all the drama over translation mistakes is a distraction and that recent debates have falsely divided parties into those who care about accuracy and those who don't. It's ridiculous to claim that certain translators don't care about basic accuracy. What those who wag the 'Gotcha!' finger often overlook is that accuracy isn't always straightforward, that getting a word 'right' is often a broader contextual matter of interpretation: of style, register, tone, mood, sound patterns, or maintaining an overall image or feel beyond individual words.

NATASHA SOOBRAMANIEN: I feel that there is something about the historical position of the translator, simultaneously being overlooked and hyper-visible (being overpoliced – albeit not literally) that is [also] true of the marginalized and powerless in society. It is the privileged who are accorded the most beneficial kind of attention – they and their right to be are acknowledged – and are not held to account for their mistakes. I wonder how this applies to privilege structures within translation. It's interesting to look at who is publicly judging translations – who feels they have the authority and expertise to do this? There seem to have been a number of recent examples of men with high-profile public platforms using their positions to 'shame' female translators, often younger/less established, in other words, with less cultural power.

SOPHIE COLLINS: On hypervisibility: translators are still often only publicly associated with their work when readers/critics/other translators identify so-called errors in the translation. For me this again comes down to 'fidelity' as a measure of quality and the connected piece of conventional wisdom that a 'good' translation is an 'invisible' one – I'm thinking here of Norman Shapiro's 'pane of glass', cited in Venuti's book on the translator's invisibility.[19]

KATRINA DODSON: I agree that there is a certain, frequently patriarchal, will to domination, of proving oneself superior to others, behind this compulsion to draw up lists of mistakes and look no further, or to minutely scrutinize a selection of slip-ups as if they were an adequate synecdoche for the work as a whole. It also arises from that sense of possessiveness mentioned earlier – that this writer, this literature, this language is mine and not yours, that you somehow weaselled your way into representing this great artist and cannot possibly understand such work on the level that *I* do.

KATE BRIGGS: Right *or* wrong, presumptuous *or* selfless, concerned with accuracy *or* just sloppy and careless, what these polarizing and – I agree – wholly distracting positions miss is that translation, of all writerly activities, involves engaging with what I called togetherness. Maybe *both-ness* is better? Because, after all, a translation is *both* the same as and different from the text that produced it. It is *both* something I wrote and it isn't. This is what is so complicated and difficult and fascinating about it. When I read these sorts of simplifying polemics around translation, what astounds me is how they seem to wilfully ignore the very mode of being of a translation. As an object, surely it *undoes* such easy oppositions? As an activity it very often requires us to recognize the value of more than one position *at the same time.* For example, how a translation error can be wrong at the level of basic comprehension but productive in terms of what it exposes, or the unlikely reading it offers. The problem, I've discovered, is that pointing these complexities out can be received as weak thinking or weak argumentation – but on the contrary: it is trying to meaningfully engage with how things actually are.

JEN CALLEJA: Judging people based on their mistakes and presuming that they're purposefully hiding them is acting in bad faith, I think. For me it's the same as claiming that people who say 'um' a lot or slip on their words aren't eloquent or worth listening to. Literature has never been error-free, and when a book goes through a string of people and a mistake still makes it through, that's life. It could also be considered a small exciting stitch of cross-reading.

But the phrase 'how things actually are' is what really jumps out at me in what you say. It's a kind of radical positivity in the face of this 'Gotcha' culture that is gatekeeping masquerading as a concern for quality in translation. I'm not one for 'what ifs' or 'optimum outcomes' or 'missed opportunities' – I think it leads to dissatisfaction and an unwillingness to accept what has come to pass, how the actual translation is being read by readers, what the real-life parameters are for translators such as time, working relationships, editing support.

KATE BRIGGS: I like this phrase! Radical positivity. Translation as a form of radical positivity. It is, though, isn't it? Without wanting to claim that all translations are equal, or that all translations are straightforwardly a force for good in the world – translations can do harm too, clearly – I do believe it is a fundamentally hopeful activity. I say this because it is an activity grounded in an attentiveness to someone else's work, to someone else's situation, premised on the hope that this work will be of interest to those who currently know nothing or only very little about it. As translators, I think we have to believe in that reach, and in what it can do, or open: in what unexpected things can happen when actual translations – not idealized, non-existent, could-have-been translations – but actual translations written, for example, by women like us, get read by actual readers.

Notes

1 See Emily Wilson's selected twitter threads, www.emilyrcwilson.com/emilyrcwilson-scholia, accessed 29 October 2021.
2 Katrina Dodson, 'Understanding is the Proof of Error', *Believer Magazine*, 11 July 2018, accessed 29 October 2021, https://believermag.com/understanding-is-the-proof-of-error/
3 Veronica Forrest-Thomson, *Poetic Artifice: A Theory of Twentieth-Century Poetry* (London: Palgrave Macmillan, 1978).
4 Clarice Lispector, *The Complete Stories*, ed. Benjamin Moser, trans. Katrina Dodson (New York: New Directions, 2015).
5 Homer, *The Odyssey*, trans. Emily Wilson (New York: Norton, 2018).
6 Kate Briggs, *This Little Art* (London: Fitzcarraldo Editions, 2018).
7 Anita Raja, 'Translation as a Practice of Acceptance', trans. Rebecca Falkoff and Stiliana Milkova, *Assymptote*, 25 November 2015, accessed 29 October 2021, www.asymptotejournal.com/criticism/anita-raja-translation-as-a-practice-of-acceptance/
8 Sophie Collins, 'Erasing the Signs of Labour under the Signs of Happiness: "Joy" and "Fidelity" as Bromides in Literary Translation', *Poetry Review* 108, no. 2 (Summer 2018), https://poetrysociety.org.uk/erasing-the-signs-of-labour/, accessed 29 October 2021.
9 Gayatri Chakravorty Spivak, 'Critical Intimacy: An Interview with Gayatri Chakravorty Spivak', interview by Steve Poulson, *Los Angeles Review of Books*, July 2016, https://lareviewofbooks.org/article/critical-intimacy-interview-gayatri-chakravorty-spivak/, accessed 29 October 2021.
10 Natasha Soobramien, *Genie and Paul* (Brighton: Myriad Editions, 2012); Natasha Soobramien, *Genie et Paul*, trans. Natacha Appanah (Paris: Gallimard, 2018).
11 Lieke Marsman, *The Following Scan Will Last Five Minutes*, trans. Sophie Collins (Liverpool: Liverpool University Press, 2019).

12 Kim Hyesoon, *The Autobiography of Death*, trans. Don Mee Choi (New York: New Directions, 2018).
13 Gonzalo Aguilar, 'Augusto de Campos: The Translation of a Name', trans. Ellen Jones and Paula Porroni, *Asymptote*, n.d., www.asymptotejournal.com/criticism/gonzalo-aguilar-augusto-de-campos-the-translation-of-a-name/, accessed 29 October 2021.
14 Michael Hofmann, 'A Dead Necktie', review of *The Collected Poems, 1956–1998,* by Zbigniew Herbert, ed. and trans. Alissa Valles, *Poetry*, 1 May 2007, accessed 29 October 2021, www.poetryfoundation.org/poetrymagazine/articles/68858/a-dead-necktie
15 Ananda Devi, *Eve Out of Her Ruins*, trans. Jeffrey Zuckerman (Dallas: Deep Vellum, 2016).
16 John Berger, *Confabulations* (London: Penguin, 2016).
17 Karen Emmerich, *Literary Translation and the Making of Originals* (London: Bloomsbury, 2017).
18 See, for example, Anthony Kwame Appiah, 'Thick Translation', in *The Translation Studies Reader*, 2nd ed., ed. Lawrence Venuti (New York: Routledge, 2004), 389–401.
19 Lawrence Venuti, *The Translator's Invisibility* (New York: Routledge, 1995).

Bibliography

Acevedo, Elizabeth. *The Poet X*. New York: HarperCollins, 2018.
Ackroyd, Peter. *English Music*. London: Penguin, 1992.
Aristotle. *Metaphysics*. Translated by C. D. C Reeve. Indianapolis: Hackett Publishing Company, 2016.
Aristotle. *The Physics, Books 5–8*. Translated by Philip H. Wicksteed and Francis M. Cornford. Cambridge, MA: Harvard University Press, 1934.
Armstrong, Richard H. 'Classical Translations of the Classics: The Dynamics of Literary Tradition in Retranslating Epic Poetry'. In *Translation and the Classic: Identity as Change in the History of Culture*. Edited by Alexandra Lanieri and Vanda Zajko, 169–202. Oxford: Oxford University Press, 2008.
Arrojo, Rosemary. 'Deconstruction and the Teaching of Translation', *Translation and Interpreting Studies* 7, no 1 (2012): 96–110.
Bakhtin, Mikhail. *Problems of Dostoevsky's Poetics*. Translated by Caryl Emerson. Minneapolis, MN: University of Minnesota Press, 1984.
Balmer, Josephine. 'Jumping Their Bones: Translating, Transgressing, and Creating'. In *Living Classics: Greece and Rome in Contemporary Poetry in English*. Edited by S. J. Harrison, 43–64. Oxford: Oxford University Press, 2009.
Balmer, Josephine. *Piecing Together the Fragments: Translating Classical Verse, Creating Contemporary Poetry*. Oxford: Oxford University Press, 2013.
Barnard, Mary, trans. *Sappho*. Berkeley, CA University of California Press, 1958.
Barnes, Julian. *Levels of Life*. London: Vintage, 2013. Barthes, Roland. 'The Death of the Author'. *Aspen* 5–6 (1967).
Barthes, Roland. *Journal de deuil*. Paris: Seuil, 2009.
Basile, Elena. 'Responding to the Enigmatic Address of the Other: A Psychoanalytical Approach to the Translator's Labour'. *New Voices in Translation Studies* 1 (2005): 12–30.
Bassnett, Susan. 'When Is a Translation Not a Translation?' In *Constructing Cultures: Essays on Literary Translation*. Edited by Susan Bassnett and André Lefevere, 25–40. Clevedon, UK: Multilingual Matters, 1998.
Beauvais, Clémentine. 'Didactic'. In *Keywords for Children's Literature 2.0*. Edited by Nina Christensen, Lissa Paul, and Philip Nel, 57–59. New York: New York University Press, 2021.
Beauvais, Clémentine. *In Paris with You: A Novel*. Translated by Sam Taylor. London: Faber, 2018.

Beauvais, Clémentine. *The Mighty Child: Time and Power in Children's Literature*. Amsterdam: John Benjamins, 2015.

Beauvais, Clémentine. *Songe à la douceur*. Paris: Sarbacane, 2017.

Beckett, Samuel. *The Letters of Samuel Beckett I: 1929–1940*. Edited by Martha Dow Fehsenfeld and Lois More Overbeck, with George Craig and Dan Gunn. Cambridge: Cambridge University Press, 2009.

Beckett, Samuel. *The Letters of Samuel Beckett II: 1941–1956*. Edited by George Craig, Martha Fehsenfeld, Dan Gunn, and Lois More Overbeck. Cambridge: Cambridge University Press, 2011.

Beckett, Samuel. *The Letters of Samuel Beckett III: 1957–1966*. Edited by George Craig, Martha Fehsenfeld, Dan Gunn, and Lois More Overbeck. Cambridge: Cambridge University Press, 2014.

Beckett, Samuel. *The Letters of Samuel Beckett IV: 1967–1989*. Edited by George Craig, Martha Fehsenfeld, Dan Gunn, and Lois More Overbeck. Cambridge: Cambridge University Press, 2016.

Bellos, David. *Is That a Fish in Your Ear? Translation and the Meaning of Everything*. New York: Farrar, Straus and Giroux, 2011.

Benjamin, Andrew. 'Translating Origins: Psychoanalysis and Philosophy'. In *Rethinking Translation: Discourse, Subjectivity, Ideology*. Edited by Lawrence Venuti, 18–41. New York: Routledge, 1992.

Benjamin, Walter. 'Die Aufgabe des Übersetzers'. In *Gesammelte Schriften*, vol. 4.1. Edited by Tillman Rexroth, 7–21. Frankfurt am Main: Suhrkamp, 1991.

Benjamin, Walter. 'The Task of the Translator'. In *Walter Benjamin: Illuminations*. Translated by Harry Zohn. Edited by Hannah Arendt, 70–82. London: Fontana Press, 1992.

Berger, John. *Confabulations*. London: Penguin, 2016.

Berman, Antoine. *La Traduction et la lettre ou l'auberge du lointain*. Paris: Seuil, 1999.

Berman, Antoine. 'Translation and the Trials of the Foreign'. Translated by Lawrence Venuti. In *The Translation Studies Reader*, 3rd ed. Edited by Lawrence Venuti, 240–53. New York: Routledge, 2012.

Bernstein, Charles. *Attack of the Difficult Poems: Essays and Inventions*. Chicago: University of Chicago Press, 2011.

Bettelheim, Bruno. *Freud and Man's Soul*. New York: Vintage Books, 1984.

Bishop, Rudine Sims. 'Mirrors, Windows, and Sliding Glass Doors'. *Perspectives* 6, no. 3 (1990): ix–xi.

Bonaparte, Marie. *Topsy: The Story of a Golden-Haired Chow*. New Brunswick: Transaction Publishers, 1994.

Bonnefoy, Yves. 'Translating Poetry'. In *Theories of Translation: An Anthology of Essays from Dryden to Derrida*. Edited by Reiner Schulte and John Biguenet, 186–92. Chicago: University of Chicago Press, 1992.

Borges, Jorge Luis. 'The Homeric Versions'. Translated by Eliot Weinberger. In *Voice-Overs: Translation and Latin American Literature*. Edited by Daniel Balderston and Marcy Schwartz, 15–20. Albany: State University of New York Press, 2002.

Borges, Jorge Luis. *The Total Library: Non-Fiction, 1922–1986.* Translated by Esther Allen, Suzanne Jill Levine, and Eliot Weinberger. Edited by Eliot Weinberger. Harmondsworth, UK: Penguin, 2001.
Boyle, T. C. *Outside Looking In: A Novel.* New York: HarperCollins, 2019.
Boyle, T. C. *Talk Talk.* Translated by Bernard Turle. Paris: Grasset, 2007.
Briggs, Kate. *This Little Art.* London: Fitzcarraldo Editions, 2017.
Brink, André. *A Fork in the Road.* London: Harvill Secker, 2009.
Brown, Brandon. *Flowering Mall.* New York: Roof Books, 2012.
Brown, Brandon. *The Persians by Aeschylus.* Ann Arbor: Displaced Press, 2011.
Brown, Brandon. *The Poems of Gaius Valerius Catullus.* San Francisco: Krupskaya Press, 2011.
Brown, Brandon. *Top 40.* New York: Roof Books, 2014.
Bužarovska, Rumena. 'On the Macedonian Translations of Alice'. In *Alice in a World of Wonderlands*, vol. 1. Edited by Jon Lindseth, 358–60. New Castle, DE: Oak Knoll Press, 2015.
Byron, George Gordon. 'Childe Harold's Pilgrimage: Canto the Second'. In *Byron's Poetry and Prose.* Edited by Alice Levine, 55–97. Norton Critical Edition. New York: Norton, 2010.
Cadden, Mike. 'Rhetorical Technique in the Young Adult Verse Novel'. *Lion and the Unicorn* 42, no. 2 (2018): 129–44.
Cadden, Mike. 'The Verse Novel and the Question of Genre'. *ALAN Review* 39, no. 1 (2011): 21–7.
Carroll, Lewis. *The Annotated Alice.* Edited by Martin Gardner. Harmondsworth, UK: Penguin, 1970.
Carson, Anne. *NOX.* New York: New Directions, 2010.
Carson, Anne. *Men in the Off Hours.* New York: Knopf, 2000.
Cassin, Barbara, Emily Apter, Jacques Lezra, and Michael Wood, eds. *Dictionary of Untranslatables: A Philosophical Lexicon.* Princeton, NJ: Princeton University Press, 2004.
Chamberlain, Lori. 'Gender and the Metaphorics of Translation'. In *The Translation Studies Reader.* 2nd ed. Edited by Lawrence Venuti, 306–32. New York: Routledge, 2004.
Chapman, George, trans. *Chapman's Homer: The Iliad.* Edited by Allardyce Nicoll. Princeton, NJ: Princeton University Press, 1998.
Chen, Janice, Yuan Chang Leong, Christopher J. Honey, Chung Hyun Yong, Kenneth A. Norman, and Uri Hanson. 'Shared Memories Reveal Shared Structure in Neural Activity across Individuals', *Nature Neuroscience* 20, no. 1 (2017): 115–25.
Chwast, Seymour. *Dante's Divine Comedy.* London: Bloomsbury, 2010.
Clausing, Kimberly. *Open: The Progressive Case for Free Trade, Immigration, and Global Capital.* Cambridge MA: Harvard University Press, 2019.
Coats, Karen. 'Teaching the Conflicts: Diverse Responses to Diverse Children's Books'. In *The Edinburgh Companion to Children's Literature.* Edited by Clémentine Beauvais and Maria Nikolajeva, 13–28. Edinburgh: Edinburgh University Press, 2017.

Colina, Sonia, and Lawrence Venuti. 'A Survey of Translation Pedagogies'. In *Teaching Translation: Programs, Courses, Pedagogies*. Edited by Lawrence Venuti, 203–15. London: Routledge, 2017.

Collins, S. 'Erasing the Signs of Labour under the Signs of Happiness: "Joy" and "Fidelity" as Bromides in Literary Translation'. *Poetry Review* 108, no. 2 (Summer 2018).

Collodi, Carlo. *The Adventures of Pinocchio*. Translated by Geoffrey Brock. New York: New York Review of Books, 2009.

Collodi, Carlo. *Le avventure di Pinocchio*. Florence: Felice Paggi, 1883. Accessed 29 October 2021, www.google.com/books/edition/Le_avventure_di_Pinocchio/BHpjAAAAIAAJ.

Connors, Sean P., and Ryan M. Rish. 'Troubling Ideologies: Creating Opportunities for Students to Interrogate Cultural Models in YA Literature'. *ALAN Review* 42, no. 3 (Summer 2015): 22–34.

Cook, Daniel Thomas. 'Interrogating Symbolic Childhood'. Introduction to *Symbolic Childhood*. Edited by Daniel Thomas Cook, 1–14. New York: Peter Lang, 2002.

Cronin, Michael. *Translation and Globalisation*. London: Routledge, 2003.

Crossan, Sarah. *Swimming Pool*. Translated by Clémentine Beauvais. Paris: Rageot, 2018.

Crossan, Sarah. *The Weight of Water*. London: Bloomsbury, 2015.

Dacier, Anne. Extract from the introduction to her translation of the *Iliad*. 1699. In *Translation/History/Culture: A Sourcebook*. Edited by André Lefevere, 10–13. London: Routledge, 1992.

Daley-Carey, Ebony. 'Testing the Limits: Postmodern Adolescent Identities in Contemporary Coming-of-Age Stories'. *Children's Literature in Education* 49 (2018): 467–84.

Damrosch, David. *What Is World Literature?* Princeton, NJ: Princeton University Press, 2003.

'Dans un rayon de soleil, de Tillie Walden'. *biblioqueer*, 5 May 2019. Accessed 31 May 2019. https://biblioqueerblog.wordpress.com/tag/gallimard-bd/.

Davis, Wade. *The Wayfinders: Why Ancient Wisdom Matters in the Modern World*. Toronto: House of Anansi, 2009.

Day, Sara K. 'Power and Polyphony in Young Adult Literature: Rob Thomas's *Slave Day*'. *Studies in the Novel* 42, nos. 1/2 (Spring and Summer 2010): 66–83.

De Campos, Haroldo. *Traduzione, transcreazione. Saggi*. Italian translation by A. Lombardi and G. D'Itria. Salerno, Italy: Oèdipus, 2016.

De la Motte, Antoine Houdar. Extract from the preface to his translation of the *Iliad*. 1714. In *Translation/History/Culture: A Sourcebook*. Edited by André Lefevere, 28–30. London: Routledge, 1992.

de Saussure, Ferdinand. *Cours de linguistique générale*. 5th ed. Edited by Charles Bally and Albert Sechehaye. Paris: Payot, 1955.

de Saussure, Ferdinand. *Troisième cours de linguistique générale (1910–1911): d'après les cahiers d'Emile Constatine*. Edited by Eisuke Komatsu. Translated by Roy Harris. Oxford: Pergamon Press, 1993.

Deacon, Terrence W. *Incomplete Nature: How Mind Emerged from Matter*. New York: W. W. Norton, 2013.
Delecroix, Vincent. *Apprendre à perdre*. Paris: Payot, 2019.
Dodson, K. 'Understanding Is the Proof of Error'. *Believer Magazine*, 11 July 2018.
Eliot, T. S. Introduction to *Ezra Pound: Selected Poems*. 1928. In *Ezra Pound: A Critical Anthology*. Edited by J. P. Sullivan, 101–9. Harmonsdsworth, UK: Penguin, 1970.
Emmerich, Karen. *Literary Translation and the Making of Originals*. Bloomsbury, 2017.
Emmerich, Michael. 'Beyond, between: Translation, Ghosts, Metaphors'. In *In Translation: Translators on Their Work and What It Means*. Edited by Esther Allen and Susan Bernofsky, 44–57. New York: Columbia University Press, 2013.
Feeney, Denis. *Beyond Greek: The Beginnings of Latin Literature*. Cambridge, MA: Harvard University Press, 2016.
Fludernik, Monika. 'Conversational Narration – Oral Narration'. In *Handbook of Narratology*. Edited by Peter Hühn, Jan Christoph Meister, John Pier, and Wolf Schmid, 93–104. 2nd ed. Göttingen, Germany: De Gruyter, 2014.
Flynn, Richard. 'Why Genre Matters: A Case for the Importance of Aesthetics in the Verse Memoirs of Marilyn Nelson and Jacqueline Woodson'. *Lion and the Unicorn* 42, no. 2 (2018): 109–28.
Forrest-Thomson, V. *Poetic Artifice: A Theory of Twentieth Century Poetry*. London: Palgrave Macmillan, 1978.
Foucault, Michel. *The Archaeology of Knowledge & The Discourse on Language*. Translated by A. M. Sheridan Smith. New York: Harper & Row, 1972.
Foucault, Michel. *Language, Counter-Memory, Practice*. Translated by Donald Bouchard and Sherry Simon. Ithaca, NY: Cornell University Press, 1977.
Fraistat, Neil, and Julia Flanders. 'Introduction: Textual Scholarship in the Age of Media Consciousness'. In *The Cambridge Companion to Textual Scholarship*. Edited by Neil Fraistat and Julia Flanders, 1–15. Cambridge: Cambridge University Press, 2013.
Freud, Sigmund. *A Case of Hysteria (Dora)*. Translated by Anthea Bell. Oxford: Oxford University Press, 2013.
Freud, Sigmund. *The Interpretation of Dreams*. Translated by James Strachey. New York: Avon Books, 1965.
Freud, Sigmund. *The Interpretation of Dreams*. Translated by Joyce Crick. Oxford: Oxford University Press, 1999.
Freud, Sigmund. *Jugendbriefe an Eduard Silberstein*. Edited by Walter Boehlich. Frankfurt am Main: Fischer, 1989.
Freud, Sigmund. *The Letters of Sigmund Freud to Eduard Silberstein, 1871–1881*. Edited by Walter Boehlich. Translated by Arnold J. Pomerans. Cambridge, MA: Harvard University Press, 1990.
Freud, Sigmund. *Neue Folge der Vorlesungen zur Einführing in die Psychoanalyse*. Vienna: Internationaler Psychoanalytischer Verlag, 1933.

Freud, Sigmund. *New Introductory Lectures on Psycho-Analysis*. Translated by James Strachey. New York: Norton, 1964.
Freud, Sigmund. *The Standard Edition of the Complete Psychological Works of Sigmund Freud*. Translated by James Strachey. London: The Hogarth Press and the Institute of Psycho-Analysis, 1955–74.
Freud, Sigmund. *The Uncanny*. Translated by David McLintock. New York: Penguin, 2003.
Freud, Sigmund, and Joseph Breuer. *Studies in Hysteria*. Translated by Nicola Luckhurst. London: Penguin, 2004.
Frost, Robert. *Collected Poems, Prose, & Plays*. New York: Library of America, 1995.
Fuentes, Carlos. *How I Wrote Aura*. London: Andre Deutsch, 1988.
Gaisser, Julia. *Catullus*. Oxford: Wiley-Blackwell, 2009.
Gallagher, Ryan. *The Complete Poems of Gaius Valerius Catullus*. Lowell, MA: Bootstrap Press, 2008.
Gansel, Mireille. *Translation as Transhumance*. Translated by Ros Schwartz. London: Les Fugitives, 2018.
Garff, Joakim. *Søren Kierkegaard: A Biography*. Translated by Bruce H. Kirmmse. Princeton, NJ: Princeton University Press, 2005.
Gentzler, Edwin. *Translation and Rewriting in the Age of Post-Translation Studies*. New York: Routledge, 2017.
Gjurčinova, Anastasija. 'Spanish Poetry in Macedonian Translations (after 1945)'. In *IberoSlavica: A Peer Reviewed Yearbook of the International Society for Iberian-Slavonic Studies*. Edited by Beata Elzbieta Cieszynska, 84–91. Lisbon: CompaRes 2011.
Gombrich, Ernst H. *Art and Illusion: A Study in the Psychology of Pictorial Representation*. Princeton, NJ: Princeton University Press, 2000.
Goold, G. P. *The Poems of Gaius Valerius Catullus*. Loeb Classical Library. Cambridge, MA: Harvard University Press, 1962.
Gray, Kes. *Oi Frog!* Illustrated by Jim Field. London: Hodder Children's Books, 2015.
Graziosi, Barbara, and Emily Greenwood. *Homer in the Twentieth Century: Between World Literature and the Western Canon*. Oxford: Oxford University Press, 2007.
Green, Peter. *The Poems of Catullus*. Berkeley, CA: University of California Press, 2005.
Gregory, Horace. *The Poems of Catullus*. New York: Grove Press, 1956.
H.D. *Collected Poems 1912–1944*. Edited by Louis L. Martz. New York: New Directions, 1983.
H.D. *Notes on Thoughts and Vision & The Wise Sappho*. San Francisco, CA: City Lights, 1982.
H.D. *Palimpsest*. Carbondale, IL: Southern Illinois University Press, 1968.
Haddad, Vincent. 'Nobody's Protest Novel: Novelistic Strategies of the Black Lives Matter Movement'. *Comparatist* 42 (2018): 40–59.
Hamilton, Hugo. 'The Island of Talking'. *Irish Pages* 4, no. 2 (2007): 23–31.

Hardwick, Lorna. *Translating Words, Translating Cultures*. London: Duckworth, 2000.
Havelock, Eric. *The Lyric Genius of Catullus*. Oxford: Blackwell, 1939.
Hegel, Georg Wilhelm Friedrich. *The Science of Logic*. Translated and edited by George di Giovanni. Cambridge: Cambridge University Press, 2010.
Hinton, S. E. *The Outsiders*. London: Penguin, 1967.
Hoffmann, E. T. A. *Fantasiestücke*. Frankfurt am Main: Deutscher Klassiker Verlag, 2006.
Hoffmeister, Adolf. 'The Game of Evenings'. Translated by Michelle Woods. *Granta*, no. 89 (2005): 239–54.
Honey, Christopher J., Christopher R. Thompson, Yulia Lerner, and Uri Hasson. 'Not Lost in Translation: Neural Responses Shared Across Languages'. *The Journal of Neuroscience: The Official Journal of the Society for Neuroscience* 32, no. 44 (October 2012): 15277–83.
Jakobson, Roman. 'On Linguistic Aspects of Translation'. In *Selected Writings*, vol. 2. The Hague and Paris: Mouton, 1971.
Jankélévitch, Vladimir. *La Méconnaissance, le malentendu*. Vol. 2 of *Le Je-ne-sais-quoi et le Presque-rien*. Paris: Seuil, 1980.
Kant, Immanuel. *Critique of Pure Reason*. Translated by Norman Kemp Smith. New York: St. Martin's Press, 1929.
Karasu, Bilge. *A Long Day's Evening*. Translated by Aron Aji. San Francisco: City Lights, 2013.
Karasu, Bilge. *Uzun Sürmüş Bir Günün Akşamı*. Istanbul: Metis Publishing, 1971.
Kaza, Madhu H, ed. *Kitchen Table Translation: An Aster(ix) Anthology*. Pittsburgh, PA: Blue Sketch Press, 2017.
Kazantzakis, Nikos. *The Odyssey: A Modern Sequel*. Translated by Kimon Friar. New York: Simon and Schuster, 1958.
Kenner, Hugh. *The Pound Era*. Berkeley, CA: The University of California Press, 1971.
Kiraly, Don. *A Social Constructivist Approach to Translator Education: Empowerment from Theory to Practice*. New York: Routledge, 2014.
Kirkpatrick, Kathryn. 'Mother, Ireland'. *Canadian Journal of Irish Studies*, no. 40 (2017): 221–4.
Knittle, Davy, 'Pretty Information', in *Jacket2*, 22 June 2015. Accessed 16 March 2016. http://jacket2.org/reviews/pretty-information
Kokkola, Lydia. *Fictions of Adolescent Carnality: Sexy Sinners and Delinquent Deviants*. Amsterdam: John Benjamins, 2013.
Lacan, Jacques. *Écrits*. Translated by Bruce Fink. New York: Norton, 2006.
Lacoue-Labarthe, Philippe, and Jean-Luc Nancy. *The Literary Absolute: The Theory of Literature in German Romanticism*. Translated by Philip Barnard and Cheryl Lester. Albany, NY: State University of New York Press, 1988.
Lafontaine, Céline. *La société postmortelle*. Paris: Seuil, 2008.
Lathey, Gillian. *Translating Children's Literature*. London: Routledge, 2016.
Lattimore, Richmond, trans. *The Iliad of Homer*. Chicago, IL: University of Chicago Press, 1951.

Laybourn-Langton, Laurie, Lesley Rankin, and Darren Baxter. *This Is a Crisis: Facing Up to the Age of Environmental Breakdown*. London: Institute for Public Policy Research, 2019.
Lecercle, Jean-Jacques. *The Violence of Language*. London: Routledge, 1990.
Lefevere, André. *Translation, Rewriting, and the Manipulation of Literary Fame*. 1992. London: Routledge, 2017.
Lispector, Clarice. *The Complete Stories*. Translated by Katrina Dodson. New York: New Directions, 2015.
Liu, Lydia H. *Translingual Practice: Literature, National Culture, and Translated Modernity—China, 1900–1937*. Stanford, CA: Stanford University Press, 1995.
Logue, Christopher. 'The Art of Poetry' *Paris Review* 127 (1993): 254.
Mahony, Patrick. 'Freud and Translation'. *Imago* 58, no. 4 (2001): 837–40.
Mahony, Patrick. 'Towards the Understanding of Translation in Psychoanalysis'. *Meta* 27, no. 1 (1982): 63–71.
Maier, Carol. 'A Woman in Translation, Reflecting'. *Translation Review* 17, no. 1 (1985): 4–8.
Malaparte, Curzio. *The Skin*. Translated by David Moore. Evanston IL: Northwestern University Press, 1997.
Márai, Sándor. *Journal: Les années hongroises, 1943–1948*. Translated by Catherine Fay. Paris: Albin Michel, 2019.
Marais, Kobus. *A (Bio)Semiotic Theory of Translation: The Emergence of Social-Cultural Reality*. New York: Routledge, 2019.
Marsman, Lieke. *The Following Scan Will Last Five Minutes*. Translated by Sophie Collins. Liverpool: Pavillion Poetry, 2019.
Martin, Charles *The Poems of Catullus*. Baltimore, MD: Johns Hopkins Press, 1979.
Mayer, Bernadette. *Eruditio ex memoria*. Lenox, MA: Angel Hair Books, 1977.
Mayer, Bernadette. *The Formal Field of Kissing*. New York: Catchword Papers, 1990.
McAnulty, Dara. *Diary of a Young Naturalist*. Beaminster, UK: Little Toller Books, 2020.
McCallum, Robyn. *Ideologies of Identity in Adolescent Fiction: The Dialogic Construction of Subjectivity*. New York: Garland, 1999.
McGough, Roger. *An Imaginary Menagerie*. London: Frances Lincoln, 2011.
McGough, Roger. *Bad Bad Cats*. London: Puffin, 1997.
McGough, Roger. *Gattacci*. Italian translation by Franco Nasi. San Dorligo, Italy: Einaudi Ragazzi, 2001.
Merrill, James. *Selected Poems*. Edited by J. D. McClatchy and Stephen Yenser. New York: Knopf, 2008.
Meschonnic, Henri. *Poétique du traduire*. Paris: Verdier, 1999.
Mezzadra, Sandro, and Brett Neilson. *Border as Method, or, the Multiplication of Labor*. Durham, NC: Duke University Press, 2013.
Mill, John Stuart. *Literary Essays*. Edited by E. Alexander. Indianapolis, IN: Bobbs-Merrill, 1967.

Moody, A. David. *Ezra Pound: Poet; A Portrait of the Man and His Work.* Vol. 1, *The Young Genius, 1885–1920.* Oxford: Oxford University Press, 2007.

Murray, Mary Alice, trans. *The Story of a Puppet, or The Adventures of Pinocchio.* By Carlo Collodi. New York: Cassell Publishing, 1892. Accessed 29 October 2021, www.google.com/books/edition/The_Story_of_a_Puppet_Or_The_Adventures/p_opAQAAMAAJ.

Nabokov, Vladimir. 'Problems of Translation: *Onegin* in English'. In *The Translation Studies Reader.* Edited by Lawrence Venuti, 113–125. 3rd ed. New York: Routledge, 2012.

Nasi, Franco. *La Melancolia del traduttore.* Milan: Medusa Edizioni, 2008.

Nasi, Franco. '"Per lei, il cui nome è scritto qui sotto": sulla traduzione di un acrostico obliquo di Edgar Allan Poe'. *Griseldaonline* 17 (2018).

Nasi, Franco. *Traduzioni estreme.* Macerata, Italy: Quodlibet, 2015.

Nasi, Franco. *Translator's Blues.* Translated by Dan Gunn. London: Sylph Editions and The American University of Paris, 2015.

Nel, Philip. *Was the Cat in the Hat Black? The Hidden Racism of Children's Literature, and the Need for Diverse Books.* Oxford: Oxford University Press, 2017.

Nikolajeva, Maria. *Power, Voice and Subjectivity in Literature for Young Readers.* London: Routledge, 2010.

Nodelman, Perry. *The Hidden Adult: Defining Children's Literature.* Baltimore, MD: Johns Hopkins University Press, 2008.

Nord, Christiane. 'Scopos, Loyalty, and Translational Conventions'. *Target: International Journal of Translation Studies* 3, no. 1 (1991): 91–109.

O'Sullivan, Emer. 'Does Pinocchio Have an Italian Passport? What Is Specifically National and What Is International about Classics of Children's Literature'. In *The Translation of Children's Literature: A Reader.* Edited by Gillian Lathey, 146–62. Clevedon, UK: Multilingual Matters, 2006.

Oittinen, Riitta. *Translating for Children.* New York: Routledge, 2002.

Olivier, Christiane. *Jocasta's Children.* Translated by George Craig. London: Routledge, 1989.

Olivier, Christiane. *Les Enfants de Jocaste.* Paris: Denoël, 1980.

Ornston, Darius Gray Jr., ed. *Translating Freud.* New Haven, CT: Yale University Press, 1992.

Ortega y Gasset, José. 'The Misery and the Splendor of Translation'. Translated by Elizabeth Gamble Miller. In *Theories of Translation: An Anthology of Essays from Dryden to Derrida.* Edited by Rainer Schulte and John Biguenet, 93–112. Chicago, IL: University of Chicago Press. 1992.

Orwell, George. *1984.* Afterword by Erich Fromm. Harmondsworth, UK: Penguin, 1981.

Oswald, Alice. *Memorial.* London: Faber, 2011.

Pattee, Amy. 'Between Youth and Adulthood: Young Adult and New Adult Literature'. *Children's Literature Association Quarterly* 42, no. 2 (Summer 2017): 218–30.

Paz, Octavio. 'Further Comments'. In *Nineteen Ways of Looking at Wang Wei: How a Chinese Poem Is Translated*. Edited by Eliot Weinberger, 45–50. Mt. Kisco, NY: Moyer Bell, 1987.

Pérez, María Calzada, ed. *Apropos of Ideology: Translation Studies on Ideology, Ideologies in Translation Studies*. New York and London: Routledge, 2003.

Plutarch. *L'arte di ascoltare, tutti i moralia*. Edited by E. Lelli and G. Pisani. Milan: Bompiani, 2019.

Poe, Edgar Allan. *The Works of the Late Edgar Allan Poe*. Edited by N. P. Willis, J. R. Lowell, and R. W. Griswold. Vol. 2, *Poems and Miscellanies*. New York: Redfield, 1850.

Pollack, John. *The Pun Also Rises: How the Humble Pun Revolutionized Language, Changed History, and Made Wordplay More Than Some Antics*. New York: Gotham Books, 2012.

Poole, Adrian, and Jeremy Maule, eds. *Oxford Book of Classical Verse in Translation*. Oxford: Oxford University Press, 1995.

Pope, Alexander, trans. *The Iliad of Homer*. Edited by Steven Shankman. New York: Penguin Classics, 1996.

Pound, Ezra. *The Cantos*. New York: New Directions, 1996.

Pound, Ezra. 'Cathay'. 1915. In *Ezra Pound: Translations*, 189–204. New York: New Directions, 1963.

Pound, Ezra. 'How to Read'. In *Literary Essays*. Edited by T. S. Eliot, 15–40. New York: New Directions, 1968. Originally published in *New York Herald Tribune*, 13, 20, and 27 January 1929.

Pound, Ezra. *Literary Essays*. New York: New Directions, 1968.

Pound, Ezra. *New Selected Poems and Translations*. New York: New Directions, 2010.

Pound, Ezra. *Poems and Translations*. Edited by Richard Sieburth. New York: Library of America, 2003.

Prins, Yopie. *Ladies' Greek*. Princeton, NJ: Princeton University Press, 2018.

Rabaté, Jean-Michel. *Cambridge Introduction to Literature and Psychoanalysis*. Cambridge: Cambridge University Press, 2014.

Rehg, Kenneth L., and Lyle Campbell. 'Endangered Languages'. Introduction to *The Oxford Handbook of Endangered Languages*. Edited by Kenneth L. Rehg and Lyle Campbell, 1–20. Oxford: Oxford University Press, 2018.

Reynolds, Matthew. *The Poetry of Translation: From Chaucer and Petrarch to Homer and Logue*. Oxford: Oxford University Press, 2011.

Ricks, Christopher. *Beckett's Dying Words*. Oxford: Oxford University Press, 1993.

Ricoeur, Paul. *On Translation*. Translated by Eileen Brennan. New York: Routledge, 2006.

Robinson, Douglas, ed. *Western Translation Theory from Herodotus to Nietzsche*. London and New York: Routledge, 2014.

Rose, Jacqueline. *The Case of Peter Pan, or The Impossibility of Children's Fiction*. Philadelphia, PA: University of Pennsylvania Press, 1984.

Sakai, Naoki. 『死産される日本語・日本人』 [The Stillbirth of the Japanese as a Language and as an Ethnos]. Tokyo: Shinyô-sha, 1996; Pocketbook version, Tokyo: Kôdansha, 2015.

Sakai, Naoki. *Translation and Subjectivity: On 'Japan' and Cultural Nationalism*. Minneapolis, MN: University of Minnesota Press, 1997.
Sakai, Naoki. *Voices of the Past: The Status of Language in Eighteenth-Century Japanese Discourse*. Ithaca, NY: Cornell University Press, 1991.
Salinger, J. D. *The Catcher in the Rye*. London: Penguin, 1951.
Sappho. *Sappho*. Translated by Mary Barnard. Berkeley: University of California Press, 1958.
Schalansky, Judith. *An Inventory of Losses*. London: MacLehose, 2020.
Schiffrin, André. *The Business of Books*. New York: Verso, 2001.
Schulte, Rainer. *Comparative Perspectives: An Anthology of Multiple Translations*. Rockville, MD: American Heritage Publishing Group, 1994.
Schulz, Kathryn. 'Losing Streak: Reflections on Two Seasons of Loss'. *New Yorker*, 13 February 2017, 66–75.
Scott, Clive. *Literary Translation and the Rediscovery of Reading*. Cambridge: Cambridge University Press, 2012.
Seferis, George. *Collected Poems*. Translated, edited, and with an introduction by Edmund Keeley and Philip Sherrard. Expanded ed. Princeton, NJ: Princeton UP, 1981.
Seferis, Yorgos, trans. 'Ezra Pound: Τρία "Κάντο"', *Nea Grammata* 4–6 (1939): 193–200.
Shakespeare, William. *Hamlet*. Edited by David Bevington. New York: Bantam Books, 1988.
Shanower, Eric. 'Twenty-First Century Troy, or How Do You Solve a Problem Like Iphigenia and Other Matters of Grave Import'. In *Classics and Comics*. Edited by George Kovacs and C. W. Marshall, 195–206. Oxford: Oxford University Press, 2011.
Shields, Kathleen. *Gained in Translation: Language, Poetry and Identity in Twentieth-Century Ireland*. Berlin: Peter Lang, 2000.
Solms, Mark. 'Extracts from the Revised *Standard Edition* of Freud's Complete Psychological Works'. *International Journal of Psychoanalysis* 99, no. 1 (2018): 11–57.
Soobramien, Natasha. *Genie and Paul*. Brighton: Myriad Editions, 2012.
Soobramien, Natasha. *Genie et Paul*. Translated by Natacha Appanah. Paris: Gallimard, 2018.
Steinbeck, Michelle. *My Father Was a Man on Land and a Whale on Water*. Translated by Jen Calleja. London: Darf Publishers, 2018.
Steiner, George, ed. *Homer in English*. London: Penguin, 1996.
Swanson, Roy. *Odi et amo: The Complete Poetry of Catullus*. New York: Liberal Arts Press, 1959.
Tandoi, Eve. 'Hybrid Novels for Children and Young Adults'. In *The Edinburgh Companion to Children's Literature*. Edited by Clémentine Beauvais and Maria Nikolajeva, 329–35. Edinburgh: Edinburgh University Press, 2017.
Tate, Nahum. *The History of King Lear*. Edited by James Black. Lincoln, NE: University of Nebraska Press, 1975.
Terrinoni, Enrico. *Oltre abita il silenzio*. Milan: Il Saggiatore, 2019.

Thomas, Angie. *The Hate U Give*. New York: HarperCollins, 2017.
Thomas, Ebony Elizabeth, Debbie Reese, and Kathleen T. Horning. 'Much Ado about *A Fine Dessert*: The Cultural Politics of Representing Slavery in Children's Literature'. *Journal of Children's Literature* 42, no. 2 (2016): 6–17.
Toury, Gideon. *Descriptive Translation Studies – And Beyond*. Amsterdam: John Benjamins, 1995.
Trites, Roberta Seelinger. *Disturbing the Universe: Power and Repression in Adolescent Literature*. Iowa City: University of Iowa Press, 2000.
Van Coillie, Jan. '*Cool, Geil, Gaaf, Chouette* or *Super*: The Challenges of Translating Teenage Speech'. In *Translating Fictional Dialogue for Children and Young People*. Edited by Martin B. Fischer and Maria Wirf Naro, 217–34. Berlin: Frank and Timme, 2012.
Venuti, Lawrence. *Contra Instrumentalism: A Translation Polemic*. Lincoln, NE: University of Nebraska Press, 2019.
Venuti, Lawrence. *The Scandals of Translation: Towards an Ethics of Difference*. London: Routledge, 2002.
Venuti, Lawrence, ed. *Teaching Translation: Programs, Courses, Pedagogies*. London: Routledge, 2017.
Venuti, Lawrence. *Translation Changes Everything: Theory and Practice*. London: Routledge, 2013.
Venuti, Lawrence. 'Translation, Interpretation, and the Humanities'. Introduction to *Teaching Translation: Programs, Courses, Pedagogies*. Edited by Lawrence Venuti, 1–14. London: Routledge, 2017.
Venuti, Lawrence. *The Translator's Invisibility: A History of Translation*. London: Routledge, 1995.
Walden, Tillie. *Dans un rayon de soleil*. Translated by Alice Marchand. Paris: Gallimard, 2018.
Walden, Tillie. *On a Sunbeam*. London: Avery Hill, 2018.
Weinberger, Eliot. 'Anonymous Sources: A Talk on Translators and Translation'. In *Voice-Overs: Translation and Latin American Literature*. Edited by Daniel Balderston and Marcy E. Schwartz, 104–18. Albany, NY: State University of New York Press, 2002.
Wideman, John Edgar. *Le Projet Fanon*. Translated by Bernard Turle. Paris: Gallimard, 2013.
Williams, William Carlos. *Paterson*. Rev. ed. Edited by Christopher MacGowan. New York: New Directions, 1995.
Wilson, Emily. 'Translator's Note'. In *Homer, The Odyssey*. Translated by Emily Wilson, 81–91. New York: Norton, 2018.
Woolf, Virginia. 'On Not Knowing Greek'. In *The Common Reader*, 39–59. New York: Harcourt, 1948.
Woolf, Virginia. *Jacob's Room*. Annotated and with an introduction by Vara Neverow. New York: Harcourt, 2008.
Wynne, Frank, ed. *Found in Translation*. London: Apollo, 2018.

Yeshurun, Yaara, Stephen Swanson, Erez Simony, Janice Chen, Christina Lazaridi, Christopher J. Honey, and Uri Hasson. 'Same Story, Different Story'. *Psychological Science* 28, no. 3 (March 2017): 307–19.

Young, Alison. *Street Art, Public City: Law, Crime and the Urban Imagination*. New York and London: Routledge, 2013.

Zadbood, Asieh, Janice Chen, Yuan Chang Leong, Kenneth A. Norman, and Uri Hasson. 'How We Transmit Memories to Other Brains: Constructing Shared Neural Representations Via Communication'. *Cerebral Cortex* 27, no. 10 (October 2017): 4988–5000.

Index

abstraction, 149, 254
accessibility, 271–2
accuracy, 280
   'gotcha' criticism, 282
acoustics, 9, 16, 51, 58, 64, 146, 147, 171–7, 280
anotation, 179
Appiah, Kwame Anthony, 280
awards. *See* prizes
awareness, 16, 25, 26, 60, 147, 165, 188, 229
   self-awareness, 21

Barthes, Roland, 115, 259, 277
Beckett, Samuel, 8–14, 179–80, 185–91
Bellos, David, 17
Berman, Antoine, 18, 25, 165, 168, 176
Bettelheim, Bruno, 127–9, 132
Borges, Jorge Luis, 118, 253
Boyle, T. C., 33, 36–8, 42
Brink, André, 37, 46
Brown, Brandon, 64–79

canon formation, 2, 4, 86, 88, 112, 114, 131, 209–25
Carson, Anne, 71, 74, 78, 91
Catullus, 64–79
children's literature, 47–62
classic texts, 4, 64–6, 68, 69, 78, 82, 91, 94, 112–24, 196, 207, 212, 215, 217, 220
Colina, Sonia, 25
Collodi, Carlo, 122
   Le avventure di Pinocchio, 122, 123
comparison, 43, 85, 87, 130, 147, 162, 175, 232, 235
constraints, 21, 28, 29, 68, 181, 262, 263
contemporary, 1, 2, 16, 21, 34, 48–50, 58, 60, 64, 67, 68, 91, 112, 117, 120, 121, 162, 163, 175, 176, 195, 210, 229, 254, 256, 258
countability of languages, 3
Craft, 266–73

creativity, 22, 24, 29, 71, 79, 270
critical thinking, 22, 24
culture, 1, 25, 85, 137, 202, 263
   American culture, 206
   internet culture, 41
   literary culture, 41, 199, 268, 279
   Macedonian Ministry of Culture, 217
   popular culture, 69
   receiving culture, 123, 273
   source culture, 176
   Western culture, 114, 115
   Wild West culture, 43
   youth culture, 53

Damrosch, David, 118
Dante, 112, 121–2, 180
defacement, 77, 78
default mode network, 149, 156
detail, 77, 85, 90, 114, 150, 153, 156, 157, 176, 179, 261, 278
didacticism, 54
domestication, 52–7, 59, 177, 217, 273
   naturalising, 268
Doolittle, Hilda. *See* H.D.

ecology, 257–8
editing, 269
embodiment, 236
emerging translators, 163, 271
Emmerich, Karen, 279
extreme texts, 21–4, 28
extreme translations
   original solutions, 270–1

fidelity, 60, 64, 88, 162, 273, 277, 278–81
financial incentives, 14, 43, 198, 201, 204, 206, 258
foreignization, 25, 50, 59, 89, 168
Freud, Sigmund, 126–37
   Standard Edition, 127, 129, 131, 136

Gadamer, Hans-Georg, 25
Global
  global textuality, 124
  globish, 32, 38
graffiti, 77–8
Gray, Kes
  Oi Frog!, 28–9
Greek, 82–101, 113, 115, 117, 128, 132, 133, 135
Greek translation history, 82–106

H.D., 83, 92, 95–6, 100
Hawthorne, Nathaniel
  The Scarlet Letter, 22
Heidegger, Martin, 25, 131
hierarchy (cortical), 145–50, 155–7
Homer, 66, 84, 87–90, 100–1, 121, 267
  Iliad, 87, 112–18, 123

impossible, 17, 18
India, 38, 254, 256
individuation of languages, 227, 232–7
international, 54, 257
  international languages, 164
  international law, 237, 247
  international literature, 162, 163, 165, 174, 195, 198, 199, 201, 206, 209, 215
  international world, 231, 235–8, 241–2, 247–8
intimacy, 274
  and authenticity, 277
invariance, 140, 141–9, 151–3
Italian, 15, 17, 18, 20, 23, 28, 29, 123, 190

Japanese, 119, 164, 227–49

Karasu, Bilge, 169–74
Kiraly, Donald, 26

Lacan, Jacques, 128–9
language of thought, 152
Lewis, Carroll, 17
Lispector, Clarice, 267, 269
literary festivals, 198, 209, 215
literary translation, 1–5, 53, 57, 58, 60, 64, 140, 149, 162–78, 194, 204, 205, 218, 268, 271, 272, 273
localization, 256
loss, 93, 123, 188, 251–63

Macedonian, 209–25
Malaparte, Curzio, 184–5
McGough, Roger, 15, 20, 28
  'Dentist Poem', 23
  Wordfish, 15
memory, 117, 141, 150, 153, 155–7, 252, 261
Meschonnic, Henri, 20

migration, 4, 179, 255, 256
Mill, John Stuart
  'On Genius', 27
minor language, 209, 224
modern regime of translation, 232, 236–48
multilingualism, 38, 162–7, 178
  polyglotism, 134, 167, 260
mythology, 229, 245
  global, 115
  Japanese, 228

neuroimaging, 147
neuroscience, 140, 143, 145, 148, 149, 152, 158
neutrality, 8, 180, 257

Olivier, Christiane, 8–9
Orwell, George
  1984
    Newspeak, 19–21
Oswald, Alice
  Memorial, 112–17

palimpsest, 83, 91, 96, 100, 137
pedagogy, 22, 24–8, 29, 268–9, 271, 273
Plutarch
  The Art of Listening, 27
Poe, Edgar Allan, 18
  'A Valentine', 18
poetry, 21, 23, 40, 49–50, 58, 64–80, 86, 90–8, 100, 112–22, 140, 209, 215, 222, 251, 253, 267, 274
Pound Pound, Ezra, 100
Pound, Ezra, 67, 89, 91–5, 98, 101
  Cathay, 118–20
prizes, 46, 112, 194, 203, 215–17, 222, 256
psychoanalysis, 126–9, 136
publishing, 1, 32, 41, 52, 194–209, 213, 215, 194–208, 220–4, 272, 279
  smaller publishers, 203

quotidian, 37

reception history, 64, 65, 70, 74
reception studies, 112
remainders, 18–21
Republic of North Macedonia, 209
responsibility, 9, 22, 26, 278–9
retranslation, 1, 4, 64–80, 137
rupture, 64, 78

sales data, 122, 195–201, 202–8, 217
Sappho, 70, 90–8, 252
schematism of cofiguration, 231, 236, 246–8
Schleiermacher, Friedrich, 25, 168
Schleiermacher–Berman line, 25

Seferis, Yorgos, 84, 98, 100–6
selection, 65, 70, 71, 119, 221
Serbo-Croatian, 210–12, 216
situation model, 153
Skopostheorie, 26
slang, 47
solitude, 7–14
Solms, Mark, 130–2

teenage fiction, 47–62
teenager, 47–62, 257
Terrinoni, Enrico, 16
textual scholarship, 88, 180
transcription, 179, 183, 184, 187, 216, 232
transference, 126, 136
translating cuisine, 37
translation
  collaborative translation, 28, 162, 165, 274, 279
  translation policy, 219–24, 256
  translation practice, 3, 4, 64, 78, 164–6, 212, 268, 273, 274
  translation technologies, 16

translation theory, 4, 50, 59, 74, 174, 179, 276
translator's identity, 7–8, 52, 207, 240, 275–6
transliteration, 132

untranslatables, 21, 86, 91, 98, 131, 185, 186, 218, 270

Venuti, Lawrence, 24, 25, 114, 122, 175, 180, 198
  Contra Instrumentalism, 114
  hermeneutic model, 25
  The Translator's Invisibility, 198
  Translation Changes Everything, 180
voice, 2, 11, 12, 13, 14, 33, 49, 50, 54, 68, 69, 82, 92–4, 98, 174, 177, 269, 276
  Homeric, 90
  lyric, 96

Williams, William Carlos, 92, 96–8
Wilson, Emily, 267
Woolf, Virginia, 84, 98–101

YA literature, 47–62
Yugoslavia, 5, 209–25

For EU product safety concerns, contact us at Calle de José Abascal, 56–1º,
28003 Madrid, Spain or eugpsr@cambridge.org.

www.ingramcontent.com/pod-product-compliance
Lightning Source LLC
LaVergne TN
LVHW011801060526
838200LV00053B/3650